The Community Rules
from Qumran

The Community Rules from Qumran

from Qumran

A COMMENTARY

CHARLOTTE HEMPEL

FORTRESS PRESS

MINNEAPOLIS

THE COMMUNITY RULES FROM QUMRAN
A Commentary

Cover design: Savanah N. Landerholm

Print ISBN: 978-1-5064-8537-9

Preface

This volume offers the first Commentary on all twelve ancient manuscripts of the Rules of the Community, a series of works which contain accounts of the organisation and values ascribed to a movement associated with the Dead Sea Scrolls. My aim is to make all the texts accessible as transparently as possible. The approach adopted here is to capture the distinctive nature of each of the manuscripts by offering a synoptic translation that presents each passage as represented in all the manuscripts at a glance. Whereas previous research has focused mainly on indicating "variants" between the manuscripts, this volume allots equal attention to the many places where several manuscripts are in close agreement. The latter evidence is as significant as the differences between the manuscripts in informing us about their inter-relationship and the literary development of this complex literary tradition.

Translations are followed by detailed Textual Notes that engage the Hebrew texts.[1] The original manuscripts were consulted alongside digital images, on which more will be said below. The most exciting inter-textual insights arose out of scribal features attested in one manuscript which gained new significance in the light of another manuscript. There is much to be gained from looking at the material synoptically in order to establish the relationships between manuscripts as well as shed light on different parts within manuscripts. I have little doubt that some of the Cave 4 manuscripts preserve a form of the text – and in some cases the very manuscripts – drawn upon by the scribes and compilers of 1QS.

The more I engaged with the riches of the evidence, the more I was struck by the extent to which so much of the scholarly debate has favoured particular selections of material. While it is widely acknowledged – and frequently lamented – that the best-preserved manuscript 1QS has dominated scholarly assessments, even with regard to this manuscript researchers frequently draw on particular segments of the text. This selective approach also extends to our engagement with the manuscripts that came to light in the closing decade of the 20th century. What follows is an attempt at a reading of the material that does justice to the evidence of each passage without losing sight of the significance of its

---

[1] The most recent edition by Sarianna Metso reached me, alas, too late to be incorporated, see Metso, *The Community Rule: A Critical Edition with Translation*. Early Judaism and Its Literature (Atlanta: SBL, 2019), 2019.

context in the individual manuscripts. What emerges are clusters of material that are shared across several manuscripts. The publication of the Cave 4 manuscripts in 1998 challenged prevalent notions of the Community Rules founded on the quasi-archetypal status of the Cave 1 copy published in 1951. This Commentary embraces the new literary landscape constituted by the Community Rules. At the same time, I relished the opportunity to evaluate the material afresh within the context of current research on the Scrolls where our maps of place and time are also being re-drafted. The etymology of the English verb "to draft" encapsulates a sense of movement ("to pull; draw") alongside precision, especially if we think of maps. This verb also applies to my own work on this book. I drafted and re-drafted to arrive at a text that is as precise as I dare to be. Etymology offers some solace by suggesting that this process implies movement and, hopefully, progress, in our thinking on the texts presented here.

Over the period of writing this Commentary I have benefitted immensely from the support of a number of organizations. First and foremost, I gratefully acknowledge the support of the British Academy for the award of a Mid-Career Fellowship matched by a term of research leave granted by the University of Birmingham's College of Arts and Law in 2013–2014. During that year I was able to spend a vital period of time in Jerusalem that included several visits to the conservation laboratory of the Israel Antiquities Authority (IAA) where I was able to examine the fragments of the Community Rules from Cave 4. I am indebted to the former Curator and Head of the Dead Sea Scrolls Unit at the IAA, Pnina Shor and her team, especially Orit Kuslansky and Lena Liebman. I am also grateful to the Curator of the Shrine of the Book, Dr Adolfo Roitman, Hasia Rimon and Irene Lewitt for their assistance and the opportunity to examine the manuscript of 1QS in the high-security vault of the Shrine as well as important photographs of that scroll in 2014. I hugely profited from the professionalism and expertise of all the staff at both institutions. Since then I have benefitted daily – and often hourly – from the multi-spectral digital images taken by the photographer Shai Halevi available at the IAA's Leon Levy Dead Sea Scrolls Digital Library (LLDSSDL; http://deadseascrolls.org.il) as well as the digital images of 1QS hosted by the Shrine of the Book and photographed by Ardon Bar-Hama (http://dss.collections.imj.org.il/community).

The Spring of 2014 was also the first time I was privileged to work in the famous library of the École Biblique et Archéologique Française in Jerusalem. I was made to feel at home in the same institution for a second time in the autumn of 2019 when I was part of a cohort of Dead Sea Scrolls Scholars in Residence at the École. I will always be grateful to the Director of the École, Jean Jacques Pérennès, O. P. and Professor Michael Langlois for the invitation as well as to my Fellow Scholars in Residence and the in-house Qumran specialist Professor Émile Puech who gave so generously of his time during both of my visits. Finally, I am grateful to the community and the staff at the École for their assistance and generous hospitality. In addition, I would like to mention the following friends and colleagues for conversations and sharing pre-published work or bibliography: Martin G. Abegg, Albert Baumgarten, George Brooke, John Collins, Idan Dershowitz, Esther Eshel, Daniel Falk, Judith Göppinger, Maxine Grossman, Kamilla Skarström Hinojosa, Jutta Jokiranta, Paul Joyce, Menahem Kister, Michael Knibb, Reinhard Kratz, Simone Laqua O'Donnell, Rebekka Luther, Daniel Machiela, Sarianna Metso, Noam Mizrahi, Candida Moss, Hindy Najman, Judith Newman, Carol Newsom, Vered Noam, Mladen Popović, Gary Rendsburg, Jean-Sébastien Rey, Alison Schofield, Annette Steudel, Michael Stone, Eibert Tigchelaar, James Tucker, and Cecilia Wassén. Special thanks goes to Ariel Feldman who generously commented on a draft of the entire manu-script. Closer to home, my immediate scholarly community at the University of Birmingham, including especially our doctoral students and colleagues in the Department of Theology and Religion and beyond, has sustained me. I would like to thank Michael DeVries who skilfully prepared the Indices of this volume with customary efficiency.

I am grateful to the Editors of the Series *Texts and Studies in Ancient Judaism*, especially Annette Yoshiko Reed, for accepting this volume into the Series and to the staff at Mohr Siebeck for their skill and professionalism in seeing it through the Press, especially Elena Müller, Katharina Gutekunst, Tobias Stäbler and Jana Trispel.

This book is dedicated to the memory of my husband, Richard Charles Cave, who together with our children – Charles and Imogen Cave – shared so much of this journey with me. The first-person voice we hear in the Final Hymn hints at our fleeting presence on this earth and offers a deep connection between ourselves and those who lived, and died, over two millennia ago when it acknowledges "a human being does not determine its path, nor humankind its steps" (1QS 11:10).

Author's Note on the Paperback Edition

I am delighted that this volume will be available in paperback and am extremely grateful to Carey C. Newman, Executive Editor of Fortress Press, for his enthusiastic support for this project. Mention should be made of the doctoral dissertation by James M. Tucker, "From Ink Traces to Ideology: Material, Text, and Composition of Qumran *Community Rule* Manuscripts" submitted since the publication of this Commentary to the University of Toronto in 2020. I have taken the opportunity to correct a small number of infelicities. For a more recent treatment of 4Q259 (with a revised presentation especially of 4Q259 2:15 and 2:18-3:1) see C. Hempel, "A Tale of Two Scribes: Encounters with an Avant-Garde Manuscript of the Community Rules (4Q259)," in *HOKHMAT SOPHER: Mélanges offerts au Professeur Émile Puech en l'honneur de son quatre-vingtième* anniversaire. Edited by Jean-Sébastien Rey and Martin Staszak. Études Bibliques 38 (Leuven: Peeters, 2021), 115–128.

Charlotte Hempel, Birmingham, UK   August 2021

Table of Contents

Abbreviations Including Frequently Cited Sources

Excluded are items listed in Billie Jean Collins, Bob Buller and John Kutsko, *SBL Handbook of Style*. Second Edition (Atlanta, GA: SBL, 2014).

CDSS	George J. Brooke and Charlotte Hempel, eds., *The T&T Clark Companion to the Dead Sea Scrolls* (London: T&T Clark, 2018).
CDSSE	Geza Vermes, *The Complete Dead Sea Scrolls in English* (London: Allen Lane, 1997).
DJD 1	Dominique Barthélemy and Józef T. Milik, *Qumran Cave 1* (Oxford: Clarendon 1955).
DJD 3	Dominique Barthélemy, Józef T. Milik and Roland de Vaux, *Les 'Petites Grottes' de Qumrân* (Oxford: Clarendon, 1962).
DJD 7	Maurice Baillet, *Qumrân Grotte 4.3 (4Q482 – 4Q520)* (Oxford: Clarendon, 1982).
DJD 10	Elisha Qimran and John Strugnell, *Qumran Cave 4.5: Miqṣat Maʿaśeh ha-Torah* (Oxford: Clarendon, 1994).
DJD 11	Esther Eshel et al., *Qumran Cave 4.6: Poetical and Liturgical Texts, Part 1* (Oxford: Clarendon, 1998).
DJD 18	Joseph M. Baumgarten, *Qumran Cave 4.13: The Damascus Document (4Q266 – 4Q273)* (Oxford: Clarendon, 1996).
DJD 21	Shemaryahu Talmon, Jonathan Ben-Dov and Uwe Glessmer, *Qumran Cave 4.16: Calendrical* (Oxford: Clarendon, 2001).
DJD 23	Florentino García Martínez, Eibert J. C. Tigchelaar and Adam S. van der Woude, *Qumran Cave 11.2: 11Q2–18, 11Q20–31* (Oxford: Clarendon, 1998).
DJD 25	Émile Puech, *Qumran Cave 4.18: Textes hébreux (4Q521–4Q528, 4Q576–4Q579)* (Oxford: Clarendon, 1998).
DJD 26	Philip S. Alexander and Geza Vermes, *Qumran Cave 4.26: Serekh Ha-Yaḥad and Two Related Texts* (Oxford: Clarendon, 1998).
DJD 29	Esther G. Chazon et al., *Qumran Cave 4.20: Poetical and Liturgical Texts, Part 2* (Oxford: Clarendon, 1999).
DJD 31	Émile Puech, *Qumrân Grotte 4.22: Textes Araméens Première Partie 4Q529–549* (Oxford: Clarendon, 2001).
DJD 34	John Strugnell, Daniel J. Harrington and Torleif Elgvin, *Qumran Cave 4.24: 4QInstruction (Mûsar leMevîn): 4Q415 ff., with a Re-edition of 1Q26* (Oxford: Clarendon, 1999).
DJD 35	Joseph M. Baumgarten, *Qumran Cave 4.25: Halakhic Texts* (Oxford: Clarendon, 1999).
DJD 36	Stephen J. Pfann et al., *Qumran Cave 4.26: Cryptic Texts and Miscellanea, Part 1* (Oxford: Clarendon, 2000).
DJD 40	Carol Newsom, Hartmut Stegemann and Eileen Schuller, *Qumran Cave 1.3: 1QHodayot^a, with Incorporation of 4QHodayot^{a-f} and 1QHodayot^b* (Oxford: Clarendon, 2009).

DSS   Dead Sea Scrolls
DSSANT   Michael Wise, Martin Abegg and Edward Cook, *The Dead Sea Scrolls: A New Translation* (London: HarperCollins, 1996).
DSSHW 1   Elisha Qimron, *The Dead Sea Scrolls: The Hebrew Writings*. 3 Volumes (Jerusalem: Yad Ben-Zvi, 2010), Volume 1.
DSSSE 1–2   Florentino García Martínez and Eibert J. C. Tigchelaar, *The Dead Sea Scrolls Study Edition*. 2 Volumes (Leiden: Brill, 1998).
EDEJ   John Collins and Dan Harlow, eds., *The Eerdmans Dictionary of Early Judaism* (Grand Rapids, MI: Eerdmans, 2010).
EDSS   Lawrence H. Schiffman and James C. VanderKam, eds., *Encyclopedia of the Dead Sea Scrolls*. 2 Volumes (New York, NY: Oxford University Press, 2000).
HAL 1   Walter Baumgartner, *Hebräisches und aramäisches Lexikon zum Alten Testament* (Leiden: Brill, 1967), Fascicle 1.
HAWTTM 1   Reinhard G. Kratz, Annette Steudel and Ingo Kottsieper, eds., *Hebräisches und aramäisches Wörterbuch zu den Texten vom Toten Meer: Einschließlich der Manuskripte aus der Kairoer Geniza*. Volume 1 א – ב (Berlin: De Gruyter, 2017).
HAWTTM 2   Reinhard G. Kratz, Annette Steudel and Ingo Kottsieper, eds., *Hebräisches und aramäisches Wörterbuch zu den Texten vom Toten Meer: Einschließlich der Manuskripte aus der Kairoer Geniza*. Volumd 2 ג – ז (Berlin: De Gruyter, 2017).
HDSS   Elisha Qimron, *The Hebrew of the Dead Sea Scrolls* (Atlanta, GA: Scholars Press, 1986).
LLDSSDL   Leon Levy Dead Sea Scrolls Digital Library
OHDSS   Timothy H. Lim and John J. Collins, eds., *The Oxford Handbook of the Dead Sea Scrolls* (Oxford: Oxford University Press, 2010).
PFES   Publications of the Finnish Exegetical Society
PTSDSSP 1   James H. Charlesworth et al., eds., *The Dead Sea Scrolls: Hebrew, Aramaic, and Greek Texts with English Translations. Rule of the Community and Related Documents*. Princeton Theological Seminary Dead Sea Scrolls Project PTSDSSP 1 (Tübingen/Louisville, KY: Mohr Siebeck/Westminster John Knox, 1994).
Pl.   Plate
ThWQ 1   Heinz-Josef Fabry and Ulrich Dahmen, eds., *Theologisches Wörterbuch zu den Qumrantexten*. 2 Volumes (Stuttgart: Kohlhammer, 2010), Volume 1.
ThWQ 2   Heinz-Josef Fabry and Ulrich Dahmen, eds., *Theologisches Wörterbuch zu den Qumrantexten*. 2 Volumes (Stuttgart: Kohlhammer, 2013), Volume 2.

Symbols

{} Corrections in the manuscripts
( ) Words or letters supplied in the English translation for clarity
[ ] Text that is reconstructed and not present in the manuscripts. The symbol is also used in references, cf. [4Q255 1:5–6].
// Parallel text in overlapping manuscripts of the Community Rules

1. General Introduction

The Community Rules contain descriptions of the organization and values of the movement associated with the Dead Sea Scrolls. The twelve manuscripts that we will be dealing with in this Commentary also offer a rich laboratory preserving first-hand evidence of how ancient Jewish texts were produced and shaped over two thousand years ago. Given the dates of the preserved manuscripts indicate the approximate range for the copying of these witnesses of almost two centuries (150 BCE–50 CE), we need to allow for an even more prolonged and vibrant period for the composition of the various building blocks and the shaping of the Community Rules (S) in several manifestations. This wealth of evidence offers us a great deal of insights into the growth of this particular literary tradition. At the same time these twelve manuscripts preserve one of the richest ancient literary traditions captured mid-flow of editorial and compositional growth. The results of our investigation, therefore, shed light on the way in which ancient Jewish literature of the kind of complexity we find in the Hebrew Bible took shape. What we are looking at is nothing short of a pristine ancient literary eco-system that allows us to access a range of living literary organisms that interact with one other. At the same time the format of a Commentary invites close attention to the final form of the various Community Rules.[1]

The fact that we are not dealing with a single text – and conceivably not even the same work in all cases – makes the task of writing a Commentary both challenging as well as exciting. The first problem that we encounter is one of terminology and conceptualization. What are we to call the material in front of us? It is essential that we avoid privileging the best-preserved manuscript of the Community Rule (1QS) since the state of its preservation is purely fortuitous and accidental.[2] It is also something of a challenge to name the creative

---

[1] A number of studies have approached the text of 1QS in an explicitly synchronic fashion see, e. g., Pierre Guilbert, "La Règle de la Communauté," in Jean Carmignac and Pierre Guilbert, *Les Textes de Qumran: Traduit et Annotés* (Paris: Letouzey et Ané, 1961), 11–80, 11–12 and Kamilla Skarström Hinojosa, "A Synchronic Approach to the Serek ha-Yahad (1QS): From Text to Social and Cultural Context" (PhD diss., Umeå University, Sweden, 2016). A sharply drawn dichotomy between both approaches is unhelpful since the evidence that points to literary development, which should be evaluated on the merits of the detailed argumentation, does not deny the importance of final texts.

[2] See Jutta Jokiranta and Hanna Vanonen, "Multiple Copies of Rule Texts or Multiple Rule Texts? Boundaries of the S and M Documents," in *Crossing Imaginary Boundaries: The Dead*

individuals behind the material in an appropriate manner. As with much ancient literature, including the Hebrew Bible, we have evidence of several levels of literary activity that go back to authors, editors and correctors. Moreover, it is rarely entirely clear whose handiwork we are looking at. Nor is it likely that these kinds of distinctions mattered as much, if at all, to the ancient professionals as they do to us. The approach adopted here draws on the terminology developed by Liv Lied in the course of her work on Old Testament Pseudepigrapha.[3] Lied distinguishes three key categories that enable us to present the complex evidence of the manuscripts dealt with in this Commentary in a nuanced manner. On Lied's definitions

1. *Works* are compositional units that are regarded either by ancient authors or modern scholars as purposeful literary units.
2. *Manuscripts* are "text-bearing objects" which on our reading of the Community Rules manuscripts often overlap with works, though they are not always representatives of the same work.
3. A *Text*, finally, is defined by Lied as the 'words on the page' which can be further divided into textual units.

In order to indicate both the concurrent family resemblance and distinctiveness of the witnesses the plural Community Rules was chosen for the title of the volume and is used throughout where appropriate. It is hoped that the remainder of this Introduction and the Commentary offer an easily accessible point of access to the complex spectrum of available manuscripts alongside nuanced discussion of the relationships between the various works, texts and manuscripts.[4]

1.1 The 'Geology' of the Rule Manuscripts

This Commentary is the first to take into account the twelve manuscripts now available, both each in their own right and as witnesses to the plurality and development of the S tradition. Close attention will be paid to areas where the manuscripts converge and diverge at different points revealing distinctive tectonic plates of various sizes in the tradition. Geologists work with a concept of continental drift to describe the movement of the components of the earth's outer shell, the lithosphere, relative to each other. On our reading of the Community Rules manuscripts scholars have often privileged the best preserved manuscript of the Rule (1QS) as the key to the outer shell of the Community Rules. The

---

Sea Scrolls in the Context of Second Temple Judaism. Edited by Mika S. Pajunen and Hanna Tervanotko. PFES 108 (Helsinki: Finnish Exegetical Society, 2015), 11–60.

[3] Liv Lied, "Text-Work-Manuscript: What is an 'Old Testament Pseudepigraph*on*'?" *JSP* 25 (2015): 150–165.

[4] See further 1.7 below.

approach adopted here is one of capturing the distinctive overall shapes, the figurative lithospheres, of Rule manuscripts. Moreover, these manuscripts share a number of major and minor tectonic plates. At their boundaries these plates reveal convergence, divergence and at times dramatic literary developments. The publication of the Cave 4 manuscripts in 1998 can be conceived as a volcanic eruption that challenged our notion of the Community Rules derived from the quasi-archetypal status of the Cave 1 copy (1QS) first published in 1951. Since then the smoke has lifted, the pieces have begun to settle and we see a fertile field of green shoots emerging in the scholarly debate. In this Commentary I have tried to embrace the post-volcanic landscape of S which I sifted carefully for clues to arrive at a fresh reading of the material. Sometimes this involves the identification of previously unrecognised S material in a manuscript inscribed on the other side of the opisthograph 4Q255 (4QS[a]).[5] At other times the reading of a single word that has previously been marginalised can open up new interpretative horizons with implications not only for our understanding of the Rule but of the movement associated with this text and its place in Second Temple Judaism.[6]

1.2 The Community Rules and the Re-Drawn Map of Second Temple Judaism

1.2.1 A Broader Literary Context Reveals an Apotropaic Safety Net

Alongside the publication and concomitant scholarly discussion of ten additional manuscripts of the Community Rules some 30 other volumes containing editions of hundreds of new compositions from Qumran have appeared in the official series Discoveries in the Judean Desert. Some of these new texts have revealed material that is intimately related to the Community Rules. A parade example is the wealth of new material that is closely related to the Penal Code in a series of documents from Cave 4 such as the Damascus Document,[7] 4QMiscellaneous Rules (*olim* Serekh Damascus)[8] as well as in a fragment from Cave 11 (11Q29 Fragment Related to Serekh ha-Yaḥad).[9]

While scholars have studied texts from Caves 4 and 11 that are variously affiliated[10] with the Community Rules over recent decades, this does not mean that compositions that do not offer immediately apparent convergence with S do not

---

[5] See 1.5.2 below.

[6] See 4Q261 1a–b: 2 and the Commentary in 6.1.4.2 below.

[7] See CD 14:18b–22 // 4Q266 10 i–ii // 4Q267 9 vi // 4Q269 11 i–ii // 4Q270 7 i.

[8] See 4Q265 4 i 2 – ii 2.

[9] See Chapter 7 below.

[10] For reflections on the notion of a family resemblance between different Rule texts, including S, see Charlotte Hempel, *Qumran Rule Texts in Context: Collected Studies*. TSAJ 154 (Tübingen: Mohr Siebeck, 2013), 1.

also contribute significantly to our understanding of the worldview, theology, ideology and anthropology of the Community Rules. In particular, the discovery at Qumran of a host of apotropaic texts such as the Songs of the Maskil (4Q510–511), Apocryphal Psalms (11Q11), the Plea for Deliverance (11Q5 [Psalms[a]] 19:15b–17a), Exorcism (4Q560), Incantation (4Q444) and 4QPhylactère T (4Q147)[11] have brought to light a rich body of evidence that testifies to the place of malevolent beings in the worldview of Second Temple Judaism. Thus, according to 4Q511 48–49+51 4 the elevated speaker – probably the Maskil – refers to wars raging in his body, and quarrelling spirits are referred to as present in the speaker's physical structure according to 4Q444 4 i – 5 2. Equally suggestive are references to the empowerment to be sourced from "the statutes of God" in the war against spirits of wickedness (4Q444 4 i – 5 4).[12] Of particular relevance are a series of "apotropaic prayers" and "incantions" based on a classification proposed by Esther Eshel.[13] The incantations include exorcistic formulae where the speaker directly addresses demonic figures with phrases such as "I adjure you, oh spirit" (4Q560 1 ii 6) which refer to expelling or otherwise controlling an evil spirit through an oath. This important new cache of ancient Jewish apotropaic literature allows us access not only to these texts but also to the beliefs and practices that shaped the thoughts of ancient Jews including the authors of the Community Rules. These texts have received a great deal of attention in recent years.[14] Moreover, Gideon Bohak's ground-breaking volume has offered a powerful critique of the marginalization of ancient Jewish magic.[15] I hope to show that the implications of the apotropaic material from Qumran for our under-

---

[11] Cf. now Ariel and Faina Feldman, "4Q147: An Amulet?," *DSD* 26 (2019): 1–29; Feldman and Feldman, "4Q148 (4QPhylactère U): Another Amulet from Qumran?," *JSJ* 50 (2019): 197–222 and Ariel Feldman, "On Amulets, Apotropaic Prayers, and Phylacteries: The Contribution of Three New Texts from the Judean Desert" In *Petitioners, Penitents, and Poets: On Prayer and Praying in Second Temple Judaism*. Edited by Ariel Feldman and Timothy Sandoval. BZAW (Berlin: De Gruyter, forthcoming).

[12] See also 4Q444 4 i – 5 1 and Tupá Guerra, "Encountering Evil: Apotropaic Magic in the Dead Sea Scrolls," (PhD diss., University of Birmingham, 2017), 64 and 5.4.1 below.

[13] Cf. "Apotropaic Prayers in the Second Temple Period," in *Liturgical Perspectives: Prayer and Poetry in Light of the Dead Sea Scrolls*. Edited by Esther Chazon with Ruth Clements and Avital Pinnick. STDJ 48 (Leiden: Brill, 2003), 69–88.

[14] See, e. g., Philip S. Alexander, "'Wrestling against Wickedness in High Places:' Magic in the Worldview of the Qumran Community," in *The Scrolls and the Scriptures: Qumran Fifty Years After*. Edited by Stanley E. Porter and Craig A. Evans. JSP Supplements 26 (Sheffield: Sheffield Academic Press, 1997), 318–337; Alexander, "The Demonology of the Dead Sea Scrolls," in *The Dead Sea Scrolls After Fifty Years. Volume II: A Comprehensive Assessment*. Edited by Peter W. Flint and James C. VanderKam (Leiden: Brill, 1999), 331–353; Armin Lange, Hermann Lichtenberger and K. F. Diethard Römheld, eds., *The Demonology of Israelite-Jewish and Early Christian Literature in Context of Their Environment* (Tübingen: Mohr Siebeck, 2003) and Farah Mébarki and Émile Puech, *Les manuscrits de la mer Morte* (Arles: Éditions du Rouergue, 2002), 270–272.

[15] *Ancient Jewish Magic: A History* (Cambridge Cambridge University Press, 2008).

standing of a broader range of literature has not yet been fully recognised. I will argue that the impact of the demonic realm on the community and its members is much more pervasive. This is not the place to rehearse the detailed analyses offered in the body of the Commentary. It will suffice to introduce two pillars of our approach here. The first is to highlight the fact that the emphatically placed first instruction in the communal rules proper is the demand to turn away from all evil.[16] Strikingly, this phrase is shared by two radically different witnesses at 1QS 5:1 // 4Q256 9:1.[17] While this instruction can be read in a number of ways, on our reading it reflects one of several instances where a belief in evil forces is a driver. The argument here functions as a boundary marker through othering not only non-members but also anyone within the Community whose commitment is lacking or waning. As I will argue more fully below, the boundaries with the "other" represented by the people of injustice across three manuscripts in the very next passage coincide with a key moment in the narratives about the movement's formation.[18] As I will show in 6.5.4.3 the restrictions on contact with the people of injustice in 6.1 represent a reversal of the admissions process which suggests the former group comprised members who were temporarily or permanently excluded. Both in Chapter 5 and 6.1 the reasons given for ostracizing this group are disagreements on the interpretation of the law, see also the case of the one who refuses to enter the covenant who is rehabilitated once he obeys the law.[19] In Chapter 5 this disagreement is outlined in the context of community formation. It is clear that a commitment to the emerging community involved a separation from fellowship and influence with an affiliate group.[20] Moreover, establishing boundaries from the same group was also expected at the moment of individual decisions to join the covenant which required the cutting of ties with the same group. The intimate connection of commitment to the covenant with separation and othering is a major theme across the Community Rules, and it is likely that the inclusion of the Teaching on the Two Spirits in a small number of manuscripts just after the case of the one who initially refuses to enter the covenant illustrates how an appeal to the influence of malevolent forces goes to the core of the community's strife to establish and preserve its identity and boundaries.[21] Carol Newsom has offered a close reading of 1QS as a skilfully

---

[16] See 1QS 5:1 // 4Q256 9:1 and 1QS 1:4 // [4Q255 1:5–6].

[17] Further, 5.4.2 below.

[18] See Chapter 5 and 6.1 below.

[19] Cf. 3.4.4 below.

[20] See Chapter 5 below.

[21] See Jutta Leonhardt-Balzer, "Evil at Qumran," in *Evil in Second Temple Judaism and Early Christianity*. Edited by Chris Keith and Loren T. Stuckenbruck. WUNT 2.317 (Tübingen: Mohr Siebeck, 2016), 17–33. Note also the study by Noam Mizrahi who has identified a technical magical loanward from Aramaic in the final part of the Teaching that refers to the invasion of the body by malevolent spirits, see Mizrahi, "תכמי בשר 'Body Parts:' The Semantic History of a Qumran Hebrew Lexeme," in *The Reconfiguration of Hebrew in the Hellenistic*

composed work that gradually draws in new members with the aim of shaping their character.[22] It emerges from our reading that threats from the world outside remain a serious permanent concern for individual members as expressed in the powerful language of a wavering or shaking (זוע) spirit in the penal code.[23] Such an offence might display in the form of physical symptoms which would allow offenders to be identified.[24] Moreover, the same terminology is used to describe the emerging community in terms of a cornerstone whose foundation shall not shake[25] in Chapter 8. The nominal form of the same root זוע "terror" occurs in Isa 28:19. Whereas it is the Temple that offers safety and stability in the face of the power of a recurring scourge in Isa 28, the Community Rules present the emerging community in comparable terms as a safe haven.[26]

Secondly, the Hymn of Praise of the Maskil[27] includes plentiful accounts of timely blessing and praise but also refers to the human vulnerability of falling victim to mysterious sudden attacks such as the onset of fear and dread,[28] to which the psalmist responds with blessing and recounting God's mighty deeds.[29] The apotropaic sub-text at work here becomes clear in the description of the Maskil as confronting a range of demonic beings by recounting God's majesty according to 4Q510 1:4–6 where we read,

And I, the Maskil, (ואני משכיל) pronounce the splendour of His glory to frighten and to te[rrify] (5) all the spirits of the destroying angels and the spirits of the bastards, the demons, Lilith, desert howlers and [...] (6) and those who strike suddenly to lead astray the spirit of understanding 30

Against this context the placement of the Hymn of the Maskil at the end of a number of manuscripts of the Community Rules is suggestive.[31] Whereas the

---

Period: Proceedings of the Seventh International Symposium on the Hebrew of the Dead Sea Scrolls and Ben Sira at Strasbourg University, June 2014. Edited by Jan Joosten, Daniel Machiela and Jean-Sébastien Rey. STDJ 124 (Leiden: Brill, 2018), 123–157 and 1QS 4:21 as well as the Commentary in 4.4.6 below.

[22] Cf. *The Self as Symbolic Space: Constructing Identity and Community at Qumran.* STDJ 52 (Leiden: Brill, 2004), 110–111.

[23] Cf. 1QS 7:18b.

[24] See "זוע I," in HAWTTM, 2:214–215 and 7.2.6.3 below.

[25] See Isa 28:16.

[26] Further, 8.2.3 and 8.4.3 below.

[27] See Chapter 15.

[28] See 1QS 10:15 // 4Q256 20:4 // 4Q258 10:3 // 4Q260 4:1; see also 1QS 10:21 // 4Q260 5:1.

[29] See also Jutta Jokiranta, "Towards a Cognitive Theory of Blessing: Dead Sea Scrolls as Test Case," in *Functions of Psalms and Prayers in the Late Second Temple Period.* Edited by Mika S. Pajunen and Jeremy Penner. BZAW 486 (Berlin: De Gruyter, 2017), 25–47.

[30] See Eshel, "Apotropaic Prayers," 79–80 and Bilhah Nitzan, *Qumran Prayer and Religious Poetry.* Trans. Jonathan Chipman. STDJ 12 (Leiden: Brill, 1994), 174–200; also David Flusser, "Qumrân and Jewish 'Apotropaic' Prayers," *IEJ* 16 (1966): 194–205.

[31] See 15.1.2 below.

protective force of curses has been recognised widely,[32] we now know more about the prominent role that blessing also serves in that capacity.[33]

An extraordinary archaeological discovery in a very different environment suggests such beliefs and associated protective practices were rather more widespread. The discovery of two small incised silver amulets in a 7th century BCE burial chamber in Ketef Hinnom revealed a form of the Priestly Blessing (Num 6:24–26) in an apotropaic context.[34] These amulets offer proof that the use of protective blessing was practiced over a period of centuries.[35] The archaeological context from Ketef Hinnom – rock hewn burial benches – would only have been available to well-to-do, elite families. It seems unlikely that more modestly produced protective amulets worn by the less advantaged would have survived, and we ought to allow for a wider practice.[36]

Moreover, counterbalanced by the Covenant Ceremony (in 1QS and 4Q256) as well as the Teaching on the Two Spirits (in 1QS) the Hymn (in 1QS, 4Q256, 4Q258, 4Q260 and 4Q264) creates a framework that addresses a struggle with the forces of evil. The same is true on a larger scale of the Scroll of 1QS-1QSa-1QSb which, like Deuteronomy, also ends with blessings, though a fuller treatment of that Scroll is beyond the scope of this Commentary.[37]

In short, on our reading of the S manuscripts those responsible for the Community Rules and their readers or hearers were immersed in the demonic belief system that the apotropaic texts from Qumran as well as the silver amulets from Ketef Hinnom, a site located to the south west of the Old City of Jerusalem, have laid bare for us. In an audacious move those behind a number of Rule manuscripts put those apotropaic fears in the service of maintaining communal discipline and boundaries while also offering an explanation for apostasy from within which recurs as a concern in this material.

---

[32] See, e. g., Robert Kugler, "Making All Experience Religious: The Hegemony of Ritual at Qumran," *JSJ* 33 (2002): 131–152 and Leonhardt-Balzer, "Evil at Qumran," 25.

[33] See also Daniel K. Falk, "Material Aspects of Prayer Manuscripts at Qumran," in *Literature or Liturgy? Early Christian Hymns and Prayers in the Literary and Liturgical Context in Antiquity*. Edited by Clemens Leonhard and Helmut Löhr. WUNT 2.363 (Tübingen: Mohr Siebeck, 2014), 33–87, 7 and Loren T. Stuckenbruck, "The Demonic World of the Dead Sea Scrolls," in *Evil and the Devil*. Edited by Ida Fröhlich and Erkki Koskenniemi (London: Bloomsbury, 2013), 51–70.

[34] See Gabriel Barkay et al., "The Amulets from Ketef Hinnom: A New Edition and Evaluation," *BASOR* 334 (2004): 41–71.

[35] Cf. also Feldman and Feldman, "4Q417: An Amulet?"

[36] On the prominence of blessings in inscriptions of the biblical and post-biblical period, see James K. Aitken, *The Semantics of Blessing and Cursing in Ancient Hebrew* (Leuven: Peeters, 2007), 4.

[37] See 1.5.1.1 below and Deut 33. On the possibility of the use of writing as a magical tool in the Dead Sea Scrolls, which may be one of the factors behind the production of these texts, see George Brooke, "4Q341: An Exercise for Spelling and for Spells?," in *Writing and Ancient Near Eastern Society: Papers in Honour of Alan R. Millard*. Edited by Pietr Bienkowski, Christopher Mee and Elizabeth Slater (London: T&T Clark, 2005), 271–282.

1.2.2 A Broader Geographical Context

At the same time as the influx of a wealth of new manuscripts from Cave 4 was felt, the dating assigned to the earliest settlement by a Jewish religious movement at Khirbet Qumran has been revised. The excavator Roland de Vaux had dated the move to Qumran to around 150 BCE.[38] A reassessment of the archaeological evidence for such a date, particularly the coins, has resulted in a significantly later dating for the communal occupation of the site beginning ca. 90–70 BCE.[39] This revised time line for the communal occupation of Qumran challenges our reading of the Community Rules as reflecting a group firmly associated with the site of Qumran.[40]

Morevover, two early copies of the Community Rules – 1QS (100–75 BCE) and 4Q259 (150–100 BCE) – presuppose a community that has been established for some time by referring to the permanent expulsion of someone who has been a member for ten years.[41] This suggests that several manuscripts of the Community Rules – not to speak of their earlier building blocks – were drafted elsewhere.[42] Moreover, Joan Taylor has challenged the view of the Essenes as a marginalized, local group.[43] While it is impossible at the moment to pinpoint the range of locations where the scribes behind the composition of this complex tradition and their communities were based, the manuscripts (including 1QS)

---

[38] *Archaeology and the Dead Sea Scrolls: The Schweich Lectures 1959* (Oxford: Oxford University Press; The British Academy, 1973).

[39] See Jodi Magness, *The Archaeology of Qumran and the Dead Sea Scrolls* (Grand Rapids, MI: Eerdmans, 2002), 47–72; Bruno Callegher, "The Coins of Khirbet Qumran from the Digs of Roland de Vaux: Returning to Henri Seyrig and Augustus Spijkermann," in *The Caves of Qumran: Proceedings of the International Conference, Lugano 2014*. Edited by Marcello Fidanzio. STDJ 118 (Leiden: Brill, 2017), 221–235; Ernest-Marie Laperrousaz, "Le cadre chronologique de l'existence à Qoumrân de la communauté essénienne du maître de justice," in *Qoumrân et les manuscrits de la Mer Morte: Un Cinquantenaire*. Edited by Ernest-Marie Laperrousaz (Paris: Cerf, 1997), 71–97 and Dennis Mizzi, "Qumran Period I Reconsidered: An Evaluation of Several Competing Theories," *DSD* 22 (2015): 1–42.

[40] See also John J. Collins, *Beyond the Qumran Community: The Sectarian Movement of the Dead Sea Scrolls* (Grand Rapids, MI: Eerdmans, 2010), 166–180. For a very early proposal that the scrolls from Qumran were inscribed in a plurality of locations, see Malachi Martin, *The Scribal Character of the Dead Sea Scrolls*. Two Volumes (Louvain: Publications Universitaires, 1958), 1:392–393 and 2:715 who bases his conclusion on an analysis of scribal features.

[41] See 7.2.6.4.

[42] See Torleif Elgvin, "The Yahad is More than Qumran," in *Enoch and Qumran Origins: New Light on a Forgotten Connection*. Edited by Gabriele Boccaccini (Grand Rapids, MI: Eerdmans, 2005), 273–279; James Nati, "The *Community Rule* or *Rules* for the Community," in *Sibyls, Scriptures, and Scrolls: John Collins at Seventy*. Edited by Joel Baden, Hindy Najman and Eibert Tigchelaar. JSJSup 175 (Leiden: Brill, 2017), 2:916–939 and Alison Schofield, *From Qumran to the Yaḥad: A New Paradigm of Textual Development for the Community Rule*. STDJ 77 (Leiden: Brill, 2009), 223–224.

[43] Joan E. Taylor, *The Essenes, the Scrolls and the Dead Sea* (Oxford: Oxford University Press, 2012).

offer accounts of diverse forms of communal life at a range of locations.[44] What we can say with some confidence, however, is that wherever the fledgling phases of the movement occurred, and an account of it was committed to writing, it was not at Qumran.

1.3 Curated Communities

Careful readers may detect that I refer to the contents of the Community Rules as descriptions or accounts of scenarios rather than actual events. This reflects an attempt to acknowledge the complex relationship between what the texts portray and social realities on the ground comparable to what scholars allow for when reading other ancient literature including the Hebrew Bible.[45] The terminology "curated communities" is meant to signal the literary nature of our sources which were selectively shaped. While it is important to guard against reading these works as "reality literature," some kind of relationship to various realities may be presumed even though it is difficult to established this with certainty.[46] The rather nuanced discussion of the emergence of Christian identity is illuminating in this regard. Thus, William Horbury's judgment, that "Jews and Christians shared a common sub-culture, the literary focus of which was the Jewish Scriptures" may be adapted to the picture offered by the Community Rules.[47] We have evidence that some "Christians-to-be" and the people behind the Scrolls shared strands of that sub-culture.[48]

There is little doubt that the scribes behind these manuscripts carefully shaped an overarching narrative that invites us – alongside those described or addressed – to perceive this idealised community as a viable reality. Despite these efforts the texts also lay bare a great many rough edges that quantitatively if not rhetorically dominate the narrative of the extensively preserved manuscripts

---

[44] See especially section 6.3 and 6.4 below; cf. also Collins, *Beyond the Qumran Community* and Schofield, *From Qumran to the Yaḥad*.

[45] See Benjamin G. Wright III, "The Dead Sea Scrolls and the Study of the Ancient World," in CDSS, 216–227, 220–221.

[46] See further Charlotte Hempel, "Curated Communities: Refracted Realities on Social Media and at Qumran," in *The Dead Sea Scrolls and Ancient Media Culture*. Edited by Travis Williams, Chris Keith and Loren Stuckenbruck. STDJ (Leiden: Brill, forthcoming).

[47] William Horbury, "Jews and Christians on the Bible: Demarcation and Convergence" in *Christliche Exegese zwischen Nicaea und Chalkedon*. Edited by Johannes van Oort and Ulrich Wickert (Leuven: Peeters, 1998), 72–103, 102; also Judith M. Lieu, *Christian Identity in the Jewish and Graeco-Roman World* (Oxford: Oxford University Press, 2004) and Annette Reed and Adam Becker, eds., *The Ways that Never Parted: Jews and Christians in Late Antiquity and the Early Middle Ages* (Minneapolis, MN: Fortress, 2007).

[48] See George J. Brooke, *The Dead Sea Scrolls and the New Testament* (Minneapolis, MN: Fortress, 2005), 27–51; also Charlotte Hempel, "The Dead Sea Scrolls: Challenging the Particularist Paradigm," in *Torah, Temple, Land: Ancient Judaism(s) in Context*. Edited by Bernd Schröter. TSAJ (Tübingen: Mohr Siebeck, forthcoming).

(1QS, 4Q256, 4Q258 and 4Q259) and challenge the rather rosy picture of communal life. On our reading this reflects much more than a skilful attempt at sugar coating the accounts of communal life, but a sophisticated attempt to address and explain – both individually and collectively – a plethora of imperfections and shortcomings.

1.4 Beyond a Sanitized Reading of the Community Rules

Our close reading of the preserved manuscripts exposes a number of prevalent readings of the Community Rules as telling only part of the story. It is important to stress, however, that several passages in the manuscripts themselves point us to rather idealised portrayals of the group described in the texts. I will introduce some of those texts below while also noting evidence, often in one and the same work, that points in a different direction.

1.4.1 Perfect Holiness with Ups and Downs

A prime example is the description of members of the community as "the people of holiness" (1QS 5:13 // 4Q256 9:8–9, 11 // 4Q258 1:7–8; 1QS 8:17, 23) and "people of perfect holiness" (1QS 8:20–9:2 // 4Q258 6:12; 7:1–3). Though even in this latter account what is said about the people of perfect holiness concerns matters of discipline laid down for this group after deliberate or inadvertent wrongdoing.[49] Further references to the aspiration to conduct themselves with perfection are found in 1QS 1:8; 1QS 2:1–2; 1QS 3:9–10 // 4Q255 2:5–6 // 4Q257 3:13–14; 1QS 8:21; 1QS 11:2; 1QS 11:17 [4Q264 4–5]. Even here the third example bears closer scrutiny. 1QS 3:9–10 // 4Q255 2:5–6 // 4Q257 3:13–14 forms part of the final section of the Covenant Ceremony that deals with the case of someone who, at least initially, refuses to enter the covenant. It is important to acknowledge that the status of such an individual is described just a little earlier as "not belonging to the fount of the perfect."[50] Moreover, the elevated language outlined above should be read alongside the multiple and at times extensive accounts of situations that deal with shortcomings.[51]

---

[49] See Chapter 10 below and Newsom, *Self as Symbolic Space*, 154–165. On the aspiration to perfection in ancient Judaism see also Hindy Najman, *Past Renewals: Interpretative Authority, Renewed Revelation and the Quest for Perfection in Jewish Antiquity*. JSJSup 53 (Leiden: Brill, 2010), esp. 219–234.

[50] Cf. 1QS 3:3–4 // 4Q257 3:5 and 3.4.4 below.

[51] See 3.4.4 and Chapters 7 and 10 below. Cf. also the idealised discourse on masculinity that has been problematized recently by Jessica M. Keady, *Vulnerability and Valour: A Gendered Analysis of Everyday Life in the Dead Sea Scrolls Communities*. LSTS 91 (London: Bloomsbury T&T Clark, 2017) and the notion of "imagined perfection" developed by Maxine Grossman,

1.4.2 Ancient Descriptions of the Essenes as Archetypes of Virtue

Another body of evidence that is often drawn upon to contextualise the movement associated with the Scrolls and the site of Qumran are the descriptions of the Essenes in a range of classical sources. While there are certainly a number of striking correspondences between the evidence of Josephus, Philo and Pliny the Elder in particular, it is also clear that each author had their own *Tendenz* in reporting on the Essenes.[52] Significantly all three authors portray the Essenes as characterized by their exemplary virtue and extraordinary lifestyle. Pliny's account claims, "They are a people unique of its kind and admirable beyond all others in the whole world" (*Nat.* 73), and Geza Vermes devotes a paragraph to noting the theme of "Essene moderation and virtuousness" with reference to the evidence of Philo and Josephus.[53] The recent analysis by Jan Willem van Henten and Luuk Huitink of Josephus' characterization of individuals and groups – not least of himself and his people – in stereotypical and well established terms also applies to his account of the Essenes.[54]

It is these idealised and exoticized accounts of the Essenes that set the tone for seminal studies on the Scrolls and the Community Rules in particular. The cumulative effect of the classical accounts of the Essenes as paragons of virtue, the Community Rules' own discourse of perfection, and the evocative location of Khirbet Qumran – a site which was for a long time considered an organic part of the identity of the people associated with the Scrolls[55] – shaped our reading of the Community Rules in powerful ways. Even the story of the discovery of

---

"Inferring Holy Perfection in a Wholly Imperfect World: Cognitive Approaches to Perfection Structures in the Dead Sea Scrolls," Paper Presented at the Annual Meeting of the SBL. San Antonio, TX. 20 November 2016. Grossman's study is due to appear in print in a forthcoming monograph entitled *Embodying Perfection: Sex, Gender, and the Social World of the Qumran Rule Scrolls*. I am grateful to the author for sharing her unpublished paper with me.

[52] The texts are conveniently accessible in Geza Vermes and Martin D. Goodman, *The Essenes According to the Classical Sources*. Oxford Centre Textbooks 1 (Sheffield: JSOT Press, 1989). For the argument that Philo and Josephus made use of a shared Jewish Hellenistic source see Roland Bergmeier, *Die Essenerberichte des Flavius Josephus: Quellenstudien zu den Essenertexten im Werk des jüdischen Historiographen* (Kampen: Kok Pharos, 1993).

[53] See Vermes and Goodman, *The Essenes*, 4.

[54] Jan Willem van Henten and Luuk Huitink, "Josephus," in *Characterization in Ancient Greek Literature: Studies in Ancient Greek Narrative 4*. Edited by Koen De Temmerman and Evert van Emde Boas. Mnemosyne Supplements 411 (Leiden: Brill, 2018), 251–270; also Steve Mason, "Essenes and Lurking Spartans in Josephus' *Judean War*: From Story to History," in *Making History: Josephus and Historical Method*. Edited by Zuleika Rogers (Leiden: Brill, 2007), 219–261 and Collins, *Beyond the Qumran Community*, 122–165 who offer a current and considered discussion. On the idealised nature of Philo's description of the Therapeutae, see Benedikt Eckhardt, "Meals and Politics in the *Yaḥad*: A Reconsideration," *DSD* 17 (2010): 180–209, 190–191. For a detailed recent study that is more confident in our ability to gain historically reliable insights from the classical authors on the Essenes while acknowledging the need to allow for ancient rhetorical conventions see Taylor, *The Essenes*.

[55] See 1.2.2 above.

Cave 1 has enduring romantic appeal.[56] A close reading of the Community Rules reveals, however, all is not what it seems, and it is to this more checkered record that I will now turn.

1.4.3 Sharing Not Always So Nicely and Sometimes with the Wrong People

Scholars have also offered some romanticising readings of the evidence on shared goods as it emerges from the Community Rules. Shared property is advocated in 1QS 1:12, 13 with no preserved text in 4QS. Incidental further references also occur in the material dealing with anyone who refuses to enter the covenant,[57] the regulations on the admission of new members[58] and infractions listed in the penal code.[59]

Two pieces of inscribed pottery initially identified as the "Yaḥad ostracon" were originally thought to refer to the handing over of an estate, including a slave, by a certain Honi in the course of being admitted into the community.[60] Subsequently Ada Yardeni has proposed a credible alternative transcription of the ostracon which lacks any reference to the communal property of the yahad.[61]

There has been a great amount of interest in the ideal of shared property in the Community Rules – perhaps partly fuelled by parallels with accounts of early Christian and rabbinic practices, the descriptions of the Esseses in the classical sources and the practices of Graeco-Roman associations. In particular, the practice of shared goods was keenly compared to accounts of the practices of early Christians (Acts 2:44–45; 3:32–35), the rabbinic *haburah*,[62] Greco-Roman voluntary associations and Pythagoreans,[63] and accounts of the Essenes in the classical sources.[64]

---

[56] See Mébarki and Puech, *Les manuscrits de la mer Morte*, 19–20.

[57] 1QS 3:2 // 4Q257 3:3, see 3.2.4 and 3.4.4.

[58] 1QS 6:17, 19, 22 no preserved parallels, see further 6.5 below.

[59] 1QS 6:25 // 4Q261 3:3; 1QS 7:6; 1QS 7:25 // 4Q259 2:8 and see Chapter 7.

[60] See Frank Moore Cross and Esther Eshel, "Ostraca from Khirbet Qumrân," *IEJ* 47 (1997): 17–28 and DJD 36:497–507.

[61] Ada Yardeni, "A Draft of a Deed on an Ostracon from Khirbet Qumrân," *IEJ* 47 (1997): 233–237; see also Collins, *Beyond the Qumran Community*, 194–196.

[62] See, e. g. m. Demai 2:2–3 which does not go as far as advocating shared goods, however.

[63] Cf. Catherine Murphy, *Wealth in the Dead Sea Scrolls and in the Qumran Community.* STDJ 40 (Leiden: Brill, 2002), 6–21 with further bibliography; also Steven D. Fraade, *Legal Fictions: Studies of Law and Narrative in the Discursive Worlds of Ancient Jewish Sectarians and Sages.* JSJSup 147 (Leiden: Brill, 2011), esp. 125–143, a chapter entitled "Qumran *Yaḥad* and Rabbinic *Ḥavurah*: A Comparison Reconsidered."

[64] See, e. g., *Good Person* 85–88 where Philo describes the Essenes' common life (κοινωνία) in hyperbolic fashion as follows, "In vain would one search elsewhere for a more effective sharing of the same roof, the same way of life and the same table." See Vermes and Goodman, *The Essenes*, 22–25, here 23. Note also Philo's gushing account of the Essene virtue of frugality in *Good Person* 84 and Josephus, *J. W.* 122, 134 and *Ant.* 20. For comprehensive discussion see Todd S. Beall, *Josephus' Description of the Essenes Illustrated by the Dead Sea Scrolls.*

When we come to read the Community Rules closely, however, we are repeatedly reminded that the romanticised accounts found in the classical sources do not reflect the picture painted in these manuscripts. Several indications suggest that members were sharing goods with the wrong people or even taking food of fellow members.[65] On closer inspection the picture of communal life that emerges from the Community Rules is much less comfortable. Rather than describing an idyllic communist outpost in the Judean desert[66] the evidence suggests at least some members joined on account of economic hardship.[67] In other words, it is likely that recourse to join a movement that offered food and shelter was, for some, a form of involuntary migration driven by economic or social circumstances.[68] Need may have been particularly acute for members responsible for menial work that was not recorded in the literature, many of whom were probably illiterate.[69] The references to punishments for lying about property – the motivation for which is a moot point – with a cut in food rations[70] suggest that hardship and deprivation persisted at least for some also during their membership.[71]

1.4.4 Men, Sex and Sexuality

An area where recent scholarship has challenged earlier analyses concerning gender, impurity and sexuality concerns male impurity and sexuality. Both the archaeological remains at Khirbet Qumran and the evidence of the texts have been heavily scrutinized on the question of the presence of women in the movement behind the Community Rules where female community members are never mentioned. One argument proffered by scholars is that the absence of women in the community would have facilitated a heightened level of ritual

---

SNTSMS 58 (Cambridge: Cambridge University Press, 1988) and Murphy, *Wealth in the Dead Sea Scrolls*, 401–446.

[65] On sharing property with the wrong people or accepting their help see 1QS 5:2 // 4Q258 1:2; 1QS 5:14–15a // 4Q256 9:9 // 4Q258 1:8; 1QS 5:16 // 4Q256 9:10–11 // 4Q258 1:9–10; 1QS 5:20 // [4Q256 9:13] // [4Q258 1:11]; 1QS 8:20–24 // 4Q258 6:12; 1QS 9:8–9 // 4Q258 7:7–8; 1QS 9:22–23 // 4Q256 18:6–7 // 4Q258 8:6–7 // 4Q259 4:3–4 and 1QS 10:18–19 // 4Q260 4:6–7.

[66] See 1.2.2 above.

[67] Cf. Albert I. Baumgarten, *The Flourishing of Jewish Sects in the Maccabean Era: An Interpretation.* JSJSup 55 (Leiden: Brill, 1997), 62–66.

[68] See, e. g., Casey Strine, "The Study of Involuntary Migration as a Hermeneutical Guide for Reading the Jacob Narrative," *Biblical Interpretation* 26 (2018): 485–498.

[69] Further, Charlotte Hempel, "Reflections on Literacy, Textuality, and Community in the Qumran Dead Sea Scrolls," in *Is There a Text in this Cave? Studies in the Textuality of the Dead Sea Scrolls in Honour of George J. Brooke.* Edited by Ariel Feldman, Maria Cioată and Charlotte Hempel. STDJ 119 (Leiden: Brill, 2017), 69–82.

[70] See 7.2.2.1 below.

[71] See also 4Q270 (4QD^e) 7 i 11–12.

purity unchallenged by female menstrual impurity.[72] Whereas the halakhic issue of impurity caused by male genital emissions is well known, the challenges that frequent and unpredictable defilement by way of nightly seminal emissions would pose for communal life has been emphasized only recently.[73]

In related recent research Maxine Grossman has offered a fresh and insightful analysis of a series of infractions that appear in the penal code and involve various scenarios of exposing oneself in front of fellow members.[74] This material offers insights into interpersonal intimacy of various kinds, including behaviour of an abusive nature as implied by the suggestion of being forcibly stripped naked.[75] To Grossman's discussion I add an example from the description of the followers of the spirit of injustice that forms part of the Teaching on the Two Spirits. Thus 1QS 4:10 // 4Q257 5:8 refers to "lustful desire that leads to abominable deeds" as one of the hallmarks of those who follow the spirit of injustice. Perhaps not entirely coincidentally this statement is followed by references to ritual impurity and defiling acts (1QS 4:10). The Damascus Document makes reference to the idea of a seminal discharge brought about "by conceiving indecent plans" or, as one would call it today, sexual phantasies, see 4Q272 (4QD^f) 1 ii 3–6 // 4Q266 (4QD^a) 6 i 14–16.[76] In short, the notion that the communities described in the Community Rules exemplify a life of virtue thanks to the absence of women no longer stands, and several well-known passages have rightly been read afresh by Grossman and suggest that sexual desire and a yearning for intimacy were an integral part of the humanity represented by the movement described in the Community Rules.

1.4.5 An Ancient Sanitized Account with Contemporary Appeal

The soft underbelly of the picture painted in the Community Rules and the works of classical authors exposes often idealised and exoticized accounts in our ancient sources.[77] Moreover, ancient descriptions of the Essenes in turn set the

---

[72] See Cecilia Wassén, "Purity Laws for Men and Women in the Dead Sea Scrolls: A Comparison of Ideals and Praxis," in *Frauen im antiken Judentum und frühen Christentum*. Edited by Jörg Frey and Nicole Rupschus. WUNT II.489 (Tübingen: Mohr Siebeck, 2019), 57–84.

[73] See Lev 15:16; Wassén "Purity Laws;" also Paula Fredriksen, "Did Jesus Oppose the Purity Laws," *Bible Review* 11 (1995): 18–25.

[74] See Maxine L. Grossman, "Postmodern Questions and Sexuality Studies," in CDSS, 246–256, 250–252; further, 7.2.5 and 7.4.5 below.

[75] See 7.4.5.1.

[76] On the latter passage see Wassén, "Purity Laws;" also "זמה" in HAWTTM 2:225–226, 226 where the editors acknowledge the sexual connotations of the reference to conceiving indecent plans.

[77] For a comparable critique in the area of orality studies see Paul S. Evans, "Creating a New 'Great Divide:' The Exoticization of Ancient Culture in Some Recent Applications of Orality Studies to the Bible," *JBL* 136 (2017): 749–764.

tone for seminal studies on the Scrolls and the Community Rules in particular. The cumulative effect of the classical accounts of the Essenes as paragons of virtue, the Community Rules' own discourse of perfection and the location of Khirbet Qumran[78] shaped our reading of the Community Rules in powerful ways.[79] In short, the notion that the communities described in the Community Rules manuscripts lived a life of virtue at an idyllic setting where nourishment and property were freely shared does not hold up to scrutiny. In fact, we are able to trace an element of fetishization of some of the most attractive passages in the Community Rules starting in antiquity and still prevalent today. Such an approach is evident already in the literature on the Essenes that predates the discovery of the Dead Sea Scrolls in 1947.[80] Moreover, Grossman's insightful fresh reading of several passages in the penal code opens up further hermeneutical vistas within other parts of the S-tradition and beyond. In short, a close reading of the texts indicates that the scribes behind the Community Rules have left us evidence of hunger, greed, jealousy, as well as sexual desire and a yearning for intimacy that significantly impacted the lives of our ancient forebears as they continue to shape the life-experiences of current generations.

1.5 The Manuscripts

1.5.1 1Q28 (1QS)

Great credit is due to Millar Burrows who published the Plates and Transcription of the Community Rule from Cave 1 promptly in 1951.[81]

1.5.1.1 The Manuscript

The original leather is of a beautiful light tan colour that is particularly visible in parts of the opening margin that precedes 1QS 1 and in the margins of columns 1–4. These columns would have been somewhat less exposed to damage as the scroll containing 1QS was rolled with the beginning on the

---

[78] See 1.4.2 above.

[79] For a more confident reading of the evidence on the Essenes which are identified with the movement behind the Scrolls that nevertheless highlights intricate utopian and idealistic strands across a range of ancient sources see Doron Mendels, "Hellenistic Utopia and the Essens," *HTR* 72 (1979): 207–222.

[80] See Charlotte Hempel, "The Essenes," in *Religious Diversity in the Graeco-Roman World.* Edited by Dan Cohn-Sherbok and John M. Court (Sheffield: Sheffield Academic Press, 2001), 65–80 and further literature cited there.

[81] See Burrows with the assistance of John C. Trever and William H. Brownlee, *The Dead Sea Scrolls of St. Mark's Monastery. Volume II, Fascicle 2: Plates and Transcription of the Manual* of Discipline (New Haven, CT: ASOR, 1951).

inside.[82] I will, however, refer to damage that affected the first sheet containing 1QS 1–3 in particular below. 1QS is inscribed on five sheets of various sizes containing between 22 and 27 lines per column and has been dated on paleographical grounds to around 100–75 BCE.[83] The final column 1QS 11 is unusual by occupying a single sheet and lacking the dry horizontal and vertical lines attested in the remaining columns. On the basis of these considerations Hartmut Stegemann suggested that 1QS 11 was added on a separate sheet after the inclusion of the Teaching on the Two Spirits had brought the original calculations out of kilter.[84] In his introduction to a volume that reproduces the earliest series of photographs of 1QS taken by John Trever in 1948 and 1949 Cross writes regarding 1QS, "The work [...] was inscribed on fine white leather regularly chosen by this scribe for his copies of manuscripts."[85]

1QS is part of a scroll that is in two pieces with a separation between columns 7 and 8. A gap between the third and fourth sheet can be seen clearly on the digital images of the manuscript hosted by the Shrine of the Book photographed by Ardon Bar-Hama (http://dss.collections.imj.org.il/community). In fact, the two parts of 1QS were originally presented separately to John Trever, who took the first photographs of the scroll at the American Schools of Oriental Research, by the Syrian Metropolitan Mar Athanasius Samuel and Father Butros Sowmy.[86] 1QS was subsequently acquired by Yigael Yadin on behalf of the State of Israel and is now housed in two cases in the vault of the Shrine of the Book. The two annexes to 1QS – 1QSa and 1QSb – went to the Palestine Archaeological Museum.[87] 1QSa follows after the final column of 1QS (1QS 11) and begins with the heading "This is the rule for the congregration of Israel in the last days" which forms the basis of the work's English title "The Rule of the Congregation" (1QSa). This work displays terminological and thematic links with the Community Rules as well as the communal rules attested in the Laws of the Damascus Document.[88] The final work on the same scroll begins with the

---

[82] See Sarianna Metso, *The Textual Development of the Qumran Community Rule*. STDJ 21 (Leiden: Brill, 1997), 13.

[83] See Frank M. Cross, "The Paleographical Dates of the Manuscripts," PTSDSSP 1: 57; also Cross, "The Development of the Jewish Scripts," in *The Bible and the Ancient Near East: Essays in Honor of William Foxwell Albright*. Edited by G. Ernest Wright (London: Routledge and Kegan Paul, 1961), 133–202.

[84] See Stegemann, "Some Remarks to *1QSa*, to *1QSb*, and to Qumran Messianism," *RevQ* 17 (1996): 479–505.

[85] See "Introduction," in John C. Trever, *Scrolls from Qumrân Cave I: The Great Isaiah Scroll-The Order of the Community-The Pesher to Habakkuk*. Edited by Frank Moore Cross, David Noel Freedman and James A. Sanders (Jerusalem: The Albright Institute of Archaeological Research and the Shrine of the Book, 1972), 1–5, 4.

[86] For an engaging first-hand account of these events see John C. Trever, *The Untold Story of Qumran* (London: Pickering and Inglis, 1965), especially 49–51.

[87] See Martin, *Scribal Character of the Dead Sea Scrolls*, 1:49–55.

[88] See Lawrence H. Schiffman, *The Eschatological Community of the Dead Sea Scrolls*.

heading "Words of blessing for the Maskil" and has been given the English title "The Rule of Blessings" (1QSb). Like 1QSa, the Rule of Blessings also displays connections to the Rules of the Community such as the reference to the figure of the Maskil[89] in connection with liturgical material as well as assigning a prominent role to the sons of Zadok, the priests.[90] On the other hand, the series of blessings and curses in the Covenant Ceremony[91] do not alot any role to the figure of the Maskil, or any other individual for that matter. It is also curious that 1QSa attests six instances where "the people of" is spelled אנושי, a spelling never found in 1QS.[92] In addition, Eric Reymond has recently identified a series of linguistic features pertaining especially to orthography and phonology that are much more prominent in 1QS than in 1QSa and 1QSb.[93]

Based on my examination of a photograph (negative number 7111a) of the end of 1QS taken by Moshe Kirschner in 1954 – kindly made available to me by the staff of the Shrine of the Book – we have clear evidence that 1QSa was stitched to the end of 1QS. A remarkably well preserved seam of stitching runs all along the left margin of 1QS 11 even though it is not visible upon inspecting the recto of the scroll either in the form of images or the original manuscript which I was able to examine.[94] These findings are confirmed in a series of photographs of the verso of 1QS that were taken in the course of a condition report prepared by the Israel Antiquities Lab in 2002–2003 where the stitching at the end of 1QS 11 is clearly visible. Tiny traces of stitching are also visible on the colour photograph taken by Trever in 1948.[95] It is clear that 1QSa was no longer connected to 1QS at this point. The same photograph also reveals a better preserved line of stitches attaching the final sheet of 1QS containing the single column 1QS 11 which suggests a considerable amount of deterioration in the intervening decades.[96]

SBLMS 38 (Atlanta, GA: Scholars Press, 1989) and Charlotte Hempel, "The Earthly Essene Nucleus of 1QSa," *DSD* 3 (1996): 253–269 [reprinted as Chapter 3 in Hempel, *Qumran Rule Texts in Context*)].

[89] See Chapter 15 below.

[90] Cf. 1QSb 3:22–23.

[91] See Chapter 3 below.

[92] See further Eibert Tigchelaar, "The Scribe of 1QS," in *Emanuel: Studies in the Hebrew Bible, Septuagint, and the Dead Sea Scrolls in Honor of Emanuel Tov*. Edited by Shalom Paul et al. VTSup 94 (Leiden: Brill, 2003), 439–452, 446.

[93] Eric Reymond, "The Scribe of 1QS, 1QSa, 1QSb, 4Q53 (4QSam^c), 4Q175 and Three Features of Orthography and Phonology," *DSD* 25 (2018): 238–254.

[94] I am grateful to the Curator of the Shrine, Dr. Adolfo Roitman, as well as Hasia Rimon and Irene Lewitt, for their assistance which allowed me to examine 1QS and the Shrine's photographs of the scroll on May 7, 2014.

[95] See *Scrolls from Qumrân Cave I*, 147.

[96] For the view that 1QSa and 1QSb were never part of the same scroll as 1QS but merely rolled together, see Emanuel Tov, *Scribal Practices and Approaches Reflected in Texts Found in the Judean Desert*. STDJ 54 (Leiden: Brill, 2004), 111, n. 149.

The top edge of the top margin of 1QS is relatively well preserved with the exception of the first sheet preserving 1QS 1–3. Evidence of moisture damage originating from the top right corner of 1QS 1 that has caused damage to the top margin of the first sheet is visible. This moisture discoloured the top right of column 1 and then made its way down the central part of columns 1 and 2. The direction of the contamination indicates that the source penetrated at an angle which suggests that the scroll was stored leaning to the right.[97] Our scroll was discovered in a storage jar alongside the Great Isaiah Scroll (1QIsa[a]) and the Habakkuk Commentary (1QpHab).[98] A detailed study of the archaeological assemblage, including more than 54 storage jars that were packed tightly into the cave, was conducted by Joan Taylor, Dennis Mizzi and Marcello Fidanzio.[99] They also suggest that the wooden pole found in the cave may have served as a yoke to transport filled jars to the cave and through its originally very small opening. It is most unlikely, then, that the scrolls remained in an upright position, and the moisture damage pattern at the top right of the first column of 1QS illustrates this. The variation in the colour of the skin in the early columns of 1QS is already mentioned by Trever.[100] Our oberservations can be checked against the digital photographs available on the website of the Shrine of the Book (http://dss.collections.imj.org.il/community). The bottom margin of 1QS displays a regular pattern of damage that was caused by rodents and which continues along the bottom margin of 1QSa as indicated by Milik.[101] Harding also refers to evidence of rats having gnawed away at non-literary finds in Cave 1.[102]

Stitching holes on the right margin of 1QS 1 where a handle sheet was once attached are visible on the Shrine's digital images. Earlier photos attest to the remains of the stitching itself on a protruding part of the seam that reaches to just below the level of line 2.[103] Moreover, the inscribed remains on the verso of a handlesheet that preceded 1QS 1 appear to refer to additional material beyond 1QS.[104]

The precise relationship of 1QS, 1QSa and 1QSb is still debated though some kind of affiliation of all three works is beyond doubt and was expressed by Milik when he published 1QSa and 1QSb as appendices ("Annexes à la règle de la communauté") and suggested they were rolled together with the end of 1QS and

---

[97] I am grateful to Noam Mizrahi for a personal conversation on this matter.

[98] See Gerald Lankester Harding, "Introductory," DJD 1:3–7.

[99] Joan E. Taylor, Dennis Mizzi and Marcello Fidanzio, "Revisiting Qumran Cave 1Q and Its Archaeological Assemblage," *PEQ* 149 (2017): 295–325.

[100] See *Scrolls from Qumrân Cave I*, 10–11 where he was concerned with some unevenness of tone in his negatives.

[101] See DJD 1:107–108 and Martin, *Scribal Character of the Dead Sea Scrolls*, 1:51.

[102] See "Introductory," 7.

[103] Cf. Trever, *Scrolls from Qumrân Cave I*, 127 and Burrows, *Dead Sea Scrolls*, n.p.

[104] See further 2.3 below.

probably also stitched on.[105] Hartmut Stegemann described the scroll containing all three works as a large scale anthology or "Großhandschrift" which he divided into five separate compositions: community rules that are mostly taken up by the topic of covenant renewal (1QS 1:1–3:12); the teaching on the two spirits (1QS 3:13–4:26); disciplinary rules (1QS 5:1–11:22); the oldest community rule of the Essenes (1QSa) and the rule of blessings (1QSb) which he describes as a twin ("Zwilling") of 1QSa.[106] A curious scribal feature shared by the scribe of 1QS and 1QSa is the large amount of empty space left at the end of 1QS 11 and 1QSa 2.[107] I would add to Martin's perceptive observations that both 1QS 11 and 1QSa 2 end after 22 lines with a paragraphos in the margin just below the last line.[108] Morever, as Tigchelaar has pointed out, the use of paragraphos hooks in the margin, which he identifies with a cryptic *ayin*, is used by this scribe in 1QS, 1QSa and 1QSb and with slight differences in appearance also in 4Q175 (Testimonia).[109] Literary connections that run across both 1QS and 1QSa have been identified in the form of the tradition that promotes the sons of Zadok in 1QS 5 and 1QSa.[110]

1.5.1.2 The Scribe

The scribe of 1QS was rather prolific and also copied 1QSa and 1QSb on the same scroll, 4QSamuel[c] (4Q53), 4QTestimonia (4Q175) as well as being responsible for a number of corrections in 1QIsa[a]. It is possible our scribe was responsible for the superlinear correction in 1QIsa[a] 33:7 (Isa 40:7) of "our God" to four dots, a practice attested for Isa 40:3 in 1QS 8:14.[111] The same corrector left the divine name in Isa 40:3, the passage quoted in 1QS 8:14, untouched in 1QIsa[a] 33:2. Martin identified a second scribe as responsible for copying 1QSa though this view has not found widespread support.[112] Perhaps the harshest judgment on the author-scribe of 1QS was expressed in 1951 by Johannes van der Ploeg who described the author as illiterate.[113]

---

[105] See DJD 1:107–108.

[106] Stegemann, *Die Essener, Qumran, Johannes der Täufer und Jesus* (Freiburg im Breisgau: Herder, 1993), 152–164; see also Stegemann, "Some Remarks."

[107] Further, Martin, *Scribal Character of the Dead Sea Scrolls*, 1:55.

[108] See also Falk, "In the Margins," 24.

[109] Tigchelaar, "Scribe," 442.

[110] See Chapters 5 and 6 below as well as Hempel, "Earthly Essenes Nucleus;" further, Robert Kugler, "A Note on 1QS 9:14: The Sons of Righteousness or the Sons of Zadok," *DSD* 3 (1996): 315–320 and 14.4.2 below. For a detailed recent examination of these issues see Michael Johnson, "One Work or Three? A Proposal for Reading 1QS-1QSa-1QSb as a Single Composite Work," *DSD* 25 (2018): 141–177.

[111] Cf. Tigchelaar, "Scribe," 441–442 and 8.3 below.

[112] Martin, *Scribal Character of the Dead Sea Scrolls*, 1:55–56.

[113] See van der Ploeg, "Le 'Manuel de Discipline' des Roulaux de la Mer Morte," *BO* 8 (1951): 113–126, 114.

Several scholars have drawn attention to the large number of scribal corrections and empty spaces that mark various parts of 1QS. Thus, Cross observed features such as the "omission of words, leaving blanks in their stead" which he attributed to the use of a poorly legible *Vorlage*. In the accompanying footnote Cross refers to 1QS 10:4, a line which attests a *nun* followed by a *vacat*.[114] The suggestion of a poorly legible *Vorlage* is supported by the observation that the heavily corrected and disrupted inscription in 1QS is located at the same part of each column in 1QS 7–8 starting with line 6. This suggests a regular damage pattern in a rolled *Vorlage*.[115] We also observe a parallel though diverse pattern of damage at either side of the major seam that once held sheets 3 and 4 of 1QS together. An examination of the vertical cracks that mark both columns 7 and 8 suggests, as one might expect, that these cracks originated after inscription. This central seam would have been subject to a great deal of pressure in antiquity and post discovery. The damage pattern on either side of this seam probably originated at different periods including during the deposit in the Cave as a series of worm holes suggest.[116]

Despite the fragmentary nature of the Cave 4 manuscripts a number of features are suggestive of the possibility that the paleographically distinctive manuscript 4Q259 may have been one of the sources used by the scribe of 1QS.[117] I already noted the possibility that the two early papyri 4Q255 and 4Q257 attest early drafts of the first four columns of 1QS.[118] In a detailed analysis of the particular character of Cave 4 I stressed that this cave contained both the bulk of multiple copies of manuscripts as well as a large proportion of workaday quality material.[119] This larger picture of the nature of the repertoire unearthed from Cave 4 supports the picture that has emerged on independent grounds from a close study of the relationship of 1QS to other S manuscripts.

As we saw, the most conspicuous columns with regard to corrections are 1QS 7–8. However, Tigchelaar has rightly indicated the need to adopt a more fine-tuned approach even within these two columns. Tigchelaar bracketed out 1QS 8:15–9:11 as attesting very few corrections at a rate that is entirely compatible with most of 1QS.[120] This methodological advancement can be pushed fur-

---

[114] Cf. Cross, "Introduction," 4 and 15.3 below.

[115] For the suggestion of a damaged *Vorlage* in 1QS 7:7–8 see Émile Puech, "Remarques sur l'écriture de 1QS VII–VIII," *RevQ* 10 (1979): 35–43 and 7.3 below.

[116] On the importance to differentiate the pre-deposit, deposit and post-deposite history of the manuscripts see Mladen Popović, "Qumran as Scroll Storehouse in Times of Crisis? A Comparative Perspective on Judaean Desert Manuscript Collections," *JSJ* 43 (2012): 551–594.

[117] For details see 1.5.6.2 below.

[118] See 1.5.2 and 1.5.4 below.

[119] See Hempel, "'Haskalah at Qumran:' The Eclective Character of Qumran Cave 4," in *Qumran Rule Texts in Context*, 303–338 and now see also Sidnie White Crawford, *Scribes and Scrolls at Qumran* (Grand Rapids, MI: Eerdmans, 2019).

[120] Tigchelaar, "Scribe," 451.

ther by observing the pristine text of 1QS 8:1–5a. As well as being alert to the significance of heavily damaged sections it is necessary to be equally attentive to the significance of passages that are more pristine, and suggest a more stable text derived from a well preserved *Vorlage*. A fascinating example is the section identified by Tigchelaar (1QS 8:15–9:11) which is also lacking from 4Q259.[121]

Several scholars have observed the work of two scribes in 1QS 7–8 with Martin identifying of two scibes on a much more comprehensive scale.[122] Dominique Barthélemy suggested that the scribe of the Rule of the Congregation (1QSa) was responsible for the corrections in 1QS 7–8.[123] In a comprehensive analysis Puech identifies the work of two corrector scribes and can be summarized as follows:

Corrections inserted by the original scribe of 1QS (Scribe A), or one of his collaborators upon re-reading the text, are found in 1QS 7:1; 1QS 7:6–7; 1QS 7:8 with the exception of the phrase "one year;" 1QS 7:10–11; 1QS 7:19 the last three words, 1QS 7:20 erasure of dittography of "rabbim" and addition of "pure liquid;" 1QS 7:21 second half; 1QS 7:22; 1QS 7:23 up until "and it (his spirit) turns back" and including the last word in the line "before." In addition, all corrections in 1QS 8 with the exception of 1QS 8:10, 12–13.

Additions and glosses that go back to a different hand (Scribe B) comprise 1QS 7:8 "one year;" the substantial superlinear addition in 1QS 8:10 and the superlinear additions "as a community" and "according to these rules" in 1QS 8:12–13.[124]

On Puech's suggestion some of the corrections in 1QS 7 may have drawn on 4Q259.[125]

1.5.1.3 Marginal Signs

1QS is one of the scrolls that attests a particularly large number of scribal signs.[126] The signs can be divided intro three categories which are listed in the following table.

---

[121] See 1.5.6 below.

[122] Cf. Guilbert, "La Règle de la Communauté;" Metso, *Textual Development*, 95–105; Tigchelaar, "Scribe;" Puech, "Écriture de 1QS VII–VIII" and Martin, *Scribal Character of the Dead Sea Scrolls*, 2:431–448 and sections 7.3 and 8.3 below.

[123] See DJD 1:107–108.

[124] Puech, "Écriture de 1QS VII–VIII," 42.

[125] This is suggested by Puech, "Écriture de 1QS VII–VIII," 43. See also 1.5.6.2 below.

[126] Cf. Tov, *Scribal Practices*, 178.

Table 1: Marginal Signs in 1QS

Marginal Signs in 1QS			
Group 1: Palaeo-Hebrew *vav*			
Reference	Description	Marginal Position	Literary Position
1QS 5:1 Cf. 4Q256 9:1 *gimel*	Palaeo-Hebrew *vav.*	Top right corner, outside of text block.	New section dealing with the formation and organization of the community.[127]
Group 2: Composite Signs			
1QS 7:26–8:1	(Paragraphos?) plus paleo-Hebrew *zayin* and unidentified triangular sign.	Bottom right corner protruding into writing block of empty line 1QS 7:26. Cf. paragraphos following 1QS 11:22.	An alternative vision of community formation following an extensive cluster dealing with the many.[128]
1QS 9:3	Paragraphos plus paleo-Hebrew *zayin* and paleo-Hebrew *samek.*	At the beginning of the line and protruding in equal parts into the writing block and the margin. The lower part extends to the top of the following line.	A new section that describes the formation of the community in cultic terms.[129]
{1QS 10:6}	Pargraphos above the remains of an erased composite marginal sign.[130]	At the beginning of the line with the lower part reaching the top of the following line.	Introducing the first person voice of the speaker.[131]

---

[127] See Chaper 5.

[128] For details see Chapter 8.

[129] Cf. Chapter 11 below.

[130] See 15.3 below.

[131] Further, Chapter 15 below and Daniel K. Falk, "In the Margins of the Dead Sea Scrolls," in *Bible as Notepad: Tracing Annotation and Annotation Practices in Late Antique and Medieval Biblical Manuscripts.* Edited by Liv Ingeborg Lied and Marilena Maniaci (Berlin: De Gruyter, 2018), 10–38, 23–24 who identifies the sign as a paragraphos.

Group 3: Paragraphoi

1	{1QS 1:20}	Erased after a double amen and before the priests speak.
2	{1QS 2:10}	Erased after a double amen and before the priests and levites take the word.
3	1QS 2:18	After a third double amen that marks the end of the Covenant Admission Ceremony to be followed in 1QS 2:19 by an Annual Ceremony for current members.[132]
4	1QS 3:12	A faint paragraphos marks the end of the Covenant Ceremony. The paragraphos is in line with the equally faint inscribed letters starting this line, perhaps suggesting the same hand added the paragraphos here.
5	1QS 3:18	Marking the crucial first reference to God's establishment of the Two Spirits.[133]
6	1QS 4:1	Marking the end of a sub-section describing the establishment of the two spirits and the beginning of the sub-section on the spirit of truth and its followers at 1QS 4:2.
7	1QS 4:8	Marking the transition from the end of the sub-section on the spirit of truth and its followers to the topic of the spirit of injustice and its followers which starts at 1QS 4:9. Significantly, remains of a paragraphos at this point are also preserved in 4Q257 5:6. The remains of the paragraphos were previously published as 4Q487 (papSap B?) 37:2 by Baillet and subsequently identified as part of 4Q257 by Tigchelaar.[134]
8	1QS 4:14	Marking the transition from the sub–section on the spirit of injustice and its followers and the final section of the Teaching which deals with the struggle of the two spirits in human hearts and judgment which begins at 1QS 4:15.
9	1QS 5:13	This is a particularly illuminating case where the paragraphos accompanies a mid-line *vacat* that marks the end of a major plus in 1QS followed by closer textual proximity between 1QS 5 with the shorter text of 4Q256 9:8–9 and 4Q258 1:7–8.[135] A further plus in 1QS follows.
10	1QS 5:25	This appears to be another case where a paragraphos coincides with a short plus in 1QS over against 4Q258 2:4, cf. 1QS 5:13 and 8:13.
11	1QS 6:8	This marks the transition from the nightly meetings of the many to the daytime meetings of the many.[136]

---

[132] See Chapters 3 and 1QS 11:15.

[133] See also 1QS 8:10.

[134] Cf. Baillet, DJD 7:5–10 and Plate 4 and Eibert Tigchelaar, "'These are the Names of the Spirits of …': A Preliminary Edition of *4QCatalogue of Spirits* (4Q230) and New Manuscript Evidence for the *Two Spirits Treatise* (4Q257 and 1Q29a)," *RevQ* 21 (2004): 529–548.

[135] Compare also 1QS 5:25, 1QS 8:10 and 1QS 8:13 below.

[136] For details see 6.5 below.

12   1QS 6:23   This marks the end of the rules on the admission of new members in the course of meetings of the many and the beginning of the penal code.[137]

13   1QS 8:4   This paragraphos coincides with the transition between two distinctive accounts of the emergence of the council of the community but may also mark the reference to a potent moment in time (עת) as is the case in 1QS 9:5; 9:11 and 9:19.[138]

14   1QS 8:10   A foreshortened paragraphos positioned higher and in line with the inscription rather than just below the line coincides with a superlinear plus in 1QS over against 4Q259 2 as well as a transition between two subsections which I identify in Chapter 8 below.

15   1QS 8:13   An unusal paragraphos that resembles what Tov calls "composite paragraphoi" at 1QIsa^a 28:23; 32:29 and 35:23.[139] Its position at the beginning of a super-linear addition of a plus in 1QS is also distinctive though the use of a paragraphos to mark an expansion or its end in 1QS occurs also in 1QS 5:13, 1QS 5:25 and possibly 1QS 8:10. It is possible the addition was added after the paragraphos was in place.

16   1QS 8:19   This is a point of transition to the new section on the conduct and discipline for the people of perfect holiness.[140]

17   1QS 9:5   This paragraphos appears to highlight a reference to a potent moment marked by the words "at this time." The reference to "at this time" is marked by a *vacat* in 4Q258 7:6.[141]

18   1QS 9:11   This paragraphos might might mark the transition to the new section containing the Statutes for the Maskil which contains another reference to time. Another possibility is that the paragraphos draws attention to the reference to the expected time of the arrival of the eschatological prophet and the messiahs of Aaron and Israel.[142]

19   1QS 9:19   This paragraphos is the third to accompany a significant moment in time in the form of a reference to Isa 40:3.[143]

20   1QS 11:15 This marks the transition to the Final Blessing and an account of the psalmist's human inadequacies. The paragraphos is supplemented by a dicolon in the text.[144]

21   1QS 11:22 This concludes the Community Rule as represented by 1QS.[145]

---

[137] Cf. 6.5 and Chapter 7 below.

[138] Further, Chapter 8 below.

[139] Tov, *Scribal Practices*, 361.

[140] See Chapter 10 below.

[141] Further, Chapter 11 below.

[142] Cf. Chapter 14 below as well as the signs in 1QS 8:4; 9:5 and 1QS 9:19.

[143] See Chapter 14 below.

[144] Cf. Tov, *Scribal Practices*, 211.

[145] See Chapter 15 below.

1.5.1.3.1 Palaeo-Hebrew Vav

A palaeo-Hebrew *vav* is found in the top right corner of column 1QS 5 which introduces a new textual unit.[146] This position is distinctive from the three composite marginal signs in 1QS by being placed in the margin without intruding into the writing block of the column. The composite marginal signs in 1QS sit almost centrally aligned on the notional vertical line that marks the beginning of the writing block. In fact, the position of the composite marginal signs at 1QS 8:1; 9:3 and erased in 10:6 corresponds to the marginal position of the paragraphoi in 1QS. An affiliation between the paragraphoi and the composite signs is reinforced by the inclusion of a paragraphos at the top of the complex sign at 1QS 9:3[147] and possibly also at the top of the complex sign marking the end of 1QS 7 and the new beginning at 1QS 8:1. Tov identifies the former as palaeo-Hebrew *zayin* combined with an unknown symbol. A paragraphos also forms part of the erased composite sign which I identify at 1QS 10:6.

In terms of its position in the margin the palaeo-Hebrew *vav* at 1QS 5:1 corresponds to the *gimel* in 4Q256 9:1.[148] Tov discusses the *gimel* in 4Q256 as a separate phenomenon in a section on "Letters and marks possibly marking sheets and units" but does not include 1QS 5:1 in the same discussion.[149] Both the palaeo-Hebrew *vav* in 1QS 5:1 and the *gimel* at 4Q256 9:1 are clearly presented apart from the text block in each manuscript making them para-textual in the strict sense. Alongside the shared paragraphos between 1QS 4:8 and 4Q257 5:6 (originally identified as 4Q487 37:2)[150] the *gimel* in 4Q256 constitutes a second confluence of paratextual features in 1QS and witnesses from 4Q, an area that deserves more attention. Tov recognized that the palaeo-Hebrew *vav* marks a new beginning in terms of content in 1QS.[151] However, given its position at a literary tectonic plate in the growth of the S tradition[152] it is more likely that the paleo-Hebrew *vav* was employed as the complex composition represented by 1QS was put together and leaves us a piece of tangible evidence for the careful planning that lies behind this text and the larger scroll of which it is a part. Rather than having a numerical value the use of paleo-Hebrew *vav* to indicate a major new

---

[146] See 5.1 below as well Tov, *Scribal Practices*, 206–208, 361 and Tov, "Letters of the Cryptic A Script and Paleo-Hebrew Letters Used as Scribal Marks in Some Qumran Scrolls," *DSD* 2 (1995): 330–339.

[147] Tov, *Scribal Practices*, 107, 363.

[148] Pace Tov, *Scribal Practices*, 179 who suggests "the signs in 1QS V are not found in the parallel of 4QS^b [4Q256]."

[149] See *Scribal Practices*, 199.

[150] Further, Baillet, DJD 7:5–10 and Plate 4; Tigchelaar, "Names of the Spirits" and 1.5.1.3 above.

[151] See also the paragraphoi at 1QS 5:13; 5:25; 8:10; 8:13 and Table 1 above.

[152] See 1.1 above and 1.6 below.

section in 1QS could be an extension of the in-text employment of the same letter in a number of paleo-Hebrew manuscripts.[153]

1.5.1.3.2 Composite Signs

The composite sign in the bottom right margin of 1QS 7 is positioned at the end of an extensive section on the meeting and business of the many.[154] It marks the transition to a new section that contains further accounts of the formation of the community as well as disciplinary and organizational rules. Its position below the text and straddling the notional vertical line where the writing block begins mirrors the paragraphos that marks the end of 1QS 11 as well as 1QSa 2.[155]

A second composite sign in 1QS 9:3 marks the beginning of a section on the formation of the community in cultic terms. The enigmatic nature of the two palaeo-Hebrew letters *zayin* and *samek* that form part of the sign at 1QS 9:3 has been interpreted by Tov as possibly conveying a cryptic message. It is curious to observe that 4Q259 3:3–4 attests two phrases in cryptic script in a passage that begins with the phrase "When these exist in Israel" which recurs here in 1QS 9:3.[156] The latter passage belongs to a larger section that stretches from 1QS 8:15b–9:11 and which is lacking from 4Q259 and likely an expansion in 1QS and 4Q258. Within the expansion, which is made up of a series of shorter sections, 1QS 9:3–6 // 4Q258 7:4–7a is distinctive in revisiting themes that were introduced in the material on the Council of the Community preserved in 1QS 8:1–16a with parallels in 4Q258 and 4Q259.[157] This chapter is preceded by the first composite marginal sign discussed above. Two sections on disciplinary issues follow and are presented in Chapters 9 and 10 below. The manuscript then returns to the topic of the formation of the community in cultic terms which is introduced with a second composite marginal sign as well as a generous *vacat*. In both cases, i. e. preceding 1QS 8 and at 1QS 9:3, the composite signs mark material relating to the formation of the community as an expected turning point.[158]

We identify a further erased composite sign at 1QS 10:6, at precisely the point in the final Hymn where the speaker's first person voice is first heard.[159]

---

[153] Cf. Tov, *Scribal Practices*, 184. I am grateful to Noam Mizrahi for suggesting the latter connection.

[154] See Chapters 6 and 7 below.

[155] See also 1.5.1 above.

[156] For details see 1.5.6 and Chapter 8 below.

[157] See Chapter 8 below.

[158] Further, Chapters 8 and 11 below.

[159] See also 1.5.1.3 above.

1.5.1.3.3 Paragraphoi

We identified 21 paragraphoi in 1QS including a number of faint or erased instances in Table 1 above.[160] As indicated in the far right column of of the table, I suggest a diverse range of functions for the paragraphoi in 1QS. A substantial number of paragraphoi mark a transition from one section to another. The positions of the erased paragraphoi in 1QS 1:20 and 1QS 2:10 as well as those in 1QS 2:18 in the Covenant Ceremony, 1QS 11:15 in the Final Hymn and the erased composite sign in 1QS 10:6 appear to mark particular portions of speech.[161] In the Teaching on the Two Spirits a paragraphos marks the crucial point which refers to the establishment of the two spirits followed by three further signs that mark sections dealing with the spirits of truth and injustice and their respective followers (1QS 3:18; 1QS 4:1; 1QS 4:8 and 1QS 4:14). Two cases in 1QS 5 coincide with (the end of) a plus in 1QS (1QS 5:13 and 1QS 5:25).[162] Noteworthy, finally, are three cases where a paragraphos accompanies a reference to a potent moment in time (1QS 9:5; 1QS 9:11 and 1QS 9:19) in the Statutes for the Maskil.[163]

It emerges from this discussion that there are intriguing connections between the position of marginal signs in 1QS and its complex literary growth of 1QS. A number of paragraphoi and marginal marks constitute indicators of the literary equivalent of continental drift in the geology of S.[164] The palaeo-Hebrew *vav* at 1QS 5:1 illustrates the meticulous planning needed for putting together a complex composition on the basis of pre-existing sources. I suspect the same is true for at least some of the paragraphoi that coincide with the location of plusses in 1QS, for instance. Moreover, the paragraphos at 1QS 3:18 marks the precise line in which the two spirits are first mentioned. This juncture in the Treatise has been identified by some scholars as a seam in the growth of the Treatise on literary grounds.[165]

1.5.1.4 Significant Textual Features

The one overriding textual characteristic of 1QS in relation to the other S manuscripts is that its text is almost always longer. This is not the same as acknowledging that 1QS is by far the best preserved manuscript of the Community Rules and preserves more text than any of the other witnesses. Rather, 1QS contains a series of plusses that were lacking in one or more of the other manuscripts.[166]

---

[160] Compare further Tov, *Scribal Practices*, 180–184.

[161] Cf. 1.5.1.3.2 above and 3.3 below.

[162] See Chapter 6.

[163] Compare Chapter 14 below.

[164] Cf. 1.1 above.

[165] Further, 4.1.3 below.

[166] See Charlotte Hempel, "The Long Text of the *Serekh* as Crisis Literature," *RevQ* 27 (2015): 3–24.

1.5.1.4.1 The Opening Framework in 1QS 1–4

The most substantial plus is represented by the material in 1QS 1–4 which is lacking from 4Q258.[167] While parts of this opening framework are also attested in other manuscripts, 1QS is often our only witness. Where other manuscripts have preserved material corresponding to the text of these four columns of 1QS there are no major discrepancies preserved. In a pioneering study that pre-dates the publication of the Cave 4 manuscripts which confirm a form of the text of the Community Rules that lacked these four columns (4Q258) Jerome Murphy-O'Connor suggested that the addition of 1QS 1–4 was the final phase in the growth of 1QS.[168]

1.5.1.4.2 1QS 5

Of the remaining columns of 1QS, 1QS 5 attests a large number of plusses of different lengths which cover a number of themes and emphases that recur such as references to the sons of Zadok, the covenant, a condemnation of obstinate behaviour, an emphasis on the correct observance of the law, as well as a series of explicit biblical quotations.[169] At times the plusses in 1QS 5 reflect the polemical stance of statements in 1QS 1–4.[170]

1.5.1.4.3 1QS 6:1c–7a Rules on Meetings in Various Dwelling Places

The material attested here is preserved in parts of four manuscripts (1QS, 4Q258, 4Q261 and 4Q263) without any significant variations where the manuscripts overlap. It is important to acknowledge, however, that 6.4.2.3 (The Need for Coninuous Torah Study in 1QS 6:6–7a) is attested only in 1QS with 4Q258 preserving a shorter text at this point.

1.5.1.4.4 1QS 6:7b–23 Meetings of the Many

Parts of this material are again preserved in four manuscripts (1QS, 4Q256, 4Q258 and 4Q261) though much more fragmentarily. There is evidence indicating a shorter text in 4Q256.[171]

---

[167] Cf. 1.5.5 and Chapter 5 below.

[168] Murphy-O'Connor, "La genèse littéraire de la Règle de la Communauté," *RB* 76 (1969): 528–549, 533–537 and the refinements offered by Jean Pouilly, *La Règle de la Communauté de Qumrân: Son évolution littéraire.* Cahiers de la Revue Biblique 17 (Paris: Gabalda, 1976).

[169] See Sarianna Metso, "Biblical Quotations in the Community Rule," in *The Bible as Book: The Hebrew Bible and the Judaean Desert Discoveries.* Edited by Edward D. Herbert and Emanuel Tov (London: The British Library, 2002), 81–92 as well as Chapter 5 and 6.1 below.

[170] Compare especially 1QS 1:6–7 and 1QS 5:4–5 as well as 2.4 below.

[171] Cf. 6.5.2.2, 6.5.2.3 and 6.5.3 below.

1.5.1.4.5 1QS 6:24–7:25 The Penal Code

This section is again preserved in four manuscripts (1QS, 4Q258, 4Q259 and 4Q261). Overall the preserved material attests a stable text across the manuscripts with the exception of 1QS 7:12 where 4Q261 attests extra space that suggests a slightly longer text.[172]

1.5.1.4.6 1QS 8:1–16a The Council of the Community

This part of 1QS is represented in three manuscripts (1QS, 4Q258 and 4Q259). In addition to some significant variants in 4Q259 the latter manuscript presents a text that is shorter than 1QS. In the first example the plus in 1QS 8:10 was added in the form of a superlinear addition. Moreover, 1QS 8:15b–1QS 9:12 is not attested in 4Q259 which lacks this substantial block of material.[173] As far as 4Q258 is concerned, this manuscript has a shorter text at 1QS 8:13–14 (and 4Q259 3:4–5) and does not attest the explicit quotation of Isa 40:3.[174]

1.5.1.4.7 1QS 8:16b–9:11 Disciplinary and Communal Rules and a Further Account of Community Formation

The material in Chapters 9–13 is partially preserved in both 1QS and 4Q258. While the disciplinary material in Chapter 9 attests only a minor variant, 1QS attests a longer text than 4Q258 in the rules of conduct for the people of perfect holiness dealt with in Chapter 10.[175] The rules on the people of holiness and the people of deceipt presented in Chapter 13 attest two plusses in 1QS over against 4Q258. None of the material in Chapters 9–13 was ever part of 4Q259.[176]

1.5.1.4.8 1QS 9:12–11:22 The Statutes for the Maskil and the Final Hymn

Both of these major sub-sections of 1QS are represented by five manuscripts each. The Statutes for the Maskil are preserved in 1QS, 4Q256, 4Q258, 4Q259 and 4Q260 whereas the Final Hymn is attested in 1QS, 4Q256, 4Q258, 4Q260 and 4Q264. Two major issues may be singled out here beyond a variety of diverse textual issues covered elsewhere. The first is the lack of the Hymn in 4Q259 which continues after the Statutes of the Maskil with a calendrical anthology known also as 4Q319 (4QOtot).[177] The second point of interest is the presence of additional text after the end of the Hymn in 4Q256 23:2–3. The remains in question are fragmentary and give little away regarding the content of

---

[172] See 7.3 below.
[173] Cf. 1.5.6 below.
[174] See Alexander and Vermes, DJD 26:107.
[175] Further textual differences will be dealt with in 10.3 and 11.3 below.
[176] See 1.5.6 below.
[177] Cf. 1.5.6 and 15.1.1 below.

the material that follows.[178] In addition, stitching pointing to a further sheet after the end of the Hymn in 4Q264 suggests this manuscript also continued beyond the Hymn, though it is impossible to know what this additional material might have contained.[179] For the most part it is noteworthy that both the Statutes and the Hymn attest a rather stable text across five manuscripts.

1.5.2 4Q255 (4QpapS[a])

1.5.2.1 The Manuscript

The papyrus manuscript 4Q255 dates from around 125–100 BCE which makes it one of the oldest manuscripts of the Community Rules.[180] This manuscript is part of an opisthograph with a text identified as 4Q433a (Hodayot-Like Text B). 4Q433a was published by Eileen Schuller and dated to around 75 BCE.[181] A number of scholars have argued that 4Q255 was written on the recto with 4Q433a on the verso.[182] Others identify 4Q255 as written on the verso despite its earlier date.[183] Ayhan Aksu has recently published a comprehensive paleographical and codicological analysis of this opisthograph where he makes a strong case for considering 4Q255 as the more crudely executed text on the verso with remains of the vertical fibres identifiable. He concludes that both 4Q433a and 4Q255 date to the early first century BCE with the inscription of 4Q255 on the verso representing an example of a reuse of an earlier text.[184]

---

[178] For further discussion see 15.3 below.

[179] See Alexander and Vermes, DJD 26:201 and Plate 21 as well as 1.5.11 below.

[180] Cf. Cross, "Paleographical Dates" and Alexander and Vermes, DJD 26:27–38 as well as 1.5.6 below. Without discussion Johann Maier proposes a date in the Herodian period, see *Die Qumran-Essener: Die Texte vom Toten Meer*. 2 Volumes. UTB (München: Reinhardt, 1995), 2:203.

[181] Schuller, DJD 29:237–245 and Plate 15.

[182] See, e. g., George J. Brooke, "Between Scroll and Codex? Reconsidering the Qumran Opisthographs," in *On Stone and Scroll: Essays in Honour of Graham Ivor Davies*. Edited by James K. Aitken, Katharine J. Dell and Brian A. Mastin. BZAW 420 (Berlin: De Gruyter, 2011), 123–138, 130 and Daniel K. Falk, "Material Aspects of Prayer Manuscripts," 54–55.

[183] See Tov, *Scribal Practices*, 68–73; Alexander and Vermes, DJD 26:28 and George Brooke in a subsequent study "Choosing Between Papyrus and Skin: Cultural Complexity and Multiple Identities in the Qumran Library," in *Jewish Cultural Encounters in the Ancient Mediterranean and Near Eastern World*. Edited by Mladen Popović, Myles Schoonover and Marijn Vandenberghe. JSJSup 178 (Leiden: Brill, 2017), 119–135, 126, 128.

[184] See Aksu, "A Palaeographical and Codicological (Re)assessment of the Opisthograph 4Q433a/4Q255," *DSD* 26 (2019): 170–188. Several others have dated 4Q255 to the second half of the second century BCE, see Alexander and Vermes, DJD 26:29 where the editors follow Cross, "Paleographical Dates."

1.5.2.2 Significant Textual Features

4Q255 comprises four fragments. Two identified fragments that preserve material corresponding to the opening lines of 1QS and the section dealing with the one who (initially) refuses to enter the covenant in the final part of the Covenant Ceremony.[185] The opening words of 4Q255 1:1 offer important supplementary text that covers a lacuna in 1QS 1:1.[186]

Two further unidentified fragements labelled 4Q255 A and B have no corresponding text in any other manuscripts of the Community Rules. *Fragment A* is a composite fragment made up of two pieces. The larger fragment preserves a generous bottom margin or empty space at the end of several lines as an inspection of the original manuscript confirmed. The smaller fragment preserves a single legible word "light" and may have been aligned with A:5 based on a preserved reference to "darkness" in line 5 of the larger fragment. The precise placement of the smaller fragment in relation to the larger one is better preserved on PAM 43.255 which is published in Eileen Schuller's edition of 4Q433a (Hodayot-Like Text B).[187] Schuller draws attention to the fact that at the time PAM 43.255 was taken the two fragments of 4Q255 A were still connected by a thread of papyrus.[188]

Very little remains of the second unidentified *Fragment B* other than a rare verb רפד "to spread, support" which occurs three times in the Hebrew Bible in Job 17:13; 41:22 and Cant 2:5.[189] The context in Job 17 describes Job's account of the hopelessness of spreading his bed in darkness and refers to a group who turn the present order upside down including merging darkness into light. Such a context displays synergies with the major concern of guarding against influential outsiders and the threat of darkness in the Community Rules.

1.5.2.3 Revisiting 4Q255 A

The contents of 4Q255 A have generally been associated with material reminiscent of, but not identical with, the Teaching on the Two Spirits.[190] Such a reading would result in a sequence of preserved text ranging from Opening lines of S – Covenant Ceremony – Teaching on the Two Spirits-Like material which is in line with the sequence of 1QS. The only other papyrus manuscript of the Community Rules, 4Q257 (4QS^c), also preserves text corresponding to the opening lines of 1QS as well as the Covenant Ceremony. Crucially, in 4Q257 this is followed by

---

185 Cf. Chapter 2 and 3.4.4 below.
186 Further, 2.3 below.
187 Schuller, DJD 29:237–245.
188 Schuller, DJD 29:243.
189 See Alexander and Vermes, DJD 26:38.
190 See, e. g., Alexander and Vermes, DJD 26:37 and Aksu, "Palaeographical and Codicological (Re)assessment," 138.

fragmentary though clear remains corresponding to the Teaching on the Two Spirits.[191] It is likely that the sequence of Introduction, Covenant Ceremony, followed by the Teaching on the Two Spirits in two better preserved manuscripts – 1QS and 4Q257 – may have been a factor in muting the same sequence for the remains of 4Q255 A. However, a close analysis of the remains of 4Q255 A reveals that the preserved terminology shares as much with the Statutes for the Maskil, the opening portion of the Final Hymn and the fragmentary introduction to the calendrical material that forms part of 4Q259 4 (4QOtot) as it does with the Teaching on the Two Spirits.[192] I will comment on a series of pertinent items of terminology and offer a fresh contextualization for this fragment.

4Q255 A:2 On "human ways" (דרכי איש) see 1QS 9:17–18 "those who have chosen the way," and the parallels in 4Q258 8:2 and 4Q259 3:16 which read "the chosen of the way." The universalism expressed by this wording in 4Q255 A:2 is reminiscent also of the association of the Maskil's remit with "all the living" in 1QS 9:12 // 4Q259 3:7.

4Q255 A:3 On the infinitive *hiphil* of "to instruct" (להשכיל) see 1QS 3:13; 4:22 but also 1QS 9:18 // 4Q256 18:1 // 4Q258 8:3 // [4Q259 3:17] and 1QS 9:20 // 4Q256 18:3 // 4Q258 8:5 with a variant "to facilitate mastery" (להמשילם) in 4Q259 3:19.[193] The preceding *resh* and *ayin* translated with "evil" by Alexander and Vermes might also be rendered "fellow," a term that occurs in 1QS 9:19.[194]

4Q255 A:3–4 The fragmentary remains of this line are deciphered and translated by Alexander and Vermes as referring to "everyone, the spirits of the sons of man" which they tentatively associate with 1QS 3:13–14 (a typographical error lists 5:13–14).[195] Metso raises the possibility of the fragment offering material similar to 1QS 3:20–25.[196] I propose that 4Q255 A:3 refers, rather, to the Maskil's role as an instructor and spiritual assessor couched in universalistic terms. The final *lamed* of what Alexander and Vermes take to be הכל "everyone" in 4Q255 A:4 more likely belongs to the infinitve *qal* לשקול ("to weigh") which forms part of the Maskil's duties according to the Statutes for the Maskil, see 1QS 9:14 // 4Q259 3:10 where he is to weigh "the children of the Zadok" (sic in 1QS) // the children of righteousness (in 4Q259) according to their spirits. It seems likely that 4Q255 A:4 preserves the earliest form of this textually difficult passage on weighing in 1QS 9:14 // 4Q259 3:10. The following table presents our proposed reading, translation and terminological connections between 4Q255 A and 1QS 9:12–21.[197]

---

[191] See Alexander and Vermes, DJD 26:65.

[192] Further, 1.5.6 and Chapters 14 and 15 below.

[193] See 1.5.6.2 below.

[194] Alexander and Vermes, DJD 26:37.

[195] Alexander and Vermes, DJD 26:36–37.

[196] Metso, *Textual Development*, 21.

[197] See further Chapter 14 below.

Table 2: 4Q255 A:3–4 and the Statutes for the Maskil

	4Q255 A:3–4 and the Statutes for the Maskil	
Hebrew	English	Terminological links to 1QS 9:12–21a
[...]³ רע להשכיל ⁴[...ל] שקול רוחות בני איש	³[...] neighbour to instruct ⁴[... to] weigh the spirits of (the) ᶜʰⁱˡᵈʳᵉⁿ of humanity	רע 1QS 9:17 להשכילם 1QS 9:18, 20 לשקול בני הצדוק לפי 1QS 9:14 רוחום לשקול בני 4Q259 3:10 הצדק לפי ר[ו]חמה

The universalistic outlook established in the opening lines of the Statutes is maintained in 4Q255 A by referring to those to be assessed as "children of humanity" or "humankind." While the term "spirit(s)" is found frequently in the Teaching on the Two Spirits it also occurs three times in the Statutes.[198]

4Q255 A:5 Similarly, whereas light and darkness feature in the Teaching, this language is also central in the early part of the Final Hymn that follows the Statutes for the Maskil in a number of witnesses to the Community Rules.[199] Light and darkness also find a fitting context in the fragmentary rubric that introduces the calendric text published as Otot (4Q319) in 4Q259 4:10–11. Those lines introduce the calendrical material against the context of the creation of the luminaries on the fourth day (Gen 1:14–19) and mention God's role as creator as well as light. Given the complementary place of light and darkness in that creation account, as well as the calendrical material in the Hymn and Otot, it is reasonable to assume a reference to darkness stood alongside light in this introduction.[200]

Importantly an identification of the remains in 4Q255 A with material reminiscent of the Statutes for the Maskil opens up the possibility that 4Q433a, the text inscribed on the recto of the opisthograph containing 4Q255, forms part of a Community Rules manuscript with Hymnic material following the Statutes. It is significant that both 4Q255 and 4Q433a stem from a buoyant period in the growth of the S tradition during which both 1QS and 4Q257 were copied. The topic of a fecund tree developed in 4Q433a is familiar from the Hebrew Bible (e. g. Isa 5:1–7 and Ezek 17) and attested elsewhere in the Scrolls.[201] It is conceivable, therefore, that 4Q433a is part and parcel of an emergent pluriform Serekh tradition that reflects the developing framework of the longer text of the Serekh.[202] After all, the Final Hymn has long been recognized as "Hodayot-

---

[198] See especially 1QS 9:14 // 4Q259 3:10; 1QS 9:15 // [4Q259 3:12] and 1QS 9:18 // 4Q258 8:2 // 4Q259 3:16.

[199] Cf. 1QS 10:1–2 // 4Q256 19:1 // 4Q258 8:11 // [4Q260] and Chapter 15 below.

[200] See 1.5.6 and 15.1.1 below.

[201] Compare, e. g., 1QHᵃ 14:17–21 and 4Q262 (4QSʰ) B, another "Unidentified" fragment.

[202] See also 1.5.1 above.

like."[203] Our reading of 4Q433a against the context of a broader S tradition offers fresh interpretative avenues. It is true that the combination of 4Q433a plus 4Q255 does not at first blush match our expectations of an S manuscript, and a number of scholars have noted the lack of a discernible relationship.[204] The loose association of the two texts contained on this opisthograph with the figure of the Maskil noted by both Brooke and Falk is appealing but has no basis in the preserved text.[205] Closer inspection reveals suggestive possibilities that challenge our preconceived notions of a Community Rules manuscript.[206] Rather than representing a draft or personal copy that would reach the extent of 1QS,[207] our analysis of 4Q255 Fragment A offers further evidence for the suggestion that the two papyrus manuscripts of S testify to the period when the framework of the Long Text of the Community Rules as most fully preserved in 1QS was being drafted.[208] Our interpretation of the liturgical material attested in the unidentified fragments of 4Q255 and in 4Q433a demonstrates the effort of scribes to collect and gather material for this framework.[209]

1.5.3 4Q256 (S^b)

1.5.3.1 The Manuscript

This manuscript comprises 14 fragments inscribed on animal skin. Excluded from this calculation and the translation below is a small fragment published in DJD 26 as 4Q256 1. Serious doubts were raised already by Alexander and Vermes about the identification of this small fragment which reads בני חשך

---

[203] Cf. 15.1.5 below.

[204] See, e. g., Brooke "Choosing Between Papyrus and Skin," 135 and Philip Alexander, "Literacy among Jews in the Second Temple Period: Reflections on the Evidence from Qumran," in *Hamlet on a Hill: Semitic and Greek Studies Presented to Professor T. Muraoka on the Occasion of his Sixty-Fifth Birthday*. Edited by Martin F. J. Baasten and Wido Th. Van Peursen. Orientalia Lovaniensia Analecta 118 (Leuven: Peeters, 2003), 3–25.

[205] For a critique along these lines see also Aksu, "Palaeographical and Codicological (Re)assessment," 182.

[206] For such a challenge on different grounds see see Jokiranta and Vanonen, "Multiple Copies of Rule Texts" and Jutta Jokiranta, "Thinking About Ancient Manuscripts as Information Processing," in *Sibyls, Scriptures, and Scrolls: John Collins at Seventy*. Edited by Joel Baden, Hindy Najman and Eibert Tigchelaar. JSJSup 175 (Leiden: Brill, 2017), 1: 611–635.

[207] See Alexander and Vermes, DJD 26:30 and Alexander "Literacy among Jews," 18.

[208] Cf. Hempel, "Long Text;" see also Metso, *Textual Development*, 20 n. 31.

[209] On the suggestion that 4Q255/4Q433a comprise a collection see also Brooke, "Choosing Between Skin and Papyrus" and Falk, "Material Aspects of Prayer Manuscripts," 54–55.

("sons of darkness").[210] 4Q256 1 has now been correctly identified as preserving parts of Job 37:19 and belonging to 4Q99 (4QJob[a]).[211]

The script is dated by Cross to ca. 30–1 BCE[212] and by Milik to ca. 50–25 BCE.[213]

1.5.3.2 Marginal Sign

4Q256 attests the single letter *gimel* positioned at the top right of 4Q256 9. This letter probably numbers the third sheet of the scroll as first suggested by Milik where he also identifies an *aleph* in the margin of 4Q266 (4QD[a]) 1 a–b though the latter identification is rightly marked as uncertain by Tov.[214] Since then Matthew Morgenstern has identified a series of letters that have been used to number sheets of the Genesis Apocryphon.[215]

1.5.3.3 Significant Textual Features

The textual evidence of this manuscript and especially its relationship to 1QS and 4Q258 is crucial for getting a sense of the literary complexity and growth of the S tradition. While detailed discussions can be found throughout the Commentary I will draw attention to the most significant pieces of evidence and reflect on what these suggest in terms of the literary development of the Community Rules. Thus, 4Q256 attests widespread convergence with 1QS for parts of the Covenant Ceremony[216] before diverging substantially – alongside 4Q258 – from 1QS beginning with the equivalent of 1QS 5:1.[217] This manuscript then presents a shorter text for the account of meetings of the many and the extended admissions process.[218] 4Q256 does not preserve any remains corresponding to the Teaching on the Two Spirits or any of the material covered in Chapters 7–13 in

---

[210] See Alexander and Vermes, DJD 26:1, 40, 47. The fragment was not included in Metso, *Textual Development* nor in Qimron, PTSDSSP 1:60 though it is identified as belonging to 4Q256 in Qimron's most recent edition in DSSHW 1:213

[211] See Rebekka Luther and Idan Dershowitz, "Four Identified Fragments from 4QJob[a] (4Q99)," *RevQ* forthcoming. I am grateful to the authors for making this publication available to me prior to its appearance in print.

[212] Cross, "Paleographical Dates;" see also Maier, *Qumran-Essener*, 2:203.

[213] Cf. Józef T. Milik, "Numération des feuilles des rouleaux dans le scriptorium de Qumrân," *Semitica* 27 (1977): 75–81, 76–79. Note that Milik designated the manuscript 4Q259 (4QS[d]) in this early publication.

[214] Milik, "Numération des feuilles," 76–79 and Tov, *Scribal Practices*, 365, see also 211–212.

[215] Morgenstern, "A New Clue to the Original Length of the Genesis Apocryphon," *JJS* 47 (1996): 345–347. For our suggestion that this marginal *gimel* in 4Q256 9:1 needs to be read alongside the palaeo-Hebrew *vav* in 1QS 5:1 see 1.5.1.3 above.

[216] See 3.2.1 and 3.2.2.

[217] Cf. Chapter 5 and 6.1.2.1 below.

[218] Further, 6.5 below.

this Commentary. When 4Q256 sets in again it begins to diplay substantial convergence with 1QS and 4Q258 in Chapters 14 and 15 below. 4Q256 is the only manuscript of the Community Rules to preserve fragmentary remains of letters that follow the end of the Final Hymn as preserved in 1QS and 4Q264.[219] Finally, the implications of an important reading in 4Q256 9:10 that contains a previously overlooked reference to ritual immersion is discussed in 6.1.4.1 below.

1.5.4 4Q257 (4QpapS^c)

1.5.4.1 The Manuscript

This payrus manuscript is inscribed on the recto and is preserved in 13 fragments. Fragment 1a preserves traces of letters that are compatible with the opening lines of the Community Rules as represented by 1QS and 4Q255. This manuscript dates from around the same period as 1QS (100–75 BCE).[220] As was the case for 4Q255 Maier again proposes a much later date in the Herodian period.[221] Elsewhere I raised the possibility that the two early papyrus manuscripts 4Q255 and 4Q257 testify to the composition of the framework of the long text of S.[222] Poorly legible remains of writing have been identified on the verso of fragment 1a. Alexander and Vermes consider the possibility that these remains belong to the title of the work or the name of the scribe.[223]

1.5.4.2 Significant Textual Features

The identified remains of 4Q257 cover the opening lines of S, the Covenant Ceremony and the Teaching on the Two Spirits. Where 4Q257 overlaps with other manuscripts, i. e. 1QS, 4Q255, 4Q256, 4Q262 and 5Q11, only a small number of minor textual divergences occur. 4Q257 is the only witness to the Teaching on the Two Spirits outside of 1QS.[224] The single unidentified Fragment A preserves parts of four fragmentary words.[225]

---

[219] For details see Chapter 15 below.

[220] Cf. Cross, "Paleographical Dates."

[221] Maier, *Qumran-Essener*, 2:205.

[222] See 1.5.2 above.

[223] Alexander and Vermes, DJD 26:69–70; see also Tov, *Scribal Practices*, 118, 120–121 and further details in 2.3 below.

[224] Cf. Chapter 4 below.

[225] See Alexander and Vermes, DJD 26:82.

1.5.5 4Q258 (4QS[d])

1.5.5.1 The Manuscript

4Q258 is the best-preserved manuscript of the Community Rules from Cave 4 and the copy dates from ca. 30–1 BCE.[226] Its beginning is preserved and indicates that this scroll does not preserve any part of the material in 1QS 1–4 and parallels.[227] Substantial remains of seven columns all of which preserve parts of the top margin as well as a wider opening margin and six inter-columnar margins survive. The best preserved columns are 4Q258 1; 2; 7; 8 and 9 with the beginnings of the opening lines of 4Q258 3 and 10 also preserved in situ. 4Q258 6 is made up of four fragments that together offer the remains of eight lines. Only four tiny fragments altogether remain of columns 5, 12 and 13.[228] According to Metso's analysis of the damage pattern at the bottom of the preserved columns the scroll was deposited rolled with the beginning on the outside.[229] Alexander and Vermes mention the variation in the appearance of the scroll's colouring.[230] In particular parts of column 1, the intercolumnar margin between columns 7 and 8 and the fragment at the bottom left of 4Q258 9 covering the ends of the lines in 4Q258 9:9–12 reveal areas of a lighter colour and preserve better preserved parts of leather. If the scroll was indeed rolled with the first column on the outside, parts of the vulnerable top margin must have been protected, and some fragments may have become detached and were deposited in a more sheltered environment than other fragments.[231] Moreover, PAM M40.581 (LLDSSDL B-278385) photographed by Albina in 1953 clearly shows the well-preserved light coloured fragment that spans the ends of five lines at the top of 4Q258 7 and the first three lines of column 8 as a detached fragment. Neatly prepared dry lines are particularly well preserved in the margin between columns 7 and 8. The orthography of 4Q258 is largely defective and distinctive from 1QS and 4Q256 in that regard.[232] The divine name is twice written in paleo-Hebrew script in this manuscript.[233]

1.5.5.2 Significant Textual Features

4Q258 is the only manuscript from Cave 4 to cover material from each of the six columns that start with 1QS 5. In terms of its textual affiliation this manu-

---

[226] See Cross, "Paleographical Dates."

[227] Cf. 5.1 for details.

[228] See Alexander and Vermes, DJD 26:83–128 and Plates 10–13.

[229] Metso, *Textual Development*, 38.

[230] Alexander and Vermes, DJD 26:82.

[231] See PAM M41.481 (LLDSSDL B-298798) which includes Milik's annotations of the assembled fragments.

[232] See Alexander and Vermes, DJD 26:20, 46.

[233] Cf. 4Q258 2 iii 9 and 4:8.

script is extremely close to 4Q256 though the former never included material corresponding to 1QS 1–4. There are, nevertheless, a small number of cases where 4Q258 and 4Q256 attest divergence which will be dealt with in the Commentary.[234] Where 4Q258 covers the same ground as 1QS it is regularly shorter, especially in 1QS 5.[235]

An interesting case is a plus in 4Q258 1:12–13 that is lacking from 1QS 5:20. The context deals with a host of restrictions on engagement of various kinds with the people of injustice. Immediately prior to the plus this group is called out for their impurity and the uncleanness of their property. The plus in 4Q258 provides details that go beyond anything in 1QS by referring to their (presumably the people of injustice's?) conduct with regard to nations (גוים), oaths, devotions and vows. It is difficult to imagine that the scribe behind 1QS would have any qualms about including this plus had it been in front of him since 1QS shares the concern to establish firm boundaries, including economic ones, with the people of injustice and, if anything, expands on those concerns. 1QS may have been working with and expanding a text like 4Q258 that lacked this plus. By the latter part of the 1st c. BCE, when 4Q258 was copied, the issue that sparked this plus may be trading relations with the Romans. The Damascus Document also attests a passage that expresses concerns about the inappropriate use of oaths and the risk of blaspheming gentiles in a scenario where their property is carried off.[236]

1.5.6 4Q259 (4QS^e)

1.5.6.1 The Manuscript

Substantial remains of seven columns and a number of fragments are preserved of this manuscript. The leather is thick and very dark in places with a variety of colour tones that suggest different micro-conditions during the scroll's deposit, or its post-discovery treatment or storage, for different pieces of the scroll even if the fragments were kept in proximity to each other. The results of Metso's material reconstruction based on recurring damage patterns suggest the scroll was rolled with the first column on the outside.[237] The hand is most unusual leading to divergent paleographical dates being proposed. Alexander and Vermes follow Cross' revised dating to around 50–25 BCE.[238] A much earlier date in the second half of the second century BCE is proposed by

---

[234] See also Alexander and Vermes, DJD 26:46–47.

[235] Cf. 1.5.1.4 above.

[236] See CD 12:6b–11a and Lawrence H. Schiffman, "Legislation Concerning Relations with Non-Jews in the Zadokite Fragments and in Tannaitic Literature," *RevQ* 11 (1989): 379–389.

[237] Metso, *Textual Development*, 48–51. See also Annette Steudel, "Reading and Reconstructing Manuscripts," in CDSS, 186–191.

[238] Alexander and Vermes, DJD 26:133–134 and see Cross "Paleographical Dates."

Milik and a little after 100 BCE by Puech.[239] The most thorough discussion to date is that of Puech who draws attention to Cross' initial assessment of an earlier date as reported by Milik in 1955.[240] Metso draws attention to the "extraordinary" and somewhat mixed script of this scribe and does not commit to a date.[241] Most recently Eibert Tigchelaar has described this manuscript as belonging to a group of manuscripts "written in unique or unusual hands (e. g. 4Q259 [4QS^e]) suggesting individual idiosyncrasy, or a different geographical provenance of the scribe."[242]

On Milik's and Puech's dating of this manuscript 4Q259 constitutes one of the earliest surviving copies of the Community Rules alongside 4Q255, and on Puech's reckoning almost contemporary with 1QS.[243] Another singular feature of this particular manuscript is the use of the Cryptic A script for two phrases in consecutive lines in 4Q259 3:3–4 which parallel 1QS 8:12–13.[244]

1.5.6.2 Significant Textual Features

Textually this manuscript is also unique in several respects. The remains of 4Q259 begin with material from the Penal Code in 1QS 7:8–15. It is impossible to know how much of the material that precedes in 1QS and parallels was part of 4Q259.[245] On the basis of her physical reconstruction of the scroll Metso suggests there would not have been sufficient space to accommodate all the columns that precede in 1QS. She raises the possibility that 4Q259, like 4Q258, began at the equivalent of 1QS 5.[246]

What is clear is that 4Q259 did not contain the Final Hymn that is attested in five manuscripts of the Community Rules.[247] Instead, a calendrical anthology that was published separately under the siglum 4Q319 (Otot) followed after the

---

[239] See Józef Milik, *The Books of Enoch: Aramaic Fragments of Qumrân Cave 4* (Oxford: Oxford University Press, 1974), 61 (N.B. 4Q259 is referred to as 4Q260); Milik, *Ten Years of Discovery in the Wilderness of Judaea* (London: SCM, 1959), 123–124 and Puech, "L'alphabet cryptique A en 4QS^e (4Q259)," *RevQ* 18 (1998): 429–435, 433–435.

[240] Milik, "Le travail d'édition," 61.

[241] Metso, *Textual Development*, 48 and, similarly, Maier, *Qumran-Essener*, 2:210.

[242] Tigchelaar, "The Scribes of the Scrolls," in CDSS, 524–532, 530.

[243] See 1.5.2 above.

[244] For discussion see Milik, "Le travail d'édition," 61; Metso, *Textual Development*, 53–54; Puech, "L'alphabet cryptique A;" Qimron, DSSHW 1: 225; Tov, *Scribal Practices*, 205–206. Cf. also Charlotte Hempel, "The Profile and Character of Qumran Cave 4Q: The Community Rule Manuscripts as a Test Case," in *The Caves of Qumran: Proceedings of the International Conference, Lugano 2014*. Edited by Marcello Fidanzio. STDJ 118 (Leiden: Brill, 2017), 74–80; Hempel, "Bildung und Wissenswirtschaft im Judentum zur Zeit des Zweiten Tempels," in *Was ist Bildung in der Vormoderne?* Edited by Peter Gemeinhardt (Tübingen: Mohr Siebeck, 2019), 229–244 and Michael E. Stone, *Secret Groups in Ancient Judaism* (Oxford: Oxford University Press, 2018), 68–71. The excellent multi-spectral images LLDSSDL B-295966 and B-314657 by Shai Halevi support the readings of Milik and Puech. See further Chapter 8 below.

[245] Cf. Alexander and Vermes, DJD 26:30–132.

[246] Metso, *Textual Development*, 49–51 and Metso, "The Primary Results of the Reconstruction of 4QS^e," *JJS* 44 (1993): 303–308.

[247] See Chapter 15 below.

Statutes for the Maskil.[248] This manuscript also attests a very significant minus represented by 1QS 8:15b–9:11 // 4Q258 6:7b–7:9.[249] In 4Q259 3:6 the heading introducing the Statutes for the Maskil follows immediately after the citation and brief interpretation of Isa 40:3 that ends in 1QS 8:15a // 4Q258 6:7 (shorter text). The minus in 4Q259 includes the famous reference to the eschatological prophet and the messiahs of Aaron and Israel in 1QS 9:11. Some scholars have attributed this minus in 4Q259 to a scribal error on the part of the scribe behind 4Q259.[250] I will argue that the long plus in 1QS and 4Q258 over against 4Q259 is secondary as proposed also by Metso and Stegemann.[251]

Finally, a close analysis of minor variants between 4Q259 and 1QS suggests that 4Q259 was, in fact, a source text used by the scribe(s) of 1QS. The following table gives a comprehensive list of variants between 4Q259 and 1QS which will be discussed in more detail in the Textual Notes of the Commentary. Almost all of them can be attributed to the scribe of 1QS struggling as much with the idiosyncratic hand of 4Q259 as modern scholars have. The suggestion that 4Q259 was the source of corrections added by a second scribe in 1QS 7 has been put forward by Puech.[252] The following table presents key variants.

Table 3: 4Q259 and 1QS

Variants Between 4Q259 and 1QS

Num.	4Q259	Notes on 4Q259	1QS	Notes on 1QS
1	4Q259 1:4		1QS 7:8 שנה אחת	
	ששה [חוד]שים "[six mon]ths"		{ששה חודשים} "one year {six months}"	Superlinear correction[253]
2	4Q259 1:13		1QS 7:14	
	ששים יום "sixty days"	The first two letters are barely legible in 4Q259 but considerations of space support the reading, see DJD 26:138.	שלושים יום "thirty days"	The scribe of 1QS may have assumed the same penalty as earlier in the same line and the two previous lines.

---

[248] This Commentary does not include a Translation, Textual Notes, and Commentary on the calendrical anthology in 4Q259 4:10-7:8. However 15.1.1. offers a comprehensive discussion of the place of the calendric material in 4Q259 including bibliography.

[249] See already Milik, *Ten Years of Discovery*, 123.

[250] Cf. James C. VanderKam, "Messianism in the Scrolls," in *The Community of the Renewed Covenant*. Edited by Eugene Ulrich and James C. VanderKam. Christianity and Judaism in Antiquity 10 (Notre Dame, IL: University of Notre Dame Press, 1994), 211–234.

[251] Metso, *Textual Development*, 72 and Stegemann, "Some Remarks," 486.

[252] "Écriture de 1QS VII–VIII," 43.

[253] See 7.3 below.

Num.	4Q259	Notes on 4Q259	1QS	Notes on 1QS
3	4Q259 2:5 עד... לו *"up to completing"* ten full years	The prepositions vary and the ethical dative appears to have been added secondarily in 4Q259.	1QS 7:22 על *"upon completing"* ten full years	The reading in 4Q259 suggests an extensive additional period of probation after which members had proven their credentials.[254]
4	4Q259 2:11 ובענוה "and with humility"	Secondary addition in the margin.[255]	1QS 8:3	
5	4Q259 2:14 [למ]שפט עולם "eternal *[judg]ment*"	Judgment is a central theme in the context of this passage.[256]	1QS 8:5 למטעת עולם "eternal *plant*"	
6	4Q259 2:17 מעוז "refuge"	See 8.3 below.	1QS 8:8 מעון "dwelling"	4Q258 agrees with 1QS.
7	4Q259 2:18		1QS 8:10 "And they shall be welcome to make atonement for the land and to determine the judgment of wickedness'	Superlinear plus in 1QS
8	4Q259 3:3–4 "[When] these [exi]st[257] *in sta-tes* they shall keep apart from the com[pa]ny of *the people of [injustice]*"	Highlighed words in cryptic script. 1QS's spelling הנשי העול with *he* rather than *aleph* might be a misreading of the cryptic sequence of *aleph nun* in the *Vorlage*.	1QS 8:12–13 "When these exist *as a community* in Israel *according to these rules* they shall keep apart from the company of the people of injustice" (הנשי העול)	1QS is supplementing text shared by 4Q259 and 4Q258.

<hr>

[254] Cf. 7.4.6.4 below.
[255] See 8.3 below.
[256] See 8.2.2 below as well as 14.4.4.
[257] The font that follows identifies words written in cryptic script, see further 1.7 below.

Num.	4Q259	Notes on 4Q259	1QS	Notes on 1QS
9	4Q259 3:4		1QS 8:13	
	"and go [to] the wil[der]ne[ss in order to prepare the]re the way of *truth*" האמת	In the context of this passage truth is a key concept and antonym of injustice.[258]	"and go to the wilderness in order to prepare there the way of *Him*" הואהא	Suspected substitute for divine name.
10		Plus in 1QS 8:15b–9:11 // 4Q258 6:7–12; 7:1–9 Lacking in 4Q259		
11	4Q259 3:9		1QS 9:13	
	לפני העתים He shall acquire every insight which has been found "*in previous* times."	4Q259 presupposes expertise across previous "rounds" of revelations.[259]	לפי העתים He shall acquire every insight which has been found "*according to* the times"	This appears to be another case where the scribe of 1QS misses a subtlety.
12	4Q259 3:10		1QS 9:14	
	בני הצדק "the children of righteousness"	*He* and *tsade* are significantly effaced.	בני הצדוק "the children of the Zadok" (sic)	The scribe of 1QS left a larger space both before and after the words "the sons of the Zadok." The possibility of a deficient exemplar was proposed by Martin.[260]
13	4Q259 3:16		1QS 9:17–18	
	לבח]ירי דרך] The Maskil is to discipline "the cho[sen of the way"]	Cf. 1QS 9:14 "the chosen ones of the time" – reconstructed in 4Q259 3:11.	לבוחרי דרך The Maskil is to discipline "those who have chosen the way."	4Q258 8:2 converges with 4Q259.

---

[258] See Chapter 8 below.
[259] For details see 14.3 and 14.4.1 as well as 1QS 1:9.
[260] *Scribal Character of the Dead Sea Scrolls*, 2: 466, see further 14.3 below.

Num.	4Q259	Notes on 4Q259	1QS	Notes on 1QS
14	4Q259 3:16 "according to the *rules* (תכוני) of time"[261]	4Q256 and 4Q258 correspond with 1QS.	1QS 9:18 "according to the *rule* (תכון) of time"	
15	4Q259 3:17–18 The Maskil is to instruct "in] the wonderful mysteries. *And if the way of the alliance* of the community *reaches perfection,* they shall con[duct themselves perfectly each] with his *neighbours"*	Where preserved 4Q258 and 4Q256 converge with 1QS.	1QS 9:18–19 The Maskil is to instruct "in the wonderful *and true* mysteries *in the midst of the people* of the community so that they may conduct themselves perfectly each with his *neighbour"*	
16	4Q259 3:19–4:1 Concerning the Maskil at the time to prepare the way in the wilderness: "*He shall facilitate their mastery over* all[that has been found to do] at th[is] time" ולהמשילם		1QS 9:20 Concerning the Maskil at the time to prepare the way in the wilderness: "*He shall instruct them with* all that has been found to do at this time" ולהשכילם	
17	Final Hymn		Otot	

Looking at the textual divergences between 1QS ans 4Q259 in the round rather than atomistically reveals a striking overall impression of visual resemblance across diverging readings. Such a body of evidence can be explained by allowing

---

[261] See 14.3 below.

for 4Q259 or a 4Q259-like *Vorlage* having served as a source for 1QS. Moreover, I will argue for a tendency on the part of the scribe of 1QS to opt for more predictable and familiar phrases such as "the sons of Zadok." On closer inspection 4Q259's readings are frequently well supported by their immediate context and at times divulge a subtle point that has escaped us based on our familiarity with 1QS. Like the scribe of 1QS who approached his *Vorlage* with his own sensibilities, we have been conditioned by our familiarity with 1QS which has impacted our approach to 4Q259, a manuscript that almost always offers a superior text.

We noted above the suggestion put forward by Philip Alexander that the papyrus manuscript 4Q255 was a private first draft copy of 1QS.[262] In our view there is stronger cumulative evidence that 1QS copied from a manuscript that resembled 4Q259 with 4Q255 more likely serving as a source for the framework of 1QS, especially 1QS 1–4.[263]

1.5.7 4Q260 (4QSᶠ)

1.5.7.1 The Manuscript

Seven preserved fragments on animal skin make up the remains of five consecutive columns.[264] Only six fragments are represented on Plate 17 since Alexander and Vermes where unable to locate fragment 2b.[265] Top margins are preserved throughout. The manuscript is carefully ruled, including the provision of an additional line to assist with positioning the first line of text. Cross dates the hand to 30–1 BCE.[266] The preserved text comes from the final lines of the Statutes for the Maskil and the Final Hymn.[267] Alexander and Vermes align the format of this scroll with 4Q264 and consider both manuscripts to be portable scrolls. Falk proposes a liturgical use for both manuscripts.[268]

The start of the Calendar for Praise[269] at the beginning of a new column in 4Q260 2:1 is suggestive of careful planning and supports the view of those who have argued for this calendar's distinctive nature and originally independent origin.[270]

---

[262] Alexander, "Literacy among Jews," 18.

[263] See 1.5.1 above.

[264] Cf. Alexander and Vermes, DJD 26:153–167.

[265] DJD 26:153.

[266] Cross, "Paleographical Dates."

[267] See Chapters 14 and 15 below.

[268] Falk, "Material Aspects of Prayer Manuscripts," 64.

[269] Cf. 15.2.2 below.

[270] See Hendrik Goedhart, *De Slothymne van het Manual of Discipline: A Theological-Exegetical Study of 1QS X, 9–XI, 22* (Rotterdam: Bronder Offset, 1965), 8–9 and Knibb, *Qumran Community*, 144.

1.5.7.2 Significant Textual Features

There is only one case where the text of 4Q260 offers a distinctive reading. 4Q260 4:10 includes a third reference to a group of people ("the people of") in a broken context after both 1QS and 4Q260 shared references to "the people of the pit" and "the people of injustice" in the immediately preceding lines.

1.5.8 4Q261 (4QS^g)

1.5.8.1 The Manuscript

4Q261 is made up of 19 fragments on animal skin that preserve text corresponding to parts of Chapters 6 and 7 of the Commentary. The script has been described by Cross as semi-cursive. He dated the manuscript to ca. 50–1 BCE.[271] Most clearly preserved are parts of the Admission and Annual Assessment of Members of the Covenant and parts of the Penal Code.[272] Sparce remains of three unidentified fragments (4Q261 A, B and C) preserve no more than traces of isolated letters.[273]

1.5.8.2 Significant Textual Features

Based on the sparse remains it is not possible to get a secure sense of the extent of this scroll, though Alexander and Vermes make a convincing case that the material on the meeting of the many is probably lacking from this manuscript.[274] Whereas they suggest the missing section comprises 1QS 6:8–23 it seems conceivable that 1QS 6:7b–8a was also lacking.[275] While 4Q261 attests a much shorter text that lacked the material in 6.5, this manuscript does preserve the opening lines of the Penal Code in 4Q261 3:2–4.[276] Preserved variants suggest independent readings of some significance[277] as well as a shorter text than 1QS where the manuscripts cover the same material.[278] A number of different numeration systems have been used to refer to the fragments of this manuscript and the following table offers an overview over a selection of major editions.

---

[271] Cross, "Paleographical Dates" and see also Alexander and Vermes, DJD 26:172.
[272] Cf. 6.1 and Chapter 7 below.
[273] See Alexander and Vermes, DJD 26:187 and Plate 19.
[274] DJD 26:170.
[275] See further 6.5 below.
[276] Cf. Alexander and Vermes, DJD 26:177–179.
[277] See especially 6.1.2.2; 6.1.4.2; 7.2.5.1 and 7.4.5.1 below.
[278] See Alexander and Vermes, DJD 26:172–173.

Table 4: Editorial Presentations of 4Q261

Commentary Below	Alexander and Vermes DJD 26	Metso *Textual Development*	Qimron DSSHW	García Martínez and Tigchelaar, DSSSE
Ch. 6.1	1a–b	1	Notes only	1
Ch. 6.3–6.4	2a–c			
Ch. 6.5 and 7	3	2	Notes only	2
Ch. 7	4a–b	5 (4b only)	4*	
Ch. 7	5a–c	3	5	3
Ch. 7	6a–e	4 (6c only)	6* (6c only)	4 (6c only)
Unidentified	A			
Unidentified	B			
Unidentified	C			

1.5.9 4Q262 (4QS^h)

4Q262 is made up of three fragments on animal skin, two of which are unidentified. The identified fragment 1 preserves fragmentary remains of parts of four lines that preserve material relating to the impurity of the one who refuses to enter the covenant.[279] There are no discernible divergences. On the basis of the sparse remains it is not clear what the manuscript comprised and whether it is indeed a copy of the Community Rules, an anthology[280] or a copy of one of its sources.[281]

Only a handful of words survive of fragment A which appears to refer to economic injustice. The second unidentified fragment, fragment B, presents a tighter spacing of lines and words and and may belong to a different scroll.[282] It describes a thriving tree of supernatural proportions which likely belongs to an eschatological promise for the elect.[283] The fact that the content of this fragment does not correspond to 1QS alone does not justify allocating it to another text.[284] Moreover, the presence of a hymn in several manuscripts of the Community Rules alongside the identification of Hodayot-like material on the opisthograph

---

[279] See 3.2.4 below.

[280] Cf. Alexander and Vermes, DJD 26:190.

[281] See further Metso, "Methodological Problems," 328–330; Metso, *The Serekh Texts*. CQS 9 (London: T&T Clark, 2007), 62–62 and Jokiranta and Vanonen, "Multiple Copies of Rule Texts."

[282] See Alexander and Vermes, DJD 26:189 and Plate 20.

[283] Cf. Ezek 17; Isa 5:1–7 and 1QH^a 14:17–21.

[284] See Jokiranta and Vanonen, "Multiple Copies of Rule Texts."

4Q255 offer strong evidence that hymnic material was transmitted as part of the pluriform S tradition beyond 1QS.[285] These considerations suggest that we cannot exclude the possibility that 4Q262 fragment B is part of a copy of the Community Rules.

1.5.10 4Q263 (4QS^i)

Only a single leather fragment is preserved of this manuscript which covers the remains of 1QS 5:26–6:4 and parallels.[286] Cross has proposed a date around 30–1 BCE which is followed by Alexander and Vermes.[287] The textual picture shows a great deal of affinity with 4Q258 including a shorter text that lacks the plus in 1QS 5:26–6:1 condemning obstinate behaviour.[288] On the other hand, there are two instances in 4Q263 line 3 where this manuscript includes the conjunction before the adjective "together" with 1QS against 4Q258.

1.5.11 4Q264 (4QS^j)

This manuscript contains parts of the Final Hymn and remains of stitching pointing to a further sheet.[289] The script is dated by Cross to 50–25 BCE which is followed by Alexander and Vermes and endorsed by Metso.[290] The size of the script is very small which may point to a portable "miniature scroll" containing liturgical material.[291] The fragments preserve the remains of ten fragmentary lines from the end of the Final Hymn.[292] The preserved material includes an account of God's righteous deeds and a blessing. The final words attested in the preserved fragment correspond to the final words of 1QS 11:22 as well as 4Q256 23:1. It is noteworthy that in all three manuscripts the rest of the line is left blank after the words "What counsel can one formed by hand convey?". The preserved stitching suggests more text followed but we have no way of knowing whether this corresponded to 4Q256 23:2 or something else. Based on the preserved content Jokiranta suggests the more accurate designation would be 4QS-Hymn.[293]

---

[285] See 1.5.2 above.

[286] Further, 6.2; 6.3 and 6.4 below.

[287] Cross, "Paleographical Dates" and Alexander and Vermes, DJD 26:197–198.

[288] Cf. 1.5.1.4.2 above.

[289] Alexander and Vermes, DJD 26:201 and Plate 21.

[290] Cross, "Paleographical Dates;" DJD 26:202 and Metso, *Textual Development*, 63.

[291] See Falk, "Material Aspects of Prayer Manuscripts," 64.

[292] Cf. Chapter 15 below.

[293] Jokiranta, "Thinking About Ancient Manuscripts."

1.5.12 5Q11 (5QS)

A single fragment comprising the remains of parts of two columns is preserved of this manuscript which has been tentatively dated to 30 BCE – 70 CE.[294] While all but traces of letters remain of 5Q11 1 ii, the contents of 5Q11 1 i 2–6 can be accommodated alongside 1QS 2:4–7 and parallels and are presented dotted underlined in the translation of 1QS 2:4–7 below. A beautifully preserved seam separates both columns. Elsewhere Milik suggests that 4Q280 (Curses) and 4Q390 were copied by the same scribe and in the same "rustic semiformal hand" as 5Q11 (S) and 5Q13 (Rule).[295] In his edition Milik acknowledges that the preserved fragmentary maledictions pertain to a topic not exclusive to the Community Rules and notes that considerations of space suggest a different amount of text was attested in the gaps between the preserved letters in 5Q11. As a result of this complex picture Alexander and Vermes classify 5Q11 as a "non-S text."[296]

Given the textual fluidity reflected across the S manuscripts the fact that 5Q11 does not offer verbatim correspondence to 1QS 2 does not support excluding it from consideration as a copy of the Rules of the Community. However, the fragmentary nature of this manuscript prevents any conclusive assessment beyond noting the close relationship to the Community Rules.

The following two tables offer a summary presentation of the manuscripts.

---

[294] Cf. Milik, DJD 3:180–181; see also James H. Charlesworth, "Possible Fragment of the Rule of the Community," in PTSDSSP 1:105–107.

[295] See Józef T. Milik, "*Milkî-ṣedeq* et *Milkî-reša'* dans les anciens écrits juifs et chrétiens," *JJS* 23 (1972): 95–144, 129.

[296] Alexander and Vermes, DJD 26:3–4; further, Alexander, "Literacy among Jews."

Table 5: Community Rules Manuscripts Found at Qumran

Cave	Number and Siglum	Paleographical Date	Writing Material	Divine Name
1Q	1Q28 (S)	100–75 BCE	Skin	Four dots Personal Pronoun
4Q	4Q255 (Sa)	125–100 BCE	Papyrus	
	4Q256 (Sb)	30–1 BCE (Cross) 50–25 BCE (Milik)	Skin	
	4Q257 (Sc)	100–75 BCE	Papyrus	
	4Q258 (Sd)	30–1 BCE	Skin	**𝕻aleo-𝕳ebrew**
	4Q259 (Se)	50–25 BCE (Cross) 150–100 BCE (Milik and Puech)	Skin	Truth (?)[297]
	4Q260 (Sf)	30–1 BCE	Skin	
	4Q261 (Sg)	50–1 BCE	Skin	
	4Q262 (Sh)	1–50 CE	Skin	
	4Q263 (Si)	30–1 BCE	Skin	
	4Q264 (Sj)	50–25 BCE	Skin	
5Q	5Q11 (S)	30 BCE – 70 CE	Skin	

---

[297] For discussion see Chapter 8 below where I argue that "truth" is not a substitute for the divine name in 4Q259.

Table 6: Overview over Preserved Material According to Chapter Numbers in the Commentary

1QS	4Q255	4Q256	4Q257	4Q258	4Q259	4Q260	4Q261	4Q262	4Q263	4Q264	5Q11
2. Introduction: Outline of Communal Aspirations											
X	X		X								
3. Admission Into and Reaffirmation of the Covenant											
X	X	X	X					X			X
4. The Teaching on the Two Spirits											
X			X								
5. Requirements and Leadership for a New Community in Two Founding Narratives											
X		X		X							
6. Rules Concerning Meetings: 1. Admission and Assessment of Members											
X		X		X			X				
6. Rules Concerning Meetings: 2. Rules Dealing with Reproof											
X		X		X					X		
6. Rules Concerning Meetings: 3. Rules of Conduct in All Their Dwelling Places											
X				X					X		
6. Rules Concerning Meetings: 4 Rules of Conduct in Every Place of Ten											
X				X			X		X		
6. Rules Concerning Meetings: 5. Meetings of the Many											
X		X		X			X				
7. The Penal Code											
X				X	X		X				

1QS	4Q255	4Q256	4Q257	4Q258	4Q259	4Q260	4Q261	4Q262	4Q263	4Q264	5Q11
8. The Council of the Community											
x				x	x						
9. Deliberate Failure to Obey a Commandment											
x				x							
10. Rules of Conduct and Discipline for the People of Perfect Holiness											
x				x							
11. The Community and the Cultic Realm											
x				x							
12. The Authority of the Sons of Aaron											
x				x							
13. The Conduct of the People of Holiness and the People of Deceit											
x				x							
14. The Statutes for the Maskil											
x		x		x	x	x					
15. Final Hymn – Otot											
x		x		x	Otot	x				x	

1.6 Related Works

The Community Rules share affinities with a number of works from Qumran, many of which will be touched upon in the Commentary.[298] It is appropriate here to draw particular attention to a small number of texts that have a close relationship to the material covered in this Commentary. Both the Rule of the

---

[298] See further Hempel, *Qumran Rule Texts in Context*.

Congregation (1QSa) and the Rule of Blessings (1QSb), both of which form part
of the same scroll as 1QS, have been dealt with in 1.5.1 above.

1.6.1 The Community Rules and the Damascus Document

While the close relationship between the Penal Codes of both of these documents
has attracted a great deal of attention,[299] there is what I have referred to elsewhere a more widespread "textual intimacy" between both works.[300] The literary
affinities between both compositions encompass a breadth of material including
regulatuions on entrance into the community by swearing an oath;[301] priestly
precedence in places of ten;[302] the designation "the people of perfect holiness"[303]
as well as structural similarities such as a liturgical conclusion in some manuscripts of both works. Intriguingly, the affiliated material in the Damascus
Document shares the following sequence with the Community Rules: oath of
admission, meetings of ten, meetings of all the camps, penal code, further penal
material and liturgical conclusion.

1.6.2 The Community Rules and 4QMiscellaneous Rules (4Q265)

4Q265 was published by Joseph Baumgarten under the title Miscellaneous
Rules. The work was previously known as "Serekh Damascus" based on its
affinities with both the Community Rules and the Damascus Document.[304]
While a relationship between 4Q265 and the Community Rules as well as the
Damascus Document is uncontested, it is important to acknowledge that neither
the term "rule" (serekh) nor Damascus occur in the preserved fragments of
4Q265. The work covers ground shared with the Community Rules concerning
the Penal Code,[305] Admission into the Community[306] as well as a section on

---

[299] Cf. Chapter 7 below.

[300] See Hempel, *Qumran Rule Texts in Context*, 20; Stephen Hultgren, *From the Damascus
Document to the Covenant of the Community: Literary, Historical, and Theological Studies in
the Dead Sea Scrolls*. STDJ 66 (Leiden: Brill, 2007); Reinhard G. Kratz, "Der *Penal Code* und
das Verhältnis von *Serekh ha-Yachad* (S) und Damaskusschrift (D)," *RevQ* 25 (2011): 199–227;
Annette Steudel, "The Damascus Document (D) as a Rewriting of the Community Rule (S),"
RevQ 25 (2012): 605–620 and Schofield, *From Qumrnn to the Yahad*, 163–173.

[301] See CD 15:5b–16:2a and parallels as well as 3.2.2 and 6.1 below.

[302] Cf. CD 13:2–3 and 6.4 below.

[303] See Chapter 10 below and CD 20:1b–8a.

[304] See Baumgarten, DJD 35:57–78; Charlotte Hempel, *The Damascus Texts*. CQS 1
(Sheffield: Sheffield Academic Press, 2000), 89–104 and Schofield, *From Qumran to the
Yahad*, 174–175.

[305] See 4Q265 4 i 2 – ii 2 and Chapter 7 below.

[306] Cf. 4Q265 4 ii 3b–9 and 6.5 below.

the make-up and function of the Council of the Community.[307] In addition to the intriguing literary correspondences between 4Q265 and the Community Rules the former work also resembles the Damascus Document both on matters of content (such as Penal Code traditions and Sabbath laws, for instance), but also in the way both works accommodate communal rules alongside Jewish legal material not associated with a particular community.[308] A close reading of correspondences alongside distinctive features between 4Q265 and the Community Rules suggests a literary relationship that predates the final forms of the S manuscripts rather than excerpts as suggested, e. g., by Martin Abegg.[309] It is important, finally, to keep an open mind on the relative priority of each work or even passage in relation to the Community Rules.

1.6.3 The Community Rules and 11Q29 (11QS?)

In 2000 Eibert Tigchelaar published a fragment from Cave 11 which he tentatively identified as a copy of the Community Rule.[310] This small fragment preserves the fragmentary remains of three lines and contains penal code material reminiscent of 1QS 7:23 and 4Q270 7 i 8.[311] Given the sparse remains of this fragment are restricted to penal code material it is preferable to refer to it as Penal Code material that cannot be securely identified as belonging to a copy of the Community Rules.[312]

1.6.4 5Q13 (Rule)

A number of intriguing terminological parallels between 5Q13 and the Community Rules were first noticed by Milik in his *editio princeps*.[313] These connections to the Rules are, however, outweighed by a substantial amount of

---

[307] See 4Q265 7:7–10 and Chapter 8 below.

[308] Further, Joseph Baumgarten, "Scripture and Law in 4Q265," in *Biblical Perspectives: Early Use and Interpretation of the Bible in Light of the Dead Sea Scrolls.* Edited by Michael E. Stone and Esther G. Chazon. STDJ 28 (Leiden: Brill, 1998), 25–33; Charlotte Hempel, *The Laws of the Damascus Document: Sources, Tradition and Redaction.* STDJ 29 (Leiden: Brill, 1998) and Hempel, "Cutting the Cord with the Familiar: What Makes 4Q265 Miscellaneous Rules Tick? in *Sibyls, Scriptures, and Scrolls: John Collins at Seventy.* Edited by Joel Baden, Hindy Najman and Eibert Tigchelaar. JSJSup 175 (Brill, Leiden, 2016), 534–541.

[309] See Abegg, DSSANT, 278.

[310] Tigchelaar, "A Newly Identified 11QSerekh ha-Yaḥad Fragment (11Q29)?," in *The Dead Sea Scrolls Fifty Years After Their Discovery 1947–1997.* Edited by Lawrence H. Schiffman, Emanuel Tov and James C. VanderKam (Jerusalem: IES, 2000), 285–292 and García Martínez, Tigchelaar and van der Woude, DJD 23:433–434 and Plate 50.

[311] See 7.4.6.3 and 7.4.6.4 below.

[312] Further, Charlotte Hempel, "The Gems of DJD 36: Reflections on Some Recently Published Texts," *JJS* 54 (2003): 146–152.

[313] DJD 3:181–183.

material that differs sharply from the contents of S. 5Q13 fragments 1–3, in particular, includes a review of history. As far as convergence with the Community Rules is concerned, 5Q13 4:2–3 shares wording that describes the one who refuses to enter the covenant preserved in 1QS, 4Q257 and 4Q262.[314] Unlike what we find in the Community Rules, such a case is associated with a summoning in front of the overseer in 5Q13, a figure not mentioned in the S Covenant Ceremony. A reference to "the covenant of God" occurs in 5Q13 28:3 though the identification of this fragment as belonging to 5Q13 has been questioned by Milik.[315] Metso explains the literary relationship between 5Q13 and the Community Rules in terms of a citation or a shared source.[316] Based on the scant remains available to us the precise relationship and direction of influence between both compositions cannot be determined. It is also possible, as suggested by Jokiranta and Vanonen, that 5Q13 is a further witness to the Covenant Ceremony.[317]

1.7 Guidance Notes for Readers and Aims

The translations below are presented synoptically. This allows readers to encounter the texts as they are preserved across the twelve manuscripts of Community Rules with ease. In addition, every instance where the manuscripts diverge – beyond purely orthographical matters – is highlighted with the use of *italics* or in-text notes in SMALL CAPS for material that is not present (rather than not preserved) in one of the manuscripts. The only exception in the synoptic presentation of the manuscripts is our approach to presenting the translations of 4Q256 and 4Q258 from the point where they converge at 4Q256 9:1 and 4Q258 1:1. Based on their close affinity from this point, these two manuscripts are translated on the basis of a "Transparent Composite Text." This is achieved by clearly indicating text that is preserved in only one of the two manuscripts. Text preserved in 4Q256 only is <u>single underlined</u> and text preserved in 4Q258 only is <u>double underlined</u>. In addition, the line numbers of each manuscript are identified in the body of the translation by indicating the distinctive column numbers alongside line numbers. 𝔒𝔩𝔡 𝔈𝔫𝔤𝔩𝔦𝔰𝔥 𝔗𝔢𝔵𝔱 𝔐𝔗 font is used for paleo Hebrew words and *Harlow Solid Italic* for text in cryptic script. In order to make this commentary accessible for students and lay readers I have almost always translated Hebrew terms where

---

[314] See 3.2.4 and 3.4.4 below.

[315] Milik, DJD 3:181.

[316] Cf. Metso, *Serekh Texts*, 25, 61; see also Lawrence H. Schiffman, "Sectarian Rule (5Q13)," in PTSDSSP1:132–143 and Schofield, *From Qumran to the Yaḥad*, 176–177, 179.

[317] Jokiranta and Vanonen, "Multiple Copies of Rule Texts."

they are used in the Commentary. Occasionally a minus in one or two manuscripts is identified by adding a note in SMALL CAPS.[318]

There are any number of editions that offer the texts and translations of the various manuscripts originally assigned to S separately. For this Commentary it is timely to lay out all the evidence in a synoptic format to allow readers to get a sense of some of the clusters and particularities of the manuscripts where they overlap. Both this introduction and the comments on particular sections and passages do, however, offer the necessary methodological context of how to work with the material. Our presentation is, to an extent, heuristic but offers value by allowing some sense of the inter-relationships of the fulsome evidence.

I have tried to balance faithfulness to the Hebrew text with arriving at a meaningful and readable English translation with the scales tipped very slightly in favour of the latter.

For pragmatic and heuristic reasons the sequence of 1QS is followed. However, both the Textual Notes and the Commentary take the full spectrum of discrete and distinctive witnesses into account. It is hoped this Introduction and the Commentary offer an easily accessible point of access to the complex spectrum of available manuscripts alongside nuanced discussions of the relationships between the various works, texts and manuscripts.

It is my hope that the chief contribution of this Commentary will be to make the fullness of the evidence accessible to a broad readership. Despite the availability of a number of editions, monographs and articles sparked by the richness of the S tradition, the material is still incredibly cumbersome to consult in its fullness. I hope this obstacle will be overcome somewhat by this book. While readers may differ on particular readings and interpretations I hope we may share the glory of beholding the richness of the evidence these ancient manuscripts have opened up before us.

---

[318] See, e. g., 5.2.6.

2. Introduction: Outline of Communal Aspirations
(1QS 1:1–15 // 4Q255 1:1–6 // 4Q257 1:1–2)

2.1 Introduction

Here we find the introduction to the longest form of the Community Rules as attested in 1QS, 4Q255 and 4Q257. The programmatic opening lines, including the only reference to the work as "the book of the rule of the community," give the strong impression that this material has been skilfully crafted as an introduction to the larger work by the editors/compilers responsible for the Rules in their long form. It is perhaps not surprising, therefore, that the terms used to convey a community ethos are reminiscent of other parts of the S tradition. The tone of these introductory lines is ideological rather than pragmatic. Current community members and those aspiring to join[1] are admonished to hold fast to what is good, keep from evil and to endeavour to please God by obedience to the law revealed to Moses and the prophets.

2.2 Translation

1QS 1	4Q255 1	4Q257 1
[1] To/for [ ] *š/śym* for his life [the book of the ru]le of the community.	[1][ ] for his [lif]e the book of the rule of the community.	[1][
(They are) to seek [2]God with [all (their) heart] and with [all (their) soul;	[2][(They are) to seek God with all (their) heart and with a]ll (their) soul;	with all (their) hea]rt and with al[l [2](their) soul;
to] do what is good and right before Him according to that which [3]He has commanded through Moses and through all His servants the prophets;	to do [3][what is good and right before Him according to that which] He has commanded through Moses [4][and through all His servants the prophets;	to do what is good and right before Him according to that which He has commanded through Moses and through a]ll [...]
to love all [4]that which He favours and hate all that	to l]ove a[l]l [that which [5]He favours and hate all that	

1QS 1	4Q255 1	4Q257 1
He despises;	He despi]ses;	
to keep away from all evil	to k[eep away from all ⁶evil	
⁵but adhere closely to all	but adhere closely to all	
good works;	good works];	
to act truthfully,	to ac[t truthfully …]	

1QS

righteously and justly ⁶in the land and no longer walk in the stubbornness of a guilty heart and prurient eyes ⁷and perform all kinds of evil. (They are) to bring into the covenant of piety all those who are fervently committed to act according to the statutes of God ⁸so that they may come together on account of God's scheme; to walk perfectly before Him (according to) all⁹ that has been revealed at the times appointed for their disclosure; to love all the children of light each one ¹⁰according to his lot in the divine scheme and hate all the children of darkness each according to his guilt ¹¹on account of the vengeance of God. And all those fervently committed to His truth shall bring all their knowledge, their strength, ¹²and their property into the community of God so that they may cleanse their knowledge according to the truth of the statutes of God and arrange their strength ¹³according to the perfection of His ways and all their property according to His righteous scheme. They shall not transgress a single one ¹⁴of all the utterances of God with regard to their time periods. They shall not bring forward their times nor fall behind ¹⁵from (adhering to) any of their appointed times. They shall not disregard any of His true statutes by walking (off course) to the right or to the left.

2.3 Textual Notes

1:1 Remains of stitching holes indicate that the opening column of 1QS was preceded by another sheet. Based on the generous width of the margin the additional sheet appears to have been a handle-sheet. Parts of the handle-sheet have survived and contain the remains of a description of the contents of the scroll on the verso. The terms used to refer to the contents of the scroll, "[rul]e of the community and from" (סר[ך היחד ומן]), are often taken to confirm that the handle-sheet refers to more than the eleven columns of the Community Rule from Cave 1.² Partly effaced remains of letters are also preserved on the verso of 4Q257 1a. Alexander and Vermes read כיבו°° לוס° and note that the position of the remains would suggest we are dealing with a title or the name of the author.³ An earlier suggestion by Stephen Pfann proposed the more expected reading סרכ הי[חד] ל.⁴ The reading כל בח[...]לוס or conveivably ליס[seems more likely.

---

² Cf. Milik, DJD 1:107 and Plate 22 as well as Tov, *Scribal Practices*, 120.

³ See Alexander and Vermes, DJD 26:69–70 and Tov, *Scribal Practices*, 118, 120–121.

⁴ Pfann, "4Q249 Midrash Sefer Moshe," in *Legal Texts and Legal Issues: Proceedings of the International Organization for Qumran Studies Published in Honour of Joseph M. Baumgarten.*

1:1 A number of restorations for the lost opening words of 1QS have been proposed, many of them agreeing on restoring "For/to [the Maskil]."[5] Guilbert boldly, but with little justification, translates a restored reference to the Maskil here and preserved references throughout 1QS with the Teacher of Rightousness ("Maître de Sagesse").[6] In light of the uncertainty involved in restoring the crucial opening words and the potential significance of such a restoration on how the text is to be read, it seems best to allow the evidence to stand. Alexander and Vermes calculate space for 21–22 letters in the first lacuna in line 1 and a slightly shorter space in the opening line of 4Q255.[7]

1:1 Brownlee and Licht have noted the semantic connection between Semitic סרך and Greek τάχις.[8] This receives support from the Aramaic Levi Document 8:6 where the Greek (Athos ms. *e*) renders Aramaic בסרך (4Q214 2:10) with ἐν τάχει.[9] Finally, Conklin has offered a cross-Semitic analysis of the derivation of the root in favour of the suggestion that it originated as a Persian loanword via Aramaic.[10]

1:1 The left margin in 4Q255 1 reveals two holes followed by an ink mark at the level of the interlinear space between 4Q255 1:1–2. This mark might have served to offer guidance for the maximum length of lines.[11] Alexander and Vermes refer to a T–shaped mark in the top left margin of 4Q255 1.[12] Examination of the original fragment reveals a series of clusters of little black dots along the top margin that are most likely insect damage, see the image B-371748 by Shai Halevi in the LLDSSDL. The surface of the same fragment also reveals several discoloured areas that may indicate water damage.

1:2 There is some evidence of a variation in inkflow in this line in 1QS with the first two letters of "what is good" (הטוב) being the clearest example. Given the naturally faded localised appearance of the final two letters, it is unlikely that the thicker inkflow at the beginning was the result of a regular topping up of ink.

Edited by Moshe Bernstein, Florentino García Martínez and John Kampen. STDJ 23 (Leiden: Brill, 199), 11–18, here 11.

[5] So, e. g., Jean Carmignac, "Conjecture sur la première ligne de la Règle de la Communauté," *RevQ* 2 (1959): 85–87 and Alexander and Vermes, DJD 26:32.

[6] Guilbert, "Règle de la Communauté," 21.

[7] Alexander and Vermes, DJD 26:32 and Jokiranta, "Thinking About Ancients Manuscripts."

[8] Brownlee, *Dead Sea Manual*, 7 and Jacob Licht, *The Rule Scroll* (Jerusalem: Bialik, 1965) [Hebrew], 66.

[9] See Jonas Greenfield, Michael E. Stone and Esther Eshel, *The Aramaic Levi Document: Edition, Translation, Commentary*. SVTP 19 (Leiden: Brill, 2004), 176; Metso, *Textual Development*, 76 and Wernberg-Møller, *Manual of Discipline*, 44.

[10] Cf. Blane W. Conklin, "Alleged Derivation of the Dead Sea Scroll Term *Serek*," *JSS* 52 (2007): 45–57.

[11] On ink guidemarks more broadly see Tov, *Scribal Practices*, 58.

[12] Alexander and Vermes, DJD 26:27.

1:6 Based on the influence of Deut 6:18 the translation "upon earth"[13] for בארץ in 1QS is unlikely.

1:7 The final radical *aleph* has been omitted in the infinitive להבי "to bring" 1QS.[14]

1:7b (and 11) The *niphal* of נדב translated here with "fervently committed to" is found only in 1QS 1:7,11 in contrast to a preference for the *hitpael* in the core columns of the Rules.[15] The verb frequently occurs in cultic contexts in the Hebrew Bible. In the present passage the context refers to avoiding all evil and embracing the statutes in a manner reminiscent of 1QS 5:1 // 4Q256 // 4Q258.[16]

1:8 (and 10) Wernberg-Møller translates the phrase rendered here "God's scheme" (עצת אל) with "council of God."[17] The parallelism with "on account of the vengeance of God" in line 11 makes this less likely.

1:8 The Hebrew simply reads "all that has been revealed" and lacks the preposition כ "according to" which we would have expected. The cause is likely a scribal error as proposed already by Brownlee.[18]

10:9 Alexander and Vermes translate "with regard to the times appointed for them (the members of the community)."[19]

1:10 Fragment 4Q256 1 has not been included in the translation above since it has now been correctly identified as belonging to 4Q99 (4QJob^a).[20]

1:13 There is evidence for a scribal correction of *bet* to *mem* in בכול in 1QS.[21]

1:13–15 Gary Rendsburg has noted the prohibitive use of לא plus infinitive here.[22]

1:14 In contrast to biblical Hebrew where קץ usually means "end," the term commonly has the meaning "time, designated time" in the Dead Sea Scrolls.[23]

1:14–15 The verb אחר *hitpael* "fall behind" followed by the preposition מן occurs in 4Q266 (4QD^a) 2 i 2 and Sir 7:34. The *piel* of קדם "bring forward" is also attested in 4Q268 (4QD^c) 1:4 where *piel* forms occur for both verbs.[24]

---

[13] Cf. Vermes, CDSSE, 98 and Alfred R. C. Leaney, *The Rule of Qumran and Its Meaning.* NTL (London: SCM, 1966), 117.

[14] Cf. Qimron, HDSS, 23.

[15] See 1QS 5:1 // 4Q258 1:1; 1QS 5:6 // 4Q258 1:5; 1QS 5:8, 10, 21–22 // 4Q258 2:1–2 // 4Q261 1a–b; 1QS 6:13 // 4Q256 11:8. Cf. Brownlee, *Dead Sea Manual,* 7 and Alexander and Vermes, DJD 26:10.

[16] For fuller discussion and further literature see 5.4 below.

[17] Wernberg-Møller, *Manual of Discipline*, 44.

[18] Brownlee, *Dead Sea Manual*, 8.

[19] Alexander and Vermes, DJD 26:35.

[20] For details see 1.5.3.1 above.

[21] Cf. Qimron, PTSDSSP 1:6 n. 7 and Qimron, DSSHW 1: 213.

[22] Gary Rendsburg, "Qumran Hebrew (with a Trial Cut [1QS])," in *The Dead Sea Scrolls at 60: Scholarly Contributions of New York University Faculty and Alumni.* Edited by Lawrence H. Schiffman and Shani Tzoref. STDJ 89 (Leiden: Brill, 2010), 217–246, 223.

[23] Cf. DCH 7:275–278.

[24] See further 2.4 below.

2.4 Commentary

1:1 Very few texts from the corpus of the Scrolls preserve the titles and conclusions of compositions.[25] In the case of the Community Rules we are fortunate to find the opening lines of the long text partially preserved in 1QS 1:1 and 4Q255 1:1 as well as the title of the shorter text in 4Q258 1:1.[26] As noted above the remains of a description of the contents of the scroll containing 1QS, 1QSa and 1QSb are also preserved on the verso of the handle-sheet of that scroll pointing towards a more complex collection.[27] There is no material case to sustain a reconstruction of "For the Maskil" as the opening words of 1QS // 4Q255.[28] One may venture the possibility of such a heading, which is doubtlessly attractive, but to assume this as a reality on which to build a larger argument seems precipitous.

1:1 Even though the opening words are lost, two manuscripts (1QS 1:1 and 4Q255 1:1) preserve remains of what appears to be a part of the title for the composition which reads "the book of the rule of the community" ספר סרך היחד. As rightly noted by Jutta Jokiranta, the titular use of these words is not secure given the lost text preceding these words.[29] The noun סרך "rule, order" occurs again in sub-headings at 1QS 5:1 and 1QS 6:8. By contrast, 4Q256 9:1 // 4Q258 1:1 read "Midrash for the Maskil" (מדרש למשכל).[30] It is curious to observe that the term סרך occurs eight times in 1QS 1; 2; 5 and 6 (with three attestations in 4QS) and is entirely unattested in 1QS 7–11 across the manuscripts. The most numerous occurrences of the term are found in the War Scroll followed by the Damascus Document. In addition it occurs four times in the Rule of the Congregation (1QSa) on the same scroll as S.[31] Given the terminology is frequently employed in headings or sub-sections of larger works suggests that the term goes back to a late stage in the growth and shaping of these documents.[32] The collocation ספר סרך "book of the rule" occurs only here and in the War Scroll at 1QM 15:4–5 in a liturgical context. The construct סרך היחד is used one more time in the Rules manuscripts with reference to the general membership of the community in 1QS 1:16 // 4Q256 2:1.[33]

---

[25] See Tov, *Scribal Practices*, 108–121.

[26] Further, 5.1.2 below.

[27] On the poorly preserved remains on the verso of 4Q257 1a see 2.3 above. Cf. also 1.5.1.1 above and Tov, *Scribal Practices*, 120.

[28] See also 2.3 above.

[29] See Jokiranta, "Thinking About Ancient Manuscripts."

[30] Cf. 5.4 below.

[31] See 1.5.1.1 above.

[32] Further, Charlotte Hempel, "Rules," in CDSS, 405–412.

[33] See Charlotte Hempel, "סֶרֶךְ *særæk*," ThWQ 2:1111–1117; Lawrence H. Schiffman, *The Halakhah at Qumran*. SJLA 16 (Leiden: Brill, 1975) and Schofield, *From Qumran to the Yaḥad*, 153–154. On the semantic field of סרך and Greek τάξις, see 2.3 above.

1:1 The noun יחד "community" – often as nomen rectum of a construct phrase – is characteristic of the Community Rules, occurring 56 times in 1QS paralleled in 31 instances in 4Q255–259 and 4Q261. Across the manuscripts the terminology is predominant in the central columns[34] and entirely absent from the Teaching on the Two Spirits in 1QS 3:13–4:26 // 4Q257 though the adverb יחד "together" is found in 1QS 4:18.[35] Rather than considering 4Q255 as comprising the remains of a "complete" copy of S based on its attestation of the title,[36] I suggest that the material preserved in 4Q255 represents a manuscript of the type employed by the compiler(s) of 1QS when drawing up the framework of the Community Rule as attested most fully in 1QS and comprising material from 1QS 1–4 and the Statutes of the Maskil.[37]

1:1– 2 For the phrase "to seek God with all (their heart) and all (their soul)" see 2 Chron 15:12. The use of infinitives here and in what follows prevents us from certainty about the subject of the verbs. Michael Wise's translation presupposes a third m. sg. subject based on a reconstruction of Maskil at the very beginning of the text.[38] The frequent references to God in this introductory section are indicative of the theological flavour of this material.[39] The position of the admonition to seek God at the very beginning of communal aims at the beginning of 1QS // 4Q255 // 4Q257 reinforces this theological orientation.

1:1b–7a and the parallels in 4Q255 1:2–6 // 4Q257 1:1–2 are reminiscent of Deut 6:17–18 with a shared emphasis on proper conduct, obedience to God's commandments and the promise of the land. The preponderance of infinitives has often been noted and is reminiscent of Prov 1:2–6.[40] Comparable programmatic passages employing infinitive chains are found in the material covered in Chapters 5, 8 and 14.[41]

---

[34] Cf. 1QS 1 x3 (4QS x2); 1QS 2 x3 (4QS x1); 1QS 3 x3 (4QS x3); 1QS 5 x10 (4QS x11]; 1QS 6 x14 (4QS x1]; 1QS 7 x8 (4QS x3); 1QS 8 x9 (4QS x5); 1QS 9 x5 (4QS x5) and 1QS 11 x1.

[35] See Eyal Regev, "יַחַד *jahad*," ThWQ 2:121–130; Collins, *Beyond the Qumran Community*, 54–55 and Schofield, *From Qumran to the Yaḥad*.

[36] So Alexander and Vermes, DJD 26:30.

[37] Cf. further 1.5.2 above.

[38] See Wise, DSSANT, 126 and 2.3 above.

[39] Further, Hempel, "Long Text" and section 5.1 below as well as the recognition of "dependence on God" as a prominent feature in the liturgical components of the Community Rules in George J. Brooke, "Aspects of the Theological Significance of Prayer and Worship in the Qumran Scrolls," in *Prayer and Poetry in the Dead Sea Scrolls and Related Literature: Essays in Honor of Eileen Schuller on the Occasion of Her 65th Birthday*. Edited by Jeremy Penner, Ken M. Penner and Cecilia Wassén. STDJ 98 (Leiden: Brill, 2012), 35–54, 50–51.

[40] See Carol Newsom, "Apocalyptic and the Discourse of the Qumran Community," *JNES* 49 (1990): 135–144, esp. 138; Michael V. Fox, *Proverbs 1–9*. AB 18 (New Haven, CT: Yale University Press, 2000), 58 and Charlotte Hempel, "Wisdom and Law in the Hebrew Bible and at Qumran," *JSJ* 48 (2017): 1–27.

[41] See also Metso, *Textual Development*, 120–124.

1:3 The reference to the prophets as an authority alongside the commandments is distinctive though also found in 1QS 8:15–16 // 4Q258 6:7–8.[42] Interestingly, 1 Thess 5:20 attests an admonition not to despise the words of the prophets[43] followed by a comparable admonition to refrain from all evil in 1 Thess 5:22. As in 1QS 6:6 and 1QS 8:15–16 // 4Q258 6:7 // 4Q259 2:6, the commandments and their application are presented here as accessible to those addressed without further mediation. It emerges from our interpretation of frequent references to the interpretation of the law at a formative stage in the community's emergence that it is halakhic disagreements between those who are able to access the revealed law that cause great friction in the Community Rules.[44] This contrasts with the emphases elsewhere in the Rules and beyond on the privileged insights of particular interpreters.[45]

1:3–4 The theme of love and hate which refers to God's favour and hatred[46] is taken up again in lines 9–10 with reference to the children of light and darkness. The topos is reminiscent of 1QS 9:16, 21 // 4Q256 18:5–6 // 4Q258 8:1, 5–6 // 4Q259 3:13; 4:2–3 where it occurs twice in the context of the Maskil's duties of love for his charges and abhorrence of the people of destruction.[47]

1:4 (and 7) The concern to keep away from "all evil" (כול רע) is taken up again in line 7. 1QS 1 juxtaposes the shunning of "all evil" with commending good deeds as part of a twofold scheme that is attested more widely in Early Jewish and Christian literature.[48] The need to reject all evil is emphasized also at the outset of the programmatic introduction in 1QS 5:1 // 4Q256 9:1 // 4Q258 1:1.[49]

1:6 The emphasis on leading a life devoted to truth, righteousness and justice in the land evokes Deut 6:18 and Jer 4:2.[50]

1:6–7 Whereas most of this introductory section lacks polemics, these lines hint at a recent lifestyle change on the part of those addressed and are reminiscent of the plus in 1QS 5:4–5 as well as CD 2:16–18. The resemblance between this polemical passage and a plus in 1QS 5 offers support for the view that the Long Text of the Community Rules builds on secondary expansions in 1QS

---

[42] Cf. Alex Jassen, "The Presentation of the Ancient Prophets as Lawgivers at Qumran," *JBL* 127 (2008): 307–337, esp. 314–322.

[43] See Knibb, *Qumran Community*, 80.

[44] Cf. Chapter 5; section 6.2 and Chapter 8 below.

[45] See, e. g., 1QS 5:8–9 (contrast 4Q256 9:7–8 // 4Q258 1:6–7); 1QS 8:11–12 // 4Q258 6:5–6 // 4Q259 3:2–3 and also CD 6:7. For further discussion see Charlotte Hempel, "Interpretative Authority in the Community Rule Traditions," *DSD* 10 (2003): 59–80 and further literature presented there.

[46] Cf. CD 2:15 and Brownlee, *Dead Sea Manual*, 7.

[47] See further 14.4 below.

[48] Cf., e. g., T.Ash. 1–3 and Rom 12:9 and Wernberg-Møller, *Manual of Discipline*, 45–46.

[49] See 1.2.1 above and 5.4 below.

[50] See Brownlee, *Dead Sea Manual*, 7 as well as 1QS 8:2–3 // 4Q259 2:10–12 and 1QS 5:3–4 // 4Q256 9:3–4 // 4Q258 1:3.

which can be described as "double long."[51] That is, 1QS is long by virtue of including the material in 1QS 1–4 over against 4Q258 in addition to a series of plusses in 1QS 5 and elsewhere.

1:7b–15 The second part of this introduction displays clear connections, at times even in sequence, to various parts of the long text of the Rule that follow, such as admission into the covenant (line 7b), the Teaching on the Two Spirits (cf. lines 8–10), communal life (lines 11–13), the Statutes for the Maskil (lines 8–9) and the Final Hymn (lines 13–15).[52]

1:8 The expression "covenant of piety" (ברית חסד) introduces the covenantal idea very early in this document.[53]

1:8 (and 10) The phrase rendered "God's scheme" (עצת אל) occurs again in line 10 and is distinctive over against the much more frequently attested "council of the community" (עצת היחד) both in the Community Rules and beyond. "God's scheme" is also found in the apotropaic Songs of the Maskil,[54] and the related expression "the people of the council of God" occurs in a fragmentary context in the Rule of Blessings 1QSb 4:23–24. In each case the context suggests a polarity in the portrayal of humanity under threat from a darker side;[55] In 1QSb 4:24 the fate of the people of the council of God is contrasted with a life in the hands of a malicious prince.[56]

1:8–9 The combination of being recipients of revelations at pre-determined times and the aspiration to perfect conduct recalls the closing lines of the Covenant Ceremony in 1QS 3:10 and parallels[57] as well as the Statutes for the Maskil.[58] Note, however, the significant variant in 4Q259 3:9 // 1QS 9:13 that refers to the expectation that the Maskil is also knowledgeable about previous revelations.[59]

1:8–10 The introduction of the sons of light and the sons of darkness is striking. This opposition is, in fact, rather localised in the Dead Sea Scrolls.[60] In the present context it sits rather awkwardly alongside the generic admonitions to do what is right and good in previous lines. One suspects that the opposition

---

[51] For further detail see Hempel, "Long Text," and 1QS plusses noted in 3.4 below.

[52] For further discussion of the language of fervent commitment see 5.4.2 below.

[53] The notion of the covenant is crucial in this text, see especially Chapter 3 and section 6.1 below as well as James M. Scott, "Covenant," in *EDEJ*, 491–494.

[54] See 4Q511 48–49+51:1.

[55] Cf. 1QS 1:10–11.

[56] See further the apotropaic setting of 4Q511; Hempel, "Long Text," 12–16; Heinz-Wolfgang Kuhn, "Zum 2. Korintherbrief: Drei wichtige Parallelen zur Qumrangemeinde (Gemeinde Gottes, neuer Bund und Neuschöpfung)," *ZNW* 110 (2019): 42–83, 46–55 and 1.2.1 above.

[57] See 3.4.4.

[58] Cf. 1QS 9:13, 19 and parallels as well as 14.4.1 and 14.4.3 below.

[59] See 1.5.6.2; 14.4.3 as well as the Commentary on 1:13–15 below.

[60] See Charlotte Hempel, "The Treatise on the Two Spirits and the Literary Development of the Rule of the Community," in *Dualism in Qumran*. Edited by Géza G. Xeravits. LSTS 76 (London: T&T Clark, 2010), 102–120.

between both of these groups was introduced here by the compiler of 1QS in order to provide a suitable link to the Teaching on the Two Spirits.[61]

1:10 This is the first occurrence of the term "lot" (גורל) in the Community Rule.[62] The term is prominent in the covenant admission and reaffirmation ceremony[63] that follows, the Teaching on the Two Spirits[64] and the diverse regulations in 1QS 5–9 and parallels.[65] The term further occurs once in the Final Hymn at 1QS 11:7 // 4Q258 12:4.[66] Outside of the central columns 1QS 5–9 "lot" refers almost exclusively to opposing forces both at a human and cosmic level, with the exception of 1QS 4:26.[67] In 1QS 5–9, by contrast, the term is used in the context of community-internal decision making structures. The present passage admonishes affection for the children of light according their lot in the divine scheme.

1:11–13 Communal life extending to sharing knowledge, property and strength is dealt with in more depth in 1QS 5–9 // 4QS.

1:12 Of interest is the distinctive designation "community of God" (יחד אל) which occurs only here and in 1QS 2:22 with no preserved parallels in 4QS. Alongside the phrase "God's scheme" in 1QS 1:8 and 10 discussed above this phrase offers a more theological concept of the community than the frequently attested phrase "the council of the community" היחד (עצת) which focuses on the human domain.[68]

1:13–15 The language employed here is reminiscent of 1QS 1:9 and 1QS 3:9–11 // 4Q255 2:4–6 // 4Q257 3:13–14 where obedience to the commandments as revealed over time is a key concern. This led a number of the earliest commentators to recognise that the issue at hand is the correct understanding of divine revelation and corresponding behaviour.[69] Such a reading now receives considerable support from the opening lines of the Damascus Document as preserved in two Cave 4 manuscripts. The same verbs קדם (here *piel* "to bring forward") and אחר *hitpael* ("to fall behind") are employed there to refer to divinely appointed times past and present as well as the final judgment (4Q266 2 i 2 // 4Q268 1:4).[70] The picture is eloquently captured by Steven Fraade's reference to "the divine orchestration of history" which presupposes close adherence to the

---

[61] See Chapter 4 below.

[62] Cf. HAWTTM 2:37–39 and Armin Lange, "גּוֹרְל *gôrāl*," ThWQ 1:593–600.

[63] See 1QS 2:2; 5 // [4Q256 2:12] // 4Q257 2:1; 1QS 2:17, 23 and Chapter 3 below.

[64] Cf. 1QS 3:24 ; 1QS 4:24, [4Q257 6:4]; 1QS 4:26, see Chapter 4.

[65] See Chapters 5 and 9 below.

[66] For details see 15.4.8 below.

[67] See 4.2.4 below.

[68] For fuller discussion see Hempel, "Long Text."

[69] See Wernberg-Møller, *Manual of Discipline*, 49; Manfred Weise, *Kultzeiten und kultischer Bundesschluss in der "Ordensregel" vom Toten Meer*. SPB 3 (Leiden: Brill, 1961), 66 and Leaney, *Rule of Qumran*, 120.

[70] See also the comment on 1QS 1:9 above and 3.2.4 below.

commandments.[71] Others favour an interpretation of this passage as a pointed endorsement of the solar calendar.[72] Sacha Stern has recently drawn attention to the fact that these lines demand faithful enforcement of the calendar without expressing a preference for a particular kind of calendar.[73] 1QS 1:9 and 1QS 3:9–11 coupled with the important witness of the Damascus Document suggest that a broader salvation historical emphasis lies at the heart of these lines. However, a commitment to "divine orchestration," to use Fraade's language, would embrace due adherence to sacred time even if the latter no longer emerges as the exclusive concern at issue here.

1:15 The Introduction ends with an admonition not to stray left or right.[74]

---

[71] Cf. Fraade, *Legal Fictions*, 231–232.

[72] So, e. g., Knibb, *Qumran Community*, 82.

[73] See Stern, "Qumran Calendars and Sectarianism," in OHDSS, 232–253, here 244.

[74] Cf. Deut 28:14 and the Commentary on 1QS 3:10–11 // 4Q255 2:6–7 // 4Q257 3:14 in 3.4.4 below.

3. Admission into and Reaffirmation of the Covenant (1QS 1:16–3:12 // 4Q255 2:1–9 // 4Q256 2:1–6, 12–13; 3:1–4 // 4Q257 2:1–8; 3:1–14 // 4Q262 1:1–4 // 5Q11 1 i[1]

3.1 Introduction

The present extensive passage describes a covenant ceremony or, to be precise, a literary account of such a ceremony.[2] The Covenant Ceremony can be classified as a description of a Rite of Passage.[3] We are not given any indication of the frequency of this procedure until the notice in 1QS 2:19 which identifies the ceremony as an annual event. A similar annual event is referred to in the closing lines of the Damascus Document[4] which refer to a gathering of all the inhabitants of the camps in the third month in order to curse those who transgress the law after a ceremony that deals with the exclusion of one who despises the preceding judgments.[5] In light of a number of passages that associate the festival of weeks with the covenant it is likely that the annual event referred to in the Communal Rules is also envisaged to occur in the third month.[6] Rather than imagining that this account intimates annual admission, it seems more likely to refer to a liturgical event that conveyed the final seal of approval on new admissions.[7]

The topic of admitting new members into the community occurs repeatedly in the Community Rules. Entry into the community by oath is described in 1QS 5, 4Q256 9 and 4Q258 1.[8] A plus in 1QS 5:7b locates the admission by oath in the

---

[1] Readings attested in 5Q11 1 i are identified with dotted underlining in the translation below.

[2] See Daniel Falk, "Liturgical Texts," in CDSS, 422–434, 422

[3] Cf. further Russell C. D. Arnold, *The Social Role of Liturgy in the Religion of the Qumran Community*. STDJ 60 (Leiden: Brill, 2006), 52–81; Falk, "Liturgical Texts" and Kugler, "Making All Experience Religious," 139–143.

[4] See 4Q266 11:1–18 // 4Q270 7 i 19c – ii 12a.

[5] Further, Daniel K. Falk, *Daily, Sabbath, and Festival Prayers in the Dead Sea Scrolls*. STDJ 27 (Leiden: Brill, 1998), 230–235 and Hempel, *Laws of the Damascus Document*, 175–185.

[6] Cf. Exod 19:1; 2 Chron 15:10–12 and *Jub.* 6:17 as well as Knibb, *Qumran Community*, 89 and James C. VanderKam, *The Dead Sea Scrolls and the Bible* (Grand Rapids, MI: Eerdmans, 2012), 149–152. For a further reference to the third month see 4Q275 Communal Ceremony 1 3 and Alexander and Vermes, DJD 26:209–216.

[7] Cf. also Friedrich Baumgärtel, "Zur Liturgie der "Sektenrolle" vom Toten Meer," *ZAW* 65 (1953): 263–265.

[8] Cf. 1QS 5:7c–9a // 4Q256 9:6b–13 // 4Q258 1:5b–13 as well as 6.1 below.

context of a communal meeting. This is followed by a more extensive account of the assessment and registration of new entrants into the Covenant in 1QS 5:20b–23a // 4Q258 2:1–3a //4Q261 1a–b: 1–4a.[9] As in the present passage this assessment of new entrants is followed by a comparable annual review of current members in 1QS 5:23b–24a // 4Q258 2:3b–4a // 4Q261 1a–b: 4b–6. A more protracted admission process that also makes reference to entering the covenant is outlined in 1QS 6.[10] In addition to being connected to those parts of the Rule that are concerned with admission into the community, in the Final Hymn the Maskil pledges to (re-)enter the covenant each morning and evening.[11]

The covenant ceremony draws heavily on biblical precedents, esp. Deut 27 and Deut 29:17–20 [Hebrew].[12] A difference is the position of the blessings and curses in advance of the rules here rather than at the end of a collection of laws as in Deut 28.[13] This difference can be accounted for by the literary development of the Rules and the fact that the communal regulations were prefaced secondarily by the material now included in 1QS 1–4 and parallels including the Covenant Ceremony.

Rather than referring to a singular event, as is the case in Deut 27–30, the covenant ceremony is presented here both as a one-off life-changing event for those joining the community for the first time, presumably with the intention of devoting the rest of their lives to its cause, and as an annual event for existing members.[14] The presence of extensive and threatening curses incorporated into the account of the ceremony leaves little doubt that the liturgy, either performed or read, served as much – if not predominantly – as a warning to insincere members.[15]

Many elements of this liturgy are shared with covenant renewal ceremonies that follow a point of crisis in an existing covenant relationship as, e. g., in Neh 9–10.[16] Note also the blessings and curses that form part of the War Scroll in 1QM 13:1–6. The composition known as Berakhot which is preserved in five fragmentary manuscripts (4Q286–4Q290) shares the building blocks of blessings and curses with the Covenant Ceremony of S as well as a number of

---

[9] For details see again 6.1 below.

[10] Cf. 1QS 6:13b–23 // 4Q256 11:8, 11–13 // 4Q261 3:1 and Chapter 6.5 below.

[11] For discussion see 15.1.3 and 15.4.3 below.

[12] See Nitzan, *Qumran Prayer*, 12; Licht, *Rule Scroll*, 54–55 and Shani Tzoref, "The Use of Scripture in the Community Rule," in *A Companion to Biblical Interpretation in Early Judaism.* Edited by Matthias Henze (Grand Rapids, MI: Eerdmans, 2012), 203–234.

[13] This is noted, for instance, by Nitzan, *Qumran Prayer*, 121.

[14] Cf. 1QS 2:19 and see also 4Q287 (Ber[b]) 4:1.

[15] On the ceremony's pronounced rhetorical function see also Falk, *Daily, Sabbath, and Festival Prayers*, 219. See further Leonhardt-Balzer, "Evil at Qumran," and Newsom, *Self and Symbolic Space* 117–127.

[16] See Baumgärtel, "Liturgie;" also Hempel, "Long Text."

other thematic and terminological links with the Community Rules. Distinctively, Berakhot is concerned with praising God in his heavenly sanctuary and lacks reference to a blessing of those entering the covenant.[17] There has been a tendency to construct an "Über–Covenant Ceremony" by drawing on a range of different fragmentary texts and tag them on to the picture that emerges from the Community Rules. Texts that have been drawn in on such terms include 4QBerakhot, though Nitzan is careful to acknowledge the lack of reference to entrance into the covenant in the latter composition.[18] In addition, the expulsion ceremony in the Damascus Document is rather problematically presented almost as Commuity Rules text by Arnold.[19] 4Q280 (4QCurse), a text that preserves an extensive curse of the malevolent figure of Melchiresha, is frequently read in light of 1QS.[20] Finally, Arnold and others associate 4Q298 (Words of the Maskil to the Sons of Dawn) with admission into the covenant community.[21] The danger of an approach that draws in material from elsewhere to construct a more comprehensive covenant ceremony by padding out what is preserved in the Community Rules is to inhibit not only our understanding of S but also preventing us from reading and interpreting other distinctive compositions in their own right before offering comparative analyses.

Finally, recently published apotropaic texts have established the apotropaic significance of blessing and the praise of God's mighty deeds.[22] Thus, compositions like the Songs of the Maskil (4Q510–511) make the role of blessing after the evocative description of the precarious situation during the rule of Belial in the Covenant Ceremony more poignant. In light of the apotropaic material from Qumran I suggest that the influence of Belial is restrained as much by the act of blessing and by recounting God's righteous and powerful acts that follow in the Covenant Ceremony as by the curses.[23]

---

[17] Further, Bilhah Nitzan, "4Q286–290. Berakhot[a-e]," in DJD 11:1–74; Daniel Falk, "Berakhot," in CDSS, 289–301 and Jutta Jokiranta, "Ritualization and the Power of Listing in 4QBerakhot[a] (4Q286), in *Is There a Text in this Cave?* Edited by Feldman, Cioată and Hempel, 438–458.

[18] See Nitzan, "Blessings and Curses," in EDSS 1:95–100.

[19] Arnold, *Social Role of Liturgy*, 55–56. For a more nuanced analysis of the material on exclusion and expulsion in the Community Rules and the Damascus Document see Aharon Shemesh, "Expulsion and Exclusion in the Community Rule and the Damascus Document," *DSD* 9 (2002): 44–74.

[20] See Bilhah Nitzan, "4Q280. 4QCurses," DJD 29:1–8.

[21] Arnold, *Social Role of Liturgy*, 60–61 and further literature there. For reservations about the evidence base for such an interpretation of 4Q298 see Hempel, *Qumran Rule Texts in Context*, 169–170.

[22] Cf. Nitzan, *Qumran Prayer*, 227–272.

[23] See further 1.2.1 above and 15.1.2 below.

3.2 Translation

3.2.1 Introduction (1QS 1:16–18a // 4Q256 2:1–3a)

1QS 1	4Q256 2
[16]And all those entering the organization of the community shall gain admittance into the covenant before God to act [17]according to all that He has commanded and not to turn their back on Him because of all the dread, terror and the crucible of [18]their testing during the rule of Belial.	[1][And all those entering] the organization of the community shall gain admittance into the covena[nt [2]before God to act according to all that He has commanded and not to turn their back on Him] because of all the dr[ead, terr]or and the crucible of [3][their testing during the rule of Belial.]

3.2.2 The Covenant Admission Ceremony (1QS 1:18b–2:18 // 4Q256 2:1–6, 12–13; 3:1–4 // 4Q257 2:1–8 // 5Q11 1 i)

1QS 1	4Q256 2
And as they are entering the covenant the priests [19]and the levites shall bless the God of salvation and all His true works. And all [20]those entering the covenant shall say after them, "Amen, Amen." *Vacat.* [21]*Vacat.* Then the priests shall enumerate God's righteous deeds as reflected in His powerful acts [22]and they shall proclaim all His loving acts of kindness towards Israel. And the levites shall enumerate [23]the trespasses of the children of Israel	[And as they are entering the covenant the priest]s and the le[vites shall bless the God of [4]salvation and all His true works. And all those entering the covenant shall say after them, "Amen, Amen." [5]*Vacat?* Then the priests shall enumerate God's righteous deeds as reflected in His] powerful [acts and they shall proclaim all His loving acts of [6]kindness towards Israel. And the levites shall enumerate the tres]passes of the children of I[srael]

1QS 1–2

and all their guilty wrongdoings and their sins during the rule of [24]Belial. [And al]l those entering the covenant shall confess after them saying, "We have trespassed, [25]we have committed [wr]ongdoings, [sin]ned and acted wickedly, we [and] our [fa]thers before us by walking [26][...] truth and righteous is [Go] d [...] His judgment is upon us and upon [our] fathers. 2[1]But He has favoured us with His kind love from eternity to eternity." *Vacat.* And the priests shall bless all [2]the people of the lot of God who walk perfectly in all His ways saying, "May He bless you with all [3]good things and keep you from all things evil. May He illuminate your heart with insight(s) for life and award you eternal knowledge. [4]May He lift the face of His love upon you for eternal well-being."

1QS 2 // 5Q11 1 i dotted underline	4Q256 2–3	4Q257 2
[4b]*Vacat*. And the levites shall curse all the people of [5]the lot of Belial and answer saying, "Cursed be you in all your guilty works of wickedness. May God hand you over [6](to) terror at the hand of all those who wreak vengeance. May He visit your followers with destruction at the hand of all those who enforce [7]reprisal. Cursed be you without compassion according to the darkness of your actions	[12]And the levites [shall curse all the people of the lot of [13]Belial and answer saying, "Cursed be you in all] your guilty [works of wicked]ness. [May God hand you over to terror at the hand of all 3[1]those who wreak vengeance? May He visit your followers with destruc]tion at the hand of all [those who enforce reprisal. Cur]sed be you without compassion according to the darkness of [2][your actions	[1]And the levites shall curse all the people of the lot of Bel[i]al and answer saying, "Cursed be [2][y]ou [in al]l your guilty [works of wickedness]. May God hand you over (to) terror at the hand of all those who wrea[k [3]vengeance. May He visit your followers with destruction at the hand of all those who enforce re]pri[sal. C]ursed be you [4][without compassion according to] the darkne[ss of your actions (EXTRA SPACE)
and damned be you [8]in the wretchedness of eternal fire. May God have no compassion for you when you cry out nor pardon you to atone for your	and damned be you in the wretchedness of] eternal [fire. May God have] no [compassion for you when] you [cr]y out nor pardon you to atone for your	ar]d damned be you] in the wretchedness of [5][eternal fire.] May [God have] no c[ompassion for you when you cry out nor pardon you to atone for] your
iniquities. [9]May He lift up His furious face to avenge you and may your wellbeing not be spoken of by all those who intercede (on your behalf)." [10]And all those entering the covenant shall say after those who bless and those who curse, "Amen, Amen." [11]*Vacat*. Then the priests and the levites shall proceed by saying, "Cursed because of	*iniquity*. [3][May He lift up His furious face to avenge you and may your well]bein[g not be spoken of by all those who intercede (on your be]half)."] And all those entering the covenant [4][shall say after those who bless and those who curse, "Amen, Amen." *Vacat*. Then the priests and the] le[vites shall proceed by sayi]ng, "Cursed[	*[ini]quity*. [6][May He lift up His furious face to avenge you and may your] wellbeing [not be spoken of by all those who intercede [7](on your behalf)." And all those entering the covenant shall say af]ter those who bless [and those who curse, [8]"Amen, Amen." *Vacat*. Then the priests and the levites shall proceed by saying, "Cur]sed because of[

1QS 2

the idols of his heart when he is about to join [12]is the one entering this covenant (who) places the stumbling block of his sinfulness before him so that he backslides because of it. And [13]when he hears the terms of this covenant he will bless himself in his heart saying, 'May I enjoy happiness [14]even though I walk with a hardened heart.' But his spirit shall be snatched away, the dry together with the moist, without [15]forgiveness. God's anger and the wrath of His judgments shall flare up against him for eternal destruction. All the [16]curses of this covenant shall cling to him. And God shall mark him out for a miserable existence, and he will be cut off from the company of all the children of light because he turned away [17]from following God because of his idols and the stumbling block of his sinfulness. He shall place his lot in the midst of those who are eternally cursed." [18]And all those entering the covenant shall answer and say after them, "Amen, Amen." *Vacat.*

3.2.3 Annual Procession and Confirmation of the Values of the Community (1QS 2:19–25a // No Preserved Parallels)

[19]*Vacat.* Thus they shall do year after year during all the days of the rule of Belial. The priests shall walk [20]at the head of the procession in order one after another (each) according to their spirits. And the levites shall go in after them. [21]And all the people shall follow in third place in order one after another according to their thousands and hundreds [22]and fifties and tens so that every Israelite may know his own position in the community of God [23]according to the eternal scheme. And no one shall be denegrated from the position of his standing nor raised up from the place of his lot. [24]For they shall all form part of a community of truth and meek humility, devoted love and righteous thoughts, [25]each one and his fellow forming part of a holy council and practising eternal friendship.

3.2.4 The One Who (Initially) Refuses to Enter the Covenant (1QS 2:25b– 3:12 // 4Q255 2:1–9 // 4Q257 3:1–14 // 4Q262 1:1–4)

1QS 2

[25b]Anyone who refuses to enter [26][the covenant of Go]d in order to walk with a hardened heart

1QS 2–3	4Q257 3
[26]shall not [gain admittance into] His true [co]mmunity because his soul [31] has detested the judicious lessons of righteous ordinances. He has not displayed the strength to turn around his life and shall not count himself as one of the upright. [2]His knowledge, his strength and his property shall not be received in the council of the community because he ploughs in the filth of wickedness, and p[ol]lution [3]attends his conversion. He shall not be justified while he seeks out the hardness of his heart and he looks upon	[1]shall not [gain admittance into His] tru[e communi]ty be[cau]se his soul has de[tes]ted [the judicious lessons of [2]righteous] ordinance[s. He has not] displayed the strength [to] turn around his life and [shall not] co[unt] himself as one of the up[right.] [3]His knowledge, [his] strength [and his wea]lth shall no[t] be recei[ved] in the council of the community be[cause] he ploughs [in] the filth of wicked[ness], [5]and po[llu]tion attends his con[ver]sion. He shall not be justified while he seeks [out] the hardness of [5]his heart and he [lo]oks

1QS 2–3	4Q257 3
darkness as the ways of light. He shall not count himself ⁴as belonging to the fount of the perfect. He shall not be purified	upon darkness as [the ways of] light. He shall not c[ount] himself as belonging to the fount of the perfect. ⁶He shall not be purified

1QS 3	4Q257 3	4Q262 1
⁴with atonement nor cleansed with the waters of purification, nor shall he (be able to) purify himself in seas ⁵and rivers nor be cleansed with any water for washing. Unclean, unclean shall he be all the days of his denial of the divine ⁶judgments so that he may not	with atone[ment no]r cleansed with the waters of purification, nor shall he (be able to) puri[fy] himself ⁷[in seas and ri]ver[s nor be cl]eansed [with an]y [water [for wash]ing. Unclean, uncl]ea[n shall he be all ⁸the days of his] deni[al of the] div[ine judg]ments	¹[with atoneme]nt nor be cleansed with [the waters of purification, nor ²shall he (be able to) puri]fy [himself] in seas and rivers [nor be cleansed ³[with any water for] washing. Uncle[an, unclean shall he be all ⁴the days of] his [deni]al of [the divine judgments so that he may not

1QS 3
⁶be admonished in the community of His council.

1QS 3	4Q257 3
⁶For it is with a spirit of true counsel concerning the ways of humanity that atonement will be made for all ⁷his trespasses so that he may behold the light of life.	⁹ [For it is with a spi]rit of true cou[nsel concerning [the ways of humanity that atonement will be made for all his trespasses ¹⁰so that he may beho]ld the li[ght of life.]

1QS 3	4Q255 2	4Q257 3
⁷ᵇAnd with *a holy spirit* joining him to His truth he shall be cleansed from all ⁸his trespasses. And with a spirit of uprightness and humility atonement shall be made for his sin. And because of his profound humility towards all the divine statutes his flesh ⁹will be cleansed through sprinkling *with*	¹And with *the spirit of His holiness* joining him to [His] truth he shall be clean[sed from all] ²his trespasses. And with a spirit of uprightness and humili[ty atone]ment shall be made for [his] si[n. and because of] his profound ³[humility] towards all the divine statutes [his] fle[sh will be cleansed through sprinkling *upon him*]	¹⁰ᵇ[and with a spirit of holiness joining him to His truth he shall be cleansed from all ¹¹his trespasses. And with a spirit of uprightness and humili]ty atoneme[nt shall be made for his sin. And because of his profound humility ¹²towards all the divine statutes] his [fle]sh [will be cleansed] through sprinkling [*with*

1QS 3	4Q255 2	4Q257 3
the waters of purification and through sanctification with the waters of cleansing.	[4]the waters of purification and through sanctification with the waters of cleansing.	the waters of purification and through sanctification with the waters of [13]cleansing.
And he shall direct his steps	*And [his] st[eps he shall direct]*	And he shall direct his steps
to walk perfectly [10]in all God's ways, as He has commanded at the times appointed	[5]to walk perfectly in all God's ways, a[s He has commanded] [6]at the times appointed	to walk perfect]ly in all [God's ways, as [14]He has commanded at the times appointed
for His disclosures, and not to depart to the right or to the left, nor	*for His disclosure,* and no[t] to depart to the right [7]or to the left, nor	for His disclosures, and not to depart to the r]ight or [to the left, nor

1QS 3	4Q255 2
[11]to disobey a single one of all His commandments. Then by means of agreeable atonement he shall be favoured *before God* and enjoy a covenant [12]with the eternal community. *Vacat.*	to disobey a single one [of all His commandments.] [8]Then by means of agreeable atonement he shall be favoured and enjoy [a covenant] [9]with the etern[al commu]nity. [...]

3.3 Textual Notes

1:16 The *bet* of הבאים "those entering" appears to have been redrawn in 1QS.

1:16 In 1QS יאבורו has been corrected to יעבורו "they shall gain admittance."[24] The error was likely caused by a weakening of the gutturals frequently reflected in Qumran Hebrew.[25]

1:16 The PAM image M43.250 shows what looks like remains of ink in superlinear position in 4Q256 2:1.[26] These traces are no longer present in the more recent full spectrum colour or infrared images of the fragment;[27] nor are they preserved on the original fragment which I examined. The possibility that a tiny piece of the fragment broke off cannot be excluded.

1:16 Further on in the same line the scribe of 1QS erased another letter at the beginning of לפני "in front of." Licht identifies the erased letter as *mem*.[28]

---

[24] See Licht, *Rule Scroll*, 66.

[25] Cf. Qimron, HDSS, 25 and PTSDSSP 1:8; Edward Y. Kutscher, *The Language and Linguistic Background of the Isaiah Scroll (1QIsaᵃ)*. STDJ 6 (Leiden: Brill, 1974), 57–60, 505–511.

[26] See LLDSSDL B- 284696 and Alexander and Vermes, DJD 26:48.

[27] Cf. LLDSSDL B-366910.

[28] Licht, *Rule Scroll*, 66.

1:18 The second letter of the first word has been corrected from *he* to *samek* and now reads נ{ה}סוים "their testing" though scholars disagree on the original reading. Our reading follows Licht.[29] Alexander and Vermes also argue in favour of a correction from *he* to *samek* resulting in the Mishnaic Hebrew noun "trials."[30] Rather than taking the term to be in apposition, I take it as part of a construct with the preceding term and translate "a crucible of their testing." Wernberg-Møller reads והיום "agony" based on Syriac *hymʾ*.[31]

1:19 ואתכול "and all" is written as one word in 1QS, a practice common with this scribe.[32]

1:20 Initial *he* of "those entering the covenant" (העוברים) has suffered from a vertical crease and possibly also the erasure of a paragraphos just below on which more will be said in what follows.

1:20 Remains of a small horizontal ink trace follow the double Amen preceding a *vacat* at the end of this line in 1QS, and faint traces of ink occur in a similar position in 2:18 discussed below.[33]

1:20 A very faint paragraphos sign in the margin just below this line in 1QS suggests a paragraphos has been erased. The same phenomenon occurs after 1QS 2:10 as well as at 1QS 10:6 where I identify an erased composite marginal sign.[34] It is significant that both erased paragraphoi were originally positioned after an existing structural marker in the form of double Amen followed by a *vacat* in 1QS. Only the third and final double Amen is followed by a faint paragraphos that has not been erased in 1QS 2:18. A second clear paragraphos marks the end of the covenant ceremony in 1QS 3:12.

1:21 The *vacat* in 1QS may have been present also in 4Q256 2:5 as indicated by a brief indentation at the start of this line in the edition of Alexander and Vermes.[35]

1:21 The reading גבורתום "His powerful acts" in 1QS may be explained as a simple error on the part of the scribe who added the final *mem* by mistake.[36] Alternatively we may have here a case of the radical *mem* having been added

---

[29] Licht, *Rule Scroll*, 66.

[30] Alexander and Vermes, DJD 26:49; see also Qimron, DSSHW 1:213; Brownlee, *Dead Sea Manual*, 9 and John Strugnell, "Notes on 1QS 1, 17–18; 8, 3–4 and 1QM 17, 8–9," *CBQ* 29 (1967): 580–582, 580.

[31] Wernberg-Møller, *Manual of Discipline*, 40, 49–50.

[32] Cf. Eugene Ulrich, "4QSamᶜ: A Fragmentary Manuscript of 2 Samuel 14–15 from the Scribe of the Serek hay-yahad (1QS)," *BASOR* 235 (1979): 1–25, 1 and Stegemann, "Some Remarks," 485.

[33] For comparable paratextual features to mark changes in speakers in papyrus book roles see William A. Johnson, *Readers and Reading Culture in the High Roman Empire: A Study of Elite Communities* (New York: Oxford University Press, 2010), 19–20.

[34] See 1.5.1.3 above and Chapter 15 below.

[35] See Alexander and Vermes, DJD 26:47–50.

[36] So Preben Wernberg-Møller, "Some Reflections on the Biblical Material in the Manual of Discipline," *ST* 9 (1955): 40–66, 45 and Alexander and Vermes, DJD 26:49.

to a word ending with an open syllable.[37] 4Q256 2:5 breaks off after *tav* with a *vav* reconstructed.[38]

1:24–26 The end of 1QS 1 is attested only in 1QS and has suffered some damage leaving us with a number of lacunae. This is the case for all eleven columns of this scroll, though no text is lost in 1QS 11. Enough text is preserved, however, for the general sense to be clear.[39]

2:1 The *gimel* of גמל "he has favoured" is faintly preserved in 1QS as a result of damage that affects the first part of the first three lines in this column, but the reading is clear on recent digital images.

2:4 An original ושא was corrected to וישא "May He lift," which included adding *vav* in the margin.[40] This error may have been influenced by a scribe familiar with the material that follows in 1QS 2:9 which starts with ישא פני.

2:4 4Q257 2:1 begins at the top of a column but lacks a *vacat*.[41]

2:4–7 5Q11 has been cautiously identified by Milik as another copy of the Rule. However, he stresses that the fragmentary maledictions pertain to a topic not exclusive to the Community Rules and notes that considerations of space suggest a different amount of text in the gaps between the preserved letters.[42] For pragmatic reasons I indicate the remains of 5Q11 1 i 2–6 <u>dotted underlined</u> in the translation of 1QS 2:4–7 above.

2:6 1QS's "May God hand you over (to) terror (יתנכה אל זעוה) is also preserved in 4Q257 2:2, again without the preposition *lamed*. The possibility that the preposition *lamed* dropped out as a result of haplography was raised already by Brownlee.[43] A textual corruption in the form of haplography of *lamed* – if that is indeed what occurred – would then have impacted directly or indirectly on both 4Q257 and 1QS. Some support for an original reading with the preposition may be drawn from 4Q280 2:2–3 (4QCurses) which reads "[may] God [give you up] to terror" ([יתנכה] אל לזעוה), a fragment that displays some terminological overlap with S.[44] The phrase is attested with *lamed* also in, e. g., Ezek 23:46 and Jer 15:4.[45] In addition, very little is left of *zayin* in 4Q257 2:2 which may have

---

[37] See Qimron, HDSS, 27.

[38] Cf. Alexander and Vermes, DJD 26:48–50.

[39] See further Brownlee, *Dead Sea Manual*, 9; Weise, *Kultzeiten*, 76–78 and S. E. Scheepstra, "True and Righteous are all the Works of God: A Proposal for the Reconstruction of 1QS I, 26," *RevQ* 16 (1995): 641–646.

[40] See Tov, *Scribal Practices*, 229.

[41] See Alexander and Vermes, DJD 26:71.

[42] Cf. DJD 3:180–181 and 1.5.12 above.

[43] Brownlee, *Dead Sea Manual*, 11. Brownlee gives credit to correspondence with Samuel Iwry. See also Wernberg- Møller, *Manual of Discipine*, 40 and Alexander and Vermes, DJD 26:71–72.

[44] See Nitzan in DJD 29:5–6 and the comments below.

[45] Cf. Weise, *Kultzeiten*, 94–95.

simply worn off. The alternative translation "may the God of terror give you over" has been proposed by Michael Wise.[46]

2:6 Our translation of אחריכה "your followers" presupposes a nominal form[47] where Alexander and Vermes opt for the preposition and translate the phrase with "visit you with destruction" in their reconstruction of 4Q257 2:3.[48] However, the references to Belial and his lot in a number of texts including in the previous line (1QS 2:5 // 4Q257 2:1) suggest that the reference here is to the associates of this leader of malevolent forces. Weise proposes taking the preposition אחר interchangeably with על (Lev 26:16) as evidence of Aramaic influence translating "Er möge über dich Vernichtung befehlen."[49]

2:7 Considerations of space suggest 4Q257 2:4 had a longer text.[50]

2:9 On the translation of כול אוחזי אבות "all who intercede (on your behalf)" see the Commentary below.

2:10 On the partially erased paragraphos sign in the margin below 1QS 2:10 see the note on 1QS 1:20 above.

2:11 לעבור "when he is about to join" is here taken as an infinitive construct with the preposition lamed in a temporal sense.[51] Others have emended the text to read לעבוד and translate "which he worships."[52] Both 4Q256 and 4Q257 break off just before this disputed verb.

2:13 *Vav* has been added above the line after *shin* in בשׁ\'מעו "when he hears" in 1QS.

2:13 The words את דברי "the terms of" and "this (covenant) he will bless himself" (הזות יתברך) are written continuously in 1QS.

2:13 and 14 These lines draw heavily on Deut 29:8–19.[53]

2:17 The opening two words "from following God" (מאחרי אל) are again written in scripta continua in 1QS.

2:18 A paragraphos follows this line.[54] Faint traces of ink remain after the double Amen just above the second *lamed* of Belial in 1QS 2:19 below. I suspect this represents traces of a horizontal line after the double Amen as is the case in 1QS 1:20.

---

[46] Wise, DSSANT, 128.

[47] See Alexander and Vermes, DJD 26:71– 72.

[48] Cf. also "hinter Dir her Vernichtung," HAWTTM1:69. For the rendering "your offspring" see Wise, DSSANT, 128.

[49] Weise, *Kultzeiten*, 95.

[50] See Alexander and Vermes, DJD 26:71 and Metso, *Textual Development*, 34.

[51] Cf. GKC 114.

[52] So Knibb, *Qumran Community*, 83, cf. 87; see also Wernberg-Møller, *Manual of Discipline*, 45–46.

[53] Further, Tzoref, "Use of Scripture," 220.

[54] See also the note on 1QS 1:20 above.

2:19 The verb יעבורו in the phrase "the priests shall pass" appears to have been squeezed in at the end of this line in 1QS.

2:20 On the Shrine's digital images the initial two letters of והלויים "and the levites" appear partially effaced, possibly a misplaced concern for dittography after זה "this."

2:21 Illegible traces of an erasure are visible just before יעברו "shall follow."[55]

2:23 איש מבית "each from the position of" is written as one word in 1QS.

2:23 I read ישפל with Qimron[56] rather than ישפול with Burrows.[57] There is a vertical crack running through the leather just before *lamed*, and the digital images confirm Qimron's reading. Kutscher reads ישפול and lists this case as an example where the Masoretic text reads imperfect with *a* where the Scroll reads *o*.[58]

2:25 Only traces of initial *aleph* and *yod* are preserved in 1QS of איש לרעהו "each one and his fellow."

2:25 Scant remains of the top left of an erased second *bet* are visible of בעצת "in the council of" in 1QS.[59]

2:25–26 For the combination of the verbs מאס "refuse" and געל "detest" see Lev 26:43.[60]

2:26 The bottom margin and this line are damaged. The opening restoration ל[בברית א] "[the covenant of Go]d" follows Brownlee.[61] The second lacuna is also restored with Brownlee and Alexander and Vermes to read "shall not [gain admittance into] His true [co]mmunity" חד אמתו בי[ויעבור].לוא[62] Licht and Qimron restore "shall not count himself" יתחשב.[63]

3:1 The form למשוב "to turn around" is an Aramaic infinitive.[64] Qimron has raised the possibility of a verbal noun.[65] It is again noteworthy that this form is shared by 1QS and 4Q257 3:2 which makes a "primitive corruption"[66] less likely.

3:2 Reading לוא יבואו "shall not be received" in 1QS with Abraham Meir Habermann.[67]

---

[55] Cf. Qimron, PTSDSSP 1:10.

[56] See PTSDSSP 1:12 n. 37 and DSSHW 1:214.

[57] Burrows, *Dead Sea Scrolls*, n.p.; also Licht, *Rule Scroll*, 24.

[58] Kutscher, *Language*, 341.

[59] See Wernberg-Møller, *Manual of Discipline*, 40.

[60] Cf. Wernberg-Møller, *Manual of Discipline*, 57 and Licht, *Rule Scroll*, 77.

[61] *Dead Sea Manual*, 11; see also Licht, *Rule Scroll*, 77; Qimron, DSSHW 1:214 and Wernberg-Møller, *Manual of Discipline*, 40.

[62] Alexander and Vermes, DJD 26:74.

[63] See Licht, *Rule Scroll*, 77; Qimron, DSSHW 1:214 and 1QS 3:1 // 4Q257 3:2.

[64] See Wernberg-Møller, *Manual of Discipline*, 58 who credits van der Ploeg.

[65] Qimron, HDSS, 65.

[66] So Alexander and Vermes, DJD 26:76.

[67] Habermann, *'Edah We-'Eduth: Three Scrolls from the Judaean Desert. The Legacy of a Community* (Jerusalem: Maḥbaroth Le-Sifruth, 1952), 63; see also Wernberg-Møller, *Manual of Discipline*, 40 and Alexander and Vermes, DJD 26:74, cf. 4Q257 3:3. Burrows, *Dead Sea*

3:2 The translation of סאון with "filth" in both 1QS and 4Q257 derives the term from Aramaic סין, סיין "filth, muck."[68] The same term occurs in 4Q525 21:6.[69]

3:2 *Aleph* has been added superlinearly in גוי״לים "pollution" in 1QS.[70]

3:3 I read במתור "while he seeks" in 1QS with Qimron.[71]

3:3 "And darkness" ends with *kaph* in medial form in 1QS while 4Q257 3:5 clearly preserves a final *kaph*.

3:3 Wernberg-Møller, following Barthélemy, emends בעין "belonging to the fount of" to עם "with."[72] The original reading of 1QS is now confirmed by 4Q257 3:5, however.

3:5 For מי רחץ "water for cleansing" in 1QS 3:5, 4Q262 reads [מי] רחיצה, attesting a verbal noun otherwise unattested in the Scrolls but well known in Mishnaic Hebrew.[73] 4Q257 is too fragmentary to permit certainty on the reading.

3:7 4Q255 2:1 reads the more commonly attested וברוח קודשו "and with His holy spirit" rather than 1QS's distinctive phrase וברוח קדושה "with a holy spirit."[74]

3:7–8 The first word in each of these lines in 1QS ("his trespasses") attests a contraction of the plural suffix from *yod vav* to *vav* (ō).[75]

3:8 In contrast to 1QS, 4Q255 2:2 attests the defective form of the noun ישר "uprightness." This is an example of the variety of orthographical practices attested by the Rule manuscripts.[76]

3:9 4Q255 2:4 lacks the preposition *bet* "with" preceding מי נדה "waters of purification." Our translation of 4Q255 follows the reconstruction of עליו "upon him" at the end of the previous line 4Q255 2:3 as proposed in Alexander and Vermes.[77] Qimron proposes restoring בכול "with any."[78] Note also final *nun* in initial position in 4Q255 2:4.

Scrolls, reads לוא יביאו "they shall not bring." On the passive translation of the active *qal* of בוא "to enter," see BDB 1j with reference to revenue being received, cf. Lev 25:22 and 1 Kgs 10:14.

[68] Cf. Hanoch Yalon, *The Dead Sea Scrolls: Linguistic Studies* (Jerusalem: Shrine of the Book, 1967), 106, 120 [Hebrew].

[69] See Puech, DJD 25:158–159 and Matthew Morgenstern, "A 'Reconstructionist' Approach to the Dead Sea Scrolls: E. Puech's Edition of Discoveries in the Judean Desert XXV," *JJS* 55 (2004): 347–353, 353.

[70] Cf. Neh 13:29.

[71] Cf. Qimron, DSSHW 1:215 and see 4Q257 3:4; further, Alexander and Vermes, DJD 26:74, 77.

[72] See Wernberg-Møller, *Manual of Discipline*, 24, 40 and Dominique Barthelemy O. P., "Notes en marge de publications récentes sure les manuscrits de Qumran," *RB* 59 (1952): 187–218, esp. 198–199.

[73] Further, Alexander and Vermes, DJD 26:192.

[74] Cf. Alexander and Vermes, DJD 26:34.

[75] See Eric D. Reymond, *Qumran Hebrew: An Overview of Orthography, Phonology, and Morphology*. RBS 76 (Atlanta, GA: SBL, 2014), 144–145.

[76] See Wernberg-Møller 26:8.

[77] DJD 26:33.

[78] Qimron, DSSHW 1:215 and PTSDSSP 1:59.

3:9 The letter preceding מי דוכי "waters of cleansing" in 4Q255 2:4 is uncertain. Our translation reads *bet* with Alexander and Vermes[79] though the large amount of space between this letter and the next is puzzling. The form דוכי "cleansing" is another Aramaism attested both in 1QS and 4Q255 2:4.[80]

3:9 The fragmentary final letter preserved in 4Q255 2:4 attests a different word order from 1QS 3: 9 for ויהכין פעמיו "he shall direct his steps."[81]

3:9 The *hiphil* imperfect with *he* prefix (להלכת) reflects Aramaic influence.[82] 4Q255 reads להלכ .

3:10 The third person plural suffix in the phrase "His appointed times" has contracted in 4Q255 2:6.[83] While 1QS reads the uncontracted suffix here the same phenomenon is attested in 1QS 3:7–8 and elsewhere.

3:11 The words לפני אל "before God" are lacking from 4Q255 2:8.[84] This is the most substantive variant in this section which has otherwise been transmitted with remarkable textual stability across the preserved manuscripts. The position of the composite preposition "before" appears somewhat irregular in 1QS by starting noticeably higher than the preceding text in this line. This suggests, at a minimum, a pause in the writing process or a secondary addition.

3:12 A faint paragraphos marks the end of the Covenant Ceremony in 1QS.[85]

3.4 Commentary

3.4.1 Introduction (1QS 1:16–18a // 4Q256 2:1–3a)

1:16 The topic of ceremonial admission into the covenant is introduced in 1QS 1:16–18a // 4Q256 2:1–3a.[86] While the subject of admission was already introduced in 1QS 1:7,[87] a shift in terminology is noticeable at 1QS 1:16 // 4Q256 2:1–2 where the phrase "to pass over into the covenant" appears for the first time. While 1QS starts at the beginning of a line, it is surprising that the scribe did not indicate a new beginning here by means of a *vacat*. None of the Cave 4 manuscripts preserve the very opening words of this section. The composite fragment 4Q256 2a does not permit any firm conclusions on what preceded in the manu-

---

[79] Wernberg-Møller DJD 26:33.

[80] See Rendsburg, "Qumran Hebrew," 242; Tigchelaar, "Scribe" and the Commentary below.

[81] Cf. LLDSSDL B-511795 and Alexander and Vermes, DJD 26:33.

[82] See Rendsburg, "Qumran Hebrew," 242; Alexander and Vermes, DJD 26:35 and Takamitsu Muraoka, "Community Rule (1QS)," *in Encyclopedia of Hebrew Language and Linguistics.* Edited by Geoffrey Khan (Leiden: Brill, 2013), 1:493–495

[83] See Reymond, *Qumran Hebrew*, 144–145.

[84] Cf. Alexander and Vermes, DJD 26:33–34 and Qimron, DSSHW 1:215.

[85] See further 1.5.1.3 above.

[86] Cf. Weise, *Kultzeiten*, 68.

[87] Compare also 1QS 1:11–12.

script. *Vacats* occur in the covenant liturgy that follows at junctures marking contributions by the ceremonial leads (priest and levites) and the congregation.[88]

1:16 The Hebrew phrase translated with "all those entering the organization of the community" could also be rendered "all the members of the organization of the community" and refer to existing members.

1:16 Both verbs בוא "to enter" and עבר "to cross over" are employed in this section with the latter predominating. The latter usage here and in 1QS 1:18 // 4Q256 2:3 mirrors the language of crossing the Jordan in the run up to the one-off covenant ceremony upon arriving in the promised land in Deut 27:12.[89] Elsewhere in the Community Rules בוא "to enter" is used to describe entry into the community alongside קרב "to draw near" and יסף *niphal* "to join."[90] Outside of the covenant ceremony עבר never occurs in the Community Rules with reference to entry into the community and is found instead in a negative sense to refer to transgressions.[91]

1:16 The noun סרך, here "organization" attested both in 1QS and 4Q256 occurs 61 times in the Qumran Dead Sea Scrolls. Only here does it refer to the membership of the community.[92]

1:16 Entering "before God" (לפני אל) contrasts interestingly with the language used in the brief account of admission into the community by oath in 1QS 5:8 (a plus in 1QS) where the oath is sworn "in the presence of all those with fervent commitment" (לעיני כול המתנדבים), i. e. the membership. On the phrase "before God" in the context of a covenant Licht points to 1 Sam 23:18.[93] The depiction of entry into the community before God sets apart the ritual ceremony led by priests before God from the mundane accounts of admission that follow.[94] This is comparable to the "cultic resolution" prescribed in Exod 22 for intractable property disputes by means of "an oath before the deity."[95]

1:17 For "according to all that He has commanded" and "not to turn their back on Him" compare Gen 7:5 and Num 14:43.[96] The former recurs in 1QS 5:8, a plus in 1QS.

---

[88] See the comments on 1QS 1:20–21 below and 1.5.1.3.3 above.

[89] Further, Steven Fraade, "Rhetoric and Hermeneutics in Miqṣat Maʿaśeh ha-Torah (4QMMT): The Case of the Blessings and Curses," *DSD* 10 (2003): 150–161, 155.

[90] Cf. 1QS 5:7 // 4Q256 9:6 // 4Q258 1:5; 1QS 5:8 (a plus in 1QS); 6:14 *niphal* and 6:15 (no preserved parallels).

[91] Compare 1QS 5:7 (a plus in 1QS); 1QS 5:14 (another plus in 1QS) and 8:22 (no preserved parallels).

[92] See Licht, *Rule Scroll*, 66; Hempel, "סֶרֶךְ *særæk*;" Leaney, *Rule of Qumran*, 124–125 and 2.2 and 2.3 above.

[93] Licht, *Rule Scroll*, 66. On the terminology in 1QS 5:8 see further 5.4 below.

[94] See 6.1 and 6.5 below.

[95] Cf. Bernard M. Levinson, *"The Right Chorale:" Studies in Biblical Law and Interpretation.* FAT 54 (Tübingen: Mohr Siebeck, 2008), 73.

[96] See Brownlee, *Dead Sea Manual*, 9.

1:17–18 The reference to terror that characterizes the rule of Belial ("terror, dread and the crucible of their testing") is reminiscent of CD 4:12b–19a where terror is part of a citation from Isa 24:17 (terror, pit and snare) that is subsequently interpreted as the three nets of Belial. All three passages share a penchant for triplets with the third element expanded here by way of a construct. In spite of the terminological differences the shared sentiment conveys a powerful sense of dread and danger.[97] Jeremy Penner has observed that threats from sudden attacks are particularly menacing at night time.[98] The figure of Belial is an important new element introduced here. The latter is one of the terms to refer to the leader of the forces of wickedness whose sphere of influence threatens those within and beyond the movement in the present time.[99] As Jutta Leonhardt-Balzer has observed it is possible that the term Belial refers here to the noun "worthlessness."[100]

3.4.2 The Covenant Admission Ceremony (1QS 1:18b–2:18 // 4Q256 2:1–6, 12–13; 3:1–4 // 4Q257 2:1–8 5Q11 1 i)

This account of a ceremony marking the admission of new members into the covenant follows the basic building blocks of Deut 28 and Lev 26 by being made up of blessings and curses[101] followed by a separate treatment of impostors whose commitment to the covenant is insincere.

1:18b–20 Priests and levites open proceedings with praise of God followed by the congregation's response of "Amen, Amen." While priests both individually and collectively continue to play an important role in the Community Rules, the levites "disappear" after the Covenant Ceremony.[102]

1:19 The levites are to bless "the God of salvation," literally "salvations." For the expression see Ps 68:20–21 (Hebrew) where it also occurs in the context of

---

[97] See also 4Q525 (Beatitudes) 2–3 ii 4–6 and Bilhah Nitzan, "Education and Wisdom in the Dead Sea Scrolls in Light of their Background in Antiquity," in *New Perspectives on Old Texts: Proceedings of the Tenth International Symposium of the Orion Center for the Study of the Dead Sea Scrolls and Associated Literature, 9–11 January 2005.* Edited by Esther G. Chazon, Betsy Halpern-Amaru and Ruth A. Clements. STDJ 88 (Leiden: Brill, 2010), 97–116, esp. 114. On the threat of sudden attacks for the wicked see Prov 3:24–25 which shares with this material a sense of apprehensiveness about the forces of malevolence. This theme recurs in 1QS 3:14–15 (see 4.4.1 below) and 1QS 10:15 // 4Q256 20:4 // 4Q258 10:3 // 4Q260 4:1 (see 15.2.3 below).

[98] Penner, *Patterns of Daily Prayer in Second Temple Period Judaism.* STDJ 104 (Leiden: Brill, 2012), 165–214.

[99] Cf. e. g. CD 4:12–13 and frequently in 1QM. See further Samuel Thomas, "בְּלִיַּעַל *beᶜlijjaᶜal,*" ThWQ 1:452–458 who rightly notes the preponderance of the phrase "the rule of Belial" (ממשלת בליעל) in the covenant ceremony, see 1QS 1:18 // 4Q256 2:3; 1QS 1: 23, 24 // 4Q256 2:7; 1QS 2:19.

[100] Leonhardt-Balzer, "Evil at Qumran," 25.

[101] See Nitzan, *Qumran Prayer*, 124–129.

[102] Cf. Martha Himmelfarb, *A Kingdom of Priests: Ancestry and Merit in Ancient Judaism* (Philadelphia, PA: University of Pennsylvania Press, 2006), 121.

a blessing. A comparable expression occurs in Isa 12:2 in a context of thanksgiving. Note, however, the interchangability of the verbs for blessing (*brk*) and thanksgiving (*ydh*) in Isa 12:1 and 38:19 where the LXX reflects blessing (ἐυλογέω) over against MT. This is reflected palpably in the superlinear scribal correction in 1QHᵃ 13:22.[103]

1:20–21 The remainder of 1QS 1:20 has been left blank and is followed by an erased paragraphos in the margin.[104] As indicated in the Textual Notes above this and other erased scribal marks can be identified at crucial moments in liturgical parts of the Community Rule as represented by 1QS.[105] The open section may be intended to highlight the start of the priest's enumeration of God's deeds. However, the presentation also draws out the double Amen and may have served to accommodate the congregational response here.[106] The double Amen is also slightly set apart from what precedes.

1:21–2:1a Analogously with biblical precedents, particularly Neh 9, the covenant ceremony comprises an enumeration of God's mighty deeds by the priests, an account of the trespasses of the children of Israel by the levites and a confession of sins.

1:24–25 Unlike biblical precedents the period of sinfulness is attributed to the activity of Belial. The order of the verbs in the congregation's confession of sins corresponds to the order of verbs used by the High Priest on the Day of Atonement.[107]

1:24b–2:1a continues with a confession of sins on the part of the congregation that closes with an acknowledgement of God's steadfast kind love that has no preserved parallels in 4QS. Similar communal confessions are attested in Dan 9, Ezra 9 and Neh 9, and it is likely that those responsible for our text drew on more widely used liturgical fare.[108]

2:1b–4a The authors of this part of the Community Rules have drawn on an elaborated version of the Priestly Blessing from Num 6:24–26.[109] The expansions

---

[103] See Newsom, Stegemann and Schuller, DJD 40:173–74; Aitken, *Semantics of Blessing*, 115 and Chapter 15 below on 1QS 11:15.

[104] See further 3.3 above.

[105] Cf. 1QS 2:10; 1QS 2:18; sections 3.3 and 1.5.1.3 above and Chapter 15 below. Further, Falk, "In the Margins," 24.

[106] See also 1QS 2:10–11 below.

[107] Cf. Weise, *Kultzeiten*, 111. The lack of a petition is striking, see Falk, *Daily, Sabbath and Festival Prayers*, 226.

[108] See Weise, *Kultzeiten*, 79. For further examples from the corpus of the Scrolls see 4Q393 (Communal Confession) in Falk, DJD 29:45–61 and 4Q504 2 v 1–vii 2 (Words of the Luminaries) in Baillet, DJD 7:145–151.

[109] Further, George J. Brooke, *Exegesis at Qumran: 4QFlorilegium in Its Jewish Context.* JSOTSup 29 (Sheffield: JSOT, 1985), 295–301; Falk, *Daily, Sabbath and Festival Prayers*, 224–225; Fraade, "The Case of the Blessings and Curses," 157; Nitzan, *Qumran Prayer*, 148–150, 357–358; James A. Loader, "The Model of the Priestly Blessing in 1QS," *JSJ* 14 (1983): 11–17 and Tzoref, "Use of Scripture," 218–219.

refer to being blessed "with all good things" and being "preserved from all things evil" alongside sapiential themes such as the granting of knowledge and insight.[110] The addition of the words "from all evil" (מכול רע) illustrates the apotropaic force of blessings that also emerges in the Final Hymn.[111] In addition to this dualistic framing and based on the addition of terms such as insight and knowledge Sarah Tanzer has identified the other major elaboration of the blessing as "sapientialisation." She goes on to suggest an independent origin of the blessing based on a lack of sapiential features in the corresponding curse.[112] The blessings are addressed to "the lot of God" (l. 2) whereas the curses are aimed at "the lot of Belial" (1QS 2:5–9 // 4Q256 2:12–3:3 // 4Q257 2:1–7a).[113] The division of humanity and their cosmic counterparts into opposing lots is developed more fully and distinctively in the Teaching on the Two Spirits.[114] In Deuteronomy, by contrast, both blessings and curses are addressed to the same constituency of people.[115]

2:4 Some have argued that the phrase "may He lift the face of His love upon you" presupposes knowledge of the Hebrew text of Esther.[116]

2:4–7 There is some overlap with the fragmentary remains of 5Q11 see 3.3 above.

2:4b–10 // 4Q256 2:12–3:4a // 4Q257 2:1–8a draw on Deut 27:14–26 in associating the role of the Levites with a series of ceremonial curses. This counterpart to the priestly blessing takes the form of a curse that is to a large extent modelled on the priestly blessing.[117] As shown by Miryam Brand, the curse does not reflect a cosmic but rather "a *socially* dualistic framework" that is concerned with those in thrall to Belial.[118]

2:5 The curses are addressed to the lot of Belial, an expression familiar from the War Scroll, cf. 1QM 1:5 // 4Q496 3:5.[119] It is noteworthy that references to Belial are confined to the Covenant Ceremony and the Final Hymn in the Community Rules. It is sometimes proposed that the designations "spirit of injustice" and "angel of darkness" are alternative names for the same role.[120] The

---

[110] See Tzoref, "Use of Scripture," 218–219 and Weise, *Kultzeiten*, 82–93.

[111] Cf. 15.1.2 below.

[112] Sarah Tanzer, "The Sages at Qumran: Wisdom in the 'Hodayot'" (PhD diss., Harvard, 1986), 174.

[113] See the Commentary on 1QS 2:5 below.

[114] Cf. Chapter 4 below.

[115] See Nitzan, *Qumran Prayer*, 125.

[116] Cf. Armin Lange, *Handbuch der Textfunde vom Toten Meer* (Tübingen: Mohr Siebeck, 2009), 499.

[117] Cf. Weise, *Kultzeiten*, 93–103 and Nitzan, *Qumran Prayer*, 151–154.

[118] Brand, *Evil Within and Without: The Source of Sin as Portrayed Within Second Temple Literature*. JAJ Sup 9 (Berlin: De Gruyter, 2013), 254–255.

[119] Further, Armin Lange, "גּוֹרָל gôrāl" and the Commentary on 1QS 1:10 above.

[120] Cf. Knibb, *Qumran Community*, 40 and comments on 1:17 above.

opposition between a lot of God and a lot of Belial emphasizes a sense of division among humanity whereas the language of "the rule of Belial" elsewhere in this ceremony highlights the temporal and temporary aspects of Belial's powers.[121]

2:5–6 Noteworthy is the close terminological relationship between this curse and the curse of Melkiresha in 4Q280 (Curse) 2:2–3. The latter fragmentary composition has been shown by Nitzan to attest an independent and to some degree less developed form of a covenantal curse.[122] It is also noteworthy that our text and 4Q280 2 attest corresponding phrases arranged in a significantly different sequence.[123] Whereas 4Q280 2 is addressed to Melkiresha, our text is introduced in lines 1QS 2:4–5 // 4QS as a curse of "the people of the lot of Belial". Even in the Community Rules the curse itself is, however, couched in the second person singular and may have originated in that form as suggested by 4Q280 2:2–3.[124]

2:6 For the phrase "to hand you over to terror" see Jer 15:4; 24:9; 29:18; 34:17; Ezek 23:46 and 2 Chron 29:8. The sense of trepidation expressed here is reminiscent of the ambience exuded by Belial according to 1QS 1:17 above. As I will argue further below, it is significant that the same root זוע occurs with reference to members whose spirit is wavering in the Penal Code as well as the foundations of the emerging community which do not shake.[125]

2:6 While God is the ultimate source of judgment a group of avengers are mentioned in 1QS 2:6 // [4Q256 3:1] // 4Q257 2:2–3. Weise reasonably suggests this group is identical with the "angels of destruction" known from 1QS 4:11–13.[126]

2:6–7 "Those who enforce reprisal" is another reference to angelic agents of the divine.

2:8–9 Further notable terminological connections can be observed here with 4Q280 2:3–4.[127]

2:9 The translation of בפי כול אוחזי אבות with "those who intercede (on your behalf)" follows the analysis of Wernberg-Møller who draws on Syriac evidence and wider Aramaic usage that left its mark on 1QS.[128] The group referred to are

---

[121] See also CD 4:12–13; 1QS 3:22–23; 4:18–19; 1QM 18 and Hanne von Weissenberg, "God(s), Angels, and Demons in the Dead Sea Scrolls," CDSS, 490–495.

[122] Nitzan, DJD 29:1–8.

[123] Nitzan, DJD 29:2.

[124] See also 4Q286 (4QBer^a) 7 ii 7–8 and Milik, "*Milkî-ṣedeq* et *Milkî-reša'*." For the need to avoid reading 4QBerakhot and 4Q280 in light of the more extensive Covenant Ceremony in the Community Rules see 3.1 above.

[125] See further 7.4.6.3 and Chapter 8 below.

[126] Weise, *Kultzeiten*, 97. For the phrase "those who wreak vengeance" see 4Q280 (Curses) 2:3; 1 Enoch 62:11 and T.Levi 3:2–3. See also Wernberg-Møller, *Manual of Discipline*, 52 and Nitzan, "Blessings and Curses," 97–98.

[127] Cf. Nitzan, DJD 29:5–7 and the comments on 2:5–6 above.

[128] Wernberg-Møller, *Manual of Discipline*, 53–54.

likely the angelic counterpart of the avengers mentioned in 1QS 2:5–7 // 4Q256 3:1 // 4Q257 2:2–3 above.[129]

2:10 I have identified a second erased *paragraphos* in the margin in 1QS which follows a double amen by those assembled. The next line is marked by a *vacat* and begins with a curse pronounced by priests and levites on insincere candidates.[130]

2:11–18 This passage deals with insincere converts. The presence of insincere converts forms a particularly vehement threat to the cohesiveness of any community. As Lewis Coser has argued, "The dissenter is, in a sense, even more dangerous to the sect than the renegade who has gone over to the enemy, for the dissenter claims belongingness."[131]

As in Deut 29:17–20 [Hebrew], a passage drawn on heavily here, insincere converts are singled out for a separate curse and harsh threats jointly pronounced by priests and levites. In addition to Deut 29 this material shares terminology that repeatedly occurs also in Ezek 14:1–11.[132] This ambiguous category of participants threatens the very foundations of the entire ceremony which is based on a clear division of those addressed into "the lot of God" who receive blessings (1QS 2:2) and "the lot of Belial" (1QS 2:4–5 // 4Q257 2:1). Finally, Nitzan rightly draws attention to structural similarities with the section of extended warnings that closes the Admonition of the Damascus Document with similarities extending to the distinctive treatment of "all those who refuse (כולמואס)" to enter the covenant.[133]

2:14 "The dry together with the moist" picks up the language of Deut 29:18 (English 29:19) in the context of insincere covenant members. The exact sense of the phrase is obscure but it likely refers to the comprehensive threat to the backslider's fate.[134] This conclusion is confirmed in a forthcoming study on the linguistic background of the same language in Pesher Habakkuk by Noam Mizrahi who also draws attention to the fact that the author of this part of 1QS understood the *nota accusativi* in Deut 29:18 as the preposition "with" (את) which is represented in 1QS with עם.[135]

---

[129] See Weise, *Kultzeiten*, 98–99.

[130] See further 1.5.1.3; 3.3 and the Commentary on 1QS 1:20 above.

[131] Coser, *Greedy Institutions: Patterns of Undivided Commitment* (New York, NY: The Free Press, 1974), 108.

[132] Cf. Knibb, *Qumran Community*, 87; Licht, *Rule Scroll*, 64; Newsom, *Self and Symbolic Space*, 120–122 and Tzoref, "Use of Scripture," 219–222.

[133] Cf. 1QS 2:25b–3:6a // 4Q257 3:1–8 // 4Q262 1:1–4 and CD 7:9–10 // 19:5–6 as well as Nitzan, *Prayer at Qumran*, 126.

[134] Cf. Knibb, *Qumran Community*, 86.

[135] Noam Mizrahi, "Saturation, that is, Drunkenness: The Interpretation of 1QpHab 11:8–16 and Its Linguistic Background," *Meghillot* 14 (2019): 105–117 [Hebrew]. I am grateful to the author for sharing a forthcoming English version of this paper prior to publication.

2:14–17 Whereas Deuteronomy is based on the paradigm of concerns about idolatry and worship of the gods of the nations on the part of individuals, families or tribes, the emphasis here is on the spiritual make-up of those joining the movement (see 2:14 "his spirit") as well as an undercurrent of a divided humanity (2:16 "the children of light"; 2:17 "his lot"). These themes are more prominently developed in the Teaching on the Two Spirits to be dealt with in Chapter 4 below.

2:16–17 Remains of a similarly worded curse are preserved in 4Q280 2:1, cf. the comment on lines 2:5–6 and 2:8–9 above. Both compositions draw on Deut 29:20.

2:18 A communal response follows by all those entering the covenant.

3.4.3 Annual Procession and Confirmation of the Values of the Community (1QS 2:19–25a // No Preserved Parallels)

This short section stands out in the midst of two blocks of material dealing with the admission of new members. It is marked off from what precedes by a *vacat* and a slightly faint paragraphos hook in the margin after a double amen and the remainder of 1QS 2:18 left blank. While the marginal paragraphos is faint it does not appear to have been erased as was the case in 1QS 1:20 and 1QS 2:10 above. It is not entirely clear whether this intervening section describes a separate annual ceremony or whether it still refers to the annual admission ceremony. The passage lays down the procedure for an annual procession to be adhered to by existing community members. In its present context the occasion is the covenant ceremony. Some scholars consider this passage as unrelated to the covenant renewal ceremony.[136] Bilhah Nitzan takes the phrase "year after year, all the days of the reign of Belial" as a "redactor's comment."[137] On our reading the reference to Belial's rule in 1QS 2:19 suggests that this annual ceremony encompasses the proceedings laid down in 1QS 1:16–3:12 and parallels.[138] An annual covenant ceremony is referred to in Jub 6:17 and 2 Chron 15. Moreover, the Damascus Document preserves an annual expulsion ceremony that comprises a priestly blessing followed by a reference to an annual ceremony in the third month that also includes curses.[139]

2:19: The transition כבה "thus" is unique in S and the Rule literature more broadly. A phrase that displays verbatim overlap with this line is found in 5Q13

---

[136] Cf. Murphy, *Wealth in the Dead Sea Scrolls*, 112–113 who describes these lines as containing "Rules of Communal Organization."

[137] Nitzan, *Qumran Prayer*, 124.

[138] Cf. also Fraade, *Legal Fictions*, 98–102.

[139] See further 3.1 above.

(Rule) 4:4 which reads "[t]hese they shall do every year" except it opens with "these" (אלה) rather than "thus" (ככה).[140] It is not entirely clear whether the opening instruction "Thus they shall do year after year during all the days of the rule of Belial" concludes the preceding ceremony or introduces what follows. This bridgeing statement introduces a procession as well as a confirmation of the values of the community. This latter material may have originated independently before its incorporation here.[141]

2:19 The notion of a confined period of time that is liminal and dangerous expressed here as "all the days of the rule of Belial" is also attested in the Damascus Document.[142]

2:19–23a The participants process in hierarchical order (priests, levites and all the people). This procession includes priests and levites as was the case in the covenant ceremony above. However, the third group is here referred to as "all the people" rather than "all those entering the covenant." This discrepancy offers further support for the suggestion that this material was integrated second-arlily into the Covenant Ceremony. A number of texts attest slight variations in the order of precedence to be adhered to at formal gatherings. Thus, the rules for formal meetings in 1QS 6:8–9 prescribe seating arrangements for priests, elders and the rest of the people.[143] Meetings of all the camps in the Damascus Document include a mustering of the members consisting of priests followed by levites, Israelites and proselytes in CD 14:3–6.[144]

2:20 The assignment of positions to the priests "(each) according to their spirits" is reminiscent of 1QS 9:14 which notes the Maskil's duty to weigh the sons of Zadok – literally "the sons of the Zadok." 4Q259 3:10 reads "the sons of righteousness." If the author-copyist of 1QS misread the remains of 4Q259 or its *Vorlage*, the idea of a spiritual ranking order for priests expressed here might have played a role in evoking such the (mis-)reading in 1QS 9:14.[145] Elsewhere, such as in the framework of the Teaching on the Two Spirits in 1QS 3:14 and 1QS 4:26, "spiritual profiling" is applied across all humanity.[146] A reference to the spiritual make-up of community members is attested especially in 1QS 5:21

---

[140] See Milik, DJD 3:183 and Plates 39–40. The editor draws on fragment 28 for the latter part of 5Q13 4:4; cf. also Schiffman, PTSDSSP 1:136–137.

[141] For further discussion and the observation that the verbs in the imperfect stress repeated action see Wernberg-Møller, *Manual of Discipline*, 56–57.

[142] See CD 6:10, 14; 12:23; 15:7 and Hempel, *Laws of the Damascus Document*, 79–81.

[143] See 6.5 below.

[144] The proselytes are lacking in one of two references in 4Q267 (4QD^b) 9 v 8–10, cf. Hempel, *Laws of the Damascus Document*, 134–135.

[145] See 1.5.6.2 above and Chapter 14 below.

[146] Cf. 4.4.1 and 4.4.4 below.

where it also occurs in the context of entry into covenant and in 1QS 5:24 //
4Q258 2:3 // [4Q261 1a–b: 4] as part of an annual ranking process.[147]

2:20–21 The noun סרך in the phrase "in order" refers to the hierarchical
positions of individuals within a larger cohort.[148] Another possible translation
would be to take the noun to refer to the "organization."[149]

2:21–22 The division into thousands, hundreds, fifties and tens is modelled
on Israel in the wilderness.[150]

2:22 On the phrase "community of God" see the comments on 1QS 1:12 above.

2:22–23: The term מעמד "position" is widely used in the War Scroll with 16
occurrences in 1QM. Peter von der Osten-Sacken suggests that this is a relic of
an earlier linguistic framework.[151] The term recurs in S in the context of strictly
assigned positions during the assembly of the many in 1QS 6:12 // [4Q258 3:3].[152]
The combination מעמד בית "position" occurs only here. The more common
terminology to refer to the hierarchical positions of community members in
S is תכון "rank."[153] Both מעמד and the parallel use of גורל "lot" in line 23 as
well as the references to "the eternal scheme" suggest a larger salvation historical scheme is in view here that reaches beyond the rather administrative
employment of תכון elsewhere.[154]

2:24–25a These lines are inspired by Micah 6:8, and this language runs
through different parts of the Community Rules.[155] Particularly noteworthy is the
shared terminology (ענוה "humility" and אמת "truth") that supplements Micah
6:8 both here and in 1QS 5:3–4. The virtue of truth is repeatedly associated with
the quotation from Micah 6:8 in the Community Rules outside of this passage.[156]
Humility is attested here and in 1QS 5:3 // 4Q257 9:3–4 // 4Q258 1:3 as well
as in a secondary addition in the margin of 4Q259 2:11. Finally, references to
"righteousness" (צדק; צדקה) supplement the language of Micah 6 several more

---

[147] See 6.1 below and 1QS 9:15 // [4Q259 3:12] as well as 1QS 9:18 // 4Q258 8:2 // 4Q259 3:16
in the Statutes for the Maskil dealt with in Chapter 14 below.

[148] Cf. Hempel, "סֶרֶךְ *særæk*."

[149] See 1QS 1:16 // 4Q256 2:1 and Wernberg-Møller, *Manual of Discipline*, 24, 56.

[150] See, e. g., Exod 18:21, 25 and CD 13:1–2; also, Alison Schofield, "Wilderness," in EDEJ,
1337–1338.

[151] Von der Osten-Sacken, *Gott und Belial: Traditionsgeschichtliche Untersuchungen zum
Dualismus in den Texten aus Qumran* (Göttingen: Vandenhoek & Ruprecht, 1969), 218.

[152] Cf. Jarod Jacobs, "עָמַד *ʿāmad*," ThWQ 3:146–150 and 6.5.4.2 below.

[153] See 1QS 6:4, 8, 9, 10, 22; 7:21; 8:19; 9:2 and parallels in 4QS.

[154] Cf. also CD 2:9; 4:5 as well as the discussion in Arjen Bakker, "תָּכַן *tākan*," ThWQ 3:1123–
1128 and Menahem Kister, "Physical and Metaphysical Measurements Ordained by God in the
Literature of the Second Temple Period," in *Reworking the Bible: Apocryphal and Related Texts
at Qumran*. Edited by Esther Chazon, Ruth Clements and Devorah Dimant. STDJ 58 (Leiden:
Brill, 2005), 153–176. On the terminology of lots see the comments on 1QS 1:10 above.

[155] See 1QS 4:5; 1QS 5:3–4 // 4Q257 9:3–4 // 4Q258 1:3 and 1QS 8:2 // 4Q259 2:10–11 as
well as Licht, *Rule Scroll*, 293; Tzoref, "Use of Scripture," 222–223, 229–230 and 4.1.2 below.

[156] Compare 1QS 5:3–4 (lacking in 4Q256 and 4Q258) and 1QS 8:2 // 4Q259 2:10–11.

times in the Community Rules.[157] The fact that one of these supplementary virtues – אמת "truth" – is lacking from the otherwise parallel text of 4Q256 and 4Q258 suggests this supplementation is the work of the compiler/redactor behind 1QS.[158] Truth and righteousness already occur alongside justice in Jer 4:2. We gain the impression that meditations on the divine will inspired by Micah 6:8 found expression in textually fluid ways across S. These meditations, though not necessarily originating with the final redactor of 1QS, were used by him across a wide spectrum of material. These ethical values are reflected already in 1QS 1:5 // 4Q255 1:4[159] and are elsewhere associated with a key moment in the formation of a community.[160]

2:25 The term "fellow" (רע) occurs frequently in accounts of the peer framework described in the Community Rules.[161]

2:25 For the terminology סוד עולמים "eternal friendship" see 1QHᵃ 11:22 and 4Q403 (ShirShabbᵈ) 1 i 34. Both of these examples operate within a framework of communion with heavenly counterparts such as the reference in 1QHᵃ 11:23 to joining "the children of heaven" and prevalently in the Songs of the Sabbath Sacrifice.

3.4.4 The One Who (Initially) Refuses to Enter the Covenant (1QS 2:25b– 3:12 // 4Q255 2:1–9 // 4Q257 3:1–14 // 4Q262 1:1–4)

The case of the one who refuses to enter the covenant is treated as part of the Covenant Ceremony. This material draws substantially on Lev 26, a chapter that contains a series of blessings and curses that mark the end of the Holiness Code. The element of reassurance and continued divine protection in spite of serious shortcomings rehearsed in Lev 26:15–43 is as unexpected in Lev 26:44–45 as it

---

[157] Cf. 1QS 4:4–5 // [4Q259]; 1QS 5:4 // 4Q256 9:3 // 4Q258 1:3 and 1QS 8:2 // 4Q259 2:10.

[158] See Hempel, "Treatise on the Two Spirits," 118. For an analysis of truth in the Community Rule see Ian W. Scott, "Sectarian Truth: The Meaning of אמת in the *Community Rule*," in *Celebrating the Dead Sea Scrolls: A Canadian Collection*. Edited by Peter W. Flint, Jean Duhaime and Kyung S. Baek. EJL 30 (Atlanta, GA: SBL, 2011), 303–343 and more recently Nati, "The *Community Rule*," 934–935.

[159] Cf. also Tzoref, "Use of Scripture," 222 as well as the thorough analysis of the semantic development of the term in the Second Temple period in Eibert Tigchelaar, "Changing Truths: אֱמֶת and קֶשֶׁט as Core Concepts in the Second Temple Period," in *Congress Volume Stellenbosch 2016*. Edited by Louis C. Jonker, Gideon R. Kotzé and Christl M. Maier. VTSup 177 (Leiden: Brill, 2017), 395–415.

[160] Cf. 1QS 5:5–6 // 4Q256 9:5–6// 4Q258 1:4–5 ("they shall form part of a community [יחד]") and 8.2.2 below; further, Hempel, *Qumran Rule Texts in Conext*, 84–93.

[161] Cf. Jutta Jokiranta and Cecilia Wassén, "A Brotherhood at Qumran? Metaphorical, Familial Language in the Dead Sea Scrolls," in *Northern Lights on the Dead Sea Scrolls: Proceedings of the Nordic Qumran Network 2003–2006*. Edited by Anders Klostergaard Petersen et al. STDJ 80 (Leiden: Brill, 2009), 173–203; Hempel, "Wisdom and Law," 16–17 and 6.5.4 below.

is in 1QS 3:6b–12 // 4Q255 2:1–9 // 4Q257 3:10–14. A good case can be made for the argument that the covenant ceremony is ultimately concerned with a crisis of commitment in an existing community.[162] Thus, the change in tone in favour of rehabilitation in 1QS 3:6b, though already present in Lev 26, appears to be directed at recalcitrant members whom the text is hoping to re-connect to the values of the movement.[163] Many of the issues and much of the language that colours this part of the covenant ceremony is developed more fully elsewhere in the Community Rules including the aspiration to perfection,[164] the role of ritual purity in the formation of boundaries[165] and the opposition of light and darkness.[166] The most likely explanation is that the redactor responsible for this part of the Community Rules drew on language and concerns developed in parts of the S tradition that predate the expansion of the long text.[167]

The Damascus Document also refers to the case of a serious betrayal of the community from within in the context of membership or entrance into the covenant (כל באי\ם ב\בריתו).[168] Moreover, the explusion ceremony at the end of the Damascus Document describes those who despise the covenantal legal obligations in similar terms and even incorporates the same phrase we find in 1QS 2:25 (וכול המואס "and anyone who refuses/despises").[169] Both in the present passage and in the Damascus Document the offender is ostracised.[170]

2:25b–26 The two key verbs "to refuse" (מאס) and "to detest" (געל) are based on Lev 26:15, 43. The sequence of curses followed by the case of someone who refuses to enter the covenant is also attested in 4Q280 (Curses).[171] However, the remains of "to enter" in 4Q280 2:7 are very fragmentary and the reading is not certain. The tops of the letters, especially *lamed*, are compatible with an infinitive "to loathe" (געל) which occurs alongside "to refuse" in Lev 26:15, 43.

3:2 A rejection of the property of those who are disobedient and impure is also emphasized in 1QS 5:20 // [4Q256 9:13] // [4Q258 1:11].[172]

---

[162] See Hempel, "Long Text."

[163] Cf. also Newsom, *Self and Symbolic Space*, 120–127.

[164] See Chapters 9 and 10.

[165] Cf. Chapters 6, 7 and 9.

[166] See Chapter 4.

[167] Further, 1.5.1.4 above.

[168] Cf. CD 8:1b–2a // CD 19:13b–14 // 4Q266 (4QD^a) 3 iii 23–25. See also CD 15:13 // 4Q266 8 i 3–4 // 4Q270 6 ii 6.

[169] See 4Q266 (4QD^a) 11:5b–14b and 4Q270 (4QD^e) 7 i 19c–21.

[170] Cf. 1QS 3:2–3 // 4Q257 3:3–5 and 4Q266 11:14–16. For further discussion see Falk, *Daily, Sabbath and Festival Prayers*, 226–235 and Hempel, *Laws of the Damascus Document*, 175–185.

[171] Cf. 4Q280 2:7 and Nitzan, DJD 29:5–7.

[172] See 6.1 below as well as 1.4.3 above.

3:3 The idea of perfection introduced here and in 1QS 3:3 and 4Q257 3:5 was referred to in the priestly blessing in 1QS 2:2.[173] The emphasis on perfection is particularly developed in 1QS 8–9.[174]

3:3–4 The opposition of light and darkness referred to here is reminiscent of the Teaching on the Two Spirits where the phrase "ways of light" recurs in 1QS 3:19–20. It is significant that the latter related passage shares an image comparable to the reading "a fount of the perfect" (עין תמימים) employed here.[175] In the Teaching "a fount of light" (מעין אור) is juxtaposed with "a well of darkness" (מקור חושך).

3:4b–6a These lines are also attested in 4Q257 3:6–8 // 4Q262 1:1–4 and deal with the ritual impurity of renegade community members which persists until they reform.[176] These lines share some overlap with 5Q13 (Rule) 4:2–3 where the process is, however, associated with a summoning in front of the overseer, a figure not mentioned in the covenant ceremony at all. A reference to "the covenant of God" occurs in 5Q13 28:3 although the identification of this fragment has been questioned by Milik.[177] Metso explains the literary relationship of 5Q13 to the Community Rules in terms of a citation or a shared source.[178] Based on the scant remains available the precise relationship and direction of influence between both compositions cannot be determined.

3:4 (and 9) The present passage shares an emphasis on purification with water and washing in the context of a covenantal discourse with 4Q284 (Purification Liturgy). Purification language is pervasive in 4Q284 and concentrated in 1QS 3:4–9 and parallels. More broadly, both the Covenant Ceremony and 4Q284 share covenant language (4Q284 4:2), blessings (4Q284 2 ii 5; 3:3; 7:1 and 1QS 1:18b–20 // 4Q256 2:3–4) and sporadic references to a division of humanity into lots (4Q284 4:3 and 1QS 2:2 and 1QS 2:5 // 4Q256 2:12–13 // 4Q257 2:1). The combination of blessings with purification rituals is prominent also in 4Q512 (papRitual of Purification B) and 4Q414 (Ritual of Purification A).[179] This issue

---

[173] Compare also 1QS 1:8 and 2.3 above.

[174] Cf. Chapters 9 and 10 below.

[175] See the Textual Note in 3.3 above.

[176] Further, John J. Collins, "Prayer and the Meaning of Ritual in the Dead Sea Scrolls," in *Prayer and Poetry in the Dead Sea Scrolls and Related Literature. Essays in Honor of Eileen Schuller on the Occasion of Her 65th Birthday.* Edited by Jeremy Penner, Ken M. Penner and Cecilia Wassén. STDJ 98 (Leiden: Brill, 2012), 69–85, 78–84; James R. Davila, *Liturgical Works.* Eerdmans Commentaries on the Dead Sea Scrolls (Grand Rapids, MI: Eerdmans, 2000), 267–295; Jokiranta, "Cognitive Theory of Blessing," 44–45; Jonathan Klawans, *Impurity and Sin in Ancient Judaism* (New York, NY: Oxford University Press, 2000), 79–80 and Cecilia Wassén, "Purity and Holiness," in CDSS, 513–523.

[177] See Milik, DJD 3:181 and 1.6.4 above.

[178] Cf. Metso, *Serekh Texts*, 25, 61; see also Schiffman, PTSDSSP 1:132–137 and Schofield, *From Qumran to the Yaḥad*, 176–177.

[179] For the use of the *hitpael* of קדש for purification here with parallels in 4Q257 3:6 // 4Q262 1:2 and 1QS 3:9 // 4Q255 2:4 // 4Q257 3:12 see 4Q512 (papRitual of Purification B) 33+35:5 and

recurs in a plus in 1QS 5:13 as well as in 4Q256 9:10, both times in the context of establishing boundaries vis-à-vis the people of injustice.[180]

3:5 The notion of not being able to achieve purification by washing also occurs in 4Q512 (papRitual of Purification B) 42–44:5.[181] The phrase "water for washing" is not attested in the Hebrew Bible.[182]

3:6–7 Alonside the thematic reversal between the description of the predicament of the one who refuses to enter the covenant and the reformed renegade noted above two unique phrases are noteworthy: "true counsel" (עצת אמת) and "light of life" (אור החיים) in 1QS and 4Q257 3:9–10 are not attested anywhere else in the Scrolls. For the latter phrase compare John 8:12 as noted by Brownlee.[183]

3:6–12 The second half of 1QS 3:6 // 4Q257 3:9 marks a turning point in the argument by introducing the option of forgiveness for the reformed renegade in 1QS 3:6b–12 // 4Q255 2:1–9 // 4Q257 3:9–14. The prominent use of the third masculine singular suffix suggests we are still dealing with the case of a renegade who is here given a second chance.[184] Whereas the hopeless fate of those who refuse to enter the covenant was at issue above, here the glorious fate of those who commit to life as part of the covenant is spelled out. A substantial number of issues and phrases recur here without the negative particle.[185]

3:8 Crucially, it is the reformed member's "profound humility towards all the divine statutes" in 1QS and parallels that evokes the efficacy of purification which lends further support to Himmelfarb's metaphorical reading of the purification language here.[186] The issue that divides insiders and outsiders is again one of legal observance.[187] The language of humility alludes to Mic 6:8, an important intertext in the Community Rules.[188]

3:9 Baumgarten suggests the sprinkling reference in 1QS 3:9 // [4Q255 2:3] // 4Q257 3:12 is to be taken at face value and refers further to 4Q512 1–6 where sprinkling and "holy ash" both feature.[189] He notes that sprinkling, as-

---

Baillet, DJD 7:264. The combination of sanctification and purification with water is found in Exod 19:10, 14, see Baumgarten, DJD 35:125.

[180] Cf. 6.1 below.

[181] See Baillet, DJD 7:275.

[182] Further, Martha Himmelfarb, "Impurity and Sin in 4QD, 1QS, and 4Q512," *DSD* 8 (2001): 9–37, 30.

[183] See Brownlee, *Dead Sea Manual*, 13. For the translation "God's true council" see Wernberg-Møller, *Manual of Discipline*, 24 and 61.

[184] Cf. Lev 26:44–45 and our introductory comments to 3.4 above.

[185] Contrast the inability to look upon light (1QS 3:3 // 4Q257 3:5) which is reversed in 1QS 3:7 // 4Q257 3:10. Similarly, the state of not being able to be cleansed (1QS 3:4–6a // 4Q257 3:6–8 // 4Q262 1:1–4) is reversed in 1QS 3:7–9 // 4Q255 2:1–3 // 4Q257 3:10–13.

[186] See also Wernberg-Møller, *Manual of Discipline*, 61.

[187] See further Chapters 5; 6.1 and 8 below.

[188] See, e. g., the Commentary on 1QS 2:24–25 above.

[189] On the breadth of impurities to be treated by sprinkling waters of purification see Baumgarten, DJD 35:83–85.

sociated with corpse impurity alone in Num 19, came to be used more widely for purification including for sexual impurity and genital discharges. The practice of sprinkling water mixed with the ashes of the red heifer (Num 19) presupposes the offering of a red heifer. In light of the revised chronology of the communal occupation of Qumran[190] this does not presuppose cultic worship at the site of Qumran.[191] It is hard to know whether the process of sprinkling is to be taken literally. Himmelfarb interprets this discourse of purification as rhetorical[192] and draws attention to the conclusion to the Teaching on the Two Spirits in 1QS 4:21 which refers to God's purification by sprinkling the spirit of truth in the course of eliminating injustice. In either case it is clear that purity is employed here and elsewhere in the Community Rules as a boundary marker.[193]

3:10 The reference to "the times appointed for His disclosures" (with the singular "disclosure" in 4Q255 2:6) alludes again to the idea of gradual revelation that was introduced in 1QS 1:9.[194]

3:10–11 The admonition "not to depart to the right or to the left, nor to disobey a single one of all His commandments" in 1QS and parallels is modelled on the closing lines of the covenant blessings in Deut 28:13–14. This admonition is placed immediately afer a reference to revelation both here and in 1QS 1:15 above, each time in connection with an emphasis on times.

3:11 The reference to agreeable atonement here is reminiscent of similar language elsewhere in S including in 1QS 2:8; 3:4, 6 and parallels above. Particularly striking is the reference to the community's eternal covenant and atonement in the context of the account of the emerging community in 1QS 5:6 in a significant plus in 1QS over against 4Q256 and 4Q258.[195] A further reference to atonement following an account of establishing the covenant is found in a superlinear addition 1QS 8:10.[196] This follows not long after an earlier reference to atonement for the land in the context of the emergence the council of the community in 1QS 8:6 // 4Q259 2:15.[197] The language draws on the promise of an

---

[190] See 1.2.2 above.

[191] The question of animal sacrifices at the site of Qumran has recently been revisited by Jodi Magness, "Were Sacrifices Offered at Qumran?" *JAJ* 7 (2016): 5–34.

[192] Himmelfarb, "Impurity and Sin," 29–34.

[193] See further on 3:8 and parallels above; also Himmelfarb, "Impurity and Sin," 33 who emphasizes the close link between purity language and exclusion from the community.

[194] Cf. 2.3 above. See also 1QS 9:13 // 4Q259 3:8 and 1QS 9:19 // 4Q258 8:4 // 4Q259 3:18 as well as 14.4.1 and 14.4.3 below.

[195] See 5.4 below.

[196] See Chapter 8 below.

[197] Cf. also 1QS 9:4 and Chapter 11 below. For a comparable context of atonement associated with the establishing of the council of the community see 4Q265 (Miscellaneous Rules) 7:9.

eternal priestly covenant to Phinehas in Num 25:13.[198] The words "before God" are lacking from 4Q255 2:8.[199]

3:12 The phrase "a covenant with the eternal community" is reminiscent of similar language that speaks of an eternal covenant in 1QS 4:22 (no preserved parallels), a plus in 1QS 5:5–6 as well as in a superlinear plus in 1QS 8:10 // [4Q258 6:3] over against 4Q259 2:18.

---

[198] See Wernberg-Møller, *Manual of Discipline*, 65 and Murphy, *Wealth in the Dead Sea Scrolls*, 150.

[199] Cf. Alexander and Vermes, DJD 26:33–34; Qimron, DSSHW 1:215 and Wernberg-Møller, *Manual of Discipline*, 65.

4. The Teaching on the Two Spirits (1QS 3:13–4:26 // 4Q257 5:1–8, 12–14 [including olim 4Q487 37:1–2 and 4Q502 16:1–4]; 4Q257 6:2–5)

4.1 Introduction

This part of the Rule was for a long time considered a definitive statement of the theology of the movement behind the Scrolls.[1] The full publication of the Scrolls has revealed that the ideas expressed in the Teaching are rather distinctive in the corpus as a whole.[2] In particular, the opposition of light and darkness – so prominent in this material – is uncommon outside of the War Scroll and the Community Rules, two long known manuscripts from Cave 1. An unusual reference to the phrase "lot of light" occurs in the Damascus Document in the context of registering new members of the congregation according to their "inheritance in the lot of light."[3] In both the mediaeval Cairo and the ancient Cave 4 manuscript the reading "light" is difficult but likely. Similarly distinctive is the occurrence of an address to the "children of light" in 4Q266 (4QD^a) 1 a–b. We also find a strongly dualistic passus especially in the Visions of Amram (4Q543–547).[4] A key passage in that document repeatedly draws on the opposition of light and darkness while also preserving references the "the children of blessing and j[oy]" as well as "the children of deception."[5]

---

[1] See Mathias Delcor, "V. Doctrines des Esséniens I. L'Instruction des Dieux Esprits," *DBSup* 9:960–970; Leaney, *Rule of Qumran*, 37, 143; Jacob Licht, "An Analysis of the Treatise on the Two Spirits in DSD," *Scripta Hierosolymitana* 4 (1965): 88–100; Paolo Sacchi, *Regola della Comunitá: Introduzione, traduzione e comment a cura di.* Studi Biblici 150 (Brescia: Paideia, 2006), 65–67. For a critique of this approach see Hempel, "Long Text," 3–8.

[2] Cf. Jörg Frey, "Different Patterns of Dualistic Thought in the Qumran Library," *Legal Texts and Legal Issues: Proceedings of the Second Meeting of the International Organization for Qumran Studies Published in Honour of Joseph M. Baumgarten.* Edited by Moshe Bernstein, Florentino García Martínez and John Kampen. STDJ 23 (Leiden: Brill, 1997), 275– 335 and already Hartmut Stegemann, "Zu Textbestand und Grundgedanken von 1QS III, 13–IV, 26," *RevQ* 13 (1988): 95–131, 127–128.

[3] See CD 13:12 // 4Q267 (4QD^b) 9 iv 9.

[4] See Michael E. Stone, "Amram," in EDSS 1:23–24.

[5] Cf. 4Q548 1 ii – 2; see Puech, DJD 31:283, 394–398 and, with reference to two spirits in the Aramaic Levi Document, see Greenfield, Stone and Eshel, *Aramaic Levi Document*, 33–34.

4.1.1 The Text of the Teaching on the Two Spirits

The text of the Teaching on the Two Spirits is most fully preserved in 1QS with fragmentary remains also in 4Q257. Beyond 1QS remains of material that is reminiscent though not identical to the Teaching has been identified in the two papyrus manuscripts 4Q255 and 4Q257.[6] Based on the clear differences between the fragmentary remains of 4Q255 A and the Teaching as represented by 1QS and partially in 4Q257 the sparse evidence of 4Q255 has played a major role in discussions on the text of the Teaching. Thus Metso notes "a real possibility that the fragment is related to" the Teaching before suggesting 4Q255 may be "more original" than the text of 1QS[7]. Similarly, Dimant suggests on the basis of the pervasive interpretation of 4Q255 A that "Dualism seems to have been part of the Qumran community's outlook from the initial phases of its existence."[8] In short, scholars have presented the very fragmentary evidence of 4Q255 A as a game-changer for our assessment of the Teaching. However, 4Q255 A shares as much with the Statutes of the Maskil and may not be related to the Teaching at all.[9]

Subsequent to the publication of 4Q257 by Alexander and Vermes in DJD 26 Eibert Tigchelaar convincingly re-assigned two fragments previously attributed to other compositions (4Q502 [4QpapRitual Marriage] 16 and 4Q487 [4QpapSap B?] 37) to 4Q257 5.[10] The translation of 4Q257 5:1–7 below is based on Tigchelaar's transcription in taking the newly identified additional fragments of 4Q257 into account. Pertinent readings are highlighted in the translation and identified in the Textual Notes. In addition, Tigchelaar has identified a further possible manuscript of the Teaching in 1Q29a (Two Spirits Treatise?) *olim* 1Q29 (Liturgy of Three Tongues of Fire) 13–17 which attests a shorter version of 1QS 4: 7–9.[11] While the evidence is fragmentary there is little doubt that the textual tradition of the Teaching, especially the material on the ways of the spirits of truth and injustice, is preserved for us in a state of fluidity.

---

[6] See especially 4Q255 A [Unidentified] and 4Q257 A [Unidentified] and Metso, *Textual Development,* 90–91, 137; Alexander and Vermes, DJD 26:36–37, 78, 82 as well as Hempel, "The Treatise on the Two Spirits and the Literary Development of the Rule of the Community," 107–108.

[7] Cf. Metso, *Textual Development,* 114 and 137.

[8] See Devorah Dimant, "The Composite Character of the Qumran Sectarian Literature as an Indication of Its Date and Provenance," *RevQ* 88 (2006): 615–30, 620 and Eibert J. C. Tigchelaar, *To Increase Learning for the Understanding Ones: Reading and Reconstructing the Fragmentary Early Jewish Sapiential Text 4QInstruction.* STDJ 44 (Leiden: Brill 2001), 194.

[9] Cf. 1.5.2.3 above.

[10] Tigchelaar, "Names of the Spirits."

[11] Cf. "Names of the Spirits," 543–545.

4.1.2 The Place of the Teaching in the S-Tradition

Scholars have long suspected that the Teaching belongs to the later strata in the textual development of the S tradition and originated independently before its integration into 1QS.[12] It has, in fact, been suggested that the scribe who prepared the 1QS parchment for copying had not made allowance for including the Teaching which necessitated the insertion of an additional sheet to accommodate the final column 1QS 11[13]. On the view put forward here the only other manuscript to preserve clear evidence of having included material from this part of 1QS is 4Q257.[14]

While it is remarkable that key ideas such as the prominent dichotomy of light and darkness developed in the Teaching are not referred to in 1QS 5–9 // 4QS, it is important to acknowledge a body of evidence that points to traces of continuity between the Teaching and the remainder of the Community Rules and suggests that the Teaching was not imported "wholesale" into the Community Rules. The following connections are noteworthy:

– Maskil headings are found in the S tradition beyond 1QS 3:13.[15]
– The juxtaposition of truth (אמת) and injustice (עולה and עול) which is prevalent alongside other oppositional terms in the Teaching[16] also plays a key role in 1QS 5–6 and some parallels where two accounts of community formation consist of a separation from the people of injustice alongside a commitment to truth on the part of the new movement.[17] Similarly, and again in the context of joining the movement, 1QS 6:14–15 (no preserved parallels) refers to being admitted "into the covenant to return to the truth and to turn away from all injustice."[18] In short, the opposition of truth and injustice is pervasive in accounts of defining moments in the movement's formation and in individuals' committing to join the group. While the language is attested in several

---

[12] See Jerome Murphy-O'Connor, "La genèse littéraire de la Règle de la Communauté," *RB* 76 (1969): 528–549; Frey, "Patterns of Dualistic Thought;" Hempel, "Long Text;" Armin Lange, *Weisheit und Prädestination: Weisheitliche Urordnung und Prädestination in den Textfunden von Qumran*. STDJ 18 (Leiden: Brill, 1995), 127–128; Porzig, "The Place of the 'Treatise of the Two Spirits' (1QS 3:13–4:26) within the Literary Development of the Community Rule," in *Law, Literature and Society in Legal Texts from Qumran*. Edited by Jutta Jokiranta and Molly Zahn. STDJ 128 (Leiden: Brill, 2019), 127–151 and Émile Puech, *La croyance des Esséniens en la vie future: Immortalité, résurrection, et vie éternelle*. 2 vols (Paris: Gabalda, 1993) 2:422.

[13] Cf. Stegemann, "Some Remarks," 482–483.

[14] See 4.1.1 above and 4.2.2–4.2.4 below.

[15] Cf. 1QS 9:12, 21 and 4Q258 1:1 // 4Q256 9:1 and, e. g., Metso, *Textual Development*, 139–140 and Hempel, "Treatise on the Two Spirits," 116.

[16] See 1QS 3: 18–19 *passim*.

[17] Cf. 1QS 5:2–3 // 4Q256 9:2–3 // 4Q258 1:2–3 where the admonition to act with truth is lacking from 4Q258 and not attested in 4Q256; 1QS 5:5 // 4Q256 9:5 // 4Q258 1:4; 1QS 5:6 // 4Q256 9:6 // 4Q258 1:5; 1QS 5:10.

[18] See Chapters 5; 6 and 8.4.4 below.

manuscripts, truth is twice a plus in 1QS and attested once in 4Q259 where 1QS reads a personal pronoun representing the divine name.[19]

– As noted by Tigchelaar, truth and injustice occur as polar qualities with reference to the covenant with Levi in Mal 2:6.[20] The intertext of Micah 6:8 ("to do justice, to love kindness and to walk humbly with your God" – highlighted with dotted underline in note 21 below) makes up a further connection between the Teaching and other parts of the Community Rules.[21]

– Further, the Teaching on the Two Spirits shares terminological links also with the Statutes for the Maskil.[22] Thus, markedly universal language known from 1QS 9:12–26 is also to the fore in the framework of the Teaching.[23] In particular, the opening line of the Teaching in 1QS 3:13 speaks of "all children of humanity" which is mirrored in the closing lines with "all the living" and "children of humanity" in 1QS 4:26. This framework corresponds to the references to "all the living" and "each person" in 1QS 9:12 // 4Q259 3:7–8 in the opening lines of the Statutes for the Maskil.

– Finally, both the Teaching and the Statutes for the Maskil share a concern with the spiritual dimensions of individuals. This theme is ubiquitous in the Teaching and also attested in 1QS 9:14–15 // 4Q259 3:11–12.[24] The predominance of connections between the framework of the Teaching, including the Maskil heading, and the Statutes for the Maskil suggest the commonalities I have identified are to be explained by their shared association with the Maskil in the final form of the Community Rules as attested in 1QS.

In short, numerous continuities between the Teaching and other parts of the Community Rules suggest we need to allow for a skilful final redaction of both the Teaching and 1QS more broadly.[25] Tigchelaar has drawn attention to a comparable phenomenon in 4QInstruction. He examines various directions of literary dependence or influence between Instruction and the Teaching or

---

[19] Cf. 8.4.4 below.

[20] Tigchelaar, *Increase Learning*, 197.

[21] Cf. 1QS 2:24–25; 1QS 4:5 // 4Q257 5:3 (humble conduct); 1QS 5:3–4 // 4Q256 9: 3–4 // 4Q258 1:3 (They shall act with truth together and humility, righteousness and justice, devoted love) and the members of the council of the community are to conduct themselves "with truth, righteousness, justice, devoted love and humble conduct each with their neighbour" according to 1QS 8:2 // 4Q259 2:10–11. See also the reference to Isa 23:6 ("solid intellect") in 1QS 4:5 // [4Q257 5:2] and 1QS 8:3 // 4Q259 2:11, see further Tzoref, "Use of Scripture" and Chapters 5 and 8 below.

[22] Cf. 1QS 9:12–26 // 4Q256 18:1–7 // 4Q258 8:1–9 // 4Q259 3:6b–4:8 // 4Q260 1:1–2. See also Jean Duhaime, "L'instruction sur les deux esprits et les interpolations dualistes a Qumrân," *RB* 84 (1977): 566–94 and Metso, *Textual Development*, 136–137.

[23] Further, Hempel, *Qumran Rule Texts in Context*, 248–250; Newsom, *Self as Symbolic Space*, 81, 88 and Chapter 14 below.

[24] Cf. further Chapter 14 below.

[25] See Hempel, "The Treatise on the Two Spirits."

even the Community Rules more broadly and explores a shared provenance as well as the possibility of a social connection.[26] In sum, the confluence of shared terminology in the framework of the Teaching and Instruction points to redactional activity across a series of at times distinctive compositions.

4.1.3 The Structure and Composition History of the Teaching

There is widespread recognition that the Teaching on the Two Spirits is a complex composition, and a number of hypotheses have been proposed.[27] There are those who argue the Teaching is a carefully crafted composition that was incorporated into 1QS in its present form.[28] Others have proposed a literary development over three main stages beginning with Peter von der Osten-Sacken who distinguishes an original core[29] from two expansions.[30] Jean Duhaime endorses the basic pattern proposed by von der Osten-Sacken. His major adjustment is to suggest two additions to Osten-Sacken's basic layer comprising the opening words in 1QS 3:13 "For the Maskil to instruct and to teach all the children of light" and a substantial portion of the Introduction in 1QS 3:18b–25.[31] Finally, Eibert Tigchelaar has suggested the Teaching comprises two major groups of material which he labels "Group 1"[32] and "Group 2."[33] He goes on to suggest three potential literary stages in the growth of the Teaching: 1QS 3:18–4:1 (Stage 1); 1QS 4:2–14 (Stage 2) and a final "framework" made up of 1QS 3:13–18 and 1QS 4:15–26 (Stage 3).[34]

In sum, a good measure of consensus is emerging in recent scholarship that the Teaching was not imported wholesale into some copies of the Community Rules. Instead it seems clear that the framework, the packaging if you will, is shaping the Teaching for the purposes of a smooth integration of this material

---

[26] Tigchelaar, *Increase Learning*, 203, 247.

[27] See, e. g., Licht, *Rule Scroll*, 87 and Metso, *Textual Development*, 137–140.

[28] Cf. Lange, *Weisheit und Prädestination*, 140; Licht, "Treatise on the Two Spirits;" and Stegemann, "Textbestand und Grundgedanken."

[29] 1QS 3:13–4:14.

[30] 1QS 4:15–23a // 4Q257 5:14 and 1QS 4:23b–26 // 4Q257 6:2–5. See von der Osten-Sacken, *Gott und Belial* and Delcor, "L'instruction," 963–964.

[31] Duhaime, "Les voies des deux esprits (1QS iv 2–14): Une analyse structurelle," *RevQ* 75 (2000): 349–67.

[32] 1QS 3:18–4:14.

[33] 1QS 3:13–17 plus 1QS 4:15–26.

[34] Tigchelaar, *Increase Learning*, 201–203, 247. Given 1QS 3:18 is assigned to both Stages 1 and 3 an implied division within this line may be assumed. Another detailed reconstruction of the literary growth of the treatise was recently proposed by Meike Christian, "The Literary Development of the 'Treatise of the Two Spirits' as Dependent on Instruction and the Hodayot," in *Law, Literature and Society in Legal Texts from Qumran: Papers from the Ninth Meeting of the International Organisation for Qumran Studies, Leuven 2016*. Edited by Jutta Jokiranta and Molly Zahn. STDJ 128 (Leiden: Brill, 2019), 153–184.

into the Community Rules. In addition, I was able to outline a cluster of red threads that tie the body of the Teaching closely to other parts of the Communiy Rule.[35] While some of the most distinctive elements of the Teaching, such as the cosmic dualism of light and darkness, are lacking from the communal legislation in 1QS 5–9 // 4QS, the material attested in the latter columns is inextricably connected with the ethical dimension of of truth and injustice that we find in the Teaching.

4.1.4 The Teaching and 4Q186 (Zodiacal Physiognomy)

Physiognomics is an ancient art that endeavours to draw conclusions about a person's character based on their physical appearance. A previously unknown and rather technical Hebrew physiognomic work (4Q186 [Zodiacal Physiognomy]) has emerged from Qumran Cave 4. This work offers a list of body parts (head, thighs, beard, teeth, etc.) which are correlated to character traits and the sign of the zodiac at the time of an individual's birth.[36] Scholars' attention was immediately drawn to suggestive formulaic statements in this text about an individual's spirit in relation to certain parts "in the house of darkness" and "the house of light." Given the prominence of the spiritual make-up of humanity developed in the Teaching on the Two Spirits, including the respective influence of spirits of light and darkness, 4Q186 was initially thought to complement the Teaching by offering physiognomic indicators on the ratio of the parts of light and darkness that characterise current or aspiring community members.[37] Since then Popović has shown that 4Q186 is unrelated to the Teaching and is concerned rather with the position of zodiacal spirits at the time of a person's birth. On this reading the terminology "house of light" and "house of darkness" refers to astronomical scenarios.[38]

4.1.5 The Search for Precursors of the Teaching's Dualistic Frame of Reference

Just as the Teaching incorporates a range of dualistic terminologies and ideas scholars have also proposed a series of precursors and influences behind the

---

[35] See 4.1.2 above.

[36] Cf. Mladen Popović, *Reading the Human Body: Physiognomics and Astrology in the Dead Sea Scrolls and Hellenistic-Early Roman Period Judaism.* STDJ 67 (Leiden: Brill, 2007).

[37] See, especially, Philip S. Alexander, "Physiognomy, Initiation, and Rank in the Qumran Community," in *Geschichte – Tradition – Reflexion: Festschrift für Martin Hengel Zum 70. Geburtstag.* Edited by Hubert Cancik, Hermann Lichtenberger and Peter Schäfer (Tübingen: Mohr Siebeck, 1996), 385–94.

[38] Further, Popović, *Reading the Human Body*, 206.

material.[39] As Prods Oktor Skjærvø has shown, direct literary dependence on Persian dualistic ideas is unlikely given Zoroastrian traditions were not committed to writing until the Sasanian period, and any influence that would have occurred in our period would have drawn on oral traditions or operated via the medium of a local, shared language.[40] Henryk Drawnel's recent assessment locates the origins of ancient Jewish dualism in the Aramaic Jewish tradition.[41] On the basis of an analysis of ancient Hellenistic perspectives on Zoroastrianism Jutta Leonhardt-Balzer has independently arrived at a comparable position that favours Jewish origins for the dualism in the Teaching.[42] These cautious assessments are welcome but do not exclude cross-fertilization, and some kind of confluence of influences seems likely even if it occurred on a non-literary basis. In this context the subtle analysis of cultural encounters between east and west proposed by Mladen Popović is suggestive.[43]

4.2 Translation[44]

4.2.1 Introduction (1QS 3:13–15a // No Preserved Parallels)

1QS 3

3[13]*Vacat* For the Maskil to instruct and to teach all the children of light concerning the birth times of the children of humanity [14]with regard to all the varieties of their spirits according to their signs, their actions during their lives and with regard to the punishments that strike them as well as [15]their times of serenity.

---

[39] See Metso *Textual Development*, 138 n. 99.

[40] Skjærvø, "Zoroastrian Dualism," in *Light Against Darkness: Dualism in Ancient Mediterranean Religion and the Contemporary World*. Edited by Armin Lange et al. JAJSup 2 (Göttingen: Vandenhoeck & Ruprecht, 2011), 55–91, esp. 55, 76–89 and n. 123; further Michael E. Stone, *Ancient Judaism: New Visions and Views* (Grand Rapids, MI: Eerdmans, 2011), 75–79 and Morton Smith, "The Common Theology of the Ancient Near East," *JBL* 71 (1952): 135–147.

[41] Drawnel, "Qumran and the Ancient Near East," in CDSS, 109–118, 116–117.

[42] Leonhardt-Balzer, "Scrolls and Non-Jewish Hellenistic Literature," in CDSS, 156–163, 159–160. See further John Collins, "The Construction of Israel in the Sectarian Rule Books," in *Judaism in Late Antiquity Part 5: The Judaism of Qumran. A Systemic Reading of the Dead Sea Scrolls*. Edited by Alan J. Avery-Peck, Jacob Neusner and Bruce D. Chilton. HdO 57 (Leiden: Brill, 2001) 1:25–42, 35–37 and Loren Stuckenbruck, "The Interiorization of Dualism within the Human Being in Second Temple Judaism: The Treatise of the Two Spirits in its Tradition-Historical Context," in *Light Against Darkness*. Edited by Lange et al., 145–168.

[43] Popović, "Networks of Scholars: The Transmission of Astronomical and Astrological Learning Between Babylonians, Greeks and Jews," in *Ancient Jewish Sciences and the History of Knowledge*. Edited by Jonathan Ben-Dov and Seth Sanders (New York, NY: New York University Press, 2014), 153–195. See also Tigchelaar, "Changing Truths," 395–415.

[44] The translation includes all the manuscript witnesses of the Teaching that have been identified as part of the Community Rules in 4.1.1 above. The evidence of 1Q29a is dealt with in the Textual Notes in 4.3 below.

4.2.2 The Glorious Plan of the God of Knowledge (1QS 3:15b–18a // No Preserved Parallels)

1QS 3

From the God of knowledge comes everything that is and will be. Before they came to be he determined all their thoughts. [16]When they come into being, at their ordained time, they complete their work exactly according to His glorious plan. In His hand [17]are the judgments of all. He supports them with regard to all their needs. He created humankind to rule [18]the world.

4.2.3 The Establishment of the Spirits of Truth and Injustice Ruled by the Prince of Lights and the Angel of Darkness (1QS 3:18b–4:1 // No Preserved Parallels)

1QS 3

And He set up two spirits for them so that they may walk in them until the appointed time of His visitation. They are the spirits of [19]truth and injustice. Within a fount of light (originate) the generations of truth and from a well of darkness (stem) the generations of injustice. [20]Power over all the children of righteousness rests with the prince of lights and they walk in the ways of light. Absolute power [21]over the children of injustice rests with the angel of darkness and they walk in the ways of darkness. And because of the angel of darkness all the children of [22]righteousness go astray, and all their sins, their trespasses, their guilt and the wrongdoings of their actions are under his rule [23]in accordance with the divine mysteries until the time determined by Him. And all their sufferings and the times of their distress are caused by the rule of his hostility, [24]and all the spirits of his lot obstruct the children of light. But the God of Israel and the angel of His truth come to the aid of all [25]the children of light. It is He who has created the spirits of light and darkness and He established all actions in accordance with them. [26][…] every task and in accordance with their ways […] the one God loves for all 4[1][app]ointed times of eternity and He delights in all its deeds for ever. As for the other, He loathes its advice and all its ways He detests forever. *Vacat.*

4.2.4 The Ways of the Spirit of Truth and the Blessed Rewards for Its Followers (1QS 4:2–8 // 4Q257 5:1–7 including olim 4Q487 37:1–2 and 4Q502 16:1–4)[45]

1QS 4

²*Vacat.* These are their ways in the world: to illuminate the heart of humankind, to straighten before them all the paths of true righteousness, to fill their hearts with respect for the commandments of ³God as well as a spirit of humility and p[at]ience and an abundance of kindness, eternal moral strength, insight, understanding, great wisdom trusting in all ⁴God's works and supported by His abundant love,

1QS 4	4Q257 5
and a spirit of knowledge of all conceived actions and enthusiasm for righteous ordinances, a holy ⁵determination with a solid intellect and an abundance of love towards all the children of truth as well as glorious purity that loathes all the idols of impurity and humble conduct ⁶with prudence in all things and discretion about the truth of the mysteries of knowledge. *Vacat.* These are the foundations of the spirit for the world's children of truth. And the reward of all those who walk in it will be healing, ⁷an abundance of happiness with a long life and many descendants together with everlasting blessings and eternal joy with everlasting life and perfect glory ⁸together with a dazzling garment in eternal light. *Vacat.*	¹[and a spirit of knowledge of all conceived] actions [and enthusiasm for righteous ordinances], a h[o]ly determination ²[with a solid intellect and an abundance of] love [towards all the children of truth] as well as glorious [puri]ty that loathes all the idols of ³[impurity and hum]ble conduct with prudence [in all things and discretion about the truth of the mysteries of] knowledge. *Vacat* These are the foundations of the spirit ⁴[for the worl]d['s children of truth. And the rew]ard of all [those who walk in it will be healing, an abundan]ce of happiness with a lo[ng li]fe and many des[cen]dants ⁵together with [everlasting blessings and eternal joy with] everlas[ting] [li]fe [and] perfect glory to[gether with a dazzling garment] in [eternal] ⁶light. […] *Vacat* […]

4.2.5 The Ways of the Spirit of Injustice and the Downfall of Its Followers (1QS 4:9–14 // 4Q257 5:7–8, 12–13)

1QS 4	4Q257 5
⁹*Vacat.* But the spirit of injustice possesses greed, sluggishness in the service of righteousness, wickedness, deception, arrogance and haughtiness, lying and treachery,	⁷[But the spirit of injustice possesses greed, sluggishness in the service of] righteousness [wickedness, deception, arrogance and haughti]ness, lying and treachery, cruel[ty ⁸and an

---

[45] Text that was initially identified as belonging to 4Q487 (4QpapSap B?) 37:1–2 is represented with dotted underline and 4Q502 (4QpapRitual Marriage) 16:1–4 with continuous underline. For further details see 4.1.1 above.

1QS 4	4Q257 5
cruelty [10]and an abundance of ruthlessness, a short temper, an abundance of folly and enthusiasm for insolence, abominable actions (performed) with a prurient spirit,	abundance of ruthlessness, a short temper, an abundance of folly and enthusi]asm for insolence, abo[minable] actions [(performed) with a prurient spirit]. *Vacat.*

1QS 4

impure ways in the service of uncleanness,[11]a tongue of blasphemous words, blind eyes, a deaf ear, a stiff neck, a hardened heart set on walking in all the ways of darkness and evil craftiness. And the punishment of [12]all those who walk in it will be an abundance of suffering at the hands of all the angels of destruction, eternal downfall caused by the avenging fierce anger of God, ceaseless terror and everlasting[13]shame together with the humiliation of destruction in the fire of darkness. And their generations will endure all their times

1QS 4	4Q257 5
in agonizing grief and bitter misery in the chasms of darkness until [14]they are destroyed without a remnant or survivors for them. *Vacat.*	[12][in] agonizing grief [13][and bitter misery in the chasms of darkness until they are destroyed without a remnant or surviv]ors for them. *Vacat.*

4.2.6 The Struggle of the Two Spirits in Human Hearts and the End of Injustice (1QS 4:15–26 // 257 5:14; 6:2–5)

1QS 4

[15]*Vacat.* All human generations are governed by these (two spirits).

1QS 4	4Q257 5
All their hosts in their generations inherit their (two) types	[14]All their hosts] in [their generations inherit their (two) types]

1QS 4

and walk in their ways. All their deeds [16]are governed by their (two) types according to the proportions of the inheritance of each person for all periods of eternity. For God has put them in place in equal measure until the last [17]time and He has placed eternal hostility between their types. The actions of injustice are abhorrent to truth, and all the ways of truth are abhorrent to injustice. A heated [18]conflict rages concerning all their judgments for they do not walk together. But God in His mysterious insight and in His glorious wisdom (pre)determined an end to the existence of injustice. At the appointed time of [19]judgment He will destroy it forever. Then truth will emerge in the world forever for it contaminated itself in the ways of wickedness during the rule of injustice until [20]the agreed appointed time of judgment. And then God will purify with His truth all human actions and He will refine for Himself the human structure to remove all (traces of) the spirit of injustice from the soft tissue of [21]its flesh and to cleanse it with a spirit of holiness from all wicked deeds. And He will sprinkle upon it a spirit of truth like purifying waters (distancing them) from all abominations of falsehood – though humanity had contaminated themselves [22]with a spirit of impurity – so that the upright may understand the knowledge of the Most High and the perfect of way may have insight into the wisdom of the children of heaven. For God has chosen them for an eternal covenant [23]and all the glory of Adam belongs to them. There shall be no more injustice and all

1QS 4	4Q257 6
deeds of deceit shall be put to shame. Until now the spirits of truth and injustice fight in the hearts of men, [24]and they walk either in wisdom or in folly. According to the inheritance of a person in truth he acts with righteousness and thus detests injustice and according to his allocation in the lot of injustice he acts wickedly because of it and thus [25]loathes truth. For God has put them in place in equal measure until the agreed end	[2]de[eds of deceit shall be put to shame. Until now the spirits of truth and injustice fight in the hearts of men, and they walk either in wisdom] [3]or in fo[lly. According to the inheritance of a person in truth he acts with righteousness and thus detests injustice and according to his allocation] [4]in [the lot of injustice he acts wickedly because of it and thus loathes truth. For God has put them in place in equal measure until [5]the agreed] en[d]

1QS 4

[25]and the renewal. And He knows the actions of their deeds for all periods of [26][eterni]ty and He has given them as an inheritance to the children of humanity so that they may know good [and evil and He deter]mines the fate for all the living according to the spirit of each person […] visitation.

4.3 Textual Notes

3:13 The beginning of this section is marked with the remainder of the previous line left blank followed by a sizeable indentation at the beginning of 1QS 3:13 accompanied by a faint paragraphos in the margin. 4Q255 2:9 shares the open section with 1QS.[46]

3:14 An initial *vav* at the very beginning of the line has been erased. In addition Qimron suspects that initial *lamed* has been corrected or retraced.[47]

---

[46] See Tov, *Scribal Practices*, 151.
[47] Qimron, PTSDSSP 1:14.

3:15 The words "Before they came to be he determined all their thoughts" in the second half of this line appear markedly different and suggest a different inkflow or even a later addition.[48]

3:15 An original *he* was corrected to *khet* in מחשבתם "their thoughts."[49]

3:16 The inclusion of "at their ordained time" is somewhat redundant.[50]

3:18 Unusually, a paragraphos occurs in the margin here without a corresponding *vacat* or open line. Lange supposes the lack of a corresponding *vacat* is an oversight.[51] Whatever the case may be, the paragraphos marks the point in the text where the two spirits are first introduced.[52]

3:19 The reading "fount of light" parallels "well of darkness" that follows. Given the frequent ambiguity regarding *yod* and *vav* in this manuscript an emendation from *vav* to *yod* (מעין) as proposed by Wernberg-Møller does not seem necessary.[53]

3:22 The last two letters of ממשלתו "his rule" are written vertically in the margin.

3:26 The last line of the column is damaged with a lacuna at the beginning and in the middle of the line which I have left untranslated.[54]

4:1 The top right corner of this column is damaged in 1QS. Our translation "[app]ointed times" follows Qimron's reconstruction מ]עדי.[55] The reading "eternity" עדי proposed by Burrows results in a margin that is about one letter's width wider than the rest of the column.[56]

4:1 Stegemann suggests reading מודה "very"[57] rather than סודה "its advice."[58]

4:1 Materially, the final phrase in this line translated "and all its ways He detests for ever" is noteworthy in 1QS. In particular, the final two words in this line are written very close together and slightly higher and further apart from what precedes as if they were added at a later time. In addition a dot occurs above the verb "he detests." There is no discernible damage on the surface of the leather nor does a hiatus make sense at this point in terms of content which is continuous up to the end of the line. In addition, "all" appears retraced. The

---

[48] See the Commentary on this line in 4.4.2 below.

[49] So Wernberg-Møller, "Reflections," 45 n. 2.

[50] Cf. also Wernberg-Møller, *Manual of Discipline*, 69 n. 50.

[51] *Weisheit und Prädestination*, 166.

[52] See further 4.4.1 below as well as 1.5.1.3 above.

[53] Wernberg-Møller, *Manual of Discipline*, 40, see also 70.

[54] For a detailed discussion see Stegemann, "Textbestand und Grundgedanken," 101–103 and Puech, *Croyance des Esséniens*, 2:427.

[55] Qimron, DSSHW 1: 216.

[56] Burrows, *Dead Sea Scrolls*, n.p. followed by, e. g., Licht, *Rule Scroll*, 93 and Eduard Lohse, *Die Texte aus Qumran: Hebräisch und Deutsch* (Darmstadt: Wissenschaftliche Buchgesellschaft, 1971), 12.

[57] See also 1QS 10:16 and Qimron, HDSS, 25.

[58] Stegemann, "Textbestand und Grundgedanken," 104; see also Puech, *La Croyance des Esséniens*, 2:427.

remainder of 1QS 4:1 is left blank, and a new section begins in 4:2 as also indicated by a marginal paragraphos and an indented start to 1QS 4:2.[59]

4:3 The second *vav* in ואורך "length" is superlinear.

4:3 There is no inter-word space in "abundant kindness."

4:4 *Khet* in מחשבת is corrected from *ayin*.[60]

4:4–6 In light of the reclassification of 4Q502 (Ritual of Marriage) 16 by Tigchelaar text <u>underlined</u> in the translation of 4Q257 5:1–4 above was previously identified as part of 4Q502.[61]

4:5 The feminine singular participle *piel* מתעבת preserved in 4Q257 5:2 is grammatically preferable to 1QS 4:5 (מתעב).[62]

4:5 "Purity" (טהרה) occurs frequently in the Community Rules tradition and is almost inevitably spelled defectively as noted already by Kutscher.[63] Since Kutscher's work appeared a plethora of further attestations of the term have materialised, the great majority spelled defectively with the exception of 4Q266 (Dᵃ) 6 ii 11 and 4Q525 (Beatitudes) 5 5.

4:6 The *khet* in וחבא is the result of a correction.[64] Coupled with the frequent effects of weakened gutturals in 1QS the remains visible to the left of the left leg of *khet* in the digital images made available by the Shrine of the Book suggest the original reading was *aleph*.

4:6 The clear *vacat* in 1QS corresponds to a small *vacat* in 4Q257 5:3 where the space between words is wider at this point.[65] This is indicated in the layout of the Hebrew text by Alexander and Vermes.[66]

4:7 The combination כול ברכות עד "all everlasting blessings" occurs also in 1Q29a (Two Spirits Treastise? *olim* 1Q29 13:2–3).[67]

4:7 The collective term "des[cen]dants" noticeably protrudes into the margin in 4Q257 5:4.[68]

4:7–8 A number of additional readings highlighted with <u>dotted underline</u> in the translation of 4Q257 5:5–6 stem from a fragment previously allocated to 4Q487 (Sapiential Work B?) 37.[69]

4:8 Following עולמים "eternal" the rest of the line is left blank in 1QS and 4Q257 5:6. A new beginning is also marked with a paragraphos in the margin

---

[59] See Licht, *Rule Scroll*, 93 and 1.5.1.3 above.

[60] Cf. Qimron, PTSDSSP 1:16 n. 72.

[61] Tigchelaar, "Names of the Spirits," 538–542 and 4.1.1 above.

[62] See Alexander and Vermes, DJD 26:79; Metso, *Textual Development*, 35 and Lohse, *Texte aus Qumran*, 12 n. i.

[63] Kutscher, *Language*, 147.

[64] See Licht, *Rule Scroll*, 96 and Qimron, DSSHW, 216.

[65] Cf. LLDSSDL B-485449, photographed by Shai Halevi.

[66] DJD 26:77.

[67] See Tigchelaar "Names of the Spirits" 543–545. For more terminological correspondence with 1Q29a see line 9 below.

[68] This is clearer in LLDSSDL B-485450 than in Alexander and Vermes, DJD 26 Plate 9.

[69] For details see Tigchelaar, "Names of the Spirits," 538–542 and 4.1.1 above.

of 1QS as well as an indented line 9. This receives support from the remains of a paragraphos in 4Q487 (*olim* papSap B?) 37:2 subsequently identified as belonging to 4Q257 5.[70]

4:9 The remains of 4Q257 5:7 begin with the word "righteousness" in what looks initially like the line above. The suggestion that this is a case of a generously sized superlinear addition has been followed in the translation above.[71]

4:9 The sequence of the words רשע ושקר גוה "wickedness, deception, arrogance" is attested verbatim in 1Q29a.[72]

4:10 The noun "ruthlessness" attests medial *pe* in final position.[73]

4:11 Another medial *pe* in final position is found in the noun "neck."[74]

4:11 It is curious to see the construct of the *qutl* form כובוד "hardness, heaviness" written with and without a *vav* in the first syllable in such close proximity in this line.[75]

4:12 נקמה as been corrected by erasing penultimate *yod* and likely also reshaping an original final *tav* into *he*.[76]

4:13 The translation "chasms" presupposes the root *hwh*.[77]

4:14 A paragraphos marks the transition to the final part of the Teaching on the Two Spirits that begins at 1QS 4:15.[78] Moreover, a *vacat* appears at the end of 1QS 4:14 and 4Q257 5:13. The beginning of 4Q257 5:14 where a paragraphos might have been expected[79] has not survived.

4:15 Wernberg-Møller astutely observes that the opening words באלה תולדות "In these the generations of" are written continuously and appear to go back to a different hand in 1QS.[80] Without this addition an indented start to the new section marked at the end of 1QS 4:14 with a *vacat* as well as a marginal paragraphos may be excpected. However, without the added words the empty space at the beginning of 1QS 4:15 would be rather excessive. I suspect the scribe of 1QS was initially unsure of the reading in the *Vorlage* which subsequently led to a supplementation.

---

[70] Cf. Tigchelaar, "Names of the Spirits" and Baillet, DJD 7:5–10 and Plate 4.

[71] See Alexander and Vermes, DJD 26:78; Puech, "Review of *Textual Development*, 449 and Qimron, DSSHW 1:217.

[72] Cf. Tigchelaar, "Names of the Spirits" and Baillet, DJD 7:5–10 and Plate 4.

[73] See Qimron, DSSHW 1:216.

[74] Cf. Qimron DSSHW 1:216.

[75] See Qimron, HDSS, 37–38.

[76] See, e. g., Qimron, PTSDSSP 1:16 n. 82.

[77] See BDB, 217 and Wernberg-Møller, *Manual of Discipline*, 82. As Wernberg-Møller notes, the term refers to the place of judgement.

[78] Cf. also 1.5.1.3 above.

[79] Compare the transition between parts of the Treatise that is marked by sizeable *vacats* in 4Q257 5:6 // 1QS 4:8 above.

[80] See Wernberg-Møller, *Manual of Discipline*, 82; further Alexander and Vermes, DJD 26:79.

4:16 Following Moshe Bar-Asher Qimron explains the *vav* in מועט "small" as the result of an assimilated *shewa* to the labial *mem*.[81]

4:17 The suffix in מפלגותם "their types" has been added above the line.

4:20 Our translation of מבני איש with "human structure" understands מבני as a noun in the singular in the construct with *yod* representing final *he*.[82] The phrase has also been translated as a reference to the children of humanity prefixed by partitive *mem*.[83] In either case the wording is reminiscent of Mal 3:3.[84]

4:24 The translation above follows the reading of the imperfect יצדק "he acts with righteousness" first proposed by Licht[85] over the reading of the noun וצדק originally read by Burrows.[86] Licht's reading results in a parallelism with what is said immediately afterwards about the followers of injustice who act wickedly.

4:24 The final *aleph* of "he detests" ישנא is the result of a scribal correction, perhaps from an original *he* as proposed by Qimron.[87]

4:26 The last line of 1QS 4 is damaged and has three lacunae I reconstruct the transition from line 25–26 to read "all periods of [eterni]ty" (עולמים), a phrase that occurred in 1QS 4:16 above, as first proposed here by André Dupont-Sommer.[88] Traces of final *mem* can be identified.

4.4 Commentary

4.4.1 Introduction (1QS 3:13–15a // No Preserved Parallels)

The introduction to the Teaching begins by laying out the Maskil's remit of instruction (1QS 3:13–15a).[89] This introduction shares a great deal with what

---

[81] Qimron, HDSS, 36.

[82] See Qimron, HDSS, 20.

[83] Compare Brownlee, *Dead Sea Manual*, 16 and Wernberg-Møller, *Manual of Discipline*, 27.

[84] Cf. Brownlee, *Dead Sea Manual*, 17.

[85] Licht, *Rule Scroll*, 104.

[86] Burrows, *Dead Sea Scrolls*. See also Stegemann, "Textbestand und Grundgedanken," 105 and Puech, *La Croyance des Esséniens*, 2:430.

[87] Qimron, DSSHW 1:216.

[88] Dupont-Sommer, "L'instruction sur les deux Esprits dans le 'Manuel de Discipline,'" *RHR* 142 (1952): 5–35, 34–35, see further Stegemann, "Textbestand und Grundgedanken," 105–110; Puech, *La Croyance des Esséniens*, 2:430 and Tigchelaar, *Increase Learning*, 196.

[89] The literature on this figure is voluminous. In addition to the bibliography in Hempel, *Qumran Rule Texts in Context*, 239–251 see more recently Joseph L. Angel, "Maskil, Community, and Religious Experience in the Songs of the Sage (4Q510– 511)," *DSD* 19 (2011): 1–27; Torleif Elgvin, "מַשְׂכִּל," ThWQ 2:802–806; Hempel, "Wisdom and Law," 165–166; Judith H. Newman, "Speech and Spirit: Paul and the Maskil as Inspired Interpreters of Scripture,"in *The Holy Spirit, Inspiration, and the Cultures of Antiquity: Multidisciplinary Perspectives*. Edited by Jörg Frey and John R. Levison. Ekstasis 5 (Berlin: De Gruyter, 2014), 243–66 and Stone, *Secret Groups*, 71–73.

we learn about the Maskil's duties in the Statutes of the Maskil.[90] Particularly noteworthy is the universal concern with "the children of humanity" even though "the children of light" are the narrower group to be instructed about humanity of which the former are nevertheless a part. It is important to note the reference to the complex spiritual make-up of humanity and its influence on their actions that is emphasized here. However, in these early lines the spiritual sphere is internal with the notion of two opposing spirits exerting their power only being introduced in 1QS 3:18–19.[91]

3:13 There is some ambiguity in translating the opening words "For the Maskil." The preposition can mean attributing the material that follows to the Maskil or refer to his role as the one to recite the material. The extensive Statutes for the Maskil in 1QS 9:12–25 and parallels suggest that the participle refers to a particular office. In the Community Rules the term Maskil occurs predominantly in headings.[92] In addition to the current reference the term occurs in the title of 4Q258 (4QS^d) 1:1 and the section heading in 4Q256 (4QS^b) 9:1 both of which read "Midrash for the Maskil" which in 4Q258 continues with "over the people of the law."[93] Finally, 1QS 9 includes two further headings that refer to the Maskil in 1QS 9:12 // 4Q259 3:6–7 and 1QS 9:21 // 4Q256 18:4–5 // 4Q258 8:5–6 // 4Q259 4:2–3, and the same figure is also the speaker of the Final Hymn that follows in a number of S manuscripts.[94] In short, the Maskil emerges as a significant figure in the Community Rules, not least in its various carefully crafted forms.[95] Some, including Wernberg-Møller, propose the term maskil was a title for each full community member and translate the term along the lines of "wise man."[96] The participle "wise one" is used in the sapiential text 4QInstruction more generically, and the role of a particular individual is in view again in the title of

---

[90] See 4.1.2 above and Chapter 14 below.

[91] Cf. also Preben Wernberg-Møller, "A Reconsideration of the Two Spirits in the Rule of the Community," *RevQ* 3 (1961): 413–441, 419.

[92] On the proposal to reconstruct למשכיל in 1QS 1:1 as part of the title of 1QS see 2.2 above.

[93] For a discussion of this heading which varies significantly from 1QS 5:1 see section 5.4.1 below.

[94] See Chapters 14 and 15 below.

[95] See Hempel, "Wisdom and Law," 11–12 and Newsom, *Self as Symbolic Space*. Émile Puech, *La croyance des Esséniens*, 2:430–431 considers the Teacher of Righteousness as the author of the Treatise and other material associated with Maskil headings in the Community Rules and the Hodayot. This is implied also in Milik, *Ten Years of Discovery*, 37. For further discussion of the view that the Maskil should be identified with a historical figure see von der Osten-Sacken, *Gott und Belial*, 163–164.

[96] Wernberg-Møller, *Manual of Discipline*, 25, 66; see also Reinhard G. Kratz, "Laws of Wisdom: Sapiential Traits in the Rule of the Community (1QS 5–7)," in *Hebrew in the Second Temple Period: The Hebrew of the Dead Sea Scrolls and of Other Contemporary Sources*. Edited by Steven E. Fassberg, Moshe Bar-Asher and Ruth A. Clements. STDJ 108 (Leiden: Brill, 2013), 133–145, 143. For the proposal to translate למשכיל with "for insight," see Robert Hawley, "On Maśkil in the Judean Desert," *Henoch* 28 (2006): 43–77.

4Q298 (Words of the Maskil to the Sons of Dawn).[97] The figure also features heavily in a number of liturgical text such as the Rule of Blessings (1QSb), the Songs of the Sabbath Sacrifice (4Q400–407; 11Q17) and Songs of the Maskil (4Q510; 4Q511). The role of the Maskil to repel demonic forces in the Songs of the Maskil is noteworthy given the association of the same figure with the Teaching on the Two Spirits which is also concerned to a large degree with encroaching malevolent forces.[98]

3:14–15 The term "signs" אותות goes back to the account of the fourth day of creation in Gen 1:14, a verse which establishes a connection between the creation of the heavenly lights and calendrical matters such as seasons, days and years.[99] This terminology is prominent in 4Q259, the only copy of the Community Rules to include a calendrical section published separately as 4Q319 (Otot) where a number of other manuscripts attest the Maskil's Hymn.[100] Even within the Hymn calendrical matters are prominent.[101] Coupled with the reference to תולדות, translated above with "birth times" in 1QS 3:13, the reference to signs suggests that the Maskil's curriculum includes a concern with the heavenly constellations at the time of an individual's birth and, indeed, other significant events.[102] That such ideas were part of the cultural and scientific repertoire reflected in the Scrolls from Qumran is clear.[103]

During their lifetime humans are either precariously exposed to sudden strikes (נגע) or periods of serenity (שלום). The latter is to be understood at the level of individual lives as indicated by the third masculine plural suffix.[104]

4.4.2 The Glorious Plan of the God of Knowledge (1QS 3:15b–18a // No Preserved Parallels)

This new section instructs those addressed on the ways in which the God of knowledge determines the fate of humankind. I noted in 4.3 above that

---

[97] On 4Q298 see 3.1 above.

[98] See further 1.2.1 above and 5.4.2 as well as 15.1.2 below.

[99] Cf. "אות II," in HAWTTM 1:50–52.

[100] For fuller discussion see 15.1.1 below.

[101] See 15.4.2 and 15.4.3 below.

[102] The complex interplay of calendars, priestly courses and historical figures is evidence for what I have called "the transient nature of the scholarly designations for the calendrical compositions" which hail mostly from Cave 4, see further Hempel, *Qumran Rule Texts in Context*, 319–329 as well as 14.1 and Chapter 15 below.

[103] Cf. Popović, *Reading the Human Body*, 119–208 and Helen R. Jacobus, "4Q318: A Jewish Zodiac Calendar at Qumran," in *The Dead Sea Scrolls in Context*. Edited by Charlotte Hempel. STDJ 90 (Leiden: Brill, 2010), 365–395. For the view that the reference is, rather, to "history" or "nature" here see Alexander, "Physiognomy, Initiation, and Rank;" Lange, *Weisheit und Prädestination*, 137; Licht, "Analysis of the Treatise" and Tigchelaar, *Increase Learning*, 196.

[104] Similar terminology is attested in 4Q418c (4QInstruction^f?) 9, see Strugnell and Harrington, DJD 34:501–503 and Tigchelaar, *Increase Learning*, 196.

the phrase "before they came to be he determined all their thoughts" in 1QS 3:15c may, on material grounds, have been added by another hand. It adds little that is new, and the text makes good sense without it. The addition is terminologically and thematically close to 1QS 11:10b–11b which juxtaposes the psalmist's lowly humanity with God's determination of humanity's path from creation. A comparable predestinarian statement is incorporated into an account of community origins in the Damascus Document in CD 2:7b–10.[105] We learn of any kind of division of humanity and the forces who hold sway over them only in the following section.

3:15–16 These lines attest a preponderance of participles and infinitives of the verb "to be" which are reminiscent of 1QS 11:11 and the much debated phrase "mystery of existence" in 4QInstruction. The latter composition also shares the epithet "God of knowledge."[106]

3:18 This is the first occurrence of תבל "world" in 1QS which is frequent in the Teaching and also occurs in 1QS 5:19 // 4Q258 1:11 and 1QS 10:15.[107]

4.4.3 The Establishment of the Spirits of Truth and Injustice Ruled by the Prince of Lights and the Angel of Darkness (1QS 3:18b–4:1 // No Preserved Parallels)

As noted above it is only with 1QS 3:18b that the eponymous topic of two spirits is introduced, and this important juncture is marked with a paragraphos in the margin.[108] It is conceivable that the paragraphos assisted in incorporating a source used by the scribe of 1QS. The careful fusing of cosmic and ethical dimensions in the dualistic framework presented here has long been recognized.[109]

3:18–19 Just as modern scholars were struck by the significance of these lines, perhaps an ancient scribe added a paragraphos in the margin. In this instance the paragraphos marks the point in the text where the two spirits are first introduced.[110] It is also possible that the marginal sign preserves a stage in the literary crafting of this material as is the case elsewhere in 1QS where the evidence from Cave 4 supports such a conclusion.[111]

---

[105] See Hempel, *Qumran Rule Texts in Context*, 70–71 as well as 1QH 9:9–11 and Newsom, Stegemann and Schuller, DJD 40:118–131.

[106] Further, Lange, *Weisheit und Prädestination*, 129 and Tigchelaar, *Increase Learning*, 197.

[107] Cf. Qimron in PTSDSSP 1:17 n. 67.

[108] Further, 4.3 above.

[109] See Brand, *Evil Within and Without*, 259; Frey "Patterns of Dualistic Thought;" von der Osten-Sacken, *Gott und Belial* and Stuckenbruck, "Interiorization." For an overview over the references to truth and injustice in the Community Rules more broadly, see Hempel, "Treatise on the Two Spirits," 116–117 and 4.1.2 above.

[110] Cf. 4.3 and 1.5.1.3 above.

[111] See 1QS 5:13, 25; 8:10, 13 as well as 1.5.3 above.

3:20–21 Tigchelaar has drawn attention to the close correspondences between 4QInstruction and the Teaching in juxtaposing truth and injustice and points to Mal 2:6 as a possible source.[112]

3:21–25 While the children of righteousness are ruled by the prince of lights they are susceptible to sin on account of the influence of the angel of darkness as determined by the divine mysteries.[113] Whereas the material that follows in 1QS 4:2–14 presents a very clear-cut picture of the paths and fate of the followers of the sprirts of truth and injustice these lines offer a much more sophisticated theological explanation to account for moments of cognitive and theological dissonance where the neat scheme outlined in 4.2.4 and 4.2.5 appears to crack. The solution offered here is to acknowledge the mysteries of God who can ultimately be relied upon to put things right. This passage preserves the only reference to the angel of darkness preserved in the Scrolls. On account of the rarity of this designation Loren Stuckenbruck has observed that "The scholarly attention devoted to this figure is disproportionate to the two times he is mentioned in the Dead Sea Scrolls."[114] While it is likely that other designations for the figurehead of demonic forces refer to the same figure, Stuckenbruck is right to give due attention to the distinctiveness of the terminology here.

3:23 "Until the time determined by Him" refers to the time at which God will put an end to the rule of the angel of darkness for ever. The term translated with "hostility" at the end of this line occurs elsewhere in the Scrolls and other early Jewish literature as the proper name Mastemah, a leader malevolent forces.[115]

3:24 The terminology of lots is here employed with reference to the sphere of influence of the angel of darkness.[116]

3:24 The designation God of Israel occurs only here in the Community Rules but is common in the War Scroll.[117]

3:25 The reference to God as the creator of the spirtis of light and darkness offers a clear statement on the relative dualism envisaged in the Treatise, something already implied by the reference to the divine mysteries above.

3:26–4:1 The opposition of love and hate referred to here resembles the Statutes for the Maskil.[118] In 1QS 9 and parallels it is the Maskil's love and hatred that is at issue whereas in the Teaching and in the opening first column in 1QS 1:3–4 // 4Q255 1:4–5 it is God's.

---

[112] Tigchelaar, *Increase Learning*, 197.

[113] On the filial phraseology typical of the Teaching, see Hempel, "Treatise on the Two Spirits," 117–118; also Jutta Jokiranta, "בֵּן *ben*," ThWQ 1:462–473.

[114] Stuckenbruck, "Demonic World of the Dead Sea Scrolls," 62; see also Hanne von Weissenberg, "God(s), Angels and Demons," in CDSS, 490–495.

[115] Cf. Wernberg-Møller, *Manual of Discipline*, 72.

[116] See also the Commentary on 1QS 1:10 in 2.4 above.

[117] Cf. 1QM 1:10; 6:6 passim.

[118] Cf. 1QS 9:16 // 4Q258 8:1 // 4Q259 3:13 and 1QS 9:21 // 4Q255 18:4–6 // 4Q258 8:5–6 // 4Q259 4:2–3.

4.4.4 The Ways of the Spirit of Truth and the Blessed Rewards for Its Followers (1QS 4:2–8 // 4Q257 5:1–7 [including olim 4Q487 37:1–2 and 4Q502 16:1–4])

This passage sets out the ways of the spirit of truth and the rich rewards that await its followers. The picture that is painted here lacks the subtle realism that crept into the previous section where we found a self-aware acknowledgement that the children of righteousness also suffer from the pervasive influence of the angel of darkness and ultimately depend on God coming to their aid in 1QS 3:21b–25a. Both this section and the following present the material almost in a bullet-point style.[119] These differences support the argument of Tigchelaar[120] that the content of 4.2.4 and 4.2.5 goes back to a different stage – and almost certainly also reflects a separate provenance – from the material in 4.2.3. Both this section and the following one have often been called catalogues of virtues and vices.[121] A number of early Christian compositions such as Barnabas and the Didache refer to "the two ways" and appear to draw on Jewish material of the kind that also underlies the Teaching.[122]

4:2 A new subheading, indentation and a paragraphos in the margin clearly mark the beginning of a new section in 1QS. While the introduction to this section identifies the topic of the ways of the spirit of truth, the very first statement to follow "to illuminate the heart of humankind" makes it clear that the influence of the spirit on humanity is comprehensive.[123]

4:2–4 The references to "respect for the commandments of God" and "enthusiasm for righteous ordinances" add a halakhic dimension to the Teaching and, by implication, the remit of the Maskil, something that comes to the fore especially in 4Q256 9:1 // 4Q258 1:1.[124]

4:3 The use of גבורה "strength" occurs in contexts such as Job 12:13 to indicate sapiential prowess.[125]

---

[119] See already Licht, "Analysis of the Treatise," 93.

[120] For details see 4.1.3 above.

[121] See Wernberg-Møller, "Reconsideration," 429–431 and Tanzer, "Sages," 175 who problematizes such an identification.

[122] Cf. Leaney, *Rule of Qumran*, 46–52 and Marinus de Jonge, "The *Testaments of the Twelve Patriarchs and the "Two Ways,"* in *Biblical Traditions in Transmission: Essays in Honour of Michael A. Knibb*. Edited by Charlotte Hempel and Judith Lieu. JSJSup 111 (Leiden: Brill, 2006), 179–194. For a nuanced assessment on the complex transmission of pre-Christian Jewish material in Christian sources – including this terminology – see Robert A. Kraft, "Setting the Stage and Framing Some Central Questions," *JSJ* 32 (2001): 371–395.

[123] On "heart" as "almost synonymous with human nature" here and in 1QS 4:23 // 4Q257 6:2 see Loren Stuckenbruck, "The 'Heart' in the Dead Sea Scrolls: Negotiating Between the Problem of Hypocrisy and Conflict within the Human Being," in *The Dead Sea Scrolls in Context: Integrating the Dead Sea Scrolls in the Study of Ancient Texts, Languages, and Cultures.* Edited by Armin Lange, Emanuel Tov and Matthias Weigold (Leiden: Brill, 2011), 437–453, 450.

[124] See 5.4 for a fuller discussion.

[125] So Wernberg–Møller, *Manual of Discipline*, 74.

4:4–5 On God's love for the spirit of truth see 1QS 3:26–4:1 above.

4:5 Micah 6:8 is an important intertext both here and in 1QS 5 as well as 1QS 8.[126]

4:5 This is the first occurrence of "purity" (טהרה) in 1QS paralleled in 4Q257. The context which includes the phrase "purity of holiness" alongside a series of qualities conveyed by the spirit of truth is rather distinctive. The term appears here to refer to an innate quality rather than the more common usage to refer to ritual purity.[127] We did come across a narrative of purity in relation to boundary formation in connection with the case of someone who refuses to enter the covenant.[128] A reference to the cleanness of hands alongside one's spiritual make-up in the context of group formation occurs also in the Statutes for the Maskil in 1QS 9:15 and parallels.[129] Finally, the Teaching ends with a portrait of a glorious future after an end has been put to the spirit of injustice which includes, according to 1QS 4:20–22, a final process of glorious purification for those who remain.[130]

4:6 "The spirit" is not defined more closely here but must be the spirit of truth since it is opposed both here (cf. 1QS 4:9) and in 1QS 3:18–19 to the spirit of injustice.

4:6 The description of the followers of the spirit of truth as "the world's children of truth" combines the tension between exclusivity and universalism.

4:6b–8 This section ends with the blessings bestowed upon the followers of the spirit of truth which include health, a long life with many descendants, life everlasting in glory and bathing well attired in eternal light.[131] This vision of a blessed existence draws on traditional themes and should not be taken literally in the case of the reference to descendants.[132]

4:7–8 Particularly close correspondences can be identified with 4Q525 (Beatitudes) 11–12.[133]

---

[126] See Hempel, "Treatise on the Two Spirits," 118–119; Menahem Kister, "Commentary to 4Q298," *JQR* 85 (1994): 237–249 and Tzoref, "Use of Scripture."

[127] Further, Wassén, "Purity and Holiness." The counterpart to purity ("impure ways in the service of uncleanness") are associated with the spirit of injustice and its followers in 1QS 4:10.

[128] See 3.4.4 above.

[129] Further, 14.4.2 below.

[130] Cf. 4.4.6 below. On the nexus of impurity and the demonic realm in the Teaching on the Two Spirits, see, e. g., Yair Furstenberg, "Controlling Impurity: The Natures of Impurity in Second Temple Debates," *Dine Israel* 30 (2015): 163–196, 186*–189.*

[131] Cf. Dan 12:3.

[132] For a comprehensive analysis see Puech, *Croyance des Esséniens*, 2:434–436.

[133] See further cf. Puech, DJD 25:141–142; Tigchelaar, "Names of the Spirits," 545–546 and Elisa Uusimäki, *Turning Proverbs Towards Torah: An Analysis of 4Q525*. STDJ 117 (Leiden: Brill, 2016), 51 n. 93, 183, 193–194.

4.4.5 The Ways of the Spirit of Injustice and the Downfall of Its Followers (1QS 4:9–14 // 257 5:7–8, 12–13)

This passage forms the counterpart to the section on the ways of the spirit of truth above and begins with a long list of attributes of the spirit of injustice followed by an account of the fate that is expected to strike those who follow it.

4:9 The qualities of "arrogance and haughtiness" that characterize the spirit of unjustice contrast with the "humble conduct" ascribed to the spirit of truth.

4:10 The reference to "impure ways in the service of uncleanness" offers the counterpart to the "glorious purity" associated with the spirit of truth in 1QS 4:5 // 4Q257 5:2 above.

4:11b–14 These lines offer a description of the judgment on those who follow the spirit of injustice who are consigned to a fate in the fiery depths meted out by God with the help of angels of destruction. A comparable scenario is described in CD 2:5b–7a // 4Q266 (D^a) 2 ii 5–6. The angels of destruction also occur in the War Scroll (1QM 13:12) and the Songs of the Maskil (4Q510 1:5).[134]

4.4.6 The Struggle of the Two Spirits in Human Hearts and the End of Injustice (1QS 4:15–26 // 4Q257 5:14, 6:2–5)

Whereas the two preceding sections treated the spirits of truth and injustice and their followers as pursuing separate paths and heading to distinctive destinies this concluding section begins with the assertion that all of humanity is governed by both spirits. Differentiations emerge as a result of the proportionate share of each person of attributes derived from each spirit. As in the opening section we are again looking at a universalistic framework that has all humanity in view. As a result of divine determination the forces of truth and injustice have been locked into opposition until the day when God brings an end to injustice. As in 1QS 3:23 the time and manner of God's ultimate intervention is described as mysterious, see also CD 3:18.

4:15 A new section is indicated in 1QS with an open paragraph in 1QS 4:14 and an indented start to 1QS 4:15 alongside a marginal paragraphos.[135]

4:15–17 The noun מפלג "type" occurs rather densely twice in the masculine and once in the feminine (מפלגה) in these three lines and only here in the Community Rules. The noun occurs predominantly with reference to people.[136]

---

[134] Further, Puech, *Croyance des Esséniens*, 436–437 as well as 1QS 2:6 and parallels.

[135] On the suggestion that the opening words were added by a different hand see the Textual Note in 4.3 above and 5.1.2 below.

[136] Cf. 1QH^a 20:26 and Holger Gzella, "פלג *plg*," ThWQ 3:287–292, esp. 290–291.

4:16 The phrase "all periods of eternity" recurs partly reconstructed in the closing framework of the Teaching in 1QS 4:25–26 as well as more widely in the Scrolls.[137]

4:18 The idea of an end to injustice is also found in a superlinear addition in 1QS 8:10 which refers to "no more injustice" (ואין עול).[138]

4:19–21 After the end of injustice truth emerges in a state that is contaminated with wickedness acquired during a period governed by injustice. This is followed by a process intended to eliminate traces of injustice deep inside the human form. The combination תכמי בשרו "the soft tissue of its flesh" occurs elsewhere in the Scrolls and mostly in the context of some kind of contamination, see, e. g., 1QHᵃ 15:7 where it occurs, as here, in parallel with מבנית "structure" applied to the human body.[139]

Two texts shed further light on this account of a conflict between the forces of truth and injustice raging deep within the human body. The first is part of the Songs of the Maskil where the speaker gives thanks to God for having placed knowledge inside his "foundation of dust" (סוד עפר). The song continues with a vivid account of the lowly origins of the speaker that includes a reference to בתכמי בבשרי "in the soft tissue of my flesh."[140] Noam Mizrahi has offered a comprehensive analysis of this lexeme and traces its etymology to the Hebrew root שכם "shoulder" that persists in Biblical Hebrew. Its Semantic range began to expand to include "back" and eventually parts of the body more broadly. Mizrahi explains the change from *shin* to *tav* and the predominence in the Scrolls of occurrences in contexts that refer to a bodily invasion by malevolent spirits as a consequence of the adoption of a technical loanword from the linguistic repertoire of Aramaic magic.[141] Both here and in the remaining references in the Dead Sea Scrolls where sufficient context survives the term always refers to an episode where malevolent forces have taken hold of or been expelled from the body of a sufferer.

The same terminology is found in Incantation (4Q444) 1–4 i + 5 2–3 which includes a description of a struggle between spirits of wickedness and a spirit of knowledge, understanding, truth and righteousness that also takes place deep inside the body of the speaker. The nature of an entity described as "spirits of dispute" (רוחי ריב) within the speaker's bodily structure (מבנית) is ambiguous and refers either to benevolent or, as elsewhere, a menacing event.[142]

---

[137] For discussion see Tigchelaar, *Increase Learning*, 196.

[138] See Chapter 8 below.

[139] For the reading "structure" in 1QS 4:20 see 4.3 above. On the term תכימים see Elisha Qimron, "Notes on the 4Q Zadokite Fragments on Skin Disease," *JJS* 42 (1991): 256–259 and Nicholas A. Meyer, "תכמים *tkmjm*," ThWQ 3:1121–1123.

[140] See 4Q511 28–29 4; Baillet, DJD 7:234–235, Plate 61.

[141] Mizrahi, "תכמי בשר 'Body Parts.'"

[142] See Chazon, DJD 29:372–377.

The passages from 4Q511 and 4Q444 offer important insights into the language and anthropological ideas attested in the Teaching on the Two Spirits. Our passage shares with 4Q511 and 4Q444 the notion of a battle of the forces of truth and injustice deep within the human body. In the Treatise this internal battle is couched within a larger narrative of contamination, purification and eschatological judgment. Comparable ideas about ethical conduct, spiritual make-up and a purity rhetoric are also attested in Ps 51 as demonstrated by Anja Klein.[143]

4:22 The designation Most High occurs here in a sapiential context.[144] Hartmut Stegemann has shown that the divine epithet Most High is particularly common in sapiential material including Ben Sira and the Dead Sea Scrolls.[145]

4:22 The idea of an eternal covenant is also found in the plus in 1QS 5:5–6 as well as in 1QS 8:10 // 4Q258 6:3 // 4Q259 2:18. The closest parallel with this passage is, however, 1QSb 1:3.[146]

4:23 On "the glory of Adam" see CD 3:20 and 1QH[a] 4:21–27. Wernberg-Møller draws on Sir 46:16 to support the translation Adam rather than human being.[147]

4:23 In view of references like the battle of opposing spirits in the heart of men Stuckenbruck has referred to the conception of the heart as a "combat zone" for opposing forces influencing humanity.[148] Note also that heart is one of the terms that is used in parallelism with "soft tissue" in 1QH[a] 15:7–8.[149]

4:26 Like the opening line to the Teaching this concluding statement offers a universalist approach by being concerned with "all the living." The reference to God's role in determining the fate for all the living uses the language of casting lots. As Stegemann has suggested, this determination of human fate refers not to the eschaton, but rather to the point of origin of each human being at the time of their conception or birth.[150] The conclusion to the Treatise, thus, offers an inclusio with the description of God's glorious plan dealt with in 4.2.2 and 4.4.2 above.

---

[143] Klein, "From the 'Right Spirit' to the 'Spirit of Truth:' Observations on Ps 51 and the Community Rule," in *The Dynamics of Language and Exegesis at Qumran*. Edited by Devorah Dimant and Reinhard G. Kratz. FAT 35 (Tübingen: Mohr Siebeck, 2009), 171–191. See also the petition for freedom from the influence of a satan and a spirit of uncleanness in the Plea for Deliverance in the Psalms Scrolls (11Q5 19).

[144] For a comparison of the "discourse of knowledge" in the Teaching and the Songs of the Maskil see Angel, "Maskil, Community and Religious Experience."

[145] See Hartmut Stegemann, "Religionsgeschichtliche Erwägungen zu den Gottes-bezeichnungen in den Qumrantexten," in *Qumrân: Sa piété, sa théologie et son milieu*. Edited by Mathias Delcor et al. (Paris: Gembloux; Leuven: Leuven University Press, 1978), 195–217, 212–216. The epithet also occurs twice in the Final Hymn in 1QS 10:12 and 11:15.

[146] See also 1QSb 2:25.

[147] Wernberg-Møller, *Manual of Discipline*, 87 and Brownlee, *Dead Sea Manual*, 17–18.

[148] Stuckenbruck, "The 'Heart' in the Dead Sea Scrolls," 452.

[149] See Meyer, "תכמים," 1121.

[150] Stegemann, "Textbestand und Grundgedanken," 120–121.

5. Requirements and Leadership for a New Community in Two Founding Narratives (1QS 5:1–7a // 4Q256 9:1–6a // 4Q258 1:1–5a)

5.1 Introduction

This section introduces a substantial portion of 1QS and 4Q256. For 4Q258 this material marks the beginning of the manuscript. In all three manuscripts this new section, which deals with matters of community formation and organization, is set apart in several significant ways.[1]

5.1.1 Material Considerations, Vacats and Marginal Signs

As we saw, at least one of the Cave 4 manuscripts (4Q258) begins here and lacks the material preceding in 1QS, 4Q256, 4Q257 and 4Q262. The start of the manuscript in 4Q258 is indicated by a sizeable uninscribed right hand margin.[2] Neither 4Q257 nor 4Q262 preserve, and may never have included, any material corresponding to 1QS 5 onwards.[3] Both 4Q256 and 1QS begin with a new heading at this juncture. In 4Q256 we are at the start of a new sheet as indicated by remains of stitching and the Hebrew letter *gimel* in the top right corner which most likely represents a system for numbering the third sheet in this manuscript.[4] 1QS marks a new sub-section with a modest though noticeable *vacat* at 1QS 5:1 and a paleo-Hebrew *vav* in the margin.[5] In 1QS, as in 4Q256, the placement of the beginning of a major new section at the top of a column presupposes careful planning on the part of the scribe(s) behind these scrolls.[6] As argued above, the paleo-Hebrew *vav* may have served the scribe(s) behind 1QS in planning

---

[1] For an overview over the preserved material across the manuscripts see Table 6 at the end of section 1.5 above.

[2] Cf. Tov, *Scribal Practices*, 108–115.

[3] See 1.5.4 and 1.5.9 above.

[4] See Alexander and Vermes, DJD 26:41 and Plate 3; Milik, 'Numération des feuilles," 78 where the manuscript is labelled 4QS^d; Tov, *Scribal Practices*, 211; LLDSSDL image B-366920 and 1.5.3.2 above.

[5] Cf. Tov, *Scribal Practices*, 207.

[6] See Stegemann, "Some Remarks," 483. I am grateful to Eibert Tigchelaar for a personal conversation on this matter.

and, conceivably, the composition of 1QS on the basis of a range of sources.[7] Both 4Q256 and 4Q258 begin writing flush with the margin. The efforts of the scribes across three otherwise diverging manuscripts to start this section in a new column is noteworthy.[8]

5.1.2 Superscriptions

We immediately notice in the translations below that 1QS, on the one hand, and 4Q256 // 4Q258, on the other hand, start with a different superscription at this important juncture. Whereas 1QS 5:1 begins with "And this is the rule for the people of the community," 4Q258 with overlap in 4Q256 reads, "Midrash for the Maskil over the people of the law."

The heading in 1QS 5:1 is followed by the participle המתנדבים shared by 1QS and 4Q258 which I translate with "they shall be fervently committed."[9] In 1QS 5:1 this participle follows immediately after the heading but looks as though it was written with a different or a generously re-dipped pen. The variations in the appearance of the thickness of the ink at precisely the place where the textual tradition of S is at its most fluid give pause for thought. There was certainly a pause in the writing process at this point. We cannot know whether this pause was simply to allow the scribe to refresh the pen, to acquire or adjust their *Vorlage*, or a sign of some hesitation about the text of the *Vorlage* just after a significant new heading.

Similar phenomena in the vicinity of headings that appear to relate to the final shaping of 1QS occur also elsewhere.[10] Notable also is the slight *vacat* at the beginning of 1QS 5:1 – the smallest in all of 1QS. The unexpectedly wide inter-word space between the demonstrative pronoun[11] and the remainder of the heading may be due to a feature on the surface of the parchment. However, we know very little about the stage at which scribes added headings and we might have here some subtle indications that set the heading apart from what follows immediately after it. It is also conceivable that adding the first word or phrase of a significant new section at the top of a new column was part of the planning process for the scribe of 1QS.[12]

---

[7] Further, 1.5.1.3.1 above.

[8] Cf. also Eibert J. C. Tigchelaar, "Dittography and Copying Lines in the Dead Sea Scrolls: Considering George Brooke's Proposal about 1QpHab 7:1–2," in *Is There a Text in this Cave?* Edited by Feldman, Cioată and Hempel, 293–302, 295–296 n. 11.

[9] See 5.4 below.

[10] Cf. 1QS 3:15b immediately following the lengthy heading that introduces the Teaching on the Two Spirits in 1QS 3:13–15a as well as 1QS 4:15 preceding the introduction of the final sub-section of the Teaching on the Two Spirits. For details see 4.3; 4.4.2 and 4.4.4.

[11] So already Licht, *Rule Scroll*, 123.

[12] See also 1QS 10:1 and 15.3 below. For some perceptive comments on the position of the demonstrative pronoun at the beginning of 1QS 5:1 and the likelihood that we are witnessing an

5.1.3 Content

In terms of subject matter we notice a significant transition in all manuscript witnesses beginning with 1QS 5 and parallels up to and including 1QS 7 and parallels. We move from the theological framework of Admission into and Reaffirmation of the Covenant (Chapter 3) and the Teaching on the Two Spirits (Chapter 4)[13] to a horizontal plane and a focus on matters of communal aspirations, organization and leadership. We also note a shrinking of the chronological horizon at this point. Where time is mentioned we are dealing with a small number of years such as phases in the process of admission into the community and a variety of temporary exclusions. In 1QS 1–4 // 4QS, by contrast, the temporal sphere is far-reaching with existential implications. Thus, nine out of ten occurrences of "rule" (ממשלה) in 1QS occur in 1QS 1–4. The term refers to a significant epoch as part of a wider cosmological scheme.[14] We also note a prepondereance of the term עולם ("eternity") in 1QS 2 (x9) and in 1QS 4 (x8), not counting parallels in 4QS. An exception is 1QS 5:13 which forms part of a substantial plus in 1QS regarding the fate of all those who hold God's word in contempt.[15]

5.1.4 The Relationship of 1QS and 4Q256 // 4Q258

Ever since Józef Milik first alluded to a series of intriguing divergences between 1QS and the still unpublished Cave 4 manuscripts in 1956[16] it has been clear that 1QS 5 is a crucial witness to the relationship of 1QS and the Cave 4 manuscripts of the Community Rules. Much of the subsequent discussion on the relationship between the longer text in 1QS and the shorter text of 4Q256 // 4Q258 has focused on significant differences between them. By longer text I include not only the presence of 1QS 1–4 in 1QS over against 4Q258 but also a number of significant plusses in 1QS over against 4QS.[17] Based chiefly on 1QS's earlier paleographical date Philip Alexander argued that the longer text preserved in

---

"element of compilation" here see already Martin, *Scribal Character of the Dead Sea Scrolls*, 1:386–387.

[13] On the theologial orientation of 1QS 1–4 // 4QS including the prevalence of references to God (אל) see Hempel, "Long Text."

[14] Cf. Barbara Schlenke, "משל II," ThWQ 2:819–826.

[15] See 6.4 below.

[16] Milik, "Le travail d'édition."

[17] Further, 1.5.1.4 above. Milik first suggested that 4Q256's shorter text is more original, see "Numération des feuilles," 78; he is followed by Metso, *Textual Development*; Geza Vermes, "Preliminary Remarks on Unpublished Fragments of the Community Rule from Qumran Cave 4," *JJS* 42 (1991): 250–255; Vermes, "The Leadership of the Qumran Community: Sons of Zadok-Priests-Congregation," in *Geschichte – Tradition – Reflexion: Festschrift für Martin Hengel zum 70. Geburtstag.* Edited by Hubert Cancik, Hermann Lichtenberger and Peter Schäfer (Tübingen: Mohr Siebeck, 1996), 1: 375–384 and others.

1QS was subsequently abbreviated in 4Q256 // 4Q258.[18] While I concur with those scholars who consider the longer text attested in 1QS as an expansion of the shorter text, it is instructive and important to take the comprehensive amount of agreement between both text forms into consideration when assessing the evidence. The translation below is given in a synoptic format that offers a composite text of 4Q256 and 4Q258 – two manuscripts that are largely in agreement where they overlap – alongside 1QS. Differences between the manuscripts are indicated in the usual manner in italics. While the amount of disagreement in italics is striking, due attention will be given to the equally significant shared material which has received less attention by scholars.[19] The most substantial divergence between 1QS and 4QS is attested in the material that spans 1QS 5 with a much more stable text in evidence from 1QS 6:1c onwards that at times spans across four manuscripts

5.2 Translation[20]

5.2.1 Diverging Headings (1QS 5:1a // 4Q256 9:1a // 4Q258 1:1a)

1QS 5	4Q256 9 // 4Q258 1
[1a]*And this is the rule for the people of the community.*	9[1a]/1[1a]*Midrash for the Maskil over* <u>*the people of the law*</u>

5.2.2 Shared Objectives (1QS 5:1b // 4Q256 9:1b–2a // 4Q258 1:1b)

1QS 5	4Q256 9 // 4Q258 1
[1b]They shall be fervently committed to turn back from all evil and to hold fast to all that He has commanded *as His wish.*	1[1b]<u>They shall be</u> fervently committed to turn back from all evil and to hold fast to all 9[2]that He has commanded.

---

[18] Alexander, "Redaction-History;" followed by Tov, *Scribal Practices*, 27 and others.

[19] Cf. Hempel, "A New Paradigm," reprinted in *Qumran Rule Texts in Context*, 109–119 and Hempel, "Long Text."

[20] On the principles behind the "Transparent Composite Text" for the translation of 4Q256 and 4Q258 from this point see 1.7 above. In short, text preserved <u>in 4Q256 only</u> is <u>single underlined</u> and text preserved <u>in 4Q258 only</u> is <u>double underlined</u>. In addition, the line numbers of each manuscript are identified in the body of the translation by indicating the distinctive column numbers in 4Q256 and 4Q258 alongside line numbers.

5.2.3 A Shared First Founding Narrative (1QS 5:1c–2a // 4Q256 9:2b // 4Q258 1:2a)

1QS 5	4Q256 9 // 4Q258 1
[1c]They shall separate from the congregation of [2a]the people of injustice to form a community with regard to law and property.	[9:2]/[1:2a]They shall separate from the congregation of the people of injustice to form a community with regard to la[w] and property.

5.2.4 A Not so Divergent Leadership Model (1QS 5:2b–3b // 4Q256 9:2c–3a // 4Q258 1:2b–3a)

1QS 5	4Q256 9 // 4Q258 1
[2b]They shall be accountable to *the sons of Zadok, the priests who keep the covenant and to the multitude of the people of [3]the community who hold fast to the covenant. On their authority decisions shall be taken* regarding any matter pertaining to law, property, *and judgment.*	[1:2b]They shall be accountable [9:3]to *the many* regarding any matter [1:3]pertaining to law and property.

5.2.5 Shared Core Principles (1QS 5:3c–5a // 4Q256 9:3b–4 // 4Q258 1:3b–4a)

1QS 5	4Q256 9 // 4Q258 1
[3c]They shall act with *truth together and* humility, [4]righteousness and justice, devoted love and modesty in all their ways. Let no one walk in the hardness of his heart in order to go astray *by following his own heart [5]and eyes and the thoughts of his own imagination.*	[1:3b]They shall act with humility, righteousness and justice, devoted [9:4]love and modesty in all their ways. [1:4]Le[t] no one walk in the hardness of his heart in order to go astray.

5.2.6 A Shared Second Founding Narrative (1QS 5:5b–7a // 4Q256 9:5–6a // 4Q258 1:4b–5a)

1QS 5	4Q256 9 // 4Q258 1
[5b]Rather	[9⁵/1⁴ᵇ]Rather
they shall reign in the imagination and the stiff neck in the community	
so as to build a foundation of truth for Israel, as a community	they shall build <u>a foundation</u> of truth for Israel, as a community
of the eternal [6]*covenant. They shall atone*	
for *all those* who *are* fervently committed to holiness in Aaron and *for the* house of truth *in* Israel	<u>for</u> *every one* <u>who 1⁵*is* fervently committed to holiness in Aaron and *a* house of 9⁶truth</u> *for* Israel
as well as those who join them as a community.	as well as those who joi<u>n</u> th<u>em</u> as a community.
With regard to lawsuits and judgments [7a]*they shall declare guilty all those who transgress the statutes.*	Lacking in 4Q256 and 4Q258 along with further text at the beginning of the next section.

5.3 Textual Notes

5:1 In 1QS we have evidence of a scribal correction which has left the remains of wet ink being wiped away.[21]

5:1 The preposition על translated here with "over" in 4Q256 9:1 // 4Q258 1:1 can also be taken as "concerning."

5:1 4Q258 1:1 reads המתנדים without *bet* which may be scribal error.[22]

5:1 4Q258 1:1 reads an infinitive *hiphil* (להשיב) "to turn back" where 1QS 5:1 has לשוב.[23]

5:1 4Q258 1:2 omits *he* in the infinitive *niphal* לבדל.[24] Only the upper and lower tips of final *lamed* remain in 4Q256 9:1.

5:2 The translation presupposes the reading ומשיבים in both 1QS and 4Q258.[25]

5:2 4Q258 1:2 has יחד over against 1QS ליחד.

5:2 The *vav* in ועל פי "and according to" is written above the line in 1QS. In the same phrase there are clear signs of a correction by erasing the surface of the

---

[21] I am grateful to Professor Émile Puech for a personal conversation on this phenomenon, see also 1QS 9:1. On the text of the opening words including the para-textual evidence see the discussion in 5.1.2 above.

[22] See Alexander and Vermes, DJD 26:54.

[23] On the use of *hiphil* in place of *qal* see Qimron, HDSS, 49 and Alexander and Vermes, DJD 26:96.

[24] For the phenomenon and discussion see Qimron, HDSS, 310, 145.

[25] Cf. Brownlee, *Dead Sea Manual*, 19 and Licht, *Rule Scroll*, 123.

leather which truncated the lower part of *lamed*. *Ayin* is the result of a correction from *aleph* in 1QS.[26]

5:3 The phrases "decisions shall be taken" and "regarding any matter" are written as one word in 1QS.

5:3 The second occurrence of יחד in this line, which is translated as an adverb above, can also be taken as a noun and rendered "unity."[27] It occurs again in close proximity to אמת in 1QS 5:10 below where the adverbial sense is clearer. As rightly noted by Licht, the corrections to the penultimate word יחד "together" (1QS 5:3) and אחר "after" in the following line (1QS 5:4) are related.[28] An examination of the Israel Museum's digital images suggests that the corrector accidentally replaced *yod* with *aleph* intended for line 4 in line 3 directly above, a slip subsequently erased in line 3. The original erroneous *yod* in line 4 may also have been influenced by original *yod* in line 3 directly above.

5:4 As observed by Guilbert the root letters of the infinitive *hiphil* of "to be humble" (והצנע) appear larger in size than the surrounding material in 1QS.[29]

5:4 The LLDSSDL infrared image B-499628 reveals that in 4Q258 1:3 the *tav* in the infinitive construct לכת was corrected from *lamed* which substantially remains but is overwritten. The error was perhaps based on homoioteleuton with the following defectively written בכל.

5:4 Both here and in 1QS 5:14, 15, 17; 8:25; 9:16 the relative pronoun with or without conjunction introduces a prohibition. This usage is attested in Late and Post Second Temple sources including the Bar Kokhba letters.[30]

5:4 As noted on 1QS 5:3 above an original *yod* has been corrected to *aleph* in אחר "after."[31]

5:5 Qimron reads ועינוהי.[32] Our translation presupposes the reading ועיניהו "and his eyes."[33]

5:5 1QS's problematic reading יאאם has been dealt with in various ways by scholars. Licht's suggestion of emending to כי אם is accepted here and has now been confirmed by both Cave 4 manuscripts (4Q256 9:5 // 4Q258 1:4) which share this terminology with 1QS.[34] Both 4Q256 and 4Q258 attest כי spelt defectively. Such a defective spelling is unusual for 4Q256.[35]

5:5 The translation "they shall reign in" is a free rendering of the idiomatic Hebrew metaphor "circumcise the foreskin of."

---

[26] See Licht, *Rule Scroll*, 123.

[27] So, e. g., Lohse, *Texte aus Qumran*, 17.

[28] Licht, *Rule Scroll*, 124.

[29] Guilbert, "Règle de la Communauté," 40.

[30] See Qimron, HDSS, 77–79.

[31] Cf. Licht, *Rule Scroll*, 124.

[32] Qimron, DSSHW 1:218; see also Reymond, *Qumran Hebrew*, 159.

[33] See, e. g., Licht, *Rule Scroll*, 124.

[34] Licht, *Rule Scroll*, 124.

[35] Cf. Alexander and Vermes, DJD 26:45.

5:6c–7a This text forms part of a significant plus in 1QS that carries over into the next section.[36]

5.4 Commentary

Beyond the substantially different headings[37] both 1QS and 4QS start the substance of this programmatic section with a call for a fervent commitment to turn away from all evil and hold fast to the divine commandments. This is followed by a warning to shun the people of injustice side by side with a directive to form a community with respect to torah and property. We are given much more detail about the different spheres of encounter with the people of injustice that are to be avoided in the following chapter. The passage then outlines the leadership structure for the emerging community in different terms before turning to its ethos. The shared text, finally, returns to the question of the formation of the community, but this time more lofty and cultic terms dominate. 4Q256 and 4Q258 end on this note whereas 1QS, somewhat incongruously, continues with a more mundane plus concerning "lawsuits and judgments." Both this plus in 1QS and several issues introduced here get picked up again in the next chapter.[38]

In light of attesting some of the most eye-watering variants in any sectarian text from Qumran the material presented in this chapter and 6.1 has been extremely influential on recent research on the Community Rules. However, once we have recovered from this rather dazzling picture, it is essential to step back and approach the full spectrum of our evidence before arriving at a more measured conclusion. The implications of an amplifying approach to these chapters have contributed to overestimating the significance of the sons of Zadok in the Scrolls.[39] It is important to acknowledge other passages that cover the same issue in very different terms.[40] The latter material offers much neglected and yet similarly radical discrepancies within 1QS 5. Moreover, in 1QS 5:20b–22c this manuscript is in close alignment with 4Q258 on the leadership of "the sons of Aaron" and "the multitude of Israel."[41]

---

[36] See 6.1 below.

[37] Cf. 5.1.2 above.

[38] Cf. 6.1 below.

[39] See Charlotte Hempel, "Consider Ourselves in Charge: Self-Assertion Sons of Zadok Style," in Hempel, *Qumran Rule Texts in Context*, 211– 227, also 14–15.

[40] Compare 1QS 5:20b–22 // 4Q258 2:1–3a // 4Q261 1a–b:1–2a and 6.1 below.

[41] Further, 6.1 below.

5.4.1 Diverging Headings (1QS 5:1a // 4Q256 9:1a // 4Q258 1:1a)

5:1 After the fragmentary title in 1QS 1:1 // 4Q255 1:1 discussed in section 2.3 above this is the second time the noun **serekh** occurs in a title of what is now a subsection of 1QS. The term introduces another sub-section on community meetings in 1QS 6:8 with no preserved parallels in 4QS.[42] Beyond the single occurrence of serekh in 4Q255 1:1 noted above the noun is not preserved in any sub-headings that survive from the Cave 4 witnesses. Several non-titular uses of serekh refer to the community (1QS 1:16 // 4Q256 2:1) or, more often, to procedural details relating to precedence during the Covenant Ceremony (1QS 2:20–21) or the written registration of members (1QS 5:23 // 4Q258 2:2; 1QS 6:22).

Both 4QS manuscripts begin with "Midrash for the maskil."[43] This use of the term **midrash** as the opening element in a heading is unique in the Rule literature, but see the closing lines of the Damascus Document as preserved in 4Q266 11 20 // 4Q270 7 ii 15 and 4QFlorilegium (4Q174) 1–2 i 14. Moreover, the reading of the title of 4QMidrash Sefer Moshe (4Q249) written on the verso of this cryptic text has recently been improved. Jonathan Ben-Dov and Daniel Stökl Ben Ezra were able to show that the second element of the title, "sefer," was, in fact, deleted by means of cancellation dots leaving us with the shorter title 4QMidrash Moshe.[44] The authors suggest that the substitution in 4Q249 of sefer with midrash testifies to ancient bibliographic sensibilities. They argue that the correction was made on the basis of a re-assessment of the contents of 4Q249 in relation to Lev 14. On this analysis, the corrector came to the view that the composition did not warrant the title "sefer." However, the oscillation in the headings attested in the S material from "sefer serekh" (4Q255 1:1), "[ser]ekh" (1QS 5:1) to "midrash" (4Q256 9:1 and 4Q258 1:1) cautions against assuming such terminology was already as canonically charged as presupposed by Ben-Dov and Stökl Ben Ezra.

The noun midrash also occurs in the latter part of the heading to the Penal Code in 1QS 6:24 (lacking in 4Q261) where it refers to a process of enquiry. There the determinative opening words of the heading are, in fact, "And these are the judgments" (ואלה המשפטים).[45] A comparable context is found in 1QS 8:26 // 4Q258 7:1 where midrash occurs as part of a series of terms referring to communal activities: meetings, study and (exchanging) counsel (1QS: במדרש

---

[42] See Chapter 7 below.

[43] Cf. Hindy Najman and Eibert Tigchelaar, "A Preparatory Study of Nomenclature and Text Designation in the Dead Sea Scrolls," *RevQ* 26 (2014): 305–325 and Schofield, *From Qumran to the Yaḥad*, 154–155.

[44] See Ben-Dov and Stökl Ben Ezra, "4Q249 Midrash Moshe: A New Reading and Some Implications," *DSD* 21 (2014): 131–149.

[45] Further, 6.5 below.

ובעצה) or study and (exchanging) counsel (4Q258 במדרש ובעצה).[46] A further important reference to the interpretation of the law (מדרש התורה) is attested in 1QS 8:15 // 4Q258 6:7 // 4Q259 3:6 where Isa 40:3 is interpreted as referring to the study of the law.[47]

The term midrash is left untranslated here since an unambiguous meaning cannot be arrived at. A number of different possible translations have been suggested. Johann Maier proposed that the meaning here is "the (official) written record."[48] Alexander and Vermes translate "the instruction for the maskil" but comment that teaching, instruction or interpretation are all possible.[49]

Out of twelve occurrences in the non-biblical Scrolls the term midrash occurs ten times in the Rule texts – eight times in the Community Rules and twice in the Damascus Document (CD 20:6 and 4Q266 11 20 // 4Q270 7 ii 15). Both occurrences in the Damascus Document are part of the construct "midrash of the torah" or "interpretation of the law." The term is also closely linked to torah in the Community Rules (cf. 1QS 8:15 // 4Q259 3:6), and the current heading in 4QS continues this by referring to the intended constituency as **the people of the law** (אנשי התורה), a phrase found only here in the DSS.[50] The divergent terminology to refer to the community in the headings of 1QS 5:1 ("the people of the community") and 4Q258 1:1 ("the people of the law") has rightly been emphasized.[51] It is crucial to acknowledge, however, that even within 4Q256 and 4Q258 other designations for the community predominate such as "the (congregation of) the people of community" (4Q256 1x; 4Q258 x5) or "the people of the covenant of the community" (4Q258 x1) and "the people of holiness" (4Q256 x1; 4Q258 x2). Moreover, the emphasis on torah reflected in 4QS here is pervasive across the S manuscripts including in this section. It is striking, also, that the otherwise remarkably diverging headings in 1QS 5:1 and 4Q258 1 include the shared element "the people of." There is little reason to doubt that 4Q256 agreed with 4Q258 in this regard. This shared term distinguishes 1QS 5:1 from the heading in 1QS 1:1 and more fully preserved in 4Q255 1:1 "the book of the rule of the community" which gave the document its name. And, as we saw, 1QS' term "the people of the community" is elsewhere attested in 4Q256 and particularly frequently in 4Q258. Taken together with the singular titular use of

---

[46] See Chapter 10 below.

[47] Cf. CD 20:6 and Chapter 8 below.

[48] Maier, "דָּרַשׁ *dāraš*; מִדְרָשׁ *midrāš*," ThWQ 1:726–738.

[49] Alexander and Vermes, DJD 26:95–96. For an insightful discussion of the lexeme in the Scrolls as well as further literature see George J. Brooke, *Reading the Dead Sea Scrolls: Essays in Method*. EJL 39 (Atlanta, GA: SBL, 2013), 107–114; further, Steven Fraade, "Midrashim," in EDSS 1:548–552; Timothy H. Lim, *Pesharim*. CQS 3. Sheffield: Sheffield Academic Press, 2002, 48–52 and Rendsburg, "Qumran Hebrew," 243.

[50] See Schofield, *From Qumran to the Yaḥad*, 155–156.

[51] Cf. Alexander and Vermes, DJD 26:96 and Schofield, *From Qumran to the Yaḥad*, 94–95.

midrash we need to acknowledge that the heading in 4Q256 // 4Q258 that has struck scholars for its distinctiveness from 1QS 5:1 is extraordinary even in 4QS as attested most fulsomely by 4Q258.

As far as the reference to the **Maskil** is concerned, this office occurs frequently in headings both in the non-biblical Dead Sea Scrolls, including in the Community Rules, as well as in the Bible.[52] While the Maskil's association with the spiritual and liturgical realm is widely recognised, it is clear that the sphere of influence of this figure also comprises assessments of adherence to the law as a prerequisite for protection from malevolent influences and a blessed future. Thus, halakhic sensibilities are attributed to the influence of the Spirit of Truth in 1QS 4:2–3 (no preserved parallels in 4QS) by filling the heart of its followers with "respect for the commandments of God."[53] Moreover, according to 1QS 4:4 // 4Q257 5:1 the same spirit "engenders enthusiasm for righteous ordinances."[54] The theme of obedience to the law is taken up again in the Statutes for the Maskil as well as the Final Hymn.[55] Even the heading "Statutes for the Maskil" in 1QS 9:12 is noteworthy. In addition, Judith Newman has drawn attention to the connection of the Maskil with the idea of engraved statutes.[56] Moreover, on our reading and translation of 1QS 9:23 and parallels the Maskil is expected to be zealous for the statute and ready for a day of vengeance, leaving little doubt about the seriousness of such concerns.[57] It is therefore entirely appropriate to have allocated a prominent role to the Maskil just at this juncture in 4Q258 and 4Q256 where we turn to the aims and regulations for the community.[58]

In short, it is clear that human conduct is part and parcel of the spiritual make-up of community members and firmly within the sphere of operations of the Maskil. Moreover, already prior to the publication of the Cave 4 manuscripts that attest a Maskil heading introducing rules of conduct Arnold Anderson astutely noted that the Maskil's duty of assessing the spiritual make-up of community members concerns "both understanding and behaviour or practical living."[59]

---

[52] See section 4.4.1 above.

[53] Cf. Wernberg-Møller, *Manual of Discipline*, 73–74.

[54] See also 1QS 2:26–3:1 // 4Q257 3:1–2.

[55] Cf. Chapters 14 and 15 below.

[56] Newman, *Before the Bible: The Liturgical Body and the Formation of Scriptures in Early Judaism* (New York, NY: Oxford University Press, 2018); see also Lange, *Weisheit und Prädestination*, 146.

[57] Cf. 14.3 and 14.4 below.

[58] On the nexus of wisdom and law in the Community Rules see also Hempel, "Wisdom and Law" and further literature cited there.

[59] Anderson, "The Use of *Ruaḥ* in 1QS, 1QH, and 1QM," *JSS* 7 (1962): 293–303, 296–297; see also Chapter 14 below.

5.4.2 Shared Objectives (1QS 5:1b // 4Q256 9:1b–2a // 4Q258 1:1b)

5:1 (and 6) The *hitpael* participle of the verb נדב occurs seven times in 1QS 5–6, five of which are also attested in manuscripts from Cave 4. The remaining two cases are conspicuous plusses in 1QS.[60] As noted above, the verb occurs only twice more in the *niphal* in 1QS 1:7, 11 with no preserved parallels in 4QS.[61] While there is no difference in meaning, it is noteworthy that the author of the Introduction displays an inclination towards the *niphal* over against the linguistic preference for *hitpael* across several manuscripts in 1QS 5–6 and 4QS.

We translate the participle with "those who are fervently committed" and take it to refer to a particular course of action or behaviour rather than as a self-designation for the community as the terminology is often understood.[62] A commitment to undertake a specific and immediate course of action is expressed by the same verb in Exod 35:21 and 29. In the present passus the participle does not represent a generic descriptor of the members of the community but rather a characteristic attribute of the latter. Its predicative syntactic function reflected in our translation is compatible to the *hiphil* participle "they shall be answerable" משיבים in 1QS 5:2 // 4Q258 9:2.[63]

In an excellent discussion of the use of the verb *ndb* in the Hebrew Bible Fitzgerald notes a preponderance of occurrences at seminal and potent moments of cultic significance for the restoration of relations to the deity.[64] The present passage, particularly as attested in the longer text of 1QS, has a pronounced priestly and cultic flavour that is more subtly shared by all three manuscripts in a second occurrence of the participle *hitpael* of *ndb* in 1QS 5:5–6 // 4Q256 9:5–6; 4Q258 1:4–5.[65]

While there is no doubt that the priestly and cultic emphases in 1QS 5 are more pronounced than in the two 4Q manuscripts it is remarkable that both 1QS 5 and 4QS also include the laity. A prominent involvement of lay members of the con-

---

[60] The passages are as follows: 1QS 5:1 // 4Q258 9:1; 1QS 5:6 // 4Q258 1:5; 1QS 5:8 (a plus in 1QS); 1QS 5:10 (a plus in 1QS); 1QS 5:21 // 4Q258 2:1; 1QS 5:22 // 4Q258 2:2 // 4Q261 1a–b 2; 1QS 6:13 // 4Q256 11:8.

[61] See Chapter 2 above. Further, Devorah Dimant, "The Volunteers in the Rule of the Community – A Biblical Notion in Sectarian Garb," *RevQ* 23 (2007): 233–245; reprinted in Dimant, *History, Ideology and Bible Interpretation in the Dead Sea Scrolls*. FAT 90 (Tübingen: Mohr Siebeck, 2014) 289–299 and Qimron, HDSS, 49

[62] So, e. g., Devorah Dimant, "Volunteers"; Dimant, "נָדַב nādab," ThWQ 2:879–883; Benedikt Eckhardt, "TheYahad in the Context of Hellenistic Group Formation," in CDSS, 86–96; Aloysius Fitzgerald F. S. C., "MTNDBYM in 1QS," *CBQ* 36 (1974): 495–502. Jacob Licht designates the large segment of the Community Rule in 1QS 5:1–6:23 as "Statutes for the volunteers" rather than following the opening heading in 1QS 5:1, see Licht, *Rule Scroll*, 19; for discussion see Hempel, "Rules," in CDSS, 405–412, especially 408.

[63] See Guilbert, "Règle de la Communauté," 39.

[64] Fitzgerald, "MTNDBYM;" see also Klein, "Right Spirit," 184–189.

[65] See 5.4.6 below.

gregation is also attested in Num 35 and 2 Chron 29. Both chapters deal with cultic contributions to the tabernacle (Num) and the Temple during Hezekiah's cultic reform (2 Chron) respectively. Each of these two chapters include the root *ndb* in this context.[66] Sara Japhet notes with reference to 2 Chron 29:31 that whereas the assembly offered sacrifices and thank offerings, a group referred as "those of a generous disposition" (כל־ נדיב לב) went above and beyond Hezekiah's instructions by also offering whole burnt offerings.[67]

Exod 35 deals with the building of the wilderness shrine as well as the offerings to be brought in the context of the new start epitomized by the renewed covenant after the idolatrous Golden Calf incident. The chapter follows the account of Moses cutting two new tablets to replace the tablets that he had shattered on coming face to face with the idolatrous worship of the Gold Calf (Exod 32–34). Likewise 2 Chron 29 deals with a new beginning represented by Hezekiah's cultic reform. As in the present passage both the root *ndb* as well as priests and non-priests *together* restore relations with God, and the fervour of the laity is particularly pronounced in each episode. A similar context accompanies the terminology in Ezra 2:68 and Neh 11:2. According to Ezra 2:68 some of the lay heads of the fathers' houses are fervently committed (התנדבו) to support the re-establishment of the Temple at the seminal moment of approaching the sanctuary for the first time. Similarly Neh 11:2 refers to a group who were fervently committed (המתנדבים) to relocating to Jerusalem, perhaps in addition to those identified by lot referred to in Neh 11:1. In short, close attention to the use of the verb *ndb* in the Hebrew Bible suggests that the choice of this language here emphasizes the fervent commitment of both the priestly and lay constituencies of the emerging movement to mark a moment to "reboot" relations with the deity.

5:1 On the combination of turning back from (שוב) and evil (רע) see Jer 44:5[68] and the requirement in the war camp "to keep yourselves from all evil" in Deut 23:10 (Hebrew).[69] The instruction "to turn back from all evil" is emphatically positioned as the first objective stated at the very beginning of the manuscript in 4Q258 1:1.[70] This admonition is also prominently placed at a major juncture in 1QS 5:1 and 4Q256 9:1, the central section of the longer text of Community Rules that on our reading predates the supplementation with 1QS 1–4 and paralells.[71]

---

[66] Cf. Num 35:21, 29 and 2 Chron 29:31; further, Fitzgerald, "MTNDBYM," 496–497 and Hugh Williamson, *1 and 2 Chronicles*. NCBC (Grand Rapids, MI: Eerdmans; London: Marshall, Morgan & Scott, 1982), 359.

[67] Japhet, *I & II Chronicles: A Commentary*. OTL (Louisville, KY: Westminster/John Knox Press, 1993), 929.

[68] Cf. Wernberg-Møller, *Manual of Discipline*, 89.

[69] See also the admonition at the end of the Lord's Prayer in Matt 6:13 and already Flusser, "Qumrân and Jewish 'Apotropaic' Prayers."

[70] See 5.1.1 above.

[71] Cf. 1.5 above.

Whether or not one is convinced of this wider argument on the composition history of the Community Rules, the emphatic position of the admonition to turn back from all evil deserves more attention than it has received. In the longer text of the Community Rules this warning comes immediately after the Teaching on the Two Spirits which is likewise concerned with a looming backdrop of opposing forces of light and darkness as well as good and evil.[72] Whereas the Teaching on the Two Spirits suggests a significant influence of a predestined spiritual make-up upon humanity, 1QS 5:1 and parallels encourage those addressed to make the right choices.[73] A concern to keep a conscious distance from all evil and cleave instead to good deeds also occurs in 1QS 1:4–5 // 4Q255 1:5–6 and is picked up again in 1QS 1:7.[74] While the reference to "all evil" is juxtaposed with "good works" in 1QS 1:4–5 // 4Q255 1:5–6, the present passage contrasts "all evil" with holding fast to the commandments as ordained by God.

5:1 (and 9) The references to God's wish (רצון) is a plus in 1QS over against 4Q256 and 4Q258. This is also the first occurrence of the noun in the 1QS manuscript. Both here and in 1QS 5:9, where God's will recurs as part of another more substantial plus in 1QS, the term is associated with the law and emphasizes the sons of Zadok as the privileged conduits of the divine will. Resembling aspects of the present context, four references to God's will in 1QS 8–9 describe the emergence of a new community in cultic terms associated with atonement[75] or pleasing freewill offerings.[76] Finally, the term is also associated with the Maskil as mediating the will of God.[77]

5.4.3 A Shared First Founding Narrative (1QS 5:1c–2a // 4Q256 9:2b // 4Q258 1:2a)

5:1c–2a The two infinitives "to keep separate" (להבדל) from the people of injustice and "to form a community" (להיות ליחד) can be taken either to refer to separate aspirations[78] or as concomitant events.[79] Several considerations sup-

---

[72] On the significance of this transition from the Teaching on the Two Spirits to the admonition to turn back from evil in the discourse of 1QS see also Hinojosa, "A Synchronic Approach," 158.

[73] See Brand, *Evil Within and Without*.

[74] On the prominence of apotropaic texts in Cave 4 and their implications for our understanding of an underlying belief in the pervasive influence of malevolent forces reflected in the Community Rules see 1.2.1 above.

[75] Cf. 1QS 8:6 // 4Q259 2:15; 1QS 8:10 // [4Q258 6:4] and 1QS 9:4 // 4Q258 7:5.

[76] See 1QS 9:5 // 4Q258 7:6. For a similarly cultic context for a reference to God's will see 4Q265 (Miscellaneous Rules) 7:9; Chapter 11 below and Hempel, *Qumran Rule Texts in Context*, 92–94.

[77] Compare 1QS 9:13 // 4Q259 3:8; 1QS 9:15 // 4Q259 3:11; 1QS 9:23 // 4Q258 8:8 // 4Q259 4:5 // 4Q260 1:1 and 1QS 9:24 // 4Q258 8:9.

[78] So, e. g., Brownlee, *Dead Sea Manual*, 18.

[79] So Knibb, *Qumran Community*, 104–105.

port the view that the two events are affiliated. Firstly, the material presented in 6.1 elaborates on a firm link between joining the community by oath and keeping away from the people of injustice. While 1QS has a much fuller text at that point, all preserved manuscripts present the separation from the people of injustice as a defining part of entering the community by oath. While such a close connection is implied in the shorter text of 4Q256 // 4Q258, it is explicit in 1QS 5:10b which reads "And he shall take upon himself a covenant oath to separate from all the people of injustice" (ואשר יקים בברית על נפשו להבדל מכול אנשי העול). Moreover, while 1QS 5:2 // 4Q258 1:2 single out law and property as key aspects of communal life, the same domains are barred with reference to the people of injustice.[80]

It is striking that we are presented with an emphatic separation from another group, rather than the Jewish world outside, at this crucial juncture in the narrative of the community's emergence.[81] The view that this passage refers to a separation from all other Jews or both Jews and gentiles is hard to uphold in light of the kinds of restrictions imposed on dealing with the people of injustice in 6.1 below.[82] In other words, the pivotal point of communal emergence as outlined here is also a momemt of communal schism. What we are about to learn regarding the people of injustice in 1QS 5:7b–20a // 4Q256 9:6b–13 // 4Q258 1:5b–13 makes it clear that this group once belonged to the author(s)'s movement and includes at least some individuals of remarkable authority as well as means.[83] The use of the verb בדל "to keep separate" from a congregation (עדה) is reminiscent of the gruesome divine response to the revolt of Korah, Dathan and Abiram and their followers in Num 16:20–21 where Moses and Aaron are instructed to separate themselves from this congregation.[84] Both here and in Num 16 the challenge that results in the need to draw a sharp differentiation comes from within.

The theme of separation from "the company of the people of injustice" also lies at the heart of the famous account of the withdrawal to the wilderness in 1QS 8:12b–16a // 4Q258 6:6b–8 // 4Q259 3:3b–6. Moreover, when the Maskil is charged with transmitting revealed instruction during the key period of preparing

---

[80] See 1QS 5:8b–11a // 4Q256 9:6–8a // 4Q258 1:5–7a.

[81] For an insightful analysis see also Jutta Jokiranta, "Black Sheep, Outsiders, and the Qumran Movement: Social-Psychological Perspectives on Norm-Deviant Behaviour," in *Social Memory and Social Identity in the Study of Early Judaism and Early Christianity*. Edited by Samuel Byrskog, Raimo Hakola and Jutta Jokiranta. NTOA/SUNT 116 (Göttingen: Vandenhoeck & Ruprecht, 2016), 151–174.

[82] See André Dupont-Sommer, *The Dead Sea Scrolls: A Preliminary Survey*. Trans. Margaret Rowley (Oxford: Blackwell, 1952), 50 and cf. Sacchi, *Regola*, 115.

[83] See Charlotte Hempel, "The Community and Its Rivals According to the Community Rule from Caves 1 and 4," *RevQ* 21 (2003): 47–81 and Jokiranta, "Black Sheep, Outsiders, and the Qumran Movement" as well as 6.1 and Chapters 9 and 10 below.

[84] Cf. Brownlee, *Dead Sea Manual*, 19.

the way to the wilderness his charges are admonished to keep away from those following paths of injustice.[85]

We also note echoes with the opening lines of the small law code in the Admonition of the Damascus Document (CD 6:14b–16a // 4Q266 3 ii 20–21) where the same verb "to separate" occurs with reference to "the children of destruction" who are accused of acquiring unclean wealth of wicked wickedness.

5:2 In addition to the separation from the people of injustice and the account of community formation being attested across otherwise divergent manuscripts, the present passage also constitutes the first occurrence of the term torah across all manuscripts with the exception of the expression "the people of the law" in the superscription in 4Q258 1:1 noted above. The prominence of torah in the context of an emerging community defining itself over against the congregation of the people of injustice suggests that matters of legal interpretation produced both communal affiliation as well as inter-communal tensions.[86] We get a flavour of the kinds of debates that were at issue between priestly groups in a number of texts from Qumran, especially in 4QMMT.[87]

The present passage envisages a principle commitment to sharing property.[88] We learn of a pooling of resources also in Acts 2:44–45. As in the present passage the context in Acts 2 describes a defining moment of decision on whether or not to join the early Christian movement. In Acts those present are overcome with fear (φόβος Acts 2:43), and salvation or judgment are at stake (Acts 2:47).

5.4.4 A Not so Divergent Leadership Model (1QS 5:2b–3b // 4Q256 9:2c–3a // 4Q258 1:2b–3a)

One of the most discussed features of the present passage is the striking difference between the manuscripts with 4Q256 and 4Q258 both lacking the reference to "the sons of Zadok" and "the multitude of the people of the community who hold fast to the covenant" and attributing an equivalent authoritative role much more succinctly to "the many."[89] The first indications of this fascinating and rich textual picture were offered by Milik in 1956.[90] The impact of the publication

---

[85] See 1QS 9:19b–21a and parallels as well as Chapter 14 below.

[86] So already Joseph Blenkinsopp, "Interpretation and the Tendency to Sectarianism: An Aspect of Second Temple History," in *Jewish and Christian Self-Definition*. Edited by Ed P. Sanders (Philadelphia, PA: Fortress, 1981), 2:1–26. Theodor Gaster's early translation of בתורה with "in a doctrinal sense" is hardly the meaning here, see *The Scriptures of the Dead Sea Sect in English Translation* (London: Secker & Warburg, 1957), 56.

[87] Cf. Qimron and Strugnell, DJD 10; Hanne von Weissenberg, "Miqṣat Maʿaśeh ha-Torah," in CDSS, 325–328 and Reinhard Kratz, ed., *Qumran 4QMMT: Some Precepts of the Law*. Sapere (Tübingen: Mohr Siebeck, forthcoming).

[88] See 1.4.3 above.

[89] Cf. also 1QS 5:9 // 4Q256 9:7–8 // 4Q258 1:7 as well as 1QS 9:14 // 4Q259 3:10.

[90] Milik, "Le travail d'édition," 61.

of this divergence between 1QS and 4Q256 // 4Q258 has dominated initial assessments of the relationship between these witnesses and the implications to be drawn from this for the literary growth of the Community Rules. It is vital, however, to come to a judgment on both of these questions on the basis of the full gamut of evidence without unduly privileging this passage. Given the diverse, and at times contradictory, portrayals of the leadership structure that emerge from various sections of the Community Rules manuscripts it is crucial to have the full picture in view. The key message to emerge from the evidence as a whole is that the precedence of the sons of Zadok in 1QS 5:2 and 5:9 does not tell the whole story even within 1QS where the sons of Aaron play a comparable leadership role in 1QS 5:21 and 1QS 9:7. In addition, 1QS 6:19 allocates precedence during the admissions process to "the priests." It is easier to explain the introduction of the sons of Zadok as prominent leaders into 1QS 5 – a rather contained part of 1QS – than to suppose that otherwise divergent manuscripts like 1QS and 4Q258 were harmonized at 1QS 5:21.[91] The only other reference to the sons of Zadok in 1QS employs the designation with reference to community member to be assessed by the Maskil.[92] In an insightful analysis Nathan MacDonald has shown that the longer text of 1QS emerges as exegetically derived from Ezek 44, Isa 56 and 1 Sam 2 – a cluster of texts that are also reflected in the interpretation of Ezek 44 in the Damascus Document (CD 3–4).[93]

The term רוב "multitude" occurs repeatedly in parts of the Teaching on the Two Spirits that deal with the innate qualities of the spirits of truth and injustice and their followers[94] and is found once in the Final Hymn where it refers to God's abundant goodness.[95] The current passage is one of four instances where a lay group designated as "a multitude of x" is referred to as an authoritative body alongside a leading priestly group.[96] It is significant, however, that the conjunction "and" that places "the multitude of the people of the community" alongside the sons of Zadok in 1QS has been added secondarily above the line.[97] This correction may preserve vestiges of the scribal adjustments to facilitate

---

[91] See further 6.1 below.

[92] Cf. 14.2.2 below. For discussion see Robert A. Kugler, "Priests," in EDSS 2:688–293; Ulrich Dahmen, "צָדוֹק ṣādôq," ThWQ 3:379–383; Hempel, *Qumran Rule Texts in Context*, 109–119; 211–227 and Alison Schofield, *From Qumran to the Yaḥad*, 114–152.

[93] MacDonald, *Priestly Rule: Polemic and Biblical Interpretation in Ezekiel 44*. BZAW 476 (Berlin: De Gruyter, 2015), 114–145. For a connection between exegetical elaboration and the Zadokite discourse in 1QS see also Puech, "Review of *Textual Development*," 451.

[94] Compare 1QS 4:3, 4, 5; 1QS 4:7 // 4Q257 5:4; and 1QS 4:10, 12, 16.

[95] See 1QS 11:14 // 4Q264 1.

[96] The terminology used in 1QS for the lay leadership is as fluid as that used to refer to priestly leaders. Some translations render רוב with "majority," see Brownlee, *Dead Sea Manual*, 18–19; for discussion see Wernberg-Møller, *Manual of Discipline*, 92. Beyond this passage see 1QS 5:9; 5:22 and 6:19.

[97] See further 5.3 above.

the supplementation of the text in 1QS with "the sons of Zadok." A comparable piece of evidence is represented by the addition of "truth" in 1QS 5:3.[98]

While the exclusive reference to the leadership of "the many" in 4Q256 // 4Q258 is striking, a close reading of the passage and its wider context in S makes it clear that we are not dealing with a fundamental difference here, or in the S manuscripts more broadly, on promoting an exclusively priestly or lay leadership model.[99] Firstly, while 1QS emphatically places the sons of Zadok first, a lay group is to act alongside them. Secondly, the language of fervent commitment expressed with the *hitpael* participle of *ndb* identifies the dedication of a particularly committed lay group for cultic renewal. Crucially, this fervour presupposes an environment inclusive of priests and laity as demonstrated in our analysis of two important inter-texts (Num 35 and 2 Chron 29) in 5.4.2 above. Thirdly, the final sub-section to be dealt with in this chapter makes it clear that both 1QS and 4QS envisage a role for both Israel and Aaron at an incipient phase of communal life.[100] And finally, the opening of the section outlining the meetings of the many in 1QS 6:8–9 ("This is the rule for the meetings of the many. Everyone shall sit according to their rank: the priests first, the elders second and then all the people shall sit each according to their rank.") makes it clear that "the many" include priests alongside laity.[101] We come across a second reference to "the many" in the context of a section on Rules Dealing with Reproof.[102] These crucial endorsements of the authority of the many have been drowned out by the captivating endorsement of the sons of Zadok here and in 6.1.2.1 below.

5:3b The Hebrew underlying the translation "decisions shall be taken" actually speaks of the casting of lots. It seems likely that the processes envisaged here relied on the authority and judgment of the sons of Zadok rather than an actual process of casting lots.[103] The sons of Zadok's oversight covers law, property and judgment (1QS) whereas "the many" have responsibility to monitor law and property (4QS). Such a remit is compatible also with what is said about the *potential* influence of the people of injustice in 6.1.2.1.[104]

---

[98] Cf. 5.4.5 below.

[99] On the terminology see Milik, *Ten Years of Discovery*, 101.

[100] See 5.4.6 below.

[101] Cf. 6.5 below and pace Hannah Harrington, "Purity," EDSS 2:724–728, 725 who takes rabbim to refer to the laity exclusively.

[102] Cf. 1QS 6:1 // 4Q258 2:5 // 4Q263 1–2 and 6.2 below.

[103] Cf. Alexander and Vermes, DJD 26:223; see also Lange, "גּוֹרְל *gôrāl*." Brownlee notes the implied divine sanction behind the decisions even if lots are not used, see *Dead Sea Manual*, 18–19.

[104] See also 6.1.4.2.

5.4.5 Shared Core Principles (1QS 5:3c–5a // 4Q256 9:3b–4 // 4Q258 1:3b–4a)

As demonstrated in some detail in 3.4.3 above, the use of the list of virtues extolled in Micah 6:8 in the Covenant Ceremony (1QS 2:24–25a) shares significant overlap with what we find here.[105] In the context of Micah 6 a series of rhetorical questions on the desirability of sacrifices culminates in an endorsement of the list of virtues drawn upon here. As in 1QS 2, Micah 6:8 is supplemented by references to truth and humility. In the present passage truth is part of a plus in 1QS over against 4QS. On the model of the growth of the S tradition adopted here, the material in 1QS 1–4 and parallels was added to regulations beginning in 1QS 5 and parallels. This suggests that the plus in 1QS attests the composition-historically earliest attestation of the supplementation of Micah 6:8 with "truth" in the Community Rules. Moreover, the evidence here suggests that the plus in 1QS was added at a time when the supplement "humility" was already present across the manuscripts. Guilbert proposes that "truth" goes back to a different hand in 1QS 5:3. If he is right this might take us to the very pen strokes of the hand that made this supplementation here. The beginning of a second plus in 1QS that continues into 5.2.6 expands the shared admonition not to stray by walking in the hardness of one's heart. Remarkably similar language recurs in the account of an emerging council of the community in 8.2.1 below which is followed in 8.2.2, as here, by an account of the emerging community in cultic terms.

5:4c–5a The plus in 1QS elaborates on a shared warning not to go astray.

5:6c–7a This is the first part of a second, longer plus in 1QS which continues into 5.2.6. The plus expands on the admonition not to stray by walking in the hardness of one's heart.[106]

5.4.6 A Shared Second Founding Narrative (1QS 5:5b–7a // 4Q256 9:5–6a // 4Q258 1:4b–5a)

In a second shared founding narrative the emerging community is described in language of construction ("laying a foundation of truth" and "a house of truth"). This language is combined with a reference to a fervent commitment to holiness in Aaron and a portrayal of the new community as a figurative Temple. The concerns with the community's role in facilitating atonement as well as the reference to judgment voiced in the two plusses in 1QS also occur in 1QS 8:1–7a // 4Q258 // 4Q259 as well as in 4Q265 (Miscellaneous Rules) 7:7–10.[107] This extensive

---

[105] See also 4.1.2 above.

[106] See further 6.1.3 below.

[107] For an earlier analysis that draws attention to intertexts within S but failed to note the allusion to Micah 6:8 see Georg Klinzing, *Die Umdeutung des Kultus in der Qumrangemeinde*

cluster of related statements that describe the foundation of a community in terms that fuse cultic and ethical terminology suggests a grappling with these issues while presenting the emergence of the community in S as well as in 4Q265. The sequence from an allusion to Micah 6:8 to an Israel and Aaron motif is also attested in 1QS 8:8b–10a and parallels.[108]

When looked at in the context of our discussion in 5.4.4, the traditional language used to refer to the priestly-lay model in terms of Aaron and Israel here and frequently elsewhere in the Community Rules is noteworthy.[109] It is, rather, the phrase "the sons of Zadok and the multitude of the people of the community" that is a new development.

5:6c The final part of the shared statement seems to introduce a third group: those who join them as a community. The *niphal* of לוה "to join" refers to stages in an emerging community also in CD 4:3. It seems unlikely that levites, in particular, are in view here[110] as opposed to community members in general.

---

und im Neuen Testament. SUNT 7 (Göttingen: Vandenhoeck & Ruprecht, 1971) and Hempel, *Qumran Rule Texts in Context*, 84–92.

[108] See Chapter 8 below. For a leadership model comprising Aaron and Israel as the priestly and lay elements see also 6.1.4.2.

[109] Cf. 6.1.4.2 below and CD 6:2–3; see also Steudel, "The Damascus Document (D) as a Rewriting," 613.

[110] So Brownlee, *Dead Sea Manual*, 21.

6. Rules Concerning Meetings (1QS 5:7b–6:23 // 4Q256 9:6b–13; 11:5–8, 11–13 // 4Q258 1:5b–13; 2:1–10b; 3:1–3 // 4Q261 1a–b:1–6; 2a–c:2b–5; 3:1? // 4Q263 1–5)

The previous chapter presented a series of objectives and presented – in 1QS and 4QS respectively – two of the many leadership models that we come across in the Community Rules. The present chapter will examine a large number of regulations that deal with meetings of various kinds. The material in 6.1 offers an account of entrance and written registration into the covenant followed by an annual assessment of existing members. It is important to acknowledge that these processes are explicitly contextualised in 1QS 5:7b as taking place during an assembly as a community (בהאספם ליחד).[1] This is followed by a section in 6.2 that deals with reproof. I will argue that the context of this material as part of a cluster of texts dealing with meetings has not been given sufficient weight in previous studies.[2] The regulations presented in 6.3 and 6.4 deal with meetings in a series of dwelling places on the one hand, and as fellowship groups of ten and above led by a priest on the other hand. A final section lays down processes to be followed during three different types of meetings of the many. It is the second of those, presented in 6.5.2.2, that is often prioritised in discussions of communal meetings in the Community Rules. While this passage offers a well thought-through framework for conducting meetings it is important to be aware that it forms part of a diverse set of rules pertaining to meetings including those of the many.

6.1 Admission and Assessment of New and Current Members

(1QS 5:7b–24a // 4Q256 9:6b–13 // 4Q258 1:5b–13; 2:1–4a // 4Q261 1a–b: 1–6)

6.1.1 Introduction

The account of admitting new members into the covenant by means of swearing an oath marks the beginning of a new topic, the substance of which is shared

---

[1] On this transition and the evidence of 4Q256 and 4Q258 see 6.1.1 below.

[2] Cf. 6.2.1 below.

across the extant manuscripts.[3] In 1QS 5:7b the transition is marked with the words, "And these are their prescribed ways according to all these statutes when they assemble as a community" which leaves little doubt that the proceedings outlined are envisaged to take place during a communal gathering. The presence of a *vacat* in 4Q258[4] as well as the conjunction in both 4Q256 and 4Q258 also indicate a new beginning, though one that follows on more smoothly from the previous section. The lack of paratextual indications such as a *vacat* or a paragraphos at the start of this section in 1QS is striking since a *vacat* and paragraphos mark the start of a new sentence within the same section at 1QS 5:13 where the manuscripts converge after a substantial plus in 1QS. Something comparable is evident in 1QS 5:25 where we find a *vacat* and paragraphos in 1QS again at a point where the manuscripts converge after a more modest plus in 1QS within the section on reproof.[5]

The regulations on admission into the community by oath are followed by rules on conducting an assessment of and compiling a register for new members (6.1.4.2) as well as rules for an annual assessment of current members (6.1.4.3).

6.1.2 Translation[6]

6.1.2.1 The Admission of New Members by Swearing an Oath and Separation from the People of Injustice (1QS 5:7b–20a // 4Q256 9:6b–13 // 4Q258 1:5b–13)

1QS 5	4Q256 9 // 4Q258 1
[7b]*And these are their prescribed ways according to all these statutes when they assemble as a community.*	LACKING IN 4Q256 AND 4Q258
[7c]Everyone who joins the council of the community	9[6] /1[5] *Vacat And* everyone who joins <u>the council of</u> 1[6][the communi]<u>ty</u>
[8]*shall enter into the covenant of God in the presence of all those with fervent commitment.*	
He shall take upon themselves a binding *oath* to return to the law of Moses *according to all that He has commanded* with all (their) [9]heart and all (their) soul *concerning* all that has been revealed from	<u>shall ta[k]e upon themselves</u> 9[7]a binding *oath* to <u>return</u> to the <u>law</u> of Mos<u>es</u> with all (their) heart and and <u>all (their) soul (concerning) all that has been revealed from</u>
it	1[7]*the L[aw*

---

[3] Cf. 6.1.4.1 below.

[4] See 6.1.3 below.

[5] Further, 1.5.1.3.3 above as well as 6.2.4 and Chapter 8 below.

[6] On the principles behind the transparent composite text for the translation of 4Q256 and 4Q258 see 1.7 and 5.2 note 20 above.

1QS 5	4Q256 9 // 4Q258 1

to the sons of Zadok the priests who keep the covenant and seek His favour and to the multitude of the people of their covenant ¹⁰*who together are fervently committed to His truth and to conduct themselves according to His will. And he shall take upon himself a covenant oath*
to keep separate from all the people of injustice
who walk ¹¹*in the path of wickedness. For they have been left out from His covenant because they have not sought nor asked for His advice concerning His statutes in order to have knowledge of the hidden things in which they have gone astray* ¹²*so as to incur guilt. As for the revealed things they have acted deliberately so that anger flares up for judgment and vengeance by the curses of the covenant, acting in the face of great* ¹³{j}*udgments for eternal destruction without a remnant. Vacat.*
He shall not
enter the waters to
touch the purity of the people of holiness,
for they are not purified ¹⁴*unless they turn away from their wickedness, for they are unclean among all those who disobey His word.*
No one shall get involved with him in matters of *work or property*
lest he burden him ¹⁵*with guilty transgression. Rather he shall keep apart from him in all things for thus it is written, "You shall keep away from every false thing".*
No one from among the people of the community ¹⁶shall be accountable to them with regard to any law or judgment.
No one shall

eat
or drink anything
from their property nor accept anything
at all

---

acc]ording [to] 9⁸*the council of the people of the community.*

They
shall keep separate from [al]l the people of injustice.

They [s]hall not

Touch the purity of the people of 9⁹
1⁸holiness,

He shall not eat with him in [co]mmunity.

No [o]ne from among the people of the community [shall be accountable] to them 9¹⁰with regard to any 1⁹law or judgment.
No one shall enter [the waters to undertake] *work* (jointly);
nor shall 9¹¹*anyone from among the people of holiness* eat

1¹⁰[from their property]nor [accept anythi]ng

1QS 5	4Q256 9 // 4Q258 1
from them *[17]which has not been paid for according to that which is written, "Shun the human being in whose nostrils is breath for what is his or her value?" For [18]all those not included in His covenant are to keep themselves and everything that is theirs separate.* *And no holy person shall* depend upon any worthless [19]deeds for worthless are all those who do not know His covenant. And He will wipe out all those who hold His word in contempt from the earth, and *all* their deeds are impure [20a]before Him, and all their property is unclean. LACKING IN 1QS	[from them]. <u>*And they shall not*</u> <u>depend upon</u> [any] [9 12]<u>worthless</u> [de]<u>eds for</u> <u>worthless are a</u>ll those who <u>do not k</u>[now [1 11]His covenant.] <u>And He will wipe out</u> [all those who hol]<u>d His word in contempt</u> [9 13]<u>from the earth and</u> their <u>deeds are</u> imp<u>ure</u> bef[ore] <u>Him,</u> [and al]<u>l</u> [their property is unclean]. [1 12][ ] mem *nations and oaths, devotions and vows are in their mouths* [ ] [1 13][ ] TRACES OF LETTERS [ ]

6.1.2.2 Assessment and Registration of New Entrants into the Covenant (1QS 5:20b–23a // 4Q258 2:1–3a // 4Q261 1a–b: 1–4a)

1QS 5
[20b]And when (a person) enters into the covenant in order to act according to all these statutes and in order to join the holy congregation they shall examine [21]his spirit in the community distinguishing between one candidate and the next according to his insight and

1QS 5	4Q258 2
and the lawfulness of *his* deeds according to the authority of the sons of Aaron who are *together* fervently committed to uphold	[1]and the lawfulness of *their* deeds according to the authority of the sons of Aaron who are fervently committed to uphold

1QS 5	4Q258 2	4Q261 1a–b
[22]His covenant and to observe all His statutes which He has commanded to obey	His covenant and to observe all His statutes which He has commanded [2]to obey	[1]His [covena]nt and to [observe all of] His [st]atutes which He has commanded to ob[ey]

1QS 5	4Q258 2	4Q261 1a–b
And according to the authority of the multitude of Israel who are fervently com- mitted	according to the authority of the multitude of Israel who are fervently com- mitted	[2] [according to the authority of the multitu]de of Is[rael who are fervently com- mit]ted
to return together to His covenant.	*to return together.*	*to dwell together.*
[23] *And they shall write them down in the register*	*And it shall be written down*	*and to writ[e down]*
each before his fellow	each before (his) fellow *in the register each*	[3] each befo]re [his] fell[ow *in the register*
according to his insight and	according to his insight [3] *and* *the lawfulness of*	according to] his insight and *the la[w]fulness of*
his deeds so that	his deeds so that	his deeds [4] [so that]
they may all obey one another,	*they may all obey one anoth[er],*	
those of inferior rank obey- ing their superiors.	those of inferior rank obeying their superiors.	those of inferior rank [may obey their superiors.]

6.1.2.3 Annual Assessment of Current Members (1QS 5:23b–24a //
4Q258 2:3b–4a // 4Q261 1a–b: 4b–6)

1QS 5	4Q258 2	4Q261 1a–b
And they shall [24] assess their spirit and	[3b] And they shall assess their spirit and	[4b] And they shall asses]s [their spirit [5] and]
their deeds	*the lawfulness of* [4] *their deeds*	*the [lawfulness of] their [deeds*
every year so as to bring prosperity to each person according to his insight	every year so to bring prosperity to each person according to [his] insight	every year so as to bring prosperity to e]ach [person according to his insight]
and the perfection of his conduct		
and to hold back (another) according to his tendency to sin.	and to hold back (another) according to his tendency to sin.	[6] [and to hold back (another) according to his ten]dency to s[in]

6.1.3 Textual Notes

5:7 The singular תכון in 1QS "These are their prescribed ways" is unexpected,
cf. the comparable formula in 1QS 9:21 ואלה תכוני למשכיל "These are the rules of

conduct for the Maskil." The sense is clearly plural here too. Either a collective sense of the singular or scribal error can account for the text we have.[7]

5:7 The word יחד "community" which immediately precedes the plus in 1QS also forms the final word of the plus. This leaves us with the same transition from "community" to "everyone who joins the council of the community" across the divergent manuscripts. A scribal lapse is therefore a possibility here.[8] However, given the large number of plusses in 1QS it is possible that this is simply another plus. From this point on all three extent manuscripts converge. Unlike 1QS, both 4Q256 9:6 and 4Q258 1:5 begin this section with a conjuction "And everyone who enters" after a clear *vacat* in 4Q258 1:5. That *vacat* is not indicated in a number of editions.[9]

5:8: קום *hiphil* is used here in the sense "to swear."[10]

5:8–9 As indicated in the translation, the text of 1QS contains substantial plusses that expand the more concise but clear account in 4Q256 and 4Q258. A good indication for the priority of the shorter text in 4Q256 9:7 and 4Q258 1:6 ("to return to the law of Moses with all [their] heart and all [their] soul") is attested in the comparable account in CD 15:9 where the shorter phrase also occurs.

5:9 The preposition "concerning" (ל) attested in 1QS is lacking in 4Q258 1:6. It has been supplied in our translation.[11]

5:10 *He* has been omitted from the infinitive *hitpael* of הלך in 1QS, a phenomenon that occurs frequently in the Scrolls.[12]

5:11 An original further third person plural perfect דרשו in 1QS has been corrected to the form with suffix דרשהו.[13]

5:12 The reading לאששמה in 1QS is commonly emended to לאשמה. This noun "guiltiness" with preposition underlies our somewhat loose translation "so as to incur guilt."[14]

---

[7] Cf. Wernberg-Møller, *Manual of Discipline*, 41. Brownlee's translation "these are to direct their ways" presupposes the verb תכן, see *Dead Sea Manual*, 20.

[8] Further, Alexander and Vermes, DJD 26:97 and Charlesworth, PTSDSSP 1:21 n. 96. Note that the reference in Charlesworth should read 1QS 5:6–7 rather than lines 7–8.

[9] Cf., e. g., Alexander and Vermes, DJD 26:93; Corrado Martone, *La "Regola della Comunità:" Edizione critica* (Turin: Silvio Zamorani, 1995), 98; Metso, *Textual Development*, 41; Schofield, *From Qumran to the Yaḥad*, n.p. and Qimron, PTSDSSP 1:72. A notable exception is García Martínez and Tigchelaar, DSSSE, 520.

[10] Cf. Wernberg-Møller, *Manual of Discipline*, 95 n. 34 and Heinz-Josef Fabry, "קום *qûm*," ThWQ 3:509–516.

[11] See Alexander and Vermes, DJD 26:95, 97 and 6.1.4.1 below.

[12] Further, Qimron, HDSS, 48.

[13] See Wernberg-Møller, *Manual of Discipline*, 41 and Qimron, PTSDSSP 1:22 n. 120.

[14] Cf. Lohse, *Texte aus Qumran*, 18. On acting "deliberately" (literally "with a high hand") see Tzoref, "Use of Scripture," 223–224.

5:12 Initial *mem* has been erased in בם{מ}שפטים "judgments" in 1QS which leaves us with a combination of the preposition *bet* followed by "judgments" which I render in context "acting in the face of great judgments."

5:13 Both a mid-line *vacat* and a paragraphos in 1QS coincide with the end of a substantial plus in this manuscript.[15]

5:14 *Nun* has been added above the line in 1QS after the scribe had erased another letter the remains of which resemble *shin*.[16]

5:15 Our translation presupposes the *hiphil* ישיב in analogy with 1QS 5:2 above.[17]

5:15 The final letter *vav* in "the people of" at the end of this line in 1QS has been added above the line.

5:16 The quiescent *aleph* has dropped out in יוכל in 1QS.[18]

5:16 Alexander and Vermes read יוחד "make common cause" in 4Q256 9:10.[19] However, based on the recent infrared image by Shai Halevi at LLDSSDL B-366921 this is not materially possible. The translation above reads "he shall (not) enter" (יבו) with García Martínez and Tigchelaar.[20] The reading יבו is also presupposed by Catherine Murphy who refers to 4Q256 as including the phrase "to go" in this context.[21] On the significance of this important variant see 6.1.4.1 in the Commentary below.

5:18–19 4Q258 1:10 reads מעשי ההבל with the article over against מעשי הבל in 1QS.

5:20 Qimron and Wernberg-Møller read להיחד "for the community."[22] The translation above is based on the reading להוחד "to join" adopted by Burrows.[23]

5:20 4Q258 1:12–13 preserves a plus that refers to nations, oaths, devotions and vows in the context of separating from the people of injustice.

5:22 The non-standard spelling of the third masculine singular suffix appended to the plural noun "statutes" in 4Q261 1a–b: 1 is the result of a contraction of the diphthong and the uniform pronunciation of long ō as suggested by Qimron.[24]

5:22 In 1QS an initial central letter *yod* in "the multitude of" was first marked for deletion with dots placed above and below and subsequently erased.[25] The

---

[15] See further 1.5.3.1 and 6.1.1 above and section 6.2 as well as Chapter 8 below.

[16] So Wernberg-Møller, *Manual of Discipline*, 41.

[17] Cf. also Wernberg-Møller, *Manual of Discipline*, 41.

[18] See GKC 69h and Ezek 42:5; also 1QS 6:13 below and Wernberg-Møller, *Manual of Discipline*, 97.

[19] See Alexander and Vermes, DJD 26:53–54.

[20] García Martínez and Tigchelaar, DSSSE, 512–513 and Metso, *Textual Development*, 28.

[21] Cf. Murphy, *Wealth in the Dead Dead Sea Scrolls*, 134.

[22] See Qimron, DSSHW 1:218 and Wernberg-Møller, *Manual of Discipline*, 41.

[23] Burrows, *Dead Sea Scrolls*, n. p. and Lohse, *Texte aus Qumran*, 18.

[24] Qimron, HDSS, 59 and see on 5:23 below.

[25] Cf. Martin G. Abegg, *The Dead Sea Scrolls Concordance. Volume One: The Non-Biblical Texts from Qumran [Parts 1–2]* (Leiden: Brill, 2003), 2:672, 684; Qimron, DSSHW1:218 and Tov, *Scribal Practices*, 192.

outline of the erased letter is visible under magnification in the digital images at the Shrine of the Book. The term "multitude" with plene spelling occurs frequently in 1QS (1QS 4:3, 4, 5, 7, 10 [x2], 12, 16; 5:2, 9; 6:19; 11:14). Wernberg-Møller, following Dupont Sommer, suggests the dots indicate that "children of" should be added and translates "the multitude of the children of Israel."[26] In support of Wernberg-Møller it is noteworthy that where רוב is used elsewhere in 1QS of a group of people it is always accompanied by "the people of" (אנשי) the yahad or the covenant, see 1QS 5:2, 9; 6:19. In all three instances the term is either lacking in or not attested in 4QS.[27] While 4Q261 1a–b: 2 only preserves remains of final *bet*, 4Q258 2:1 clearly reads "the multitude of Israel" (רוב ישראל) which makes it likely the same was intended in 1QS.

5:22 4Q261 1a–b: 2 reads "[and according to the authority of the multitu]de of Is[rael who have voluntee]red "to dwell (לשבת) together" where 1QS and 4Q258 2:2 read לשוב "to return together."

5:23 4Q258 reads a plus comprising a second "each" (איש) in 4Q258 2:2, perhaps the result of dittography in איש לפי "each according to" arising from the preceding איש לפני "each before."

5:23 On the spelling of the suffix in "his deeds" in 4Q261 1a–b: 3 see the note on 5:22 (4Q261 1a–b: 1) above.

5:23 The words "all of them" shall obey "one another" are lacking from 4Q261.[28]

5:24 "Their spirits" (את רוחם) is written in scripta continua in 1QS.

6.1.4 Commentary

6.1.4.1 The Admission of New Members by Swearing an Oath and Separation from the People of Injustice (1QS 5:7b–20a // 4Q256 9:6b–13 // 4Q258 1:5b–13)

We suggested in 6.1.1 that the plus in 1QS 5:7 clearly locates the admission into the covenant as part of a community assembly (בהאספם ליחד) in the longer text of 1QS.[29] This is the only instance where אסף occurs in the Community Rules in the sense of a gathering or assembly. The verb is found in the Calendar for Praise that forms part of the Final Hymn where it refers to the cycle of heavenly lights being gathered in.[30] Translations that take this verb here as referring to the

---

[26] Wernberg-Møller, *Manual of Discipline*, 29, 99.

[27] Cf. Chapters 5 and 10.2.3.

[28] Cf. Qimron, PTSDSSP 1:24 and Alexander and Vermes, DJD 26:101.

[29] See Heinz-Joseph Fabry, "אָסַף *'āsap*," ThWQ 1:251–255, 253; also Brownlee, *Dead Sea Manual*, 20; Lohse, *Texte aus Qumran*, 19 and "אסף I," HAWTTM 1:157–159.

[30] See 1QS 10:1, 2, 3 // 4Q256 19:1.

process of joining the community in 1QS 5:7 are less convincing.[31] It is unlikely, moreover, that the act of joining the community by swearing an oath is envisaged to take place in private in the shorter text found in 4Q256 and 4Q258.

This first sub-section takes up a good deal of the vocabulary and concerns introduced in the immediately preceding section, such as the prominence of the sons of Zadok in 1QS.[32] Beyond radical differences between 1QS and 4QS on the question of leadership, the shared language to refer to the community which new entrants join in terms of "the council of the community" in both 1QS and 4Q258 needs to be acknowledged also. As the passage continues, 4QS retains this terminology by referring to the leadership as "the people of the council of the community" (4Q256 9:7–8 // 4Q258 1:7). 1QS refers instead again to the leadership of the sons of Zadok and the people of their covenant (1QS 5:9b) which resembles what we saw in 5.2.4 above. The next sub-section (6.1.2.2) offers a leadership model comprised of the sons of Aaron and the multitude of Israel attested across three manuscripts including those that here promote the sons of Zadok or the people of the council of the community.[33]

The rules on admitting new members by swearing an oath to return to the law of Moses laid down here differ in complexity from the better-known admission process in several stages to be discussed in 6.5 below. They are also more closely related to the Covenant Ceremony in Chapter 3 above as well as the process described in CD 15:5b–10a and parallels.[34] Finally, this account presents a simpler admissions procedure than the protracted process laid out in 6.5.2.3.

As was the case in 5.2.2 above, admission into the community is closely associated across the manuscripts with a separation from the people of injustice. What is said about the areas where co-operation is forbidden makes it clear that this group of opponents are potential or, more likely, former affiliates.[35]

5:9 As noted in 6.1.3 above, 1QS reads "according to everything that has been revealed" לכול הנגלה where 4Q258 1:6 attests כל הנגלה without the preposition. The translation requires a preposition. Given the same phrase recurs in 1QS 8:15 where 1QS reads ככול הנגלה with 4Q258 6:7 again lacking the preposition, a repeated scribal error appears unlikely.[36]

---

[31] Cf., e. g., Knibb, *Qumran Community*, 107; Metso, "Biblical Quotations," 82; Leaney, *Rule of Qumran*, 161 and Wernberg-Møller, *Manual of Discipline*, 28.

[32] See 5.4.2–5.4.3 above.

[33] For further discussion see 6.1.4.2 below.

[34] For further details see Hempel, *Qumran Rule Texts in Context*, 28–31; Hempel, *Laws of the Damascus Document*, 73–90 and John Kampen, "'Torah' and Authority in the Major Sectarian Rules Texts from Qumran," in *The Scrolls and Biblical Traditions: Proceedings of the Seventh Meeting of the IOQS in Helsinki*. Edited by George J. Brooke et al. (Leiden: Brill, 2012), 231–254.

[35] See further 5.4.3 above as well as Chapters 9 and 10 below and Hempel, "The Community and Its Rivals."

[36] See Alexander and Vermes, DJD 26:97.

5:11 The verb "to be reckoned" recurs in a citation and interpretation of Isa 2:22 in 1QS 5:17 below.[37]

5:13 A mid-line *vacat* and paragraphos in 1QS mark a significant place in the textual development of the Community Rules just at a point where 1QS converges briefly with 4Q256 and 4Q258 in between two significant plusses.[38]

5:13–14 According to 1QS the people of injustice are denied the opportunity of entering the waters in order to touch the purity followed by a reminder of the need for repentance. The thrust of the prohibition is to indicate that such immersions would have been to no avail.[39] Scholars have often noted the lack of a reference to ritual immersion in the 4QS evidence.[40] However, as suggested in our reading and translation of the crucial remains of 4Q256 9:10, a very significant reference to ritual immersion is preserved in 4Q256 and almost certainly also 4Q258.[41]

The idea of touching the purity covers much more than eating as we will argue more fully in 6.5.4.3 below. 4Q256 // 4Q258 continue after the plus in 1QS with a separate prohibition of not eating in community (ביחד) with the people of injustice in language that denies the fellowhip of eating together (יחד). Comparable measures are laid down for the people of holiness who are admonished to preserve their property and purity vis-à-vis the people of deceit in Chapter 13 below.

5:14b–15 Here we have another plus in 1QS that includes and interprets a biblical quotation from Exod (LXX) 23:7.[42]

5:15b–16a The language used to prohibit honouring the authority of the people of injustice by "not being accountable to them with regard to any law or judgment" (שוב *hiphil* plus על פי) across the manuscripts mirrors the terminology with which deference to the authority of the sons of Zadok and the many is asserted in 5.2.4 and 5.4.4 above. In the latter passage the remit covers "law, property and justice" in 1QS and "law and property" in 4QS. This rather unexpected equivalence of referring, albeit in the negative, to the people of injustice in terms used elsewhere to refer to legitimate community leaders suggests the decried people of injustice are former or temporarily excluded members including discredited authority figures. It is hardly credible that non-members would be invested with that much kudos and respect. Such a scenario supports our reading of the account of the movement's foundation narrative in terms of a schism in 5.4.5 above. Moreover, read against the background of the regulations on being admitted into the community in 6.5.2.3 the status of the people of injus-

---

[37] Cf. also Tzoref, "Use of Scripture," 208–210.

[38] See further 1.5.1.3 and 6.1.3 above.

[39] See Cecilia Wassén, "The (Im)purity Levels of Communal Meals within the Qumran Movement," *JAJ* 7 (2016): 102–122, 109.

[40] So, e. g. Himmelfarb, "Impurity and Sin," 34.

[41] See 6.1.3 above and the comments on 1QS 5:16b below.

[42] Cf. Metso, "Biblical Quotatations," 83 and Tzoref, "Use of Scripture."

tice is equivalent to a temporary or permanent reversal of the admission process, a sanction known from the Penal Code.[43]

5:16b In 4Q256 9:10 and 4Q258 1:11 we find strong evidence for the presence of the prohibition "No one shall enter [the waters (in order to undertake)] work (jointly)" as argued on 5:13–14 and 6.1.3 above. This prohibition ties in with the emphasis on ritual purity attested both in halakhic texts from Qumran such as 4Q284a (Harvesting) and 4Q274 (Tohorot A) as well as the archaeological record which has revealed ritual immersion installations in agricultural contexts.[44] The possibility of reading "enter the covenant" is less likely in view of the considerable overlap with the continuation after the reference to immersion in 1QS 5:13 // 4Q256 9:9 // 4Q258 1:7–8 ("not to touch the purity of the people of holiness") above and a warning to individual people of holiness not to eat with them (i. e. the people of injustice), see 4Q256 9:10–11 // 4Q258 1:9. Moverover, as is the case here in 4QS, the reference to immersion in 1QS 5:13 is followed immediately by a prohibition of collaborating in matters of work.

5:17 1QS again attests a plus that includes an explicit biblical quotation, this time from Isa 2:22, which is then, as Metso has demonstrated, followed by a brief interpretation that plays on the verb "being counted, have esteem." Metso suggests the interpretation is rather removed from the context of Isaiah and concerns "an entirely different matter."[45] The context of Isa 2:22 in the book of Isaiah is a warning that the day of the Lord will deal harshly with the arrogant and haughty (Isa 2:12–22) which culminates in a warning to shun the one whose worth is questionable. A rhetorical question concludes this extended warning with a *niphal* participle of the root חשב which in Isaiah refers to such an individual's misled account of themselves. However, the semantic ambiguity of this verb also permits the sense of "being esteemed" which is perfectly suited for the present context as part of an admonition not to fall for the appearance of esteem of the people of injustice whose worth is questionable and their influence dangerous.[46] Moreover, while we know that the 1QS manuscript, which includes this quotation from Isa 2:22, was brought to Qumran from elsewhere,[47] it is likely that the immediately preceding description of repentant humanity seeking refuge on the day of the Lord in rocky caves and crevices in cliffs would have resonated with the location of Qumran once some of the movement had relocated there.[48] We seem to have here a further quotation from the book of Isaiah that

---

[43] For details see 6.5.4.3 below.

[44] Cf. Yonatan Adler, "Second Temple Period Ritual Baths Adjacent to Agricultural Installations: The Archaeological Evidence in Light of Halakhic Sources," *JJS* 59 (2008): 62–72 and Hempel, "Who is Making Dinner" as well as 6.5.4.3 below.

[45] Metso, "Biblical Quotations," 84.

[46] Cf. the Commentary on 1QS 5:15b–16a and paralles above.

[47] See 1.2.2 above.

[48] Further, George J. Brooke, "Isaiah in Some of the Non-Scriptural Dead Sea Scrolls," in *Transmission and Interpretation of the Book of Isaiah in the Context of Intra- and Interreligious*

resonates where hopes are pinned on a remote location that stands in the shadow of the famous reference to Isa 40:3 in 1QS 8:14. As we will see in our analysis of that famous passage below, it is striking that this second explicit quotation from Isaiah again occurs in the context of an admonition to separate from the people of injustice at a foundational momemt in the movement's emergence.[49]

5:19 The language warning those who despise the word of the Lord in 1QS 5:19 // 4Q256 1:11 // 9:12–13 is interesting since it draws on Jer 23:17–40. The latter passage is found in the context of material on false prophets. This subtext is most appropriate in a passage concerned with the formidable appeal of the people of injustice who on our reading are influential former members.[50]

5:20 The plus in 4Q258 1:12–13 shares some terminological overlap with 4Q275 (Communal Ceremony), especially the concern with the nations.[51] It is unusual for 4Q258 to depart from the text of 4Q256 where they preserve the same material. Another instance is attested in 1QS 9:22 and parallels below.

6.1.4.2 Assessment and Registration of New Entrants into the Covenant (1QS 5:20b–23a // 4Q258 2:1–3a // 4Q261 1a–b: 1–4a)

Whereas the immediately preceding section shares covenantal language with the beginning of the current section, a key difference is the lack of reference to – let alone emphasis on – a separation from the people of injustice here.

5:20–21 It is noteworthy that the overarching aim of assessing candidates for admission is their spiritual make-up. However, as the passage continues it becomes clear that tangible access to a person's spirit is achieved by paying close attention to their insight and deeds. This approach is borne out by the account in the Teaching on the Two Spirits which stresses that the nature of the Spirit of Truth manifests itself in actions and deeds.[52]

5:20c–22 While this outline of leadership roles is structurally very similar to what we find in 5.2.4 and 6.1.2.1 above, the terminology differs substantially. In Chapter 5 leadership was set out in terms of "the sons of Zakok and the multitude of the people of the community" (1QS 5:2–3) and "the many" in 4Q256 9:2–3 // 4Q258 1:2–3.[53] In 6.1.2.1 it was the sons of Zadok and the people of their covenant (1QS) and the council of the people of the community (4Q256 and 4Q258).[54] The terminology Aaron and Israel that is used to refer to the priestly and lay elements in the community here has a strong biblical pedigree

---

Debates. Edited by Florian Wilk and Peter Gemeinhardt. BETL 280 (Leuven: Peeters, 2016), 243–260, especially 251–254 and Kratz, "Der *Penal Code.*"

[49] See 8.4.4 below.

[50] Cf. Brownlee, *Dead Sea Manual*, 21 n. 49 who refers to 1QS 3:2–3.

[51] See Alexander and Vermes, DJD 26:209–216.

[52] For details see 1QS 3:25–4:1 as well as 4.2.3 and 4.4.3 above.

[53] Cf. 5.2.4 and 5.4.4 above.

[54] See 6.1.4.1 above.

and is also found in several passages in the Community Rules that describe the emergence of a community.[55] Martha Himmelfarb has aptly described the use of Aaron and Israel as referring to "the totality of the sect" in the Admonition of the Damascus Document (CD 1:7; CD 6:2–3) as well as in S, including in cultic contexts (1QS 8:5–9).[56]

5:22 As noted in 6.1.3 above, 4Q261 1a–b:2 reads "[and according to the authority of the multitu]de of Is[rael who are fervently commit]ted to dwell together" (לשבת יחד). Steudel seems to take 4Q261's reading to refer to the sabbath.[57] Both 1QS and 4Q258 read "to return together." Outside of this particular instance the root ישב almost always indicates an allotted place in the hierarchical order set out in the Community Rules. An exceptional instance occurs in the Final Hymn in 1QS 10:14 to refer to times of praise when the psalmist "settles down and rises" (לשבת וקום).[58] We take the verbal form ישב in the rhetorical question "What is one born of a woman to reply before You?" as a defectively spelled *hiphil* of שוב which occurs in a comparable question and plene spelling in the following line 1QS 11:22.[59] Alison Schofield writes about the written registration that is dealt with just after the infinitive "to dwell together" and concludes "4QS^g is extant here and probably preserves a reading closest to the original."[60] As far as I was able to establish the significantce of the variant "to dwell" in 4Q261 1a–b:2 has received very little scholarly attention. We may ask why this variant did not provoke more interest? Alexander and Vermes suggest it is a fix for an awkward text in 4Q258 which reads "to return" (לשוב) without complement.[61] However, we cannot assume that 4Q261 had access to 4Q258. It is equally possible that the scribes behind 1QS and 4Q258 depended on a text like 4Q261, misread the unexpected reading "to dwell," and and wrote "to return." In any case, it is methodologically preferable to take the witness 4Q261 seriously.

We suspect the reasons scholars were initially disinclined to engage closely with 4Q261's reading relate to the fact that it was felt there was little to be gained from it. Many scholars assumed for a long time that the movement behind the Community Rules had settled at Khirbet Qumran. Since Laperoussaz and Magness made a strong case for a revised chronology regarding the communal occupation of the site, the answer to the question "where and when did the movement settle" is less clear.[62] While the date of the copying of 4Q261 (50–1 BCE) falls within the revised chronological window of Qumran occupation, the passage gives way to a pertinent set of regulations on gatherings

---

[55] Cf. 5.4.5 above as well as 8.4.2 and Chapter 11 below.

[56] Himmelfarb, *Kingdom of Priests*, 121–122.

[57] Steudel, "The Damascus Document (D) as a Rewriting," 615.

[58] Further, 15.2.3 below.

[59] See 15.3 below.

[60] Schofield, *From Qumran to the Yaḥad*, 92, 128 n. 181.

[61] Alexander and Vermes, DJD 26:175.

[62] Cf. 1.2.2 above.

in "all their dwelling places" (מגורהם) in 1QS 6 and parallels which include 4Q261.[63] In this distinctive material yahad repeatedly features as an adverb. 1QS was copied around 100–75 BCE and includes evidence suggesting a significant time had passed for the movement it describes.[64] Given 1QS already includes the material on different dwelling places where fellowship activities are undertaken together (yahad), we are beyond the window of the occupation of the site on the revised chronology. Another reason this important reading did not chime with scholars to date is because it does not highlight a schism or withdrawal but refers to rather benign acts of fellowship.

To sum up, we are dealing here with a case where an apparently minor variant has been neglected. I tried to argue that rather than testifying to a slip of the pen or a subtle improvement on 4Q258, the single word לשבת is a potential gem in our evidence on the picture of community formation as portrayed in the S manuscripts.

6.1.4.3 Annual Assessment of Current Members (1QS 5:23b–24a // 4Q258 2:3b–4a // 4Q261 1a–b: 4b–6)

The previous sub-section was concerned with determining the suitability for membership of aspiring members on the basis of their spiritual make-up as reflected in their insight and deeds. This section deals with an annual assessment of existing members along similar lines. The sequence of topics from admission into the covenant to an annual assessment of existing members is very much reminiscent of the Covenant Ceremony.[65]

5:24a The closing statement across all three manuscripts approaches the evaluation of current members pragmatically with an expectation that some members will fall short of what is expected and are therefore liable to face the consequences. This may reflect experience and is also in line with the fulsome evidence of a rather unvarnished picture of communal life that follows in Chapters 7, 9. and 10 below. Our approach to the Community Rules resists playing down the rough edges in the portrayal of communal life.[66]

6.2 Rules Dealing with Reproof

(1QS 5:24b–6:1b // 4Q258 2:4b–6a // 4Q263 1–2a)

---

[63] Cf. 6.3 below.
[64] See 7.4.6.4.
[65] Cf. Chapter 3 above.
[66] See further 1.4 above.

6.2.1 Introduction

The scriptural basis for the law of reproof that is promoted in several compositions from Qumran is found in Lev 19:17 which reads, "You shall not hate your brother in your heart, but you shall certainly rebuke your neighbour so as not to bear sin because of him." As in Lev 19:17 the current passage emphasizes not only the need to reprove fellow members but to do so in the right spirit.[67]

Remarkably, a small manuscript comprising five fragments from Qumran Cave 4, 4Q477 (Rebukes by the Overseer) appears to have preserved such a record.[68] Daniel Falk has plausibly suggested that such a record of rebuked members was used in a public setting for the purpose of ranking community members.[69] On our reading such a public setting is evident in the literary context of this section on reproof within the Rule. The topic of reproof occurs as part of a cluster of texts that deal with different kinds of meetings, each of them referring to the principle of a hierarchical order of members, with some mentioning a rigorous process for assessing members. More particularly, the previous section ended with a reference to an annual assessment process that specifically singles out members' tendency to sin.[70] During this kind of annual assessment – and just at this point in the Community Rules' narrative – the overseer's written record of the previous year's rebukes might have played a role. Even without such a record, the references to hierarchical seating arrangements in 6.3, 6.4 and 6.5 make it clear that the question of one's place during a gathering could create tensions and invite conflict especially upon arrival and trying to claim one's place in the hierarchy. The present passage paints a picture of just such a scenario by referring to members dealing with unfinished business or even indulging in deep-seated rivalries without following due process during a meeting of the many.

---

[67] Cf. James Kugel, "On Hidden Hatred and Open Reproach: Early Exegesis of Leviticus 19:17," *HTR* 80 (1987): 43–61 and Lawrence H. Schiffman, *Sectarian Law in the Dead Sea Scrolls: Courts, Testimony and the Penal Code.* BJS 33 (Chico, CA: Scholars Press, 1983), 89–109. For an analysis of the wider context, including in the New Testament and rabbinic sources, see Menahem Kister, "Divorce, Reproof, and Other Sayings in the Synoptic Gospels: Jesus Traditions in the Context of 'Qumranic' and Other Texts," in *Text, Thought and Practice in Qumran and Early Christianity.* Edited by Ruth A. Clements and Daniel R. Schwartz. STDJ 84 (Leiden: Brill, 2009), 195–209, esp. 212–229.

[68] For details see Esther Eshel, "4Q477: The Rebukes by the Overseer," *JJS* 45 (1994): 111–122 and Alexander and Vermes, DJD 36:474–483.

[69] Falk, "Liturgical Texts," 427.

[70] See 6.1.2.3 and 6.1.4.3 above.

6.2.2 Translation

1QS 5	4Q258 2
[24b]They shall repro[ve] [25]one another *tr[uthful]ly and humbly and* with devoted love *to each. Vacat.* No one shall speak *to his brother* in anger or with grumbling [26]or	[4b]They shall reprove one another (with) devoted love. [5]No one shall speak *to his fellow* in anger or with grumbling or

1QS 5–6	4Q258 2	4Q263
with a [stiff] neck [or a jealous] sprit of wicked-ness. No one shall hate [ ] his heart. Rather he shall re-prove him him on the same day{..} [6]and thus not be-come guilty because of him.	*wicked jealousy.* LACKING IN 4Q258	[1][wick]ed [jealousy.] *Vacat.* PROBABLY LACKING IN 4Q263
	END OF MINUS IN 4Q258	
Nor shall anyone bring up a matter against his fellow *before* the many without (prior) re-proof before witnesses.	Nor shall anyone bring up a matter against his fellow *to* the many without (prior) reproof before wit[nesses].	[Nor] shall anyone bring [a matter against his fellow to (?) the many without (prior) [2a]re]proof before witnesses.

6.2.3 Textual Notes

5:24 The final *khet* of "to reprove" (להוכיח) has been added above the line in 1QS in an attempt to correct a quiescent *khet*.[71] Looking at images of the manuscript makes it clear, however, that the secondary intervention goes beyond adding *khet* with *kaph* and *yod* showing evidence of having been adjusted in some way.

5:25 This line displays two notable spacing features in 1QS. Firstly, there is a larger than expected space in the middle of the phrase opening the line "one another" (איש את רעהו). The cause for leaving extra space was damage to the surface of the skin perhaps caused by an erasure which left the surface darker just at this point. A second longer *vacat* in 1QS more or less divides the line in half and disrupts the thematic continuity. It is curious that a paragraphos accompanies this longer *vacat* which is lacking in 4Q258 2:4–5.[72] There are no signs of

---

[71] So Reymond, *Qumran Hebrew*, 108.
[72] See 6.2.4 below as well as 1.5.1.3; 6.1.1 and 6.1.3 above. Further, Chapter 8 below.

damage to the surface of the skin at this point. The longer *vacat* is marked generously by García Martínez and Tigchelaar who leave two empty lines.[73]

5:25 After the shared phrase "devoted love" 1QS attests the plus "to each" (לאיש).

5:25 The translation of 1QS "to his brother" reflects an emendation of אלוהיהו to אל אחיהו.[74] 4Q258 2:5 reads "to his fellow" (אל רעהו).

5:25 The text of 4Q258 2:4 is shorter than 1QS 5:25 at this point.[75]

5:26–6:1a A substantial plus in 1QS is clearly missing from 4Q258 and almost certainly also lacking from 4Q263. The latter manuscript attests a *vacat* just before all three manuscripts converge.[76]

5:26 "Jeaslousy" (קנאת) has been restored in 1QS on the basis of 4Q258.

5:26: The restoration "[stiff] neck" can draw support from the fact that in the other three cases where neck occurs in 1QS (4:11; 5:5 and 6:26) it is always accompanied by a form of קשה "to be hard."

5:26 Two letters have been erased following "on the same day" in 1QS. García Martínez and Tigchelaar identify the erased letters as *yod* and *vav*.[77]

6.2.4 Commentary

This passage outlines the position on the importance of reproof between community members. As in the Damascus Document the process is a judicial one in front of witnesses.[78] According to CD 9:18 the overseer is to keep a written record of rebukes brought against community members by their fellow members and, as we saw in 6.2.1 above, 4Q477 appears to preserve a record of rebukes. The present passage does not mention the overseer but addresses concerns about exposing wrongdoing without prior rebuke before witnesses in the course of a meeting of the many. For an account of such meetings of the many see 6.5 below.

5:26b–1QS 6:1a The plus in 1QS results in a closer engagement with the text of Lev 19:17 and forms part of a broader tendency in 1QS to add or enhance biblical references including to Lev 22:16.[79]

6:1 This is the first occurrence of the designation "the many" in 1QS. Curiously the term occurs extremely frequently in this manuscript from now on with 31 attestations in 1QS 6–7. The current reference appears rather abruptly but shares a

---

[73] García Martínez and Tigchelaar, DSSSE, 82–83.

[74] See Brownlee, *Dead Sea Manual*, 63 n. 61 who credits Samuel Iwry; cf. also Qimron, DSSHW 1:218.

[75] Cf. Alexander and Vermes, DJD 26:101.

[76] See Alexander and Vermes, DJD 26:199–200.

[77] García Martínez and Tigchelaar, DSSSE, 82.

[78] See CD 9:16–10:3; Deut 17:6; 19:15 and Hempel, *Laws of the Damascus Document*, 93–100.

[79] Cf. also Metso, *Textual Development*, 83; Metso, "Biblical Quotations," 83 and Tzoref, "Use of Scripture."

great deal with the cluster of rules on the many that follow in 6.5 below.[80] Given the series of rather disparate passages on a variety of fellowship activities that come between this reference to the many and 6.5 it is conceivable that the current dispersion of material dealing with the business of the many emerged in the course of the literary development of the manuscripts.[81] I would be inclined, furthermore, to include the material now attested in 4Q256 // 4Q258 which defers authority to "the many" in 5.2.4.[82] Given the prominent and well established place of "the many" in 1QS beyond 1QS 5, it is likely that 4QS preserves a version that was at one time part of a proto-1QS 5 text. This argument will be developed further in 6.5 below.

6.3 Rules of Conduct in All Their Dwelling Places

(1QS 6:1c–3a // 4Q258 2:6b–7b // 4Q263 2b–3)

6.3.1 Introduction

Partly because it forms part of a series of disparate statements outlining a distinctive lifestyle within S, this statement is frequently read together with what follows on gatherings of ten in 6.4 and nightly meetings of the many in 6.5.2.1. All three passages describe a plurality of settlements or gatherings and attest partly overlapping activities such as praying, studying and exchanging counsel. Several scholars treat this material together as dealing with peripheral meetings.[83] Licht groups this section together under regulations for a *haburah*.[84] However, the lack of any concern with ritual purity sets this material apart from what follows in 6.5.2.2 and the descriptions of the *haburah* attested in the Mishnah and Tosefta. While the regulations on small scale gatherings that follow share a number of features that set this material apart from other parts of the Community Rules, it is preferable to let each passage speak in its own right rather than harmonising various distinctive passages with one another.

---

[80] See Schofield, *From Qumran to the Yahad*, 144–147.

[81] Cf. Sarianna Metso, "Whom Does the Term Yahad Identify?," in *Biblical Traditions in Transmission*. Edited by Hempel and Lieu, 213–235.

[82] See also 5.4.4 above.

[83] So, e. g., Leaney, *Rule of Qumran*, 180–186 and Sacchi, *Regola*, 122.

[84] Licht, *Rule Scroll*, 19, 138–140. On the relationship of the Community Rules to the rabbinic accounts of the *haburah* see 6.5.4.3 below.

6.3.2 Translation

1QS 6	4Q258 2	4Q263
[1c]*With* th[es]e (rules) [2]they shall conduct themselves in all their dwelling places, everyone who is found (there)	[6b]*And with* these (rules) they shall conduct themselves in all their dwelling places, everyone who is found (there)	[2b]*And with* these (rules) they shall con[duct themselves in all their dwelling places, everyone who is found (there)
each with their fellow. Those of inferior rank shall obey (their) superiors in matters of work	*with their fellow.* [Those of inferior rank] shall ob[ey] [7](their) superiors in matters of work	*each with their fellow.]* [3]Those of inferior rank [shall ob]ey (their) superiors in matters of work
and money. And together they shall eat, [3a]*and together*	*and wea[lth. Together* they shall e]at, *to[ge]ther*	*and we[alth. And together* they shall eat, *and together]*

1QS 6	4Q258 2	4Q261 2a–c	4Q263
they shall pray and together they shall exchange counsel.	they shall pray and together they shall exchange couns[el.]	[1] they [shall pra]y	[they shall pray and together they shall exchange counsel.]

6.3.3 Textual Notes

6:1 1QS lacks the conjunction attested by 4Q258 and 4Q263 ("And with these rules"). In addition, *aleph* has been added above the line by a different hand with noticeably finer strokes in באלה "with these" in 1QS.

6:2 4Q258 2:6 lacks "each" (איש) before "their fellow."

6:2 4Q263 reads "work and we[alth]" ([ון]ה)" where 1QS has "work and money" (ממון). Based on the scarce remains preserved the reading in 4Q258 is unclear.

6:3 "As one they shall exchange counsel" has been corrected to "and together …" in 1QS.[85] The corrected reading is clearly preserved in 4Q258 2:7. The remains of 4Q261 extend to no more than ink traces here.[86]

---

[85] Cf. Wernberg-Møller, *Manual of Discipline*, 41.

[86] See Alexander and Vermes, DJD 26:176. Others, such as Metso, *Textual Development*, 57–61; García Martínez and Tigchelaar, DSSSE, 540–541 and Qimron, DSSHW 1:220–221 do not include this group of fragments in their editions. See also 1.5.8.2 and Table 4 above.

6.3.4 Commentary

This short statement contains rules for living in a series of dwelling places. The referent for the opening demonstrative pronoun (באלה) which refers to rules of conduct serves to introduce these particular rules. The immediately preceding section on reproof with its reference to the many and the overseer shares more with what follows in 6.5.[87] This short passage on communal life in a series of dwelling places stands out from the remainder of the Community Rules even though it shares the notion of multiple dispersed gathering with what follows. On our reading the organizational requirements outlined here and in 6.4 describe a more seminal state of communal fellowship from what follows on meetings of the many in 6.5 below. Here I am in agreement with Michael Knibb who proposed that this material was incorporated into the Community Rules from elsewhere.[88]

6:2 Some commentators translate the phrase "everyone who is found (there)" in 4Q258 2:6 with "according to all that has been discovered."[89] Our rendering follows Licht and takes כול as referring to "each one." Alexander and Vermes suggest that כל stands for ככל and should be rendered "according to all that has been discovered" in 4Q258 2:6 in analogy with 4Q258 1:6.[90] However, while 1QS lacks the preposition here, it is attested with reference to revelation in 1QS 5:9 and 1QS 8:15 where 4Q258 1:6 and 4Q258 6:7 lack it.[91] In any case, the text makes good sense as it stands, and I translate the phrase with "everyone who is found there each with their fellow."[92]

6:2 No leadership structure is outlined here, though it is likely that senior members were considered responsible for overseeing matters of work and property. It is not stated whether those of priestly descent formed part of the fellowship groups. Some kind of economic collaboration or trading standards are also presupposed in CD 13:15.[93]

6:2c–3a This list of shared activities comprises meals, prayer and exchanging counsel. All of these fellowship activities occur in more developed regulations throughout the Community Rules. The present passage gives the impression of describing an incipient form of such fellowship activities where yahad occurs as an adverb rather than as a designation for a more developed community. Several of the joint activities recur in the material that follows in 6.4 and 6.5

---

[87] See also 6.2.4 above.

[88] Knibb, *Qumran Community*, 115.

[89] So, e. g., Alexander and Vermes, DJD 26:102 and Wernberg-Møller, *Manual of Discipline*, 29, 101.

[90] See Alexander and Vermes, DJD 26:102.

[91] Cf. further 6.1.4.1 above and Chapter 8 below.

[92] See also Brownlee, *Dead Sea Manual*, 22–23.

[93] On shared assets in the Community Rules, see, e. g., 6.5.2.3 below.

below though the emphasis on the study of the law that is prominent in 6.4.2.3 and 6.5.2.1 is lacking here.

6.4 Rules of Conduct in Every Place of Ten

(1QS 6:3b–7a // 4Q258 2:7c–10a // 4Q261 2a–c: 2b–5 // 4Q263 4–5)

6.4.1 Introduction

Whereas we have come across a range of dual authority structures such as Aaron and Israel in Chapter 5 and 6.1.2.2 above, the present passage demands the presence of a priest in gatherings of ten. Gatherings of ten also occur in the Damascus Document (see CD 13:2–3) and the Rule of the Congregation (see 1QSa 2:21–22).[94] The opening reference to "every place where" suggests the gatherings in view occur in a number of places as was the case in 6.3 above. Both this section and 6.3 deal with three types of communal activities. The first two – exchanging counsel (6.4.2.1)[95] and shared meals (6.4.2.2) – are presided over by a priest. The final activity concerns a member of the group whose credentials are not further specified who is to be engaged in studying the law day and night. I will deal with each of these items in turn.

The opening stipulation calls for priestly oversight in communal deliberation and picks up an issue that concluded the previous instructions for life in a series of dwelling places ("together they shall exchange counsel").[96]

6.4.2 Translation[97]

6.4.2.1 Meetings Presided over by a Priest (1QS 6:3b–4b // 4Q258 2:7c–8 // 4Q261 2a–c: 2b–4a // 4Q263 4–5)

1QS 6	4Q258 2	4Q261 2a–c	4Q263
[3b]And in every place where there are found ten people for the commununal exchange	[7c][And] in [ev]ery [place where there are found ten] [8]people for [the commununal ex-	[2b][And in every place where the]re [are found] ten [people[3] for the commununal ex-	[4][And in every] pl[a]ce where there are found [ten people for the commununal ex-

---

[94] See also m. Sanh. 1:6.

[95] For a detailed overview over the noun counsel/council as well as the verb יעץ see Hempel, "Wisdom and Law," 12–15 and further bibliography there.

[96] Cf. 6.3 above.

[97] Shading is used here to facilitate continuous reading for 4Q261.

1QS 6	4Q258 2	4Q261 2a–c	4Q263
of counsel a priest must be [4]found. They shall sit before him each *according to* his rank	change of counsel] a prie[st must be fou]nd. [They shall] si[t before him ea]ch *according to* his rank	change of counsel a priest shall be found. They shall sit before him each] *according to* [his] ran[k	change of counsel priest must be [5]found. They shall sit before him ea]ch *in* [his] ra[nked (*place*)

1QS 6	4Q258 2	4Q261 2a–c
[4]and thus they shall be asked for their counsel regarding any matter.	[and thus they shall be asked for their counsel regarding any matter.]	[4]and thus they] shall be ask[ed for their counsel regarding any matter.

6.4.2.2 Meals Presided over by a Priest (1QS 6:4c–5 // 4Q258 2: 9–10a // 4Q261 2a–c: 4b–5)

1QS 6	4Q258 2	4Q261 2a–c
[4c]And when they prepare the table to eat or the new wine [5]to drink the priest shall stretch out his hand	[9]And when [they prepare the table to eat or the new] wine [to drink the] priest shall stre[tch out his hand	[4b]And when] they [pre]pare [5][the table to eat] or the [new wine to drink the priest shall stretch out his] hand

1QS 6	4Q258 2
first to bless the first fruits of the bread and the new wine.	first to bless the first fruits of the bread] [10a]and the new wine.

6.4.2.3 Continuous Torah Study (1QS 6:6–7a)

1QS 6
[6]And in every place where there are ten there shall be present a person who studies the law continually day and [7]night one replacing the other.

6.4.3 Textual Notes

6:3 The translation of מעצת החיד with "for the communal exchange of counsel" is based on an emendation to מעצת היחד.[98] Both 4Q258 and 4Q263 are recon-

---

[98] See, e. g., Alexander and Vermes, DJD 26:200; García Martínez and Tigchelaar, DSSSE, 82–83; Qimron, DSSHW 1:220; Licht, *Rule Scroll*, 139 and Wernberg-Møller, *Manual of Discipline*, 30, 41. Reymond identifies the scribal error of metathesis, see *Qumran Hebrew*, 25.

structed at this point with only the top right of the initial letter *mem* preserved in 4Q258 2:8.[99] I take the preposition *min* in the causative sense "for (reason of)."[100]

6:3–4 1QS reads איש כוהן "a priest" where 4Q258 partially preserves כוהן alone.

6:4 In the description of the hierarchial seating order during meetings of ten which is preserved by four manuscripts 4Q263 5 reads "[ea]ch in [his] ra[nked (place)]." The remaining three witnesses read "according to his rank."[101]

6:4 The scribe of 1QS skilfully wrote the word "table" by accommodating a pre-existing hole in the leather.

6:5–6 Our translation does not include a sizeable dittography repeating the words "or the new wine to drink the priest shall stretch out his hand first" in 1QS.

6:5 and 6 *Yod* has been omitted in the infinitive *hiphil* here and in 1QS 8:6 and 8:10.[102]

6:6–7a None of the Cave 4 manuscripts of the Rules preserve these words. On the basis of the size of the lacuna in 4Q258 it is clear that its text was considerably shorter than 1QS.[103]

6:7a The rendering "one replacing the other" is based on a widely adopted emendation of the Hebrew על יפות to חליפות.[104] Some scholars leave the text as it is, and Steven Fraade, for instance, translates "concerning the correct conduct."[105]

6.4.4 Commentary

6.4.4.1 Meetings Presided over by a Priest for the Purpose of Exchanging Counsel (1QS 6:3b–4b // 4Q258 2:7c–8 // 4Q261 2a–c: 2b–4a // 4Q263 4–5)

This passage lays down a requirement for priestly oversight over communal deliberations in gatherings of ten and forms part of a diverse section of the Community Rules. It picks up the theme of communal deliberation from the preceding rules on meetings in a variety of dwelling places and also displays close terminological overlap with CD 13:2–3.[106] The emphasis in the Damascus

---

[99] Cf. Alexander and Vermes, DJD 26:98–99 and Plate 10.

[100] See DCH 5:337.

[101] See Alexander and Vermes, DJD 26:198–200.

[102] Further, Reymond, *Qumran Hebrew*, 40–41.

[103] Cf. Alexander and Vermes, DJD 26:99–100, Plate 10 and Metso, *Textual Development*, 43.

[104] So Preben Wernberg-Møller, "Observations on the Interchange of *Ayin* and *Het* in the Manual of Discipline," *VT* 3 (1953) 104–107; Bakker, "Figure of the Sage," 168–169 and Ben Sira 42:19 as preserved in Mas 1h 5:8 // SirB 12r:12.

[105] Fraade, "Interpretive Authority in the Studying Community at Qumran," *JJS* 44 (1993): 46–69, 56 and for discussion see Isaiah Sonne, "Remarks on 'Manual of Discipline," Col. VI,6–7," *VT* 7 (1957): 405–408.

[106] See, e. g., Brownlee, *Dead Sea Manual*, 23 and Édouard Cothenet, "Le Document de Damas," in *Les Textes de Qumrân*. Edited by Jean Carmignac, Édouard Cothenet and Hubert Lignée (Paris: Letouzey et Ané, 1963), 2:129–204, 199.

Document is firmly on the issue of the priest's authority ("And in every place of ten a priest [who is] learned in the book of hagu shall not be lacking. All of them shall obey him."). We will return to the shared context in both the Damascus Document and the Community Rules as part of a series of loosely connected rules below.

In the present string of passages a number of fellowship activities are identified as requiring appropriate oversight. Two of the activities associated with life in all their dwelling places in 6.3 – exchanging counsel and sharing meals – recur here and in 6.4.2.2 but are now subject to priestly oversight. The fact that 6.3 ends with a form of the verb יעץ in the *niphal* "to exchange counsel" may well have been the hook that led to connecting this passage with what came before.

A key phrase for gauging the type of social environment described here is commonly translated with "from the council of the community."[107] The preposition "from" can be interpreted as indicating that the passage is concerned with a small group of community members travelling or residing in satellite settlements that have spawned out of the well-developed community described elsewhere in the Rules as "the council of the community."[108] However, the Damascus Document preserves a related version of the requirement for priestly oversight over meetings of ten that does not refer to the council of the community (CD 13:2–3). The evidence of CD indicates that accounts of geographically spread out and modest gatherings circulated without being associated with the more tightly structured council of the community.[109] CD 13:2–3 suggests that the self-designation "the council of the community" was not originally associated with accounts of meetings in groups of ten. It is clear that by the time 1QS was copied the phrase "the council of the community" had become a prominent self-designation. As a consequence the scribe of 1QS as well as ancient and modern readers could read the phrase in this way with some justification. The particular context of the present passage introduces gatherings of ten and ends by stressing the need for priestly oversight over communal deliberation. In 6.3 we learnt of a series of dwelling places where deliberation took place. Our translation of מעצת היחד as a reference to communal deliberation prefaced by the preposition *min* in a causative sense "for the communal exchange of counsel" mirrors the immediate context and concerns of this material which has not received the attention it deserves.[110] The scenario described is one where small groups gather for the purpose of communal deliberation.

---

[107] On the emendation from מעצת החיד to מעצת היחד see 6.4.3 above.

[108] Cf. John Collins, "The Nature and Aims of the Sect Known from the Dead Sea Scrolls," in *Flores Florentino: Dead Sea Scrolls and Other Early Jewish Studies in Honour of Florentino García Martínez*. Edited by Anthony Hilhorst, Émile Puech and Eibert Tigchelaar. JSJSup 122 (Leiden: Brill, 2007), 31–52, 43; Knibb, *Qumran Community*, 115 and Metso, "Whom Does the Term Yaḥad Identify?"

[109] Further, Hempel, *Qumran Rule Texts in Context*, 97–105.

[110] See also 6.5.4.2 below.

A piece of distinctive textual evidence offers further support for a literary relationship between this material and the Damascus Document. An important indicator that has not, to my knowledge, been referred to in this context is the reading היחיד in the phrase "the unique teacher" (מורה היחיד) attested in CD 20:1.[111] As is the case here, the latter reading is frequently emended to "the teacher of the community" (מרה היחד).[112] Given the passage on groups of ten is one of the clusters of material shared between the Damascus Document and the Community Rules, the attestation of a comparable and unusual textual particularity and wide-spread emendation in both the Damascus Document and the Community Rules is thought-provoking and should caution us from assuming the error goes back to the mediaeval scribes of CD B as proposed by Regev.[113] Chaim Rabin astutely recognised the appeal of the emendation(s) in CD 20 but makes a good case for taking the reading "unique teacher" seriously by appealing to the expectation of "a unique prophet" (μονογενοῦς προφήτου) in an eschatological context in T. Benj. 9:2.[114] By connecting CD 20:1, 14 with the expectation of "one who teaches righteousness at the end of days" in CD 6:11 Rabin uncovered substantial evidence in support of CD's original reading.[115] It is likely that an original reading "the unique teacher" was, over time, read by both ancient readers and modern scholars of CD as a reference to "the teacher of the community." I suggest that ancient scribes and modern readers of the Community Rules, similarly, read this passage in light of the familiar designation "the council of the community." It is likely that the present passage was composed at a time that predates these developments. It is at that level that the passage represents a cluster that is closely related to CD 13:2–3.[116] Given its present macro-context, and in keeping with the dynamic engagement with texts of this period,[117] the interpretation proposed here can be read side by side with interpretations that privilege the larger context of this passage in the Community Rules.

---

[111] Cf. also CD 20:14.

[112] See, e. g., Knibb, *Qumran Community*, 70, 72 and Qimron, DSSHW 1:20.

[113] Regev, "יַחַד *jaḥad*," 124.

[114] Rabin, *The Zadokite Documents: I. The Admonition II. The Laws* (Oxford: Oxford University Press, 1954), 36–37.

[115] On the expectation of a prophet in the messianic age see further 1QS 9:11 and Chapter 13 below.

[116] Cf. also the chapter on "Rewritten Rule Texts" in Hempel, *Qumran Rule Texts in Context*, 137–150 and Florentino García Martínez, "¿Sectario, no-sectario, o qué? Problemas de una taxonomía correcta de los textos qumránicos," *RevQ* 23 (2008): 383–394.

[117] See, e. g., Hindy Najman, "The Vitality of Scripture Within and Beyond the 'Canon,'" *JSJ* 43 (2012): 497–518.

6.4.4.2 Meals Presided over by a Priest (1QS 6:4c–5 // 4Q258 2: 9–10a // 4Q261 2a–c: 4b–5)

The next activity for which priestly precedence is required concerns communal meals. In its current literary context the opening statement "And when they prepare the table to eat" picks up the reference to shared meals in 6.3 above. A significant difference is the inclusion here of shared drinking alongside the consumption of solid food though we are rather removed from the pronounced concern with the susceptibility of liquids to defilement by touch that is emphasized in 6.5.2.3 below.

A good case has been made for locating deliberation and meals in one and the same setting. Such a connection is based on the conjunction of communal meals, prayer and deliberation in 6.3 above, the seamless sequence from 6.4.4.1 to the present passage as well as analogies attested for Hellenistic voluntary associations.[118]

While food looms large in much of the Community Rules the present passage is the only description of a shared meal. Though sharing food is more frequently part of a discourse of boundary formation that is closely linked to questions of ritual purity in the Rules,[119] the present passage shows no concern with ritual purity.[120] Moreover, given the broader geographical context indicated by the revised chronology of the communal occupation of the site of Qumran,[121] I will not draw on the archaeological remains for meals at Qumran in our analysis of the Community Rules.[122]

What is outlined here is very much in line with what we know of shared meals in ancient Judaism including blessings prior to eating and drinking.[123] The only other place in the Scrolls where we come across a comparable scenario is a statement appended to the account of the messianic banquet in the Rule of the Congregation. The account of a messianic banquet in 1QSa 2:17–22 is reminiscent of the current narrative by referring to the act of preparing for a meal which comprisies bread and (new) wine.[124] As here the priest blesses bread and wine before the meal begins. The priest in 1QSa is often taken as the priestly messiah though this is debated.[125] 1QSa refers to the messiah of Israel partaking of the

---

[118] See Collins, *Beyond the Qumran Community*, 79–84; Eckhardt, "Meals" and Cecilia Wassén, "Daily Life," in CDSS, 547–558, 554–556.

[119] Cf. 6.1.2.1 and 6.1.4.1 above and 6.5.2.3 and 6.5.4.3 as well as Chapter 7 below.

[120] See further Charlotte Hempel, "Who is Making Dinner at Qumran?," *JTS* 63 (2012): 49–65 and Wassén, "The (Im)purity Levels of Communal Meals."

[121] For details see 1.2.2 above.

[122] For a recent analysis of those remains see Magness, "Were Sacrifices Offered at Qumran?" and the remaining contributions in the same issue *JAJ* 7 (2016).

[123] See David Kraemer, *Jewish Eating and Identity through the Ages* (New York, NY: Routledge, 2007); Lawrence Schiffman, "Communal Meals at Qumran," *RevQ* 10 (1979): 45–56 and Schiffman, *Sectarian Law*, 194.

[124] Cf. Eckhardt, "Meals," 201–205 and Schiffman, *Eschatological Community*, 53–67.

[125] See Hartmut Stegemann, "Some Remarks."

bread before the hierarchically organized congregation offer another blessing. Bringing the account of 1QSa even closer to our passage is the final instruction to proceed in this manner every time when at least ten come together (1QSa 2:21b–22). Something of a bridge between the messianic framework of 1QSa and the gatherings of ten presided over by a priest in 1QS is found in CD 12:22b–13:3a where the rule for life in the camps is similarly restricted to the age of wickedness which will come to an end with the appearance of the Messiah of Aaron and Israel. The reference to the messiah in CD 12:23 is followed by the regulation for groups including those comprising ten members. What are we to make of these connections across several texts? For the purposes of this commentary, which is concerned with elucidating the S manuscripts, the most likely reason for such a wide-spread attestation of related – if not identical – statements on meals and gatherings suggests that this material had a wider circulation than other parts of the Community Rules. The distinctive content of this account vis-à-vis more developed and restrictive regulations on shared meals elsewhere in the Community Rules suggests a separate provenance for both. All this points to shared interests and practices among a range of related groups which generated clusters of texts that were absorbed into a variety of manuscripts. Such literary cross-fertilization developed in all likelihood from shared interests alongside either direct or indirect social contact.

6:4–5 On one level bread and wine are the staples of the ancient Mediterranean diet.[126] However, this account also displays significant correspondences to the First Fruits Festival described in the Temple Scroll (11Q19 19:11–21:10).[127] Suggestive connections between both accounts include the sequence from grain (see especially the term "first fruits of the bread" in 1QS 6:5) to "new wine" (תירוש in S while 11Q19 attests יין חדש alongside תירוש). The fact that the treatment of bread and new wine are listed as separate occasions, as suggested by the use of או "or" both in S and in the Temple Scroll bears further reflection. Finally, priestly precedence is promulgated in 1QS, 1QSa as well in 11Q19. Schiffman is right that this short account in 1QS gives little away about the particular occasions on which these meals would take place.[128] What we can say is that language used in this passage and the connections with the description of harvest festivals in the Temple Scroll suggest a seasonal context. תירוש has been taken to refer rather broadly to a range of stages in the process of wine production or

---

[126] See further David M. Freidenreich, "Food and Table Fellowship," in *The Jewish Annotated New Testament*. Edited by Amy-Jill Levine and Marc Zvi Brettler (New York, NY: Oxford University Press, 2011), 521–24 and Magness, *Archaeology of Qumran*, 116.

[127] Cf. Yigael Yadin, *The Temple Scroll: Volume Two. Text and Commentary* (Jerusalem: IES, 1983), 78–95. See also Ed P. Sanders, "The Dead Sea Sect and Other Jews," in *The Dead Sea Scrolls in Their Historical Context*. Edited by Timothy H. Lim et al. (Edinburgh: T&T Clark, 2000), 7–43, here 21–22.

[128] Schiffman, *Sectarian Law*, 192.

understood figuratively.[129] It is not helpful, however, to conflate what is said here with 6.5.2.3 below and introduce an enhanced concern with ritual purity into the present passage.[130] While we cannot be sure how frequently the meals described here took place, the seasonal language needs to be taken seriously. Finally, as suggested above, the immediate context speaks of two separate events to coincide with the harvests of grain and grapes. The widely accepted suggestion that the Festival Calendar comprises a discrete source that has been integrated into the Temple Scroll leaves us with a potentially broad literary and social horizon behind the accounts here and in the Temple Scroll.[131]

Moreover, the language of priests stretching out their hands first is attested in the Laws of the Damascus Document. The pertinent passage in the Damascus Document prohibits consuming freshly harvested produce from the garden prior to the priests stretching out their hands first.[132] A lacuna is restored to refer to a priestly blessing but it seems possible that the stretching out of hands by priests may refer to the collection of priestly dues. A comparable scenario is envisaged in CD 12:9–10 where we find a prohibition of selling grain and wine to the gentiles straight from the threshing floor and wine press in what we may call a "tithe loophole."[133] A gathering associated with the harvesting season is described in m. Bik. 3:2 which is considered an early mishnah by Saul Lieberman.[134] As Lieberman points out, this mishnah portrays the collection of first fruits as a collective enterprise whereas Deut 26:1–11 presupposes this to be an individual duty to collect and hand over to a priest in Jerusalem. As in the present context the mishnah also presupposes a local, small scale context as suggested by meeting in the local small town. Pertinent also is the language put in the mouth of the Psalmist in the Final Hymn to refer to the daily consumption of food as "before I raise (רום *hiphil*) my hand to taste the delights of the fruits of [4]the earth."[135] By contrast, the Community Rules here offer an account of a meal at harvest time in the course of which the season's produce was blessed by a local priest who may also have overseen the collection of first fruits or tithes.

---

[129] So Michael Becker, "תִּירוֹשׁ *tîrôš*," ThWQ 3:1118–1120.

[130] Cf. Becker, "תִּירוֹשׁ *tîrôš*," 1120.

[131] See Andrew Wilson and Lawrence Wills, "Literary Sources of the Temple Scroll," *HTR* 75 (1982): 275–288; Michael Wise, *A Critical Study of the Temple Scroll from Qumran Cave 11* (Chicago, IL: Oriental Institute of the University of Chicago, 1990) and Sidnie White Crawford, *The Temple Scroll and Related Texts*. CQS 2 (Sheffield: Sheffield University Press, 2000), 49–57.

[132] Cf. 4Q271 2:1–6 // 4Q270 3 iii 13–15; Baumgarten, DJD 18:174 and Hempel, *Laws of the Damascus Document*, 56–57.

[133] See Lawrence H. Schiffman, "Legislation Concerning Relations with Non-Jews in the *Zadokite Fragments* and in Tannaitic Literature," *RevQ* 11 (1983): 379–389.

[134] Lieberman, *Hellenism in Jewish Palestine: Studies in the Literary Transmission, Beliefs and Manners of Palestine in the I Century B. C. E.–IV Century C. E.* (New York, NY: Jewish Theological Seminary of America, 1962), 144.

[135] See 1QS 10:15 // 4Q256 20:3–4 and 4Q258 10:2–3.

6.4.4.3 Continuous Torah Study (1QS 6:6–7a)

This passage formally resembles the requirement for priestly oversight over communal deliberations in 6.4.2.1. In fact, the opening words "And in every place where there are ten there shall be present" (במקום אשר יהיו שם העשרה ואל ימש) correspond closely to 1QS 6:3b–4b and parallels. The distinctive element introduced here for the first time is a requirement for one member of the gathering to be engaged in the study of the law continuously day and night with one replacing another. As has often been pointed out, a comparable requirement forms part of a divine address to Joshua in the course of preparations for crossing the Jordan in Josh 1:8.[136] Joshua is instructed to ensure that the book of the law is present and to meditate upon it day and night. Both Joshua 1:8 and Ps 1:2 reflect a comparable milieu to that represented by our passage.[137] While our passage shares with Joshua 1:8 the admonition to devote day and night to the law, the direction to meditate upon (הגה) and study (דרש) the mystery of being (רז נהיה) continuously day and night in 4QInstruction (4Q417 1 i 6 // 4Q418 43:2) offers a closer terminological parallel for the activity (הגה) to Josh 1:8.[138] Moreover, the continuous meditation on the law is also emphasized in 4Q525 (Beatitudes) 2–3 ii 6.[139] While a different verb is used to refer to attentive engagement with the law in 4QMMT, we note a reference to a previous correspondence that was dispatched to facilitate the addressees careful consideration (בין *hiphil*) of the book of Moses, see 4Q397 14–21 i 10.[140] As Isaiah Sonne has shown, some early rabbinic voices extol a similar routine of continuous study, while others considered the twice daily recitation of the Shema as sufficient.[141] Our passage removes any ambiguity by adding "continually" (תמיד) to qualify the requirement to study the law day and night.[142]

This passage is best understood in its literary context which describes a variety of gatherings. While this statement shares a terminological framing with 6.4.2.1, the absence of an individual or collective authority makes this

---

[136] Cf., e. g., Brownlee, *Dead Sea Manual*, 24 and Otto Betz, *Offenbarung und Schriftforschung in der Qumransekte*. WUNT 6 (Tübingen: Mohr Siebeck, 1960), 21.

[137] For this suggestion see Hempel, *Qumran Rule Texts in Context*, 285–299. See also Alexander Rofé, "The Piety of the Torah-Disciples at the Winding-Up of the Hebrew Bible: Josh. 1:8; Ps 1:2; Isa. 59:21," in *Bibel in jüdischer und christlicher Tradition: Festschrift für Johann Maier zum 60. Geburtstag*. Edited by Helmut Merklein, Karlheinz Müller and Günter Stemberger (Frankfurt a. M.: Hain, 1993), 75–85.

[138] See also Sir 6:37 and Arjen Bakker, "The Figure of the Sage in *Musar le-Mevin* and *Serek ha-Yahad*" (PhD diss., Katholieke Universiteit Leuven, 2015) 159–175.

[139] Cf. Bakker, "Figure of the Sage," 173–174 and Puech, DJD 25:122–123.

[140] A connection between this passage in 4QMMT and the instruction to study the law in the Community Rules is suggested by H. Gregory Snyder, *Teachers and Texts in the Ancient World: Philosophers, Jews and Christians* (London: Routledge, 2000), 156–158.

[141] Sonne, "Remarks."

[142] See also 4Q417 (Instruction^c) 1 i 6.

passage distinctive.[143] Its flavour is also distinct from what follows in 6.5. Given its context, this injunction is best understood as applying for the duration of gatherings, perhaps alongside prayer, deliberation and seasonal meals. A comparable scenario is attested in Neh 8 where the reading of the law is followed by a shared meal.[144] If 4Q258 2:10 did preserve a shorter version of this instruction – conceivably without the opening words – the connection between the account of seasonal meals with torah study would be more immediate.[145]

6:6b Related termininology to "a person who studies the law" is found in the phrase "the scholar" (1QS 8:11–12 // 4Q258 6:6 // 4Q259 3:2) and "the study of the law" (1QS 8:15 // 4Q258 6:7 // 4Q259 3:6).[146] A related title "the interpreter (or student) of the law" occurs with reference to a historical figure in CD 6:7–8 and in an eschatological context in CD 7:18–19 and 4Q174 (Florilegium) 1:11.[147] Steven Fraade has aptly described this broad chronological span in terms of "Study as a Bridge between Communal Origins and the End of Time."[148]

Finally, the emphasis on continuous study of the law both here and conceivably also in Josh 1:8 is now illuminated by our fuller appreciation of the significance of apotropaic beliefs. Elsewhere I emphasized a series of references to the role of adherence to the law in apotropaic contexts for keeping harmful demonic forces at bay.[149] As Bilhah Nitzan has pointed out, the admonition to meditate and study the law continuously is explicitly connected to times of trial, distress and fear in 4Q525 2–3 ii 6.[150] One reason why a heightened state of watchfulness may have been required in the context of the meetings described in 6.4 would have been the process of admitting and assessing new members into the covenant. As far as admitting new membes is concerned, we know from the case of those who initially refuse to enter the covenant[151] that these decisions could be challenging and complex. As for as annual assessments of current members are concerned, the references to an evaluation of members' spirits and (the lawfulness of their) deeds undoubtedly required extreme vigilance since a member compromised by the influence of dark forces would have exposed the movement to the reach of perilious powers from within.[152]

[143] Pace Johann Maier, "Early Jewish Biblical Interpretation in the Qumran Literature," in *Hebrew Bible/Old Testament: The History of Its Interpretation. Volume 1: From the Beginnings to the Middle Ages (Until 1300)*. Edited by Magne Sæbø (Göttingen: Vandenhoeck & Ruprecht, 1996) 108–129.

[144] Cf. Hugh Williamson, *Ezra, Nehemiah*. Word Biblical Commentary 16 (Waco, TX: Word Books, 1985), 277–299.

[145] See 6.4.3 above.

[146] Cf. Chapter 8 below.

[147] For details see Michael A. Knibb, "Interpreter of the Law," EDSS 1:383–384.

[148] Fraade, "Interpretive Authority," 58–63.

[149] See 1.2.1 and 5.4.1 above.

[150] Nitzan, "Education and Wisdom in the Dead Sea Scrolls," 113–114.

[151] Cf. 3.2.4 above.

[152] See 1.2.1, 4.2.5 and 4.2.6 above. On the particular dangers of exposure to such forces during the night see 6.5.4.1.

6.5 Meetings of the Many

(1QS 6:7b–23 // 4Q256 11:5–8, 11–13 // 4Q258 2:10b; 3:1–3 // 4Q261 3:1?)

6.5.1 Introduction

In this section I group together three types of meetings of the many. This material includes a paradigmatic account of meetings of the many.[153] Two sets of regulations frame this well-known account. The two framing sections concern the nightly meetings of the many, on the one hand, and the material laying down the rules for admitting new members during meetings of the many, on the other hand.[154] I will deal with each of these three accounts in turn. While the material preserved in 4Q256 and 4Q258 is fragmentary, it is clear that both these manuscripts contained a shorter text for all three sets of regulations on meetings of the many.[155] Significantly, Alexander and Vermes note the possibility that 4Q261 lacked the account of the meeting of the many in 1QS 6:8–23 altogether.[156] In fact, we cannot be sure that this manuscript contained any of the passages dealt with in this chapter including 1QS 6:7b–8a // 4Q258 2:10b.

6.5.2 Translation

6.5.2.1 Nightly Meetings of the Many (1QS 6:7b–8a // 4Q258 2:10b)

1QS 6	4Q258 2
[7b]And the many shall take care together for a third of all the nights of the year to read the book, study the law [8a]and to pray together. *Vacat.*	[10b][the many shall take c]ar[e

6.5.2.2 Rules on Conducting Communal Meetings (1QS 6:8b–13a // 4Q256 11:5–8a // 4Q258 3:1–3[157]

1QS 6
[8b]This is the rule for the meetings of the many. Everyone shall sit according to his rank: the priests first, the elders second and then [9]all the people shall sit each according to his

---

[153] Compare 1QS 6:8b–13a // 4Q256 11:5–8a // 4Q258 3:1–3.

[154] See Knibb, *Qumran Community*, 119.

[155] Cf. Alexander and Vermes, DJD 26:55, 99–100 and Metsc, *Textual Development*, 23.

[156] Alexander and Vermes, DJD 26:170.

[157] On the principles behind the transparent composite text for the translation of 4Q256 and 4Q258 see 1.7 and 5.2 note 20 above.

rank. And thus they shall be asked about judgment or about any counsel or issue which concerns the many,

1QS 6	4Q256 11 // 4Q258 3
each one contributing their knowledge [10]to the deliberations of the community. No one shall interrupt his fellow's speech	3[1]each one [contributing their] know[ledge
before his brother has finished speaking. {.} Nor shall anybody speak before one whose rank [11]precedes them. The person who is consulted shall speak in his turn.	11[5]Nor shall anybody] speak [
And during a meeting of the many no one shall raise any issue which does not have the approval of the many, and, indeed, the overseer [12]over the many. Anyone who has a matter to raise with the many who is not leading the deliberations of [13a]the community (by asking members for their counsel), he shall rise to his feet and say, "I have a matter to raise with the many."	11[6][and during a meeting of] 3[2]the many no one shall rai[se …] 11[7][… any] member who has [a matter to raise] 3[3]with the many even though [he is not leading the deliberations
If they tell him to he may speak.	11[8a][if they tell him to] he may speak.

6.5.2.3 Rules on the Admission of New Members (1QS 6:13b–23 // 4Q256 11:8b, 11–13 // 4Q261 3:1?)

1QS 6	4Q256 11
[13b]And everyone who is fervently committed from Israel	[8b]And everyone who is fervently co[mmitted from Israel …]

1QS 6
[14]to join the council of the community, the official presiding over the many shall examine (each) one with respect to his insight and deeds. If he attains the (appropriate standard of) discipline he shall allow him to enter [15]into the covenant to return to the truth and to turn away from all injustice, and he shall [in]struct him in all the ordinances of the community. And afterwards when he comes in to stand before the many

1QS 6	4Q256 11
they shall all be asked [16]about his affairs.	[11][they shall] all [be asked]

1QS 6	4Q256 11
And when the decision is taken on the advice of the many he shall either approach or keep away. And when he approaches the council of the community he shall not touch the purity of [17]the many until he has examined him (again) with regard to his spirit and his deeds and he has completed a full year. Nor shall he be permitted to share the property of the many.[18]And when he has c°mpleted *a year in the midst of the community* the many shall be consulted	SHORTER TEXT [12][he shall not touch the] purity of the many until [he has] com[pleted][158] SHORTER TEXT [13][and whe]n h[e has completed *a full year* [the many] shall be consul[ted

1QS 6

about his affairs with regard to his insight and the lawfulness of his deeds. And if the decision is taken for him [19]to approach the alliance of the community on the authority of the priests and the multitude of the people of their covenant they shall hand {.} over both his property and his goods to the [20]overseer over the property of the many. He himself shall write it down in an account, but he shall not spend it on the many. He shall not touch the pure liquids of the many until [21]he has completed a second year in the midst of the people of the community. And when he has completed a second year he shall examine him on the authority of the many. And if the decision [22]is taken for him to approach the community he shall enrol him in the order of his rank in the midst of his brothers with reference to law, judgment, pur[it]y and for sharing his property.

1QS 6	4Q261 3?
And his counsel shall [be] accessible [23]to the community	[1][And] his [c]ounsel [shall be accessible] to the communi[ty]

1QS 6

as shall his judgment. *Vacat.*

---

[158] Our reading here follows James M. Tucker, "From Ink Traces to Ideology: A Reassessment of 4Q256 (4QSerekh ha-Yaḥad[b]) Frags. 5 a–b and 1QS 6:16–17," in *Law, Literature and Society in Legal Texts from Qumran.* Edited by Jutta Jokiranta and Molly Zahn. STDJ 128 (Leiden: Brill, 2019), 185–206.

6.5.3 Textual Notes

6:8 A paragraphos and small *vacat* mark a new beginning in 1QS.[159] Moreover, the initial letter of the new section has been corrected from *he* to *vav* in 1QS.[160]

6:10 There are traces of an erasure after the infinitive "to speak" (לדבר) in 1QS.

6:10–11 As noted by Alexander and Vermes, 4Q258 3:1–2 has a shorter text than 1QS at this point, see also the scarce remains of 4Q256 11. Alexander and Vermes propose a conjectural restoration for the lacuna in 4Q258.[161]

6:11 The first letter of the Hebrew term for "approval" should be amended from *he* to *khet*.[162]

6:12 Alexander Rofé has proposed reading "he shall restrain" יכיל rather than וכול "and anyone" after the reference to the overseer over the many in 1QS.[163] While Rofé's suggestion is materially and philologically excellent it is very difficult to see how it fits in with what follows as explained more fully in 6.5.4.2 below.

6:13 *Aleph* has been omitted in "they tell him (יומרו) in 1QS.[164]

6:13 The definite article that determines "the one who is fervently committed" has accidentally been appended to the previous word "everyone" (כול) in 1QS. The reading is preserved without this error in 4Q256 11:8.[165]

6:14 The translation "presiding over the many" follows Milik.[166]

6:15 The second letter of "and he shall instruct him" (והבינהו) is added above the line after initial *vav* was erased and an original *lamed* crudely re-shaped into what is now intial *vav*.[167] Van der Ploeg suggests the uncorrected text read ויבינהו.[168]

6:16 The text of 4Q256 11 is shorter at this point.[169]

---

[159] See also 1.5.1.3 above.

[160] Cf. Brownlee, *Dead Sea Manual*, 24 and Qimron, DSSHW, 220.

[161] Alexander and Vermes, DJD 26:103.

[162] See, e. g., Edmund F. Sutcliffe, "The General Council of the Qumran Community," *Biblica* 40 (1959): 971–983, 978–979 and Reymond, *Qumran Hebrew*, 109.

[163] Rofé, "A Neglected Meaning of the Verb כול and the Text of 1QS vi:11–13," in *"Sha'arei Talmon:" Studies in the Bible, Qumran, and the Ancient Near East Presented to Shemaryahu Talmon*. Edited by Michael A. Fishbane and Emanuel Tov (Winona Lake, IN: Eisenbrauns, 1992), 315–321; see also DCH 4:371–372 as well as Qimron, DSSHW 1:220. Qimron acknowledges the important alternative reading proposed by Rofé without fully committing to it. Charlesworth's English translation in PTSDSSP 1:29 follows Rofé.

[164] Cf. Qimron, HDSS, 20–21.

[165] Cf. Alexander and Vermes, DJD 26:55, Plate 3 and LLDSSDL B-366897.

[166] Józef T. Milik, "Manuale Disciplinae," *Verbum Domini* 29 (Rome: Pontificium Institutum Biblicum, 1951), 129–158, 145.

[167] See Wernberg-Møller, *Manual of Discipline*, 41.

[168] Van der Ploeg, "Manuel de Discipline," 121; similarly Brownlee, *Dead Sea Manual*, 25.

[169] See Alexander and Vermes, DJD 26:57 and Metso, *Textual Development*, 84.

6:16 The phrase translated here "and when the decision is taken" takes the reference to casting lots figuratively.[170]

6:16–17 James Tucker has convincingly argued that the longer reading in 1QS includes a secondarly addition.[171]

6:17 The plural suffix ō in "his works" is the result of a contraction of the diphthong āw.[172] The same phrase recurs in the next line (1QS 6:18) without contraction. The contracted form occurs in the longer and likely expanded text of 1QS.

6:17 *Vav* has been added above the line in the infinitive construct מולאת in 1QS.[173] The same form recurs inclusive of *vav* in 1QS 6:18.

6:17 The phrase "until he has examined him" is sometimes translated with a plural. On our reading the current process is a re-run of what happened at the first level of examination by the official who presides over the many in 1QS 6:14.[174] I follow the same approach in translating 1QS 6:21 and 22.

6:19 A letter that has been identified by Qimron as *yod* or *vav* has been erased in "they shall hand over" (יקר{י}בו).[175]

6:20 Initial *ayin* has been corrected from *aleph* in the preposition "over" (על) near the beginning of the line.

6:20 "He himself" is a somewhat free translation of "in his hand" (בידו) which I take to refer back to the overseer who is to keep a written ledger of assets brought to the community.[176] Maier takes the expression to mean "for his purposes" ("zu seiner Verfügung").[177] Yet another translation is favoured by Brownlee who renders בידו "in his credit" as a reference to the new member's interim account.[178]

6:22 *He* has been added secondarily and above the line in "to purity" (לטוהרה) in 1QS. Another superlinear addition of *yod* occurs at the end of the verb "it shall be (accessible)" (ויהי) in the same line.

6:22–23 Only ink traces are preserved of this material in 4Q261 3:1. They are tentatively identified by Alexander and Vermes as corresponding to 1QS 6:22–23.[179] In their assessment of the remains of 4Q261 3 Alexander and Vermes allow

---

[170] Cf. Lange, "גּוֹרָל *gôrāl*."

[171] Tucker, "From Ink Traces to Ideology."

[172] See Qimron, HDSS, 33–34 and Reymond, *Qumran Hebrew*, 144–145.

[173] Cf. Qimron, HDSS, 35–36, 110.

[174] So also Wernberg-Møller, *Manual of Discipline*, 31, 108.

[175] Qimron, DSSHW 1:220.

[176] See also Knibb, *Qumran Community*, 119.

[177] Maier, *Qumran-Essener*, 1:183.

[178] Brownlee, *Dead Sea Manual*, 26.

[179] Alexander and Vermes, DJD 26:177–178 and Plate 18. See also García Martínez and Tigchelaar, DSSSE, 540 and Martone, *Regola*, 174. A slightly different reading is proposed by Metso, *Textual Development*, 60.

for the possibility that this manuscript did not include the rules on the meetings, including the rules on admission of new members of the many.[180]

6:23 The rest of this line has been left blank in 1QS which, together with a paragraphos sign in the margin and a *vacat* at the beginning of the next line, indicates the end of this section which is followed by the Penal Code.

6.5.4 Commentary

6.5.4.1 Nightly Meetings of the Many (1QS 6:7b–8a // 4Q258 2:10b)

The topic of the study of the law including during (parts of) the night shared between this passage and what precedes in 6.4.2.3 likely gave rise to the combination of two otherwise distinctive regulations on meetings at this point. A number of scholars take this passage with what precedes.[181] Both Leaney and Metso go further by suggesting that we have here a passage linking the string of rules on communal activities in more dispersed settings to material that deals with the particular context of the many.[182] While the passage does de facto serve as a link, it belongs with what follows. In our view its contribution goes far beyond that of a literary bridge created by a redactor for this purpose as envisaged by Metso. Firstly, this passage introduces nightly meetings of "the many" which include three activities: reading the book, studying the law and blessing. Moreover, these meetings are to take place during a part of every night of the year. While the previous passage offered no particulars on the occasion(s) when continuous study of the law is required, I stressed the need to take the context of communal gatherings that precede the stipulation into account.[183] In addition to the thematic connection between 6.4.2.3 and 6.5 the current brief statement must be understood as an integral part of what follows on meetings of the many that take place during the daytime. On our reading section 6.5 includes a significant cluster of regulations devoted to meetings of the many. We came across an earlier reference to the authority of the many in 4Q256 9:3 and 4Q258 1:2[184] as well as a first reference to the many in 1QS in 1QS 6:1.[185] The lack of reference to the many in sections 6.1, 6.3 and 6.4, and the likelihood that one of the Cave 4 manuscripts (4Q261) lacked the comprehensive regulations on

---

[180] Alexander and Vermes, DJD 26:11, 70; see also 6.5.1 above.

[181] See, e. g., Leaney, *Rule of Qumran*, 175–186; Knibb, *Qumran Community*, 112–117 and Licht, *Rule Scroll*, 138–140.

[182] Cf. Metso, *Textual Development*, 133. Leaney, in line with the standard view at the time, associated the contents of 6.5 exclusively with Qumran, see *Rule of Qumran*, 185–186; see now 1.2.2 above.

[183] See 5.4.4.3 above.

[184] Cf. 5.2.4 and 5.4.4 above.

[185] See 6.2 above.

meetings of the many found in 6.5,[186] suggests we ought to allow for a stage in the growth of the Community Rules at which the regulations of the many were inserted. It is important to understand the much-discussed reference to the many in 4Q256 9:3 and 4Q258 1:2 as also belonging to a larger cluster of rules concerning the many across the S manuscripts including elsewhere in 1QS. It is crucial to respond proportionately to the dramatic variant between 1QS 5:2 and 4Q256 // 4Q258 where 1QS has "the sons of Zadok and the multitude of the people of the community" over against "the many" attested in 4QS. The particular case of 1QS 5:2 and parallels cannot speak pars pro toto on the picture of communal leadership in 1QS. And, similarly, whereas the singular and most unexpected reference to the many in 4Q256 9:3 // 4Q258 1:2 is indeed striking at that point, it needs to be read alongside a sizeable cluster of a comparable material across the Community Rules as attested in several manuscripts.

Jeremy Penner has drawn together a wealth of evidence on prayer patterns in ancient Judaism and offered perceptive reflections on the relationship of prayer to the cycle of day and night. By building on recent research on the anthropology of sleep in antiquity Penner is able to throw fresh light on the present passage when he observes, "A sustained culture of nocturnal activities existed in the ancient world, activities such as prayer and study, that for most individuals today have lost a meaningful connection to nighttime."[187] He further makes a strong case for the night as a period during which the ancients felt particularly exposed to demonic threats which can be addressed by ritualised nocturnal prayers as advocated in the present passage.[188] Penner's insightful analysis on nocturnal prayer can be developed further by referring also to the apotropaic impact of the study of the law discussed in 5.4.1 and 6.4.4.3 above. Finally, George Brooke has paid close attention to the triad of nocturnal activities referred to here, including the references to reading the book.[189] He offers a comprehensive survey of references to reading as an engaged and perhaps even performative act.[190] Brooke's conclusion emerges in a new light when we add that a substantial number of community members at Qumran and elsewhere may well have been illiterate and in need of "text brokers" to allow them access to and protection from dangers, particularly at night.[191] Be that as it may, a strong case

---

[186] Cf. 6.5.1 above.

[187] Penner, *Patterns of Daily Prayer*, 171.

[188] Penner, *Patterns of Daily Prayer*, 178–208.

[189] See George J. Brooke, "Reading, Searching and Blessing: A Functional Approach to Scriptural Interpretation in the יחד," in *The Temple in Text and Tradition: A Festschrift in Honour of Robert Hayward*. Edited by George J. Brooke and Timothy McLay. LSTS 83 (London: Continuum, 2015), 140–156.

[190] Brooke, "Reading, Searching and Blessing," 145–146.

[191] On the idea of "text brokers" and the larger question of literacy see Snyder, *Teachers and Texts*, 165; Chris Keith, *Jesus's Literacy: Scribal Culture and the Teacher from Galilee*. LNTS (London: T&T Clark, 2011), 112 and Hempel, "Literacy, Textuality, and Community."

emerges to suggest that the nocturnal activities of the many were ideally placed
to keep threats at bay during the night.

6.5.4.2 Rules on Conducting Communal Meetings (1QS 6:8b–13a // 4Q256 11:5–8a // 4Q258 3:1–3)

We began this chapter by noting the predominant place of this material in discussions of meetings as they emerge from the Community Rules. This focus
is partly suggested in the text itself which in 1QS 6:8b begins, after a closed
paragraph, with the heading "This is the rule for the meetings of the many." Such
an apparently clear structure can obscure our alertness to alternative narratives of
meetings, including those dealt with in the earlier sections of this chapter. Moreover, a close look at 1QS reveals a lack of certainty on the reading of this heading
at two important junctures. Thus, I noted in the Textual Notes that the first letter
of the heading has been corrected.[192] Moreover, the first word of the introduction
to the material on communal life in all their dwelling places in 1QS 6:1 has also
been corrected and lacks a conjunction found in both parallel 4QS manuscripts.[193]
While it is impossible to say which reading was original, material considerations
such as these do support literary analyses that have stressed unevenness in 1QS 6
and parallels. Unfortunately the beginning of the current section is not preserved
in any of the Cave 4 manuscripts.

While the material preserved in 4Q256 and 4Q258 is fragmentary, it is clear
that both manuscripts contained a shorter text, as is the case throughout the
section on meetings of the many.[194]

The business of day-time meetings of the many is expected to be conducted
on the basis of hierarchical principles. The hierarchical order[195] is expressed
with the verb "to sit" suggesting a hierarchical seating order rather than a
chronological order of taking seats.[196] The idea of the great majority of those
present being seated is mirrored by the lack of explicit involvement by any of
the leading figures in what follows. Immediate leadership of proceedings lies
with a chair of deliberations (the one who asks for counsel), and the latter's role
is associated with a standing position in 1QS 6:12 on which more will be said
below. The meetings cover the areas of judgment (משפט), deliberation (עצה) and
"any other matters" (דבר אשר יהיה). Occasions for judgment might refer to the
kinds of issues laid down in the penal code which is introduced with the words
"These are the judgments according to which they shall judge" (אלה המשפטים
אשר ישפטו).[197] Another area that falls in the remit of the many concerns rebukes

---

[192] Cf. 6.5.3 above.

[193] See 6.3.3.

[194] Cf. Alexander and Vermes, DJD 26:55; Metso, *Textual Development*, 23 and 6.5.1 above.

[195] Cf. Wernberg-Møller, *Manual of Disciplins*, 30.

[196] So Brownlee, *Dead Sea Manual*, 24; see also M. Chan, "יָשַׁב jāšab," ThWQ 2:302–309.

[197] See Chapter 7 below.

by fellow members which can be brought before the many after having been raised in front of witnesses.[198] The references to deliberation, on the one hand, and other issues that might arise, on the other hand, evoke a formal and closely regulated process in the accounts of these meetings.

1QS 6:11–12 The reference to the overseer over the many in 1QS 6:12 is somewhat disruptive since it is the many who make decisions elsewhere. This is the case also in the case mentioned in the wake of a reference to the overseer. Thus, 1QS 6:13 reads "if they tell him he may speak." Moreover the individual who is leading the deliberations is referred to as "the one leading the deliberations of the community" (האיש השואל את עצת היחד).[199] This way of proceeding is laid out already in 1QS 6:9 "And thus they shall be asked about judgment or about any counsel or issue which concerns the many" (כן ישאלו למשפט ולכול עצה ודבר אשר יהיה לרבים). In other words, the person leading the deliberations asks members for their input. Given the poor integration of the role of the overseer in the passage as a whole I suspect the reference to this office was one of the areas where 1QS's longer text includes a supplementation of what we find in 4QS. This title occurs only one more time in 1QS in the rules on admission in 1QS 6:20 below. As we will see below the immediate context of this second reference to the overseer in 1QS is terminologically at odds with the rest of the admissions passage.[200]

1QS 6:12–13a The use of the term מעמד (literally "the place where one stands") to refer to the chair of proceedings is significant in light of the account that everyone, including leading members, are seated. The next line instructs members wishing to speak to rise and to declare their desire to speak. This nuanced use of the standing position is lost by emending מעמד to read מחמד "desire, will" as proposed by Wernberg–Møller.[201]

There is some overlap with the various meetings described above where communal deliberation is to take place with senior members guiding those of lesser rank in all their dwelling places[202] and overseen by a priest in places where ten meet.[203] The literary connections to 6.4 go further since both passages share the language used in the Damascus Document with regard to the meeting of all the camps in CD 14:3–12a and parallels.[204] Overlapping termininology includes the

---

[198] Cf. 1QS 6:1 // 4Q258 2:5 // 4Q263 1–2.

[199] See 1QS 6:1 // 4Q258 2:5 // 4Q263 1–2. For the translation "the investigator" for האיש השואל see Reinhard Kratz, "The Teacher of Righteousness and His Enemies," in *Is There a Text in this Cave?* Edited by Feldman, Cioată and Hempel, 515–532. For a translation along the lines put forward above see Sutcliffe, "General Council."

[200] Cf. further 6.5.4.3 below.

[201] Wernberg–Møller, *Manual of Discipline*, 30, 41 and 106, see also 7.2.4.5 below.

[202] Cf. 6.3 above.

[203] See 6.4 above and Metso, "Whom Does the Term Yaḥad Identify?."

[204] For details see Hempel, *Laws of the Damascus Document*, 131–138 and Hempel, *Qumran Rule Texts in Context*, 33 as well as further literature cited. See also Steudel, "The Damascus

heading "this is the rule for the meeting," a hierarchical order of precedence, members sit (ישב) and speak (דבר) when invited to (שאל *niphal*).

The meeting is clearly referred to as "the session of the many" (מושב הרבים), and "the many" occurs seven times in this relatively brief account. The passage also includes two references to what is often translated with "the council of the community" (עצת היחד), a phrase that is very much to the fore in 1QS 8 // 4Q259 2.[205] Whatever its meaning in the rather distinctive account of 1QS 8 and parallels, it is clear that the phrase as it is used here refers to parts of the sessions that are devoted to "deliberation" which is why I translate collectively with "the deliberations of the community." It is significant that each time the phrase "deliberations of the community" occurs, the context is concerned with verbal contributions of members.[206]

We are not given any indication of the frequency of these meetings, though the fact that the many meet for part of every night[207] suggests a degree of geographical proximity for day-time meetings as well. There is, however, no need to presuppose that members of the movement were settled at Qumran until well into the first century BCE.[208]

6:8b–9a The division of the assembled community into priests, elders and the rest of the people differs markedly from the division into priests, levites and all the people in 1QS 2:19–21a.[209] Moreover, in the otherwise related passage on the meeting of all the camps in the Damascus Document the movement includes priests, levites, Israelites and proselytes.[210] As far as the Community Rules are concerned, the language used here is at odds with the binary division into priests and laity in 5.2.4; 6.1.2.1 and elsewhere. This passage includes the only reference to elders in the Community Rules. The idea of elders as chosen representatives of the people of Israel is familiar from the Hebrew Bible,[211] and the order of precedence described in these terms is modelled on the organization of biblical Israel.[212] On the other hand, both male and female elders appear in a number of texts from Qumran, and what seem to be male elders are assigned a role during the meetings of the many even if they are not otherwise referred to in the Community Rules.[213] As Himmelfarb notes, the term elders suggests a significant

---

Document (D) as a Rewriting," 609. In addition, a remarkably similar procedure is referred to in 1QSa 2:9, see, e. g., Licht, *Rule Scroll*, 144.

[205] See Chapter 8 below.

[206] Compare also 6.4.4.1 above.

[207] Cf. 6.5.4.1 above.

[208] Further, 1.2.2 above.

[209] See 3.4.3 above and Knibb, *Qumran Community*, 117.

[210] On the latter category see Carmen Palmer, *Converts in the Dead Sea Scrolls: The Gēr and Mutable Ethnicity*. STDJ 126 (Leiden: Brill, 2018).

[211] Cf., e. g., Exodus 19:7.

[212] Further, Leaney, *Rule of Qumran*, 186–188.

[213] See Cecilia Wassén, "זָקֵן zāqen," ThWQ 1:865–869 and "זקן III," in HAWTTM 2:236–237.

element of merit in achieving this status.[214] However, the dual authority poles for priests and elders sits somewhat awkwardly alongside the role of the overseer over the many referred to in 1QS 6:12. The difficulty of placing the role of the elders alongside other hierarchies is acknowledged also by Himmelfarb.[215]

6.5.4.3 Rules on the Admission of New Members (1QS 6:13b–23 // 4Q256 11:8b, 11–13 // 4Q261 3:1?)

This section contains detailed regulations on the admission of new members into the community and is often discussed independently of its context.[216] A simpler admission process by oath was introduced in 1QS 5:7c and parallels. The relationship of what is envisaged here to the brief earlier passage on admission into the community by swearing an oath has been the subject of debate. The traditional view, most recently supported by James VanderKam, argues that the oath referred to in 6.1.2.1 above is an integral part of the procedure described here.[217] However, the simpler process of admission into the community by swearing an oath is attested more widely[218] and reflects a more modest affair than the procedure laid down in the present passage. Moreover, as I will demonstrate below, there are a number of affinities between this passage and 6.1 above that indicate literary developments both within 1QS and across several manuscripts in 5.2.4 and 6.1 above.

One reason why the complex admissions process described here was often discussed almost as a self-contained unit are the many striking connections with descriptions of the initiation of members into the *haburah*, a fellowship network attested in the Mishnah and Tosefta,[219] on the one hand, and Josephus' account of the admissions procedures of the Essenes, which he claims to have experienced himself,[220] on the other hand. I have dealt with methodological reservations about reading the classical sources in order to arrive at a better understanding of the primary evidence of the Dead Sea Scrolls in 1.4.2 above. As far as the rabbinic accounts of the *haburah* are concerned, Steven Fraade has offered an excellent review of scholarship that judiciously reminds us, in concluding, that we are not comparing two historical movements but rather literary accounts that offer a particular "rhetorical reconstruction" of features the respective authors, and conceivably already their sources, wanted to emphasize.[221] Fraade

---

[214] Himmelfarb, *Kingdom of Priests*, 121.

[215] Himmelfarb, *Kingdom of Priests*, 127.

[216] Cf., e. g., Leaney, *Rule of Qumran*, 191 and Wernberg-Møller, *Manual of Discipline*, 106.

[217] VanderKam, "The Oath and the Community," *DSD* 16 (2009): 416–432.

[218] See 1QS 5:7c–9a and parallels; CD 15:5b–10a and parallels as well as Neh 10.

[219] Cf., e. g., m. Demai 2:2–3 and t. Demai 2:2–3:10.

[220] See *J. W. 2.137–142* and *Life* 10–11.

[221] Fraade, *Legal Fictions*, 125–143; see also the cautious assessment by Lawrence H. Schiffman, *Reclaiming the Dead Sea Scrolls: The History of Judaism, the Background to*

demonstrates in passing how various confessional perspectives have had an impact on the reading of the sources. His constructive solution to point at "morphological" correpondences in our sources rather than offering historical conclusions presents a way forward. The key morphological features shared by this account of admission into the community and both Josephus and the descriptions in the Mishnah and Tosefta on the *haburah* concern a gradual process of admission that extends over a period of years and a pronounced concern for purity.[222] In addition, the rabbinic sources on the *haburah* share particular terminology with our passage including רבים (*rabbim*) to refer to members of the חבורה (*haburah*) or חברים (*haberim*), טהרות (*tohorot*) to refer to ritually pure items as well as משקין (*mašqin*) to refer to pure liquids. The latter are referred to as טהרה (*tohorah*) and משקה (*mašqeh*) in the Scrolls.[223] As Friedrich Avemarie points out, comparable terminology occurs, for instance, in the Temple Scroll (11QT 47:7) and on potsherds from Masada.[224] The widely shared purity terminology suggests the authors of the Community Rules drew on a wider usage.

Finally, a teared process of admission that is ratified in a plenary meeting is also attested in the statutes of Greco-Roman associations.[225] Not unlike Fraade with reference to the *haburah*, Benedikt Eckhardt acknowledges "structural similarities" with Hellenistic associations but is aware that explaining how these came about is far from straight forward.[226]

Christianity, the Lost Library of Qumran (Philadelphia, PA: Jewish Publication Society, 1994), 104–105.

[222] Cf. Beall, *Josephus' Description of the Essenes*, 73–78.

[223] See Saul Lieberman, "The Discipline of the So-Called Dead Sea Manual of Discipline," *JBL* 71 (1952):199–206. Jacob Licht developed the comparison with rabbinic purity regulations further, see *Rule Scroll*, 294–303 and Licht, "Some Terms and Concepts of Ritual Purity in the Qumran Writings," in *Studies in the Bible Presented to Professor M. H. Segal*. Edited by J. M. Grintz and Jacob Liver (Jerusalem: Kiryat Sefer, 1964), 300–309 [Hebrew]. I am grateful to Noam Mizrahi for bringing the latter study to my attention. Licht's contribution has been assessed in light of the publication of fresh evidence from Qumran Cave 4 by Friedrich Avemarie, "'Tohorat Ha-Rabbim' and 'Mashqeh Ha-Rabbim:' Jacob Licht Reconsidered," in *Legal Texts and Legal Issues: Proceedings of the Second Meeting of the IOQS in Honor of Joseph M. Baumgarten*. Edited by Moshe Bernstein, Florentino García Martínez and John Kampen. STDJ 23 (Leiden: Brill, 1997), 215–229.

[224] Avemarie, "Tohorat Ha-Rabbim," 20.

[225] Cf. Collins, *Beyond the Qumran Community*, 79–85; Eckhardt, "Yahad in the Context of Hellenistic Group Formation;" Bruno W. W. Dombrowski, *Wider die Hellenisierung jüdischer Religion: Die Qumran-Assoziation nach dem 'Manual of Discipline' (QS)*. Qumranica Mogilanensia (Krakow: Enigma, 1998), 262–272; Yonder Gillihan, *Civic Ideology, Organization, and Law in the Rule Scrolls: A Comparative Study of the Covenanters' Sect and Contemporary Voluntary Associations in Political Context*. STDJ 97 (Leiden: Brill, 2011) and Matthias Klinghardt, *Gemeinschaftsmahl und Mahlgemeinschaft: Soziologie und Liturgie frühchristlicher Mahlfeiern*. TANZ 13 (Tübingen: Francke, 1996), 227–249 as well as further literature cited in these contributions.

[226] Eckhardt, "Yahad in the Context of Hellenistic Group Formation," 94.

The shared descriptions of communal life along orderly parameters in this part of the Community Rules (especially 6.5.2–3 and 7.2.4 below) and pagan Hellenistic associations are intriguing. They reflect two rather different social phenomena of individuals coming together to achieve integration into organizations that operated in similar ways.[227] Such perhaps unexpected correspondences support recent scholarly re-assessments of the narrative of narrow sectarianism for the movement behind the Dead Sea Scrolls.[228] The similarities between the meetings of the many and Hellenistic associations should also be seen against the context of a series of studies that have identified significant connections between Jewish and Greek practices in unexpected places.[229] To this I would add the close relationship between types of pottery and the chemical composition of the clay from which it was produced between the Hasmonean Palaces at Jericho and the site of Qumran[230] and the emergence of an ancient commentary tradition.[231] The suggestion by Albert Baumgarten, that the emergence of Hellenistic associations in the wake of the conquests of Alexander the Great inspired upwardly-mobile, disaffected Jews to up their game offers a compelling explanation for the administratively highly developed accounts of communal life in this part of the Community Rules. Baumgarten's analysis contextualises the emergence of ritual immersion pools in the Hasmonean palaces of Jericho as indicative of "intra-elite competition" on the part of Hasmonean rulers in the Hellenistic period.[232] Along similar lines Cynthia Baker's analysis of rabbinic literature refers to this phenomenon as "'mimicking' dominant culture practices."[233] This leaves us with the credible hypothesis that the elaborate written account of structures such as meetings and admission at least partly served the leaders of the movement to present themselves and aspiring members as "players" in the intra-elite competiton Baumgarten has drawn attention to.[234] Whether or not

---

[227] See, e. g., Collins, *Beyond the Qumran Movement*, 80–81.

[228] Cf. Hempel, "Challenging the Particularist Paradigm."

[229] See Martin Hengel, "Qumran und der Hellenismus," in *Qumrân: Sa piété, sa théologie et son milieu.* Edited by Mathias Delcor. BETL 46 (Paris-Gembloux: Duculot; Leuven: University Press, 1978), 333–372; Yonatan Adler, "The Hellenistic Origins of Jewish Ritual Immersion," *JJS* 69 (2018): 1–21; Danielle Steele Fatkin, "Invention of a Bathing Tradition in Hasmonean Palestine," *JSJ* 50 (2019): 155–177, 174. I am grateful to Joseph Scales for bringing the latter article to my attention.

[230] See Rachel Hachlili, "Communal Meals at Qumran Revisited." *RevQ* 28 (2016): 215–256.

[231] Cf. Pieter B. Hartog, *Pesher and Hypomnema: A Comparison of Two Commentary Traditions from the Hellenistic Roman Period.* STDJ 121 (Leiden: Brill, 2017).

[232] Baumgarten, "Graeco-Roman Voluntary Organizations and Ancient Jewish Sects," in *Jews in a Graeco-Roman World.* Edited by Martin Goodman (Oxford: Oxford University Press, 1999), 93–111, esp. 106–111.

[233] Cynthia Baker, "When Jews were Women," *History of Religions* 45 (2005): 114–134.

[234] Cf. also recent nuanced research on the subtle yet "ambitious maneuverings of provincial sub-elites" in the Eastern Roman Empire in Late Antiquity, see Annette Yoshiko Reed and Natalie B. Dohrmann, "Rethinking Romanness, Provincialising Christendom," in *Jews,*

all of these rules were put into practice, the ambition projected by committing
the regulations to writing is a powerful statement.[235] George Brooke has made a
comparable case concerning the use of papyrus imported from Egypt as a writing
material attested from Qumran, including 4Q255 and 4Q257. Brooke describes
the use of imported papyrus as "an attempt by some Jews to emulate at least
one feature of high culture as that might be recognized through such material
artefacts in the Eastern Mediterranean."[236] Finally, Yehudah Cohen has argued
that *tefillin* are an "invented tradition" in response to Greek practice.[237] The
striking similarity between our movement's innermost organizational structures
and what Michael Stone has aptly described as "outsider texts"[238] should be ap-
preciated as a reciprocal proximity. Rather than following the standard view that
assumes knowledge of the practices of the rabbim reached the outside world, I
would emphasize the subtle influence of outside, including elite Greco-Roman
practices, on this part of the Community Rules and those responsible for crafting
them.

Our reading of this passage will resist approaching this material in a decon-
textualised manner and pay close attention to its context in the Community Rules.
In its immediate literary context the discussion on the admission of new members
forms part of a large block of material on meetings (6.1–6.5), and a significant
cluster that deals with meetings of the many in particular (6.5). The many play
a key role in the Community Rules more broadly in 5.2.4 (as the authoritative
body in 4Q256 and 4Q258), 6.2 (in the context of rebuke), 6.5 (in meetings), as
well as in 7.2.4 and 7.2.5.2 (in parts of the Penal Code). Moreover, the contexts
where the many play an active role suggest we are dealing with a "judicial body."[239]

From a material perspective it is clear that the two manuscripts which preserve
the opening lines of this section (1QS 6:13b and 4Q256 11:8b) present the rules
on admission as an integral part of the section on the communal meetings of the
many that precedes with no trace of a *vacat* or, in the case 1QS, a paragraphos.[240]
Moreover, the account of the admissions process contains an explicit reference
to aspiring members being questioned (1QS 6:15) before the many after a period
of instruction by a presiding officer. Decisions are ultimately taken on the ad-

---

Christians, and the Roman Empire: The Poetics of Power in Late Antiquity. Edited by Annette
Yoshiko Reed and Natalie B. Dohrmann. Jewish Culture and Contexts (Philadelphia: Univer-
sity of Pennsylvania Press, 2013), 1–22, 14. Further, Hayim Lapin, "The Law of Moses and the
Jews: Rabbis, Ethnic Marking, and Romanization," in *Jews, Christians, and the Roman Empire.*
Edited by Reed and Dohrmann, 79–92.

[235] See 1.3 above and Hempel, "Curated Communities."

[236] Brooke, "Choosing Between Papyrus and Skin," 131–133, citation from 132.

[237] Yehudah Cohen, *Tangled Up in Text: Tefillin and the Ancient World.* BJS 351 (Providence
RI: Brown University, 2008).

[238] Cf. Stone, *Secret Groups*, 96.

[239] So Schofield, *From Qumran to the Yaḥad*, 146–147.

[240] See also Knibb, *Qumran Community*, 119–120.

vice of the many (1QS 6:16; 1QS 6:18 // 4Q256 11:13; 1QS 6:21) as was the case in the rules on the meetings of the many, see especially 1QS 6:11 and 6:13. All of these scenarios can only be envisaged as taking place when the many are assembled. What is less clear is where the initial assessment by an official presiding over the many takes place or its time-frame. The requirement to instruct those wishing to join in the ordinances of the community does suggest this induction process took place outside of the confines of a meeting of the many, as does the phrase "and afterwards when he (i. e. the candidate) comes in to stand before the many" (1QS 6:15). 1QS 6:13b–15a // 4Q256 11:8b constitutes, therefore, a brief narrative that introduces the topic of admission as it is to play out in a meeting of the many according to 1QS 6:15b–23a // 4Q256 11:11–13 // 4Q261 3?. Given the bulk of what is described here takes place during a meeting of the many – and the period of induction is led by a chair over the many and is in essence preparing for the meeting itself – suggests that this section forms an integral part of the rules on the meetings of the many.

If we follow the material evidence and read the rules on meetings and admission continuously, the present passage sets in just after the invitation to members to stand and declare their intention to raise a matter with the many. This would be a natural moment for the admission of new candidates to be flagged up.

6:13b Both 1QS and 4Q256 begin with a reference to a fervent commitment. As I demonstrated in detail above, the root *ndb* is frequently used, both in the Hebrew Bible and at Qumran, to refer to the fervour of a lay element in a larger group that also comprises priests.[241] We also know that the many are made up of priests and laity.[242] It is likely, therefore, that the concept of Israel includes both priests and laity here. This is particularly explicit in 8.2.2 below where the expectation of "a holy house for Israel and a most holy assembly for Aaron" forms part of a series of events that are described in 1QS 8:4b // 4Q259 2:13b in terms of "when these exist in Israel."[243] We cannot exclude the possibility, however, that Israel refers to lay candidates.

6:14 The phrase "the council of the community" (עצת היחד) appears to be used synonymously here and in 1QS 6:16 as a designation for the community with yahad in 1QS 6:22 and frequently with "the many."

6:14 An official presiding over the many, or paqid (האיש הפקיד ברואש הרבים), closely resembles the title and role of "the priest [in cha]rge (המ[ופקד]) over the many" who is chairing a disciplinary process introduced as "[These are the l]aws by wh[ich] all who are disciplined (המתיסרים) [shall be judged]" in a ceremony

---

[241] See 5.4.2 and 5.4.4 above.

[242] Cf. 6.5.2.2 above.

[243] See 1QS 8:5–6 // 4Q259 2:14–15; also 8.1.1 and for a detailed study on the issue Collins, "Construction of Israel," 30–34.

near the end of the Damascus Document.[244] Even though the present passage talks about the paqid's concern with instructing and testing, the root יסר occurs here also.[245]

6:14b–15a Here we have the first of two outliers in this passage in the form of a reference to entering a covenant. In fact, this part of the admissions process is very close to the admission by oath in 6.1.2 which never mentions "the many" but continues instead with a detailed list of joint enterprises and activities to avoid in relation to the people of injustice. I already noted that the activities prohibited with what appear at first sight a group of outsiders are encounters that only insiders would share with one another.[246] A closer inspection of what we find in 6.1 alongside the current passage leaves no doubt that what is said regarding the people of injustice in 6.1 is nothing short of a reversed admissions process that forbids touching the purity of the people of holiness (1QS 5:13 // 4Q256 9:8–9 // 4Q258 1:7–8) and making common cause in matters of work and property (1QS 5:14. cf. 4Q256 9:10–11 // 4Q258 1:9–10) or share property and work (jointly) with (only in 4Q256 and lacking in 1QS).[247] As is the case here, a number of Cave 4 witnesses preserve a shorter account that was expanded in 1QS. The following table highlights correspondences with dotted underlining. The two shaded columns on the left present manuscripts that cover the same passage in 1QS and 4QS with the Cave 4 witnesses preserving a shorter account.

Table 7: Entrance by Oath and Renouncing Injustice in 6.1.2 and 6.5.2.3

4Q256 9:6–8b// 4Q258 1:5–7b	1QS 5:7b–8	1QS 6:13b–15 converges with 4Q256 11:8b)
And everyone who joins the council of [the community]	Everyone who joins the council of the community	[1]And everyone from Israel who is fervently committed to join the council of the community [...]
	shall enter into the covenant of God in the presence of all eager volunteers.	he shall allow him to enter into the covenant to return to the truth
shall ta[k]e upon themselves a binding *oath* to return to the law of Moses [...]	He shall take upon themselves a binding oath [...]	
They shall keep separate from [al]l the people of injustice.	to keep separate from all the people of injustice ...	and to turn away from all injustice ...

---

[244] See 4Q270 7 i 15–16; cf. also 4Q266 11:8 and CD 14:6–7.

[245] Cf. the wording "If he attains the (appropriate standard of) discipline" (ואם ישיג מוסר).

[246] See 6.1.4 above.

[247] Cf. 6.1.2.1 and 6.1.4.1 above.

6:15 The initial induction of candidates ends with the candidate being directed "to come in and stand before the many." As we saw in our discussion in 6.5.4.2 above, almost everyone attending the meeting of the many is seated which implies that being on your feet signalled participation even if it was of a liminal sort – and was certainly conspicuous.

6:16b After having passed the first year of induction and assessment the candidate is permitted to approach the council of the community. As Noam Mizrahi has recently argued, the verb "to draw near" (קרב) occurs here in a specialised sense that is also attested in rabbinic accounts of social gatherings. Mizrahi concludes that the evidence reflects a particular linguistic usage among Jewish authors of the Graeco-Roman period.[248] This additional connection between the admission process and wider Jewish practices offers further support for our analysis of the cross-fertilization reflected in this part of the Community Rules with practices attested more widely.[249]

1QS 6:16b–17 It is at this point in 1QS and 4Q256 11:12 that the issue of the purity of the many occurs for the first time. This aspect of the tiered admissions process displays intriguing links to the accounts of the *ḥaburah* in rabbinic sources which we discussed in the early part of 6.5.4.3 above. Recent scholarship has been able to draw on a much richer pool of evidence on ritual purity in the texts from Qumran.[250] The movement's vigilance about matters of ritual purity both in the daily life of the membership as well as at liminal moments were committed to writing just at a time when a number of archaeological phenomena emerge that signal a heightened concern with ritual purity much beyond Qumran.[251] In short, while purity concerns are highlighted in the material that describes the intricate organization of the many in the core of the Community Rules, this same narrative counter-intuitively also displays the strongest connections to a much broader literary and material landscape beyond the Community Rules.

A plus in 1QS refers to an examination of candidates' spiritual make-up and deeds. As James Tucker has shown the language of this plus in 1QS is reminiscent of the language and concerns of the Teaching on the Two Spirits.[252] Elsewhere in the Community Rules it is the Maskil who is credited with particular expertise in

---

[248] Cf. Noam Mizrahi, "Priests of *Qoreb*: Linguistic Enigma and Social Code in the *Songs of the Sabbath Sacrifice*," in *Hebrew of the Late Second Temple Period: Proceedings of a Sixth International Symposium on the Hebrew of the Dead Sea Scrolls and Ben Sira.* Edited by Eibert Tigchelaar and Pierre van Hecke. STDJ 114 (Leiden: Brill, 2015), 37–64.

[249] See our introductory remarks in 6.5.4.3 above.

[250] Cf., e. g., Avemarie, "'Tohorat Ha-Rabbim;" Hannah Harrington, *The Purity Texts.* CQS 5 (London: T & T Clark, 2004); Vered Noam, "4QMMT and Rabbinic Halakhah," in *Qumran 4QMMT.* Edited by Kratz et al. and Wassén, "Purity and Holiness."

[251] See, e. g., Adler, "Second Temple Period Ritual Baths."

[252] Tucker, "From Ink Traces to Ideology."

assessing the spiritual make-up of members and humanity more broadly.[253] We need to be mindful, also, of the nexus between spiritual inclination and deeds which would have facilitated an assessment of a candidate's spirit by a third party.

1QS 6:18b–19a This passage is again replete with terminology that appears out of place in its present context by referring to those in charge of decisions as "the priests and the multitude of the people of their covenant" (1QS 6:19). Given the many are repeatedly charged with making key decisions (1QS 6:16; 1QS 6:18a // 4Q256 11:13; 1QS 6:21), this passage almost constitutes a "variant" within 1QS that is on a par with what we find in 5.2.4 and 6.1.2.1 between different manuscripts. This passage is almost certainly part of the same literary process of supplementation that I outlined with reference to 1QS 6:14b–15 and parallels above. This picture offers strong support for our argument that the endorsement of the many in 4Q256 9 // 4Q258 1 is closely aligned with a cluster of texts where the many occupy a crucial role in 1QS.[254] The following table summarizes the evidence.

Table 8: Leadership Models in 5.2.4, 6.1.2.1 and 6.5

Section 5.2.4	Section 6.1.2.1	Section 6.5
4Q256 9:3 // 4Q258 1:2 the many	4Q256 9:8 // 4Q258 1:7 the council of the people of the community	1QS 6:16 the many 1QS 6:18a // 4Q256 11:13 the many
1QS 5:2b–3a the sons of Zadok, the priests who keep the covenant and to the multitude of the people of ³the community who hold fast to the covenant.	1QS 5:9 the sons of Zadok the priests who keep the covenant and seek His favour and to the multitude of the people of their covenant.	1QS 6:18b–20a the authority of the priests and the multitude of the people of their covenant.
		1QS 6:21 the many

1QS 6:19b If a candidate proves themselves worthy after a year's instruction and testing they are to "hand over both their property and goods to the overseer over the property of the many. He himself shall write it down in an account, but he shall not spend it on the many." Joan Taylor has suggested that women and children would have been considered as belonging to the property of male community members.[255]

---

[253] Cf. 14.2.1 below and 5.4.1 above.

[254] See 6.5.4.1 above.

[255] Taylor, "Women, Children, and Celibate Men in the Serekh Texts," *HTR* 104 (2011): 171–190.

As I have argued more fully elsewhere, the language of touching the purity and pure liquids of the many needs to be read in light of halakhic compositions that refer to purity concerns in an agricultural context.[256] In short, the issue at hand goes far beyond shared meals and might even extend to avoiding any physical contact that might contaminate not only food but also clothes, vessels and other people.[257] Both purity and property serve as boundary markers between those inside the community and those outside.[258]

6:20c–21a Candidates are instructed to wait a second year before they may come into contact with the pure liquid of the many and be fully integrated economically.

6:22 The account ends with the climactic moment of a member taking his place "among his brothers" just at the point where kinship property rights are given away in a manner that would have been life-changing for the members of the biological kinship group.[259] On the terms suggested by Tammas David-Barrett and Robin I. Dunbar, the movement emerges here as employing "quasi-kin linguistic cues to trigger kin-like relationships among their followers."[260]

6:22–23 The account ends in 1QS 6:22–23 // 4Q261 3 with granting full speaking rights to new members in deliberation and judgment after two probationary years. This implies that during the second probationary year candidates were permitted to be present and observe but not contribute their views and judgments. Such an interim state concerning formal spoken contributions mirrors the more well-known restricted spheres of membership during first probationary year pertaining to property and purity.

---

[256] See 4QTohorot A (4Q274) 3; 4QHarvesting (4Q284a) and Hempel, "Who is Making Dinner at Qumran;" see also Wassén, "Purity and Holiness."

[257] Cf. Avemarie, "'Tohorat Ha-Rabbim.'"

[258] On the benefits of shared goods for maintaining ritual purity see David Flusser, *Judaism of the Second Temple Period: Volume 1. Qumran and Apocalypticism*. Trans. Azzan Yadin (Grand Rapids, MI: Eerdmans; Jerusalem: Magnes, 2007), 36.

[259] See Baumgarten, *Flourishing of Jewish Sects*, 64.

[260] David-Barrett and Dunbar, "Fertility, Kinship and the Evolution of Mass Ideologies," *Journal of Theoretical Biology* 427 (2017): 20–27, 25; see also Jokiranta and Wassén, "A Brotherhood at Qumran?"

7. The Penal Code (1QS 6:24–7:25 // 4Q258 5:1 // 4Q259 1:4–15; 2:3–9 // 4Q261 3:2–4; 4a–b:1–6; 5a–c:1–9; 6a–e:1–5)

7.1 Introduction

The beginning of the Penal Code is preserved in two manuscripts and is clearly marked materially in 1QS with the rest of 1QS 6:23 left blank followed by a *vacat* at the start of 1QS 6:24 as well as a paragraphos in the margin.[1] Alexander and Vermes tentatively mirror the *vacat*s in their restoration of 4Q261. Despite clear indications that we are at the beginning of a new section there are also connections between this code of violations by members of the community and what precedes.[2] The first close connection to the end of the previous section is the term "judgment" (משפט) that closes the rules on admitting new members and forms part of the heading of the penal code. In closing the rules on admission the term appears somewhat as an afterthought in 1QS 6:22–23: "And his counsel shall be accessible to the community, as shall his judgment." Alexander and Vermes note the awkward syntax which is mirrored in the cautiously proposed decipherement of 4Q261 3:1.[3] Since the reference to judgment is an integral part of the conclusion to the admissions process in 1QS in its present form it offers a catchword link with the heading of the penal code that follows. Beyond this catchword link the content of the penal code functions well as part of the proceedings of the meetings of the many. Thus, Lawrence Schiffman has argued in favour of a close connection between the description of admission into the community (see 6.5.2.3) and the penal code. He argued, more particularly, that the latter offers a selection of judicial scenarios that were intended for the instruction of novices.[4] Aharon Shemesh has also observed the connections between the Penal Code and the material on admission into the community and meetings that precedes.[5]

I would go further and highlight that the primary description of the business to be covered in the meetings of the many in 1QS 6:9b–10a // 4Q258 3:1 requires

---

[1] Cf. 1.5.1.3 above.

[2] See also Hinojosa, "A Synchronic Approach," 159–160.

[3] Alexander and Vermes, DJD 26:178.

[4] See Schiffman, *Sectarian Law in the Dead Sea Scrolls*, 155–157.

[5] Aharon Shemesh, "The Scriptural Background of the Penal Code in the *Rule of the Community* and *Damascus* Document," *DSD* 15 (2008): 191–224, 196–197.

members to "be asked about judgment or about any counsel or issue which concerns the many, each one contributing their knowledge to the deliberations of
the community." The rules on the meetings of the many, therefore, depict the
forum where the judgments and punishments for the kinds of offences listed
in the penal code are dealt with. On our reading the penal code makes up an
integral part of regulations that are associated with meetings of the many. The
following further considerations support such an interpretation. Firstly, a large
number of offences pick up issues of concern to the deliberations of the many as
described in 6.4–6.5 above by referring to behaviour such as appropriate speech[6]
and conduct during meetings of the many.[7] Secondly, the case of someone who
blasphemes while reading the book or praying in 1QS 6:27b–7:2a // 4Q261 4a–b:
1–4a refers to a scenario that is very reminiscent of the nightly watches of the
many outlined in 6.5.1 above. I argue below, therefore, that the nightly gatherings
are suggestive occasions during which members might sleep, intentionally or
from exhaustion.[8] Finally, while the penal code includes a number of generic
terms for punishment, the precise meaning of which is at times difficult to establish, the more concrete punishments include a barring of access to the purity
of the many or permanent exclusion – precisley the kinds of questions that are
dealt with by the many in 6.5.2.3 above.

Until the publication of the contents of Cave 4 the only parallel to the penal
code attested in the Community Rules were the remains of a very similar heading
in the Damascus Document in CD 14:18b.[9] While nothing is preserved of the
penal code proper in CD 14, four fragmentary manuscripts of the Damascus
Document from Cave 4 include a substantial part of a penal code that displays
both remarkable overlap as well as dramatic differences from the penal code in
the Community Rules.[10] Of particular interest are a number of additional offences
preserved in the Damascus Document but not included in the Community Rules
that refer to women leaders in the congregation as well as wives. This evidence
amplifies the silence on the role of women in the movement described in the
Community Rules further without offering a clear-cut solution to the debate
on whether or not (some) male community members had families outside of
their involvement in communal life.[11] While the penal code material shared by
the Community Rules and the Damascus Document is highly significant, it is
important to consider this particular area of convergence between those two
texts alongside a series of other close literary connections that at times occur

---

[6] Cf. 7.2.2 below.

[7] See 7.2.4 and 7.2.5.2 below.

[8] Cf. 7.2.4.3 and 7.2.4.5 below.

[9] See Hempel, *Laws of the Damascus Document*, 141–148.

[10] See 4Q266 (4QD^a) 10 i–ii // 4Q267 (4QD^b) 9 vi // 4Q269 (4QD^d) 11 i–ii and 4Q270 (4QD^e)
7 i.

[11] On this issue see recently Cecilia Wassén, "Daily Life," in CDSS, 547–558.

in sequence.[12] Additional penal material forms part of 4Q265 (Miscellaneous Rules, see 4Q265 4 i 2 – ii 2) and 11Q29 (Serekh ha-Yahad?).[13] While there are close relationships between the penal code material in the Community Rules, the Damascus Document and 4Q265, each text displays distinctive features, and scholars continue to debate the particulars and their implications.[14]

Carol Newsom has offered the fascinating observation that the penal code is written from the point of view of "the disciplinary power" rather than ordinary members.[15] The same point could be made about the admission process and other parts of the Community Rules in which boundaries, control and power are a dominant theme. The repeated concern with control suggests a sense of insecurity, perhaps in view of the lack of commitment of members and the sway held by the potentially influential people of injustice.[16] Finally, Schiffman has argued, convincingly, that the code is intended for instruction and to a certain extent intimidation of novices. This might explain the circumstance that someone could be reduced to a trembling state which is suggested by our interpretation of 7.2.6.3 in 7.4.6.3 below.[17]

7.2 Translation

7.2.1 Introduction (1QS 6:24a // 4Q261 3:2a)

1QS 6	4Q261 3
[24a]*Vacat.* And the[se] are the judgments according to which they shall judge/be judged	[2a][And these are the judgments (according to) wh]ich they shall judge/be judged
at an inquiry of the community according to the cases.	according to [the cases.

---

[12] See further 1.6.1 above.

[13] Cf. 1.6.2 and 1.6.3 above.

[14] See, e. g., Joseph M. Baumgarten, "The Cave 4 Versions of the Qumran Penal Code," *JJS* 43 (1992): 268–276; Charlotte Hempel, "The Penal Code Reconsidered," in *Legal Texts and Legal Issues.* Edited by Bernstein, García Martínez and Kampen, 337–348; Kratz, "Der *Penal Code*" and Schofield, *From Qumran to the Yahad*, 180–183. For a comparison of the Penal Code with Graeco-Roman associations see Moshe Weinfeld, *The Organizational Pattern and the Penal Code of the Qumran Sect: A Comparison with Guilds and Religious Associations of the Hellenistic Roman Period.* NTOA 2 (Göttingen: Vandenhoeck & Ruprecht; Fribourg: Éditions Universitaires, 1986).

[15] Newsom, *Self as Symbolic Space*, 148.

[16] See especially, 1.2.1; Chapter 5 and 6.1 above.

[17] Cf. also 1.2.1 above.

7.2.2 Offences Involving the Spoken Word

7.2.2.1 Fraudulent Speech (1QS 6:24b–25a // 4Q261 3:2b–4)

1QS 6	4Q261 3
24bIf someone is found among them who lies 25aknowingly about *property* they shall exclude him from the purity of the many for a year and withhold a quarter of his food.	2bIf someone is found among them 3who lies] knowingly [about] *money* they shall ex[clude him from the purity 4of the many for a year and withhol]d [a quar]ter of [his] foo[d.]

7.2.2.2 Unguarded or Disrespectful Speech (1QS 6:25b–27a)

1QS 6
Whoever talks back at 26his neighbour obstinately or speaks with a short temper, not paying regard to the dignity of his companion by rebelling against the word of his neighbour who is registered before him, 27is [ta]king the law into his own hand and shall be punished for on[e] year.

7.2.2.3 Blasphemy (1QS 6:27b–7:2a // 4Q261 4a–b:1–4a)

1QS 6–7	4Q261 4a–b
27b[... Whoev]er invokes the name of the Honoured One concerning any [...] 71Or if someone has blasphemed either while suddenly befallen by terror brought on by distress or for whatever reason he may have {...} while he is reading in the book or praying they shall exclude him 2never to return again to the council of the community.	1[Whoever invokes the name of] the Ho[noured One concerning any [...] 2[Or if someone has blasphemed either while suddenly befallen by terror brought on by] distress [or for whatever reason he may have while he is 3reading in the boo]k or [praying they shall exclude him never to return again to the council of 4the community.]

7.2.2.4 Verbal Outburst Against Registered Priests (1QS 7:2b– 3b // 4Q261 4a–b:4b–6)

1QS 7	4Q261 4a–b
2bAnd if someone speaks in anger against one of the priests who are written down in the book he shall be punished for one 3ayear and be excluded on his own from the purity of the many.	4b[And if someone speaks in anger] against on[e of the priests who are written down in the book 5he shall be punished] for o[ne] year [...] 6 [...] the many [...]

1QS 7

---

³ᵇBut if he speaks inadvertently they shall be punished for six months.

7.2.2.5 Deliberate Deception (1QS 7:3c–4a)

1QS 7

---

³ᶜAnd whoever deceives knowingly ⁴shall be punished for six months.

7.2.2.6 Unjustified Reproach (1QS 7:4b–5a)

1QS 7

---

⁴ᵇThe person who knowingly reproaches his neighbour without justification shall be punished a year ⁵ᵃand be excluded.

7.2.2.7 Deceptive Speech (1QS 7:5b–6a)

1QS 7

---

⁵ᵇThe person who speaks to his neighbour with bitterness or knowingly acts deceptively shall be punished for six months. If ⁶ᵃ*vacat* he ᵈᵉᶜᵉⁱᵛᵉˢ his neighbour he shall be punished for three months.

7.2.3 Offences Involving Behaviour

7.2.3.1 Fraudulent Actions (1QS 7:6b–8a)

1QS 7

---

⁶ᵇ*Vacat.* But if he acts deceptively with regard to the property of the community as to cause its loss he shall restore it {…} ⁷in full. *Vacat.* TWO EMPTY LINES ⁸But if he does not have the means to restore it he shall be punished for ˢⁱˣᵗʸ ᵈᵃʸˢ.

7.2.3.2 Bearing a Grudge or Retaliating (1QS 7:8b–9a // 4Q259 1:4)

---

⁸ᵇWhoever bears a grudᵍᵉ against his neighbour which is not ʲustified shall be punished

---

1QS 7	4Q259 1
for {six months}ᵒⁿᵉ ʸᵉᵃʳ.	⁴[for six mo]nths. […]

1QS 7

---

⁹ᵃAnd the same applies to the one who himself takes revenge for anything.

7.2.4 Misconduct During Communal Meetings

7.2.4.1 Foolish Speech (1QS 7:9b)

1QS 7
Whoever says anything foolish: three months.

7.2.4.2 Interrupting a Fellow Member (1QS 7:9b–10a // 4Q261 5a–c: 1–2a)

1QS 7	4Q261 5a–c
[9b]And the one who interrupts his neighbour's speech: [10]ten days.	[1][And the one who interru]pts [2a][his neighbour's speech: ten days.]

7.2.4.3 Lying Down to Sleep (1QS 7:10b // 4Q259 1:6 // 4Q261 5a–c: 2b–3a)

1QS 7	4Q259 1	4Q261 5a–c
[10b]Whoever lies down and sleeps during a meeting of the many: thirty days.	[6][…] Whoever lies down […]	[2b][Whoever lies down and] sleeps during a mee[ti]ng of [3a][the many: thirty days.]

7.2.4.4 Leaving Without Permission (1QS 7:10c–11a / 4Q259 1:7a // 4Q261 5 a–c: 3b)

1QS 7	4Q259 1	4Q261 5a–c
[10c]And the same applies to the person who lea[v]es *during* a meeting of the many [11a]without permission.	[7a][And the same applies to the person] who lea[ves] a meeting of the many with[out permission.]	[3b][And the same applies to the person who leaves during a meeting of the] man[y] without per[mi]ssion.

7.2.4.5 Dozing Off Repeatedly (1QS 7:11b // 4Q259 1:7b–8a // 4Q261 5a–c: 4)

1QS 7	4Q259 1	4Q261 5a–c
[11b]And he who drops off up to three times in the course of a single meeting shall be punished for ten days.	[7b][And he who drops off up to three times [8a]in the cour]se of a single meeting shall be punished for te[n days.]	[4][And he who drops off up to three times in the course of a single meeting shall be pu]nished [te]n days.

7.2.4.6 Leaving While the Assembled are on Their Feet (1QS 7:11c–12a // 4Q259 1:8b–9a // 4Q261 5a–c: 5a)

1QS 7	4Q259 1	4Q261 5a–c
[11c]But if they are stan[di]ng *vacat* [12a]and he leaves	[8b][But if they are standing and he leaves]	[5a][But if they are standing and he leaves *EXTRA SPACE*
he shall be punished for thirty days.	[9a]he shall be punished for thirty days.	he shall be punished for th]ir[ty d]ays.

7.2.5 Indecent and Socially Unacceptable Behaviour

7.2.5.1 Walking Naked Without Duress (1QS 7:12b // 4Q259 1:9b–10a // 4Q261 5a–c: 5b–7a)

1QS 7	4Q259 1	4Q261 5a–c
[12b]Whoever walks about naked in front of his neighbour	[9b]Whoever wa[lks about naked in front of his neighbour	[5b]Whoever [6][walks about naked in front of his neighbour *EXTRA SPACE*
shall be punished for six months unless there are mitigating circumstances.	shall be [10a]pu]nished [for s]ix mo[nths unless] there are mitigating circumstances.	with]out having been coerced [[7a]shall be punished for six months.]

7.2.5.2 Spitting (1QS 7: 13a // 4Q259 1:10b–11a // 4Q261 5a–c: 7b–8a)

1QS 7	4Q259 1	4Q261 5a–c
[13a]The person who spits into the midst of a meeting of the many shall be punished for thirty days.	[10b][The person who spits into the midst of a meeting of] [11a]the many [shall be punished for thir]ty days.	[7b][The person who spits into the midst of a mee]ting of the many [8a][shall be punished for thirty days]

7.2.5.3 Exposure (1QS 7:13b–14a // 4Q258 5:1 // 4Q259 1:11b–13a // 4Q261 5a–c: 8b–9a)

1QS 7	4Q258 5	4Q259 1	4Q261 5a–c
[13b]Whoever brings out his hand from underneath his garment	[1] [Whoever brings out] his hand from under[neath his garment]	[11b][Whoever brings out] [12]his hand [from undernea]th [his] garment	[8b][Whoever brings out his hand from under]neath his garment

1QS 7	4Q259 1	4Q261 5a–c
so that it [14a]blows up and his nakedness is seen shall be punished for *thirty days.*	and i[t blows up and his nakedness can be seen] [13a]shall be punished for *sixty days.*	[9a][and it blows up and his nakedness can be seen shall be punished for thirty days.]

7.2.5.4 *Ill-Mannered Laughter (1QS 7:14b–15a // 4Q259 1:13b–14a // 4Q261 5a–c: 9b)*

1QS 7	4Q259 1	4Q261 5a–c
[14b]Whoever	[13b]Whoever	[9b]Whoever

1QS 7	4Q259 1
laughs foolishly and raucously shall be punished for thirty [15a]days.	laughs [foolishly and [14a]rau]cously shall be punished for thirty d[ays].

7.2.5.5 *Gesticulating with the Left Hand (1QS 7:15b // 4Q259 1:14b–15 // 4Q261 6a–e: 1a)*

1QS 7	4Q259 1
[15b]The one who brings out his left hand	[14b]The [one who brings out his left hand]

1QS 7	4Q259 1	4Q261 6a–e
to gesticulate with it shall be punished for ten days.	[15]to gesticulate with [it shall be punished for ten d]ay[s].	[1a][to gesticulate with it shall be pu]nished [for te]n [days].

7.2.6 *Undermining Shared Values*

7.2.6.1 *Slander (1QS 7:15c–17a // 4Q261 6a–e: 1b–3a)*

1QS 7	4Q261 6a–e
[15c]The person who goes about maligning his neighbour: [16]they shall exclude him for one year from the purity of the many and he shall be punished. As for the person who goes about maligning the many, they	[1b][The person who goes about maligning his neighbour: [2]they shall exclude him for o]ne [y]ear from the puri[ty of the many and] he shall be punished. [As for] the pers[on [3a]who goes about maligning the

1QS 7	4Q261 6a–e
shall send him away from among them [17a]never to return again.	many,] they shall send him away from am[ong] them n[ever to return] again.

7.2.6.2 Expressing Discontent (1QS 7:17b–18a // 4Q261 6a–e: 3b–5)

1QS 7	4Q261 6a–e
[17b]The person who grumbles against the basic principles of the community: they shall send him away not to return. If he grumbles against his neighbour [18a]without justification he shall be punished for six months.	[3b][The per]son [4][who grumbles against the basic prin]ciples of the community: they shall send (him) away not to [return. If he grumbles against [5]his neighbour without justification he shall be punished] for s[i]x mon[ths.]

7.2.6.3 Wavering Loyalty to the Principles of the Community (1QS 7:18b–21 // 4Q259 2:3–5a)

1QS 7
[18b]The person whose spirit wavers with regard to the basic principles of the community so as to betray the truth [19]and to walk with a hardened heart, if he repents, he shall be punished for two years. During the first (year) he shall {.} not touch the purity of the many. *Vacat* [20a] *Vacat* {…} During the second (year) he shall not touch the [pure liquid] of the many

1QS 7	4Q259 2
[20b]and he shall be seated at the back of all the people of the community. And when he has completed [21]the two years, the many shall be consulted *vacat* about his affairs. If they permit him to draw near he shall be enrolled according to his rank and afterwards he may be consulted concerning judgment.	[3][and he shall be sea]ted [at the back of all the people of the community.] And when he has complete[d [4][the two years, the many shall be consulted about his affairs. If they permit him to draw near he shall be enrolled according to] his [r]ank and afterwards he may be consulted [5a][concerning judgment.]

7.2.6.4 Betrayal on the Part of a Member of Long Standing (1QS 7:22–25 // 4Q259 2:5b–9a)

1QS 7	4Q259 2
[22]{…} [But] anyone who has been a member of the council of the community {…} *upon*	[5b][EXTRA SPACE]ut anyone who has been a member of the counci]l of the community *up to*

1QS 7	4Q259 2
completing ten full years *vacat* [23]*vacat* {…} *vacat* and his spirit turns back so as to betray the community and he departs from *vacat* [24]the many in order to walk with a hardened heart shall never return to the council of the community again. A person from among the people of the commu[nity who has de]alings [25]with him regarding his purity or his property whi[ch …] the many, his penalty shall be the same: he shall be se[nt away].	completing [6][ten years and his spirit turns back so as to betray the community and he departs fro]m the many in order to walk [7][with a hardened heart shall never return to the council of the community again. A person from among] the people of the community who [8][has dealings with him regarding his purity or his property which … the many], his penalty shall be [9a][the same: he shall be sent away.]

7.3 *Textual Notes*

6:24 The *he* in "and these" (ואלה) has been added above the line in 1QS.

6:24 4Q261 3:2 lacks the words "at an inquiry of the community" (בם במדרש יחד).

6:25 Brownlee proposes translating the participle יודע "and it become known" rather than "(lies) knowingly" by taking the verb to be a *niphal* or *hophal* rather than *qal*.[18]

6:26 The lower part of the second and third letter in "not paying regard to; neglect" (לפרוע) are damaged in 1QS though enough remains to support the reading.[19]

6:26 The infinitive *hiphil* of the verb "rebelling" (מרה) is spelled with initial *aleph* rather than *he* as a result of a weaking of the gutturals.[20] The idiom is based on 1 Kgs 13:26.

6:27 The bottom margin of this column is damaged in 1QS resulting in two significant lacunae in this line.

6:27 Despite a scribal correction involving an erasure of *aleph* the reading "shall be punished" is still in need of emending in light of accidental metathesis of *ayin* and *nun*.[21]

6:27 Willem Smelik has offered a detailed study of the expression "invoking the name of the Honoured One" in the context of an oath.[22]

---

[18] Brownlee, *Dead Sea Manual*, 26–27.

[19] See Qimron, DSSHW 1:220.

[20] Cf. Qimron, HDSS, 25; Wernberg-Møller, *Manual of Discipline*, 112 and Tigchelaar, "Scribe," 445.

[21] So already Kutscher, *Language*, 509 and more recently Qimron, DSSHW 1:220.

[22] Willem F. Smelik, "The Use of הזכיר בשם in Classical Hebrew: Josh 23:7; Isa 48:1; Amos 6:10; Ps 20:8; 4Q504 III 4; 1QS 6:27," *JBL* 118 (1999): 321–332.

7:1 I translate the *niphal* infinitive construct לֹהבעת with "suddenly befallen by terror."[23]

7:1 The words "or for whatever reason he may have" are clearly written by a different hand in 1QS and are followed by an erasure. Puech tentatively proposes reading the traces of the erased text as "he may have" (אשר לו) which would result in a repetition.[24]

7:1 The third occurrence of "or" (או) in this line in 1QS has been damaged by a finger of moisture damage that extends from the top margin to the next line.

7:2 Our translation follows Wernberg-Møller by emending the preposition על to אל in the phrase "never to return again to the council of the community."[25] The scribe may have been misled by the occurrence of the preposition על immediately below in 7:3, the first letter of which appears in turn to have been corrected from *aleph* to *ayin*.[26]

7:2 With Brownlee I emend *bet* to *mem* in "of the priests."[27]

7:2 The letter *khet* in "in anger" has suffered from the finger of moisture that also affected 1QS 7:1 immediately above.

7:3 The form "from the purity of" (מן טהרת) in 1QS constitutes an example of non-assimilation of *nun* in nouns without the definite article.[28]

7:3 Baumgarten suggests translating "knowingly" (במדעו) with "against a friend," a term attested in the *Qere* of Ruth 2:1.[29] Though this suggestion is attractive, the translation "knowingly" is more likely here. The Community Rules frequently use terms such as רע – with twenty two occurrences in 1QS, ten of which are found in the penal code – and עמית (cf. 1QS 6:26 and Lev 5:21 [Hebrew]) to express the notion of a friend or fellow. It seems feasible that the placement of this offence at this juncture was inspired by the antonym "inadvertently" earlier in the same line as well as a further reference to knowingly misbehaving in the following line. Finally, the phrase comprising the last three words of line 3 ("And whoever deceives knowingly") appears to have been squeezed in with barely any inter-word space.

7:4 The verb צחה "to reproach" is an Aramaism.[30]

7:4 For the expression "without justification" (בלו משפט), which is written continuously, see Ezek 22:29.[31]

---

[23] Cf. HALAT 1:141 ("v. plötzlichem Schrecken befallen werden"); see also Wernberg-Møller's translation "terror-stricken" which he connects with the perilous existence of the wicked in Job 15:24, *Manual of Discipline*, 31 and 113.

[24] Puech, "Écriture de 1QS VII–VIII," 37; see also Guilbert, "Règle de la Communauté," 49.

[25] Wernberg-Møller, *Manual of Discipline*, 42.

[26] See García Martínez and Tigchelaar, DSSSE, 86.

[27] Brownlee, *Dead Sea Manual*, 29. The original *bet* is reconstructed by Habermann, *Three Scrolls*, 75.

[28] See Qimron, HDSS, 30–31.

[29] See 4Q265 (Miscellaneous Rules) 4 i 9 and Baumgarten, DJD 35:65.

[30] See Qimron, HDSS, 116; also Wernberg-Møller, *Manual of Discipline*, 114.

[31] Cf. Wernberg-Møller, *Manual of Discipline*, 114.

7:5 Based on the difficulty of distinguishing *vav* and *yod* in this hand the reading translated "with bitterness" (במרים) can also be deciphered as "with arrogance" (במרום).[32] Maier's translation suggests a deceptive note in parentheses by translating "in Bitterkeit (betrügerisch?)."[33]

7:5 The first two letters of the verb "and acts" (יעשה) are damaged in 1QS as are a series of letters immediately above in 1QS 7:2–4.

7:6 The word "he deceives" (יתרמה) has been added above the line. Puech proposes that the unexpected *vacat* at the beginning of the line reflects a defective *Vorlage* which may have contained the verb "he deceives."[34]

7:6 This line ends with an erasure in 1QS. Qimron identifies an initial erased *aleph*[35] whereas Puech suspects an original partial dittography.[36]

7:7 After the word "in full" the rest of line 7 and two further lines are left uninscribed in 1QS. Guilbert has argued that the single word in this line goes back to a second scribe.[37] There is little justification for a break in terms of content. Imperfections in the leather towards the end of the lines may have been a factor.[38] Martin suspected gaps left for later inscription.[39] Puech has convincingly suggested that a major cause of the empty spaces was a damaged *Vorlage*, perhaps representing the more vulnerable bottom of a column.[40] Puech's argument receives further support from the material evidence of the following column where empty spaces occur at about the same point in 1QS 7 and 8 at either side of the seam connecting sheets 3 and 4, see further 1.5.1.2. I do not include the uninscribed lines in the numeration of the 1QS 7. Some scholars do which can result in divergent line numbers in the discussion of this material in the literature. Where relevant I draw attention to this when citing others.

7:7 Metso identifies the remains of 4Q256 7a (numbered fragment 9) as paralleling ברוש]ו ("in full").[41] However, 4Q256 fragment 7a is more commonly identified with either the first or second occurrence of בריש]ית ("before; at the beginning") in 1QS 10:13 where it is discussed more fully, see 15.3 below.

7:8 The punishment "for sixty days" has been added above the line in 1QS.

7:8 Final *resh* in "bears a grudge" (יטור) has been added above the line in 1QS after an erasure that has now left a hole in the leather.[42]

---

[32] See Brownlee, *Dead Sea Manual*, 28–29 and Qimron, DSSHW 1:222.

[33] *Qumran-Essener*, 1:184.

[34] Puech, "Écriture de 1QS VII–VIII," 37–38 and Guilbert, "Règle de la Communauté," 51.

[35] Qimron, DSSHW 1:222.

[36] Puech, "Écriture de 1QS VII–VIII," 38.

[37] Guilbert, "Règle de la Communauté," 51.

[38] Cf. Stegemann, "Some Remarks," 483 and Metso, *Textual Development*, 98.

[39] Martin, *Scribal Character of the Dead Sea Scrolls*, 1:117.

[40] Puech, "Écriture de 1QS VII–VIII," 43.

[41] Metso, *Textual Development*, 23, 29.

[42] On the corrections in this line see Puech, "Écriture de 1QS VII–VIII," 38.

7:8 The preposition *bet* of במשפט "with justification" has been added above the line after an erasure in 1QS.

7:8: An original punishment of "six months" has been been marked for deletion by the addition of faintly preserved parentheses in 1QS.[43] The use of parentheses evolved from the Greek practice of using the letter *sigma* and its inverted form *antisigma* to identify text that had been inserted in the wrong place.[44] A clear example of this usage in the Dead Sea Scrolls is attested in the Paleo Leviticus Scroll at Lev 18:27 to mark the end of a portion of Lev 20:23–24 in the middle of this verse.[45] In 1QS 7:8 a corrected punishment of "one year" was added above the line. As Tov notes, the use of parentheses is most unusual in this manuscript where corrections are mostly executed by erasure or cancellation dots.[46] Given the parentheses were clearly added after the orginal text it is hard to see why they are much more faintly visible. I suggest another scribe disapproved of this method of correction and erased the parentheses somewhat imperfectly, leaving the top and bottom points which now resemble imperfectly aligned cancellation dots. The superlinear correction here is one of the few cases that Puech attributes to a second hand (Scribe B).[47] 4Q259 1:4 preserves remains of the uncorrected reading of the first hand in 1QS.[48] The earlier date proposed by Milik and Puech for 4Q259 suggests the first hand may have drawn on 4Q259, see 1.5.6.2 above.

7:10 The scribe of 4Q259 accidentally omitted final *bet* of מושב "meeting" in 4Q259 1:7.[49] 1QS reads במושב where 4Q259 has the preposition *min* (ממוש). 4Q259's reading supports the suggestion by Schiffman[50] that 1QS's text is the result of an interchange of the prepositions *bet* and *min*.[51]

7:10 The letter *tet* has been added superlinearly in 1QS after an erasure.

7:11 The letter *ayin* is added above the line in 4Q261 5a–c in "without permission" (אשר לא ב"צה).[52] One of the copies of the Damascus Document, 4Q266 (4QD[a]) 10 ii 7, reads "without the consent of the m[a]n[y]."

---

[43] See Tov, *Scribal Practices*, 225.

[44] Cf. Emanuel Tov, *Textual Criticism of the Hebrew Bible* (2nd ed. Minneapolis, MN: Fortress; Assen: van Gorcum, 2001), 54–55.

[45] See David N. Freedman and Kenneth A. Mathews, *The Paleo-Hebrew Leviticus Scroll (11QPaleoLev)* (Winona Lake, IN: Eisenbrauns for ASOR, 1985), 36–37, 103 (Plate 3).

[46] Tov, *Scribal Practices*, 225.

[47] Puech, "Écriture de 1QS VII–VIII," 42.

[48] See Alexander and Vermes, DJD 26:134–137 and Schofield, *From Qumran to the Yaḥad*, 106–107 where the line is numbered 7:9.

[49] Cf. Alexander and Vermes, DJD 26:135–137.

[50] Schiffman, *Halakhah at Qumran*, 27–28 n. 44, 69.

[51] Cf., e. g., Alexander and Vermes, DJD 26:137.

[52] See now DSSLLDL B-365864, photo by Shai Halevi.

7:11 The second letter *he* of והנם "he who dozes off" has been crudely corrected in 1QS.[53] Puech proposes an original *aleph* or *khet*.[54]

7:11 The final word in this line in 1QS, "they are standing" (יזקפו), has been corrected with the addition of *qoph* above the line. Sutcliffe suggests an original reading יזעפו which stood for יזאפו as a result of a weakening of the gutturals and yielded "if he loses his temper and leaves."[55]

7:12 Alexander and Vermes have calculated additional space in 4Q261 5a–c: 6 and cautiously propose reconstructing "in a house or in a field" with the Damascus Document (4Q270 7 i 2).[56]

7:14 Our translation "it blows up" derives the verb פוח which is preserved only in 1QS.[57] Others take the verb to be a form of פוחח "to be raggedly dressed."[58]

7:14 *Aleph* in "and it is seen" (ונראתה) has been corrected from *ayin*.[59] Wernberg-Møller reads *ayin* and proposes an emendation to *aleph*.[60]

7:14 The first two letters in the penalty laid down in 4Q259 1:13 "sixty days" are illegible. 1QS reads "thirty days." The scribe of 1QS may have misread a *Vorlage* of the text type of 4Q259 since both numerals in Hebrew resemble each other closely, see 1.5.6.2. In the related penal code material preserved in the Damascus Document the penalty is not preserved in 4Q269 11 ii 1, restored in 4Q270 7 i 3 and ambiguous in 4Q266 10 ii where only the final *shin*, *yod* and *mem* are preserved.

7:15 The translation "gesticulate" is based on the root שיח "to sprout; figuratively to speak."[61] The reading is preserved in 1QS and 4Q259 1:15.[62] It is also preserved in the Damascus Document's penal code in 4Q270 7 i 5. The alternative translation "to recline" takes the root to be שחח attested in Sir 43:10.[63]

7:16–17 1QS and 4Q261 6a–e: 3–4 attest some variation in the precise formulation of the punishment for expulsion both between these manuscripts and internally.[64]

---

[53] See Alexander and Vermes, DJD 26:136.

[54] Puech, "Écriture de 1QS VII–VIII," 38.

[55] Sutcliffe, "General Council," 975–976. Puech proposes reading "and if he drops off" ואם יהנם for the original hand, "Écriture de 1QS VII–VIII," 38.

[56] Alexander and Vermes, DJD 26:183; for the Damascus Document see Baumgarten, DJD 18:162–166.

[57] See, e. g., Maier, *Qumran-Essener*, 1:185 and Levy, *Wörterbuch* 4:12.

[58] So Brownlee, *Dead Sea Manual*, 30–31 and Wernberg-Møller, *Manual of Discipline*, 118.

[59] See García Martínez and Tigchelaar, DSSSE, 86.

[60] Wernberg-Møller, *Manual of Discipline*, 42.

[61] See Levy, *Wörterbuch* 4:517 and van der Ploeg, "Manuel de Discipline," 122.

[62] Cf. Alexander and Vermes, DJD 26:139.

[63] So Wernberg-Møller, *Manual of Discipline*, 118. The latter has recently been endorsed by Yonder Moynihan Gillihan, "Posture or Gesture? A Note on לשוח/לשח in the Qumran Penal Codes," *RevQ* 24 (2009): 291–296.

[64] Cf. Alexander and Vermes, DJD 26:186.

7:19 One or two letters have been erased before "not" (לוא) in 1QS. Puech suggests the negative particle אל was underlying the erasure.[65]

7:19 The last two words of this line "the purity of the many" (בטהרת רבים) have been identified as going back to a second hand by Guilbert whereas Puech suggests the original scribe was responsible for adding the last three words.[66]

7:20 The beginning of the line has been left blank in 1QS, and an original first word "the many" was marked by deletion dots and erased, according to Puech by Scribe A or his associates.[67]

7:20 The term "pure liquid of" (משקה) has been added above the line in 1QS where an original "the purity of" (בטהרת) has been erased.[68] Guilbert attributes this superlinear addition and the final word "And when he has completed" (ובמלואת) to the second scribal hand.[69]

7:21 Guilbert identifies the first word of this line as written in the second hand in 1QS.[70]

7:21 There is an unexpected *vacat* after "the many" in 1QS with no indication of any flaws in the leather, see the note on 1QS 7:22–23 below. Puech attributes what follows this *vacat* to an addition added by Scribe A.[71]

7:21 *Vav* is added above the line in "in his rank" in 4Q259 2:4 as part of a correction for which Puech proposes an original reading of *kaph he*.[72]

7:22 Puech deciphers the remains of the first erasure in this line in 1QS to read "and he shall be consulted concerning judgment and concerning" (ישאל אל המשפט ואל).[73] Most of this wording is found at the end of the previous line. For the second erasure in this line, which sets in after the reference to the council of the community, Puech proposes reading "to betray the community" (לבגוד ביחד), a phrase that occurs in 1QS 7:23.[74]

7:22 The first preserved word in this line in 1QS "and every" (וכול) has the conjunction added above the line.

7:22 1QS employs the preposition על "upon completing" whereas 4Q259 2:5 reads עד "even for (or: up to)" ten full years. Alexander and Vermes suggest that

---

[65] Puech, "Écriture de 1QS VII–VIII," 39.

[66] See Guilbert, "Règle de la Communauté" 53 and Puech, "Écriture de 1QS VII–VIII," 42.

[67] Puech, "Écriture de 1QS VII–VIII," 39, 42.

[68] See Puech, "Écriture de 1QS VII–VIII," 39; García Martínez and Tigchelaar, DSSSE, 86, where the line number is given as 7:22 as a consequence of including the two empty lines after 1QS 7:7 in the numeration; cf. also Qimron, DSSHW 1:222.

[69] See Guilbert, "Règle de la Communauté," 53; also Martin, *Scribal Character of the Dead Sea Scrolls*, 2:440.

[70] Guilbert, "Règle de la Communauté," 53.

[71] Puech, "Écriture de 1QS VII–VIII," 42.

[72] See Alexander and Vermes, DJD 26:139–140; Puech, "Review of *Textual Development*," 449 and García Martínez and Tigchelaar, DSSSE, 528. Both DSSSE, 528 and Qimron, DSSHW 1:222 take the superlinear *vav* to a the pronominal suffix.

[73] Puech, "Écriture de 1QS VII–VIII," 39.

[74] Puech, "Écriture de 1QS VII–VIII," 39.

this is a case where these two prepositions are interchangeable.[75] In addition, an ethical dative לו was added secondarily at the end of the line in 4Q259 2:5. Both *lamed* and *vav* are written slightly higher than the rest of the line and are rather squeezed in right at the end of the margin, see also the note on 1QS 8:3 below.

7:22–23 Large gaps in these lines contain traces of erased text in 1QS. This preponderance of corrections in particular portions of 1QS is a feature noted by Tigchelaar.[76] I would want to add that even within the penal code as a whole this last portion – which stands out from the rest of the code in other respects also – is the subject of much more correction and erasion than the remainder. Wernberg-Møller oberserves that, "erasions and empty spaces suggest that the text before the scribe was illegible in parts."[77] The question presents itself why this particular part of the *Vorlage* was more illegible than the rest. Brownlee suggests the damage was caused by heavy use.[78] Puech attributes the entirety of 1QS 7:22 as well as the text up until "and it (his spirit) turns back" and including the last word "before" in 1QS 7:23 to a correction added later and associated with Scribe A.[79]

7:23 While several scholars have identified the work of two scribes in this line, there is no agreement on the particulars. Puech's assessment that attributes the phrase "to betray the yahad and depart" to the first hand A is convincing, with the first and last words "and it turns back" and "before" attributed to scribe B.[80]

7:23 The preposition "from" prefixed to the final word in this line in 1QS has suffered from a vertical crack in the surface of the skin.[81]

7:25 I have refrained from restoring the lacuna in the middle of this line in 1QS or 4Q259 1:8 but the suggestion by Licht to restore "[without the consent of (לוא בעצת) the many]⁺" is suggestive.[82] The damaged end of this line in 1QS likely refers to expulsion as suggested by the opening letters of the infinitive of שלח "to send away."[83]

7:26 On the composite marginal sign in the uninscribed line 26 of this column see 1.5.1.3 above and 8.1 below.

---

[75] Cf. Alexander and Vermes, DJD 26:143.

[76] See Tigchelaar, "Scribe."

[77] Wernberg-Møller, *Manual of Discipline*, 120. See also Guilbert, "Règle de la Communauté" who attributes the second half of 1QS 7:21, all of 1QS 7:22 and the first half of 1QS 7:23 to the second scribe; further, Puech, "Écriture de 1QS VII–VIII" and Tigchelaar, "Scribe."

[78] Brownlee, *Dead Sea Manual*, 31.

[79] Puech, "Écriture de 1QS VII–VIII," 42.

[80] Puech, "Écriture de 1QS VII–VIII," 39; also Martin, *Scribal Character of the Dead Sea Scrolls*, 2:441.

[81] See also Martin, *Scribal Character of the Dead Sea Scrolls*, 2:441.

[82] Licht, *Rule Scroll*, 166.

[83] Cf. Alexander and Vermes, DJD 26:141.

7.4 Commentary

7.4.1 Introduction (1QS 6:24a // 4Q261 3:2a)

The title of the penal code is preserved in two manuscripts and introduces what follows as the judgments according to which members of the community are to be judged, see 7.1 above. The title in 1QS is slightly longer and includes the plus "at a communal enquiry."[84]

It is clear from this introduction that the community – perhaps represented by senior members who took their seats in the front[85] – came to judgments about cases. The need for prior rebuke and witnesses is not mentioned and may be assumed, though the accounts of meetings of the many in 6.5 above also leave room for items to be brought up from the floor. The observation by Albert Baumgarten on Josephus' description of Essenes informing on one another is suggestive also in the context of the Penal Code.[86] The disciplinary pocess that follows the penal code at the end of the Damascus Document appeals to offenders to come forward and confess. Our reading of the condition of suffering from a wavering spirit as provoking at times pronounced physical distress might, in fact, suggest that confession would bring relief to a terrified soul expecting imminent discovery and communal as well as divine judgment.

7.4.2 Offences Involving the Spoken Word

The first group of six misdemeanours are all concerned with speech. Jacob Licht proposed that the code was structured with more serious offences in the opening and closing parts.[87] The most serious item in the opening segment is the offence of blasphemy which results in permanent exclusion.[88]

7.4.2.1 Fraudulent Speech (1QS 6:24b–25a // 4Q261 3:2b–4)

A member who speaks deliberately with deception about property is to be excluded from the purity of the many for a year and deprived of a quarter of his food rations. Milik takes this to refer to a cut to a quarter of the food rations.[89]

---

[84] On the term midrash see 5.4.1 above.

[85] See 6.5 above.

[86] See *J. W.* 2.141 and Albert I. Baumgarten, "Information Processing in Ancient Jewish Groups," in *Sectarianism in Early Judaism: Sociological Advances*. Edited by David Chalcraft (Cambridge: Cambridge University Press, 2014), 246–255, 248. Cf. also Jer 20:10.

[87] Licht, *Rule Scroll*, 157. For a recent analysis of the structure of the Penal Code see also Stefan Beyerle and Andreas Ruwe, "A Comparison of the 'Penal Code' in the Damascus Document and in the Serekh ha-Yaḥad from a Literary Perspective," *DSD* 25 (2018): 359–384.

[88] See 7.2.2.3 above.

[89] Milik, "Manuale Disciplinae," 146.

The use of the verb עָנַשׁ in the *niphal* to refer to a cut in rations might suggest a similar sense where the same verb occurs without specifying food reductions. Given the emphasis on being permitted to touch the purity or the pure liquid of the many during the admissions process outlined in 6.5 above, I have suggested elsewhere that touching pure solids or liquids refers also to the process of harvesting, food preparation and consumption rather than meals in a narrower sense.[90] Avemarie proposes that the exclusion from the purity refers to avoiding any personal contact because the individual in question might contaminate not only food but also clothes, vessels and other people.[91]

6:25 The punishment seems to involve complete exclusion from touching the pure solids of the community as well as a cut in the food the offender is allowed to consume.

7.4.2.2 Unguarded or Disrespectful Speech (1QS 6:25b–27a)

Intemperate speech in reply to a fellow member, particularly one registered at a higher rank, is punished for a year. The accusation that this behaviour constitutes taking the law into one's own hand alludes to Judges 7:2 and 1 Sam 25:26.

7.4.2.3 Blasphemy (1QS 6:27b–7:2a // 4Q261 4a–b:1–4a)

Invoking the divine name or blaspheming while reading the book, even if the outburst is the result of severe anxiety and fear, leads to permanent expulsion. Reading is one of the activities to be performed during the nightly meetings of the many which include reading the book.[92] Brooke has noted the close connection of reading the book and blessing both here and in the context of nightly study sessions of the many.[93] We argued above that the times of these nightly meetings to study the law and bless coincided with a period during which members felt particularly vulnerable to attacks from demonic forces.[94] Such a febrile atmosphere may explain why this passage refers to fear and distress in the context of reading the book. For a comparable situation fraught with distress and terror during which the sustained pursuit of wisdom is admonished see 4Q525 (Beatitudes) 2 ii+3:3b–5 which reads, "Blessed is the human being who obtains wisdom and whose conduct is in accordance with the law of the Most High, [...] who does not abandon it in the face of [their] trials, nor forsake it during periods of distress nor forget it [on a day of] terror."

---

[90] See Hempel, "Who is Making Dinner?"
[91] Avemarie, "Tohorat Ha-Rabbim."
[92] See 6.5.2.1 and 6.5.4.1 above.
[93] Brooke, "Reading, Searching and Blessing," 143.
[94] See 6.5.4.1 and 1.2.1 above.

Respect for the divine name is evident also in the widespread avoidance of the tetragrammaton at Qumran, see especially 1QS 8:14 where the divine name that occurs in a citation of Isa 40:3 is represented by four dots.[95]

7.4.2.4 Verbal Outburst Against Registered Priests (1QS 7:2b–3b // 4Q261 4a-b:4b–6)

This offence mirrors speaking intemperately against senior members dealt with in 7.4.2.2 above. Here the anger is directed at one of the priests whose name is registered in the book. While the length of the punishment is the same as in 7.4.2.2 above, the year long punishment here includes an exclusion from the purity of the many by himself which has been taken to refer to solitary confinement.[96] If the offender spoke inadvertently the penalty is reduced by half.[97]

7.4.2.5 Deliberate Deception (1QS 7:3c–4a)

A member of the community who knowingly misleads is punished for six months. No details are given about the kind of deception that is in view.

7.4.2.6 Unjustified Reproach (1QS 7:4b–5a)

A deliberate false accusation against a fellow member leads to a year long punishment as well as exclusion. Wernberg-Møller takes exclusion to refer to "confinement."[98]

7.4.2.7 Deceptive Speech (1QS 7:5b–6a)

This offense refers to a bitter exchange with a fellow member or a negligent act which provoke a punishment of six months. This combination of offences that pertain to speech and then behaviour forms something of a bridge into the next sub-section of the code.

7.4.3 Offences Involving Behaviour

7.4.3.1 Fraudulent Actions (1QS 7:6b–8a)

Anyone who misappropriates another's property suffers a three month penalty. The one who misappropriates communal property is expected to restore it. The parallel formulation suggests that a fellow member's possessions are in view in

---

[95] Cf. Stegemann, "Gottesbezeichnungen in den Qumrantexten" and Tov, *Scribal Practices*, 218–221.

[96] See Brownlee, *Dead Sea Manual*, 29 and Wernberg-Møller, *Manual of Discipline*, 114.

[97] On inadvertent wrongdoing see Lev 4.

[98] Wernberg-Møller, *Manual of Discipline*, 32.

the first scenario. Even though the Community Rules portray property as a communal asset there are cases where members in the process of joining hand over their belongings which are not immediately allocated fully to the community. For those not able to restore misused property allowance is made for their circumstances which brings with it a sixty day punishment to make amends.[99]

7.4.3.2 Bearing a Grudge or Retaliating (1QS 7:8b–9a // 4Q259 1:4)

The Community Rules include strict rules on how to reprimand fellow community members which are based on a particular interpretation of Lev 19:17. As spelled out in more detail in 6.2, members of the movement are expected to rebuke fellow members promptly and in a constructive spirit rather than bearing a grudge. Any public accusation in front of the many needs to be raised before witnesses beforehand, though we also noted the possibility to raise issues from the floor during meetings in 6.5 above.

7.4.4 Misconduct During Communal Meetings

This section includes six misdemeanours that take place during meetings of the many, be that during the nightly study and prayer meetings or the sessions of the many that take place in daytime.[100]

7.4.4.1 Foolish Speech (1QS:9b)

The reference to foolish speech is very brief and somewhat casually added to the previous item of bearing a grudge. It is entirely likely that foolish speech was particularly out of place during a meeting of the many, though such a context is not explicitly referred to.[101] Our placement of this item as a form of misconduct during meetings is more tentative than in the following five cases.

7.4.4.2 Interrupting a Fellow Member (1QS 7:9b–10a // 4Q261 5a–c: 1–2a)

This passage echoes one of the rulings laid down concerning the meetings of the many and specifies a ten day penalty for those who fail to comply.[102]

7.4.4.3 Lying Down to Sleep (1QS 7:10b // 4Q259 1:6 // 4Q261 5a–c: 2b–3a)

The offence of lying down to sleep suggests an element of intent to go to sleep rather than repeatedly dozing off unintentionally as described in 7.2.4.5. While

---

[99] See Lev 12:8; 4Q266 6 ii 12 and Tzvi Novick, "Overt Acknowledgement of Practical Considerations in Legal Texts from Qumran," *DSD* 21 (2014): 64–81, 69–70.

[100] See 6.5 above.

[101] See, however, 1QS 10:21–22 // 4Q260 5:2–3.

[102] Cf. 1QS 6:10b and 6.5.2.2 above.

hard labour or illness are as likely as sheer idleness to lie behind such a course of action at any time, the nightly study and prayer meetings of the many may have been particularly in mind.[103]

7.4.4.4 Leaving Without Permission (1QS 7:10c–11a // 4Q259 1:7a // 4Q261 5 a–c: 3b)

Leaving a meeting without permission is dealt with by a thirty day penalty. The most likely arbiter of comings and goings during the meetings of the many would have been the person leading the deliberations or the overseer over the many.[104]

7.4.4.5 Dozing Off Repeatedly (1QS 7:11b // 4Q259 1:7b–8a // 4Q261 5a–c: 4)

This passage addresses the offence of dropping off to sleep up to three times during the same meeting which implies dozing off was rather common. Sutcliffe speculates that "sessions were apt to be long and wearisome. [...] The moving force might, of course, be sheer fatigue, or it might be a way of entering a protest against a long-winded and dull speaker."[105] Another occasion when weariness may have been especially acute where the nighty vigils for study and prayer dealt with in 6.5.2.1 and 6.5.4.1 above. Such a reading would offer a smooth transition to the following offence of departing from a meeting while standing.[106]

7.4.4.6 Leaving While the Assembled are on Their Feet (1QS 7:11c–12a // 4Q259 1:8b–9a // 4Q261 5a–c: 5a)

A more serious offence concerns departing from a meeting while the community is standing up. This practice may refer to prayer as suggested by Knibb[107] or a vote as proposed by Sutcliffe.[108] Given prayer – or blessing – is associated with the nightly meetings of the many, a departure during those sessions would have been particularly frowned upon.[109]

7.4.5 Indecent and Socially Unacceptable Behaviour

This part of the penal code deals with five cases of indecent or otherwise unacceptable behaviour. Three relatively innocuous acts concern "spitting into

---

[103] See 6.5.2.1 above and 7.4.4.5 below.

[104] See 1QS 6:11–12 and 6.5.4.2 above.

[105] Sutcliffe, "General Council," 974.

[106] Cf. 7.4.4.5 below.

[107] Knibb, *Qumran Community*, 126.

[108] Sutcliffe, "General Council," 974 and Weinfeld, *Organizational Pattern*, 29–30. For further discussion see Wernberg-Møller, *Manual of Discipline*, 116–117.

[109] Cf. 6.5.2.1 above.

the midst of a meeting," raucous and presumably disruptive laughter and gesticulating with the left hand. Interspersed are two offences that refer to being in a state of partial or full undress and imply more serious social tensions. The issue of nudity may have received renewed attention in the wake of the arrival Greek and Roman empires. The topic is developed, for instance, in the book of Jubilees, a second century BCE composition attested in fifteen copies at Qumran.[110]

7.4.5.1 *Walking Naked Without Duress (1QS 7:12b // 4Q259 1:9b–10a // 4Q261 5a–c: 5b–7a)*

The first offence refers to an incident where someone walks about naked. The offender is to be punished for six months unless mitigating circumstances apply. The language used in 1QS and 4Q259 refers to sickness (אונש) as a legitimate reason for being undressed. Licht presupposes undressing for a medical examination.[111] In 4Q261 the verb employed (אונס) suggests a more sinister scenario of someone being coerced to be naked which, as discussed in 1.4.4 above, may suggest a scenario we would today call sexually abusive. Note the comments by Alexander and Vermes, "The root expresses strong, even violent physical compulsion."[112] An interchange of sibilants, in either direction, cannot be ruled out.[113]

This leaves us to consider the unmitigated offence of simply walking about naked as a matter of choice, the motivations for which are unknown. In the absence of mitigating circumstances the text describes the culprit as exposing themselves in front of another. We cannot discount that this is an insight into times when members of the community acted with erotic intent.[114]

Finally, it is rather puzzling that we are told of the lenience towards those who have been coerced into nakedness but learn nothing of the punishment of those who are coercing others to to walk about naked.

7.4.5.2 *Spitting (1QS 7:13a // 4Q259 1:10b–11a // 4Q261 5a–c: 7b–8a)*

The offence of spitting into the midst of a meeting occurs in between two items dealing with a lack of proper dress. It is difficult to know what exactly is meant here. We might be dealing with carelessness or malicious intent. Similar sensitivities are ascribed to the Essenes in Josephus, *J. W.* 2.147. Jodi Magness has noted the possible connection to the defiling nature of the spit of one afflicted with a genital discharge according to Lev 15:8.[115] However, the lack of reference to such an affliction would be surprising. Nor would the spit of such a person be

---

[110] See, e. g., Jub 7; Licht, *Rule Scroll*, 164; also Martin Goodman, *Rome and Jerusalem: The Clash of Ancient Civilizations* (London: Allen Lane, 2007), 286–292.

[111] Licht, *Rule Scroll*, 164; see also the translation of Michael Wise in DSSANT, 136.

[112] Alexander and Vermes, DJD 26:138.

[113] See Qimron, HDSS, 28–30.

[114] Cf. Grossman, "Postmodern Questions and Sexuality Studies."

[115] Magness, *Stone and Dung, Oil and Spit: Jewish Daily Life in the Time of Jesus* (Grand

the only concern during meetings. Since members were seated anyone suffering from a discharge would be contaminating the area they were occupying, see 1QS 6:8–9 and 6.5.4.2 above. Magness' discussion of rabbinic evidence prohibiting spitting suggests ritual defilement or a lack of decency may lie behind this prohibition. The immediate context of this offences in the Penal Code favours considering spitting as socially unacceptable though the lines between social mores and ritual impurity may not be entirely clear-cut.

7.4.5.3 Exposure (1QS 7:13b–14a // 4Q258 5:1 // 4Q259 1:11b–13a // 4Q261 5a–c: 8b–9a)

The exposure of one's nakedness as a result of taking one's hand from under a garment is widely recognised as a euphemism for exposing oneself.[116] The difference in punishment from thirty days in 1QS to sixty in 4Q259 may be a scribal lapse since visually the difference between both numbers in Hebrew is slight.[117] On the issue of accidental priestly exposure in the course of serving at the altar see Exod 20:26 and 28:42–43 which, on Christoph Berner's analysis, may be part of a Hellenistic strand in Exodus and reflect similar concerns to Jub 3:30–31 and the present passage.[118]

7.4.5.4 Ill-Mannered Laughter (1QS 7:14b–15a // 4Q259 1:13b–14a // 4Q261 5a–c: 9b)

We are not privy to the social context during which foolish or raucous laughter provokes a formal punishment but the meetings of the many – as mentioned explicitly in 7.2.5.2 with respect to spitting – would offer the sort of social space where the disruption of laughter would be acutely felt.

7.4.5.5 Gesticulating with the Left Hand (1QS 7:15b // 4Q259 1:14b–15 // 4Q261 6a–e: 1a)

The offence of bringing out one's left hand to gesture with it was socially unacceptable. As Michael Wise has mooted, a plausible background may have been "the common practice of using the left hand to clean oneself after defecation."[119]

Rapids, MI: Eerdmans, 2011), 125–129; also Licht, *Rule Scroll*, 164 and Leaney, *Rule of Qumran*, 206–207.

[116] See, e. g., Takamitsu Muraoka, "Sirach 51:13–30: An Erotic Hymn to Wisdom," *JSJ* 10 (1979): 166–178.

[117] Cf. also 1.5.6.2 above.

[118] See Berner, "'Mind the Step' (Exod. 20:26), or, even better: 'Wear Breeches!' (Exod. 28:42–43): The Issue of (Un)Covering One's 'Shame' in Cultic Legislation," in *Clothing and Nudity in the Hebrew Bible*. Edited by Christoph Berner et al. (London: Bloomsbury, 2019), 417–434.

[119] Wise, "Review of Michael A. Knibb, The Qumran Community," *JNES* 49 (1990): 200–202.

7.4.6 Undermining Shared Values

The last section of the penal code deals with a series of offences that challenge the principles and values of the community.[120] In the first two sections serious offences against the community are dealt with alongside the same transgressions against a fellow community member which are punished less severely.

7.4.6.1 Slander (1QS 7:15c–17a // 4Q261 6a–e: 1b–3a)

This is the first of two pairs of offences that comprise malicious talk against the community, here referred to as "the many," and the same offence against a fellow community member which is treated more leniently. The concerns at issue here are dealt with in Leviticus 19.[121]

7.4.6.2 Expressing Discontent (1QS 7:17b–18a // 4Q261 6a–e: 3b–5)

This passage deals with two levels of "grumbling." Whereas grumbling against the basic principles of the community leads to expulsion, grumbling without a legitimate cause against a neighbour is punished for six months. A structurally similar pair of offences occurs in the Damascus Document, and the passage draws on Num 16–17.[122]

7.4.6.3 Wavering Loyalty to the Principles of the Community (1QS 7:18b–21 // 4Q259 2:3–5a)

This offence concerns a member "whose spirit wavers with regard to the basic principles of the community so as to betray the truth and to walk with a hardened heart; if he repents, he shall be punished for two years." As I tried to show in the discussion of the admissions ceremony and elsewhere, we cannot assume an entirely interior spirituality here. Rather, a lack of commitment manifests itself in certain actions.[123] On the face of it this extremely serious offence provokes a punishment that amounts to undergoing the admissions process again, which is more lenient than we may have expected given that serious acts of disloyalty result in expulsion in 7.2.6.1 and 7.2.6.2 above. The leniency offered here is reminiscent of the case of the one who refuses to enter the covenant in 3.2.4 who can be forgiven and reinstated.[124] On the reconstruction offered by García Martínez, Tigchelaar and van der Woude the remains of 11Q29 appear to pro-

---

[120] See also Jokiranta, "Black Sheep."

[121] For analysis see Tzoref, "Use of Scripture," 224 (numbered 1QS 7:17–18) and Shemesh, "Scriptural Background of the Penal Code."

[122] Cf. 4Q270 7 i 13b–15a and Shemesh, "Scriptural Background of the Penal Code."

[123] Cf. 1QS 6:17 and 6.5.4.3 above.

[124] See 3.4.4 above.

vide a shorter version of this offence, though the comments suggest a closer correspondence to 1QS 7:23 and 4Q270 (D^e) 7 i 8.[125]

Given the semantic field of the verb זוע in the *qal* is to shake, tremble or rock to and fro and includes being frightened, it is likely that the description of "the person whose spirit wavers" (האיש אשר תזוע רוחו) implies physical symptoms.[126] Such symptoms might be caused by inner turmoil, mental health issues, or even being subjected to a serious allegation. The Maskil's role in assessing the spiritual make-up of humanity (14.2.1) and the sons of Zadok (1QS) // children of righteousness (4Q259)[127] offers insights into the need to monitor a person's fluctuating spirit. It is probable that malevolent demonic influences would have been a cause of concern.[128]

7.4.6.4 *Betrayal on the Part of a Member of Long Standing (1QS 7:22–25 // 4Q259 2:5b–9a)*

This passage deals with the particularly severe threat to the integrity and survival of the community by the departure of a longstanding member which requires ostracization. Remains of an offence compatible to this scenario are preserved in 11Q29.[129] While 1QS refers to a membership period beyond (על) ten full years, the preposition used in 4Q259 2:5 (עד) might also mean "up to" a full ten years. The latter reading would imply an extended probation after which the author is suggesting enduring commitment would have been established. Shemesh has argued that a betrayal on the part of a long-standing member presupposes a more deliberate act on a par with the severity of intentional disobedience to the law as opposed to inadvertent transgression.[130] We learn more about the kinds of ongoing relationships that might tempt members to continue seeking fellowship with former members from what is said about the people of injustice in 6.1.2.1 above. A ten year "career" in the community is suggestive of a level of seniority and authority that would have left a mark on relationships with more junior members. Moreover, in an environment where food was rationed – and it is hard to know whether rations were generous or even sufficient under ordinary circumstances – former members' ability to cater for material needs such as food may have played a role in maintaining close ties.[131] Finally, we ought to make

---

[125] For details see García Martínez, Tigchelaar and van der Woude, DJD 23:433–434 as well as 1.6.3 above and 7.4.6.4 below.

[126] See "זוע I," in HAWTTM 2:214–215.

[127] Cf. 14.2.2 below.

[128] Further, 1.2.1 above.

[129] See García Martínez, Tigchelaar and van der Woude, DJD 23:433–434 as well as 1.6.3 and 7.4.6.3 above.

[130] Shemesh, "Expulsion and Exclusion," 63–72.

[131] Cf. 6.1.2.1 where accepting goods and nourishment from the people of injustice is explicitly forbidden.

allowance for emotional ties.[132] Such ties may have been of a sexual or erotic nature as discussed in 7.4.5 above. Nor can we exclude kinship ties even if these are not part of the formal discourse. We find occasional glimpses of kinship ties clashing with community structures as in 4Q477 (The Rekukes by the Overseer) 2 ii 8 which objects to loving a blood relative.[133] It is conceivable also that close affiliates of defectors may have become "targeted" as potentially marred by a wavering spirit.[134]

Unlike the relative lenience towards the serious offence described in 7.2.6.3 a second chance is denied to long-term members of the council of the community who defect and those who fail to cut all ties with them.[135]

---

[132] On the challenges of cross-cultural insights on emotional ties in antiquity see Mark Golden, "Did the Ancients Care When Their Children Died?" *Greece and Rome* 35 (1988): 152–163. I am grateful to Candida Moss for this reference.

[133] See further Charlotte Hempel, "Self-Fashioning in the Dead Sea Scrolls: Thickening the Description of What Rule Texts Do," in *Social History of the Jews within the Ancient World*. Edited by Jonathan Ben-Dov and Michal Bar-Asher Siegal. TSAJ (Tübingen: Mohr Siebeck, forthcoming).

[134] Cf. 7.2.6.3 above.

[135] See also Chapter 13 below.

8. The Council of the Community (1QS 8:1–16a // 4Q258 6:1–8a // 4Q259 2:9b–3:6a)

8.1 Introduction

This section starts a new theme at the top of a column in 1QS and 4Q258 and is marked also by a major scribal sign in the bottom right corner of 1QS 7 which indicates the end of the Penal Code.[1] The material in this part of the Community Rules refers to a time before the community had come into being as indicated by a formula that looks ahead to a time "when these exist in Israel" which occurs in 1QS 8:4.12; 9:3 and in some corresponding material in 4Q258 and 4Q259. Based on this language scholars have suggested that this material should be associated with a community in the making. Murphy-O'Connor introduced the idea of a Manifesto of which this section was a part.[2]

An alternative interpretation holds that this passage describes an inner council of community leaders.[3] The latter position is difficult to reconcile with the fact that the Community Rules frequently employ the terminology "the council of the community" with reference to the community as a whole.[4] Moreover, a sub-group *within* the council of the community is singled out below.[5] A third approach is represented by Hartmut Stegemann who argued that 1QS 8–9 contains a string of secondary material.[6]

While the programmatic tone adopted here shares a great deal with the material discussed in Chapter 5, several features depict a context of community formation in modest numbers with a commitment to the study of the law and remind us of the rules in 6.3 and 6.4. It is important not to read this material in isolation from other accounts of incipient communal life in the Community Rules. On the one hand, the small scale of the community envisaged here, i. e. fifteen members according to 1QS 8:1 // 4Q259 2:9 invites comparison with 1QS

---

[1] Cf. 1.5.1.3.2 above.

[2] Murphy-O'Connor, "La genèse littéraire;" see also Sacchi, *Regola*, 132.

[3] Joseph M. Baumgarten, "The Duodecimal Courts of Qumran, Revelation, and the Sanhedrin," *JBL* 95 (1976): 59–78.

[4] Cf. especially 6.5.2.3 above.

[5] See 8.2.5 and 8.4.5 below.

[6] Stegemann, *The Library of Qumran: On the Essenes, Qumran, John the Baptist, and Jesus* (Grand Rapids, MI: Eerdmans, 1998).

6:2c–4a // 4Q258 2:7–8 // 4Q263 lines 3b–5a. A fifteen strong council is also outlined in 4Q265 (Miscellaneous Rules) 7:7–10, a passage that shares a number of other themes with this part of the Community Rules.[7] By contrast, the level of organizational complexity associated with the many is lacking in this programmatic account, though we return to highly developed disciplinary processes where rabbim terminology recurs in Chapters 9 and 10 that follow. In contrast to 6.5 members do not seek out to join this movement which is described here as coming into being.

8.2 Translation

8.2.1 Expectations for the Emerging Council of the Community (1QS 8:1–4b // 4Q259 2:9b–13a)

1QS 8	4Q259 2
[1]In the council of the community (there shall be) twelve (lay)people and three priests flawless concerning all that has been revealed from all of [2]the law. They shall conduct themselves with truth, righteousness, justice, devoted love and humble conduct each with his neighbour. [3]They shall remain faithful in the land with a solid intellect and a broken spirit. They shall make up for trespasses *by practising* justice [4a]and by (standing up to) the challenge of distress. Their conduct with everyone shall adhere to the {.} standard of truth and the rule of time.	[9b][In the council of the community (there shall be) twelve] (lay)people [and] three priests [10][flawless concerning all that has been revealed from all of the law. They shall conduct themselves with] truth, righteousness, justice, [11][devoted love and humble conduct each with his neighbour. They shall remain faith]ful in the land with a solid intellect, *humility* [12][and a b]roken [spirit]. They shall make up for tres[passes *with acts of* justice and by (standing up to)] the challenge of [distress.] Their conduct with everyone [13a][shall adhere to the standard of] truth and the rule of [time].

8.2.2 The Emerging Community is Likened to a Temple in a Context of Looming Judgment (1QS 8:4c–7a // 4Q258: 6:1 // 4Q259 2:13b–16a)

1QS 8	4Q259 2
[4c]When these exist in Israel [5]the {.}council of the community shall be established in truth *vacat* *as an eternal p*[la]*nt,*	[13b][When these exist in] Israel the council of the community shall be established [14][in truth for] eternal [judg]ment,

---

[7] See Baumgarten, DJD 35:57–78; Hempel, *Damascus Texts*, 89–104; Hempel, *Qumran Rule Texts in Context*, 79–96 and 1.6.2 above.

1QS 8	4Q259 2
a holy house for Israel and a most holy [6]assembly for Aaron, witnesses of truth for judgment and ch{.}os[e]n by the will (of God) to atone for the land	[a holy house for Israel and] a most holy [assembly] for Aar[o(n)],[15]witnesses of truth for judgment and chose[n] by the wi[l]l (of God) [to atone for] the land

1QS 8	4Q258 6	4Q259 2
and to bring back upon [7]the wicked their reward. *Vacat.*	[1][and] to bring back upon the wicked [2][their reward.]	[and] to [b]rin[g ba]ck upon the wicked [16a]their reward.

8.2.3 The Emerging Community is Likened to a Fortified City (1QS 8:7b–8a // 4Q258: 6:2b // 4Q259 2:16b)

1QS 8:7b–8a	4Q258 6	4Q259 2
It shall be a tried wall, a splendid corner(stone) whose *vacat* [8]*foundations* shall neither shake nor move from their place. *Vacat.*	[2b][It shall be the tried wall, a splendid corner(stone) *whose foundations* shall neither shake nor move from] their [p]lace.	[16b]It shall be the tried wall, a [splendid] co[rner(stone); *they* shall nei]ther [shake no]r move from their place.

8.2.4 The Emerging Community is Likened to a Temple as Part of a Covenantal Relationship (1QS 8:8b–10a // 4Q258: 6:2c–4a // 4Q259 2:16c–18a)

1QS 8	4Q258 6	4Q259 2
[8b](It shall be) a most holy *dwelling* [9]for Aaron with all of their knowledge for the sake of the covenant of justice and in order to offer up a soothing [odour]. And (it shall be) a house of perfection and truth in Israel [10a] {…} in order to establish a covenant according to the eternal sta{.}[tu]tes. *And they shall be welcome to make atonement for the land and to determine the*	[2c](It shall be) a most holy *dwelling* [3][for Aaron with all of their knowledge for the sake of the covenant of justice and in order to offer up a sooth]ing odour. And (it shall be) a house of perfection and truth in Israe]l in order to establish a covenant according to the eternal statutes. [4a][And they shall be welcome to make atonement	[16c](It shall be) [17]a m[o]st holy *refuge* for Aar[on with all of their knowledge] for the sake of the covena[nt of justice and] in order to [o]ff[er up] a soothing odour. And (it shall be) a house of [18a]perfection and truth in [Israe]l in order to [establish a covenant according to the] e[te]rnal [statut]es. Lacking in 4Q259

1QS 8	4Q258 6	4Q259 2
judgment of wickedness {with perfect conduct}.	for the land and to determine the judgment of wickedness.]	

8.2.5 A Sub-Group is Set Apart as Holy and to be Granted Access to the Findings of the Scholar (1QS 8:10b–12a // 4Q258 6:4b–6a // 4Q259 2:18b–3:1–3a)

1QS 8	4Q258 6	4Q259 2–3
[10b] When these have been established according to the basic principles of the community for two years with {…} perfect conduct *and without injustice* [11] they shall be set apart as holy in the midst of the council of the people of the community. And nothing that has been hidden from Israel but was found by the [12] scholar shall the latter hide from these out of fear of a renegade spirit. *Vacat.*	[4b] [When these have been established according to the ba]sic principles of the community for two years [5] [with perfect conduct *and without injustice,* they shall be set apart as holy in the midst of the council of the peo]ple of the communi[ty. And nothing that has been] hi[dden from Is]rael but was found [6a] by the scho[lar shall the latter hide from these out of fear of a renegade spirit]. *Vacat.*	[18b] When these have been established. *Vacat.* [19] EMPTY LINE [3][1] [according to the basic principles of the community for two years with perfect conduct they shall be set apart] as holy in the midst of the council of the peo[ple of] [2] [the community. And nothing that has been hidden from Israel but was fou]nd by the scholar shall the latter h[i]d[e] [3a] [from] these [out of fear of a] rene[gade spi]rit. [*Vacat*]

8.2.6 The Emerging Council is to Keep Apart from the People of Injustice and Devote Themselves to the Study of the Law (1QS 8:12b–16a // 4Q258 6:6a–8a // 4Q259 3:3b–6a)

1QS 8	4Q258 6	4Q259 3
[12b] When these exist *as a community* in Israel [13] *according to these rules* they shall keep apart from the company of the people of injustice and go to the wilderness	[6a] When these exist [in Israel] they shall keep apart from [the company of] [7] the people of [injustice	[3b] [When] these [exi]st *in Israel* they shall keep apart from the com[pa]ny of [4] *the people of* [*injustice*] and go [to] the wil[der]ne[ss

1QS 8	4Q258 6	4Q259 3
to prepare there the way of *Him*	to prepare there the way of *Him*?]	to prepare the]re the way of *truth*
[14]as it is written: "In the wilderness prepare the way of …. vacat, make straight in the desert a highway for our God."	SHORTER TEXT	a[s] [5]it is written: ["In the wilder]ness pre[pare the way of the *truth* (?), make strai]ght in the desert a highway for our God."
[15]This is the study of the law w[hic]h He has commanded through Moses to carry out	[This is the study of the la]w which He has commanded thr[ough Moses to ca]rry out	[6a]This is [the stu]d[y of the law whi]ch He has commanded through Moses.
according to all	*all*	
that has been revealed from time to time [16a]and according to that which the prophets have revealed by His holy spirit. *Vacat.*	[that has been revealed] [8a]from ti[me to time according to that which the prophets have revealed by His holy spirit.]	A SUBSTANTIAL MINUS

8.3 Textual Notes

8:2 The preposition "with" is spelled with *aleph* rather than *ayin* in 1QS, a common feature in the Hebrew of the Scrolls which attests a weakening of the gutturals.[8]

8:3 The plus ובענוה "and with humility" appears to have been added in a fairly compressed style in the margin of 4Q259 2:11, see also the final word in 4Q259 2:5 (another plus over against 1QS 7:22).[9]

8:4 A letter that stood originally between the preposition *bet* and the construct "standard of" was erased in 1QS.[10] Puech and Qimron identify the erased letter as *ayin*.[11]

8:4 A paragraphos marks either the transition between two distinct outlines of the emergence of the community or is the first of several paragraphoi in 1QS that mark a potent moment in time (עת) or – in the case of 1QS 9:11 – the coming of the eschatological prophet and the messiahs of Aaron and Israel.[12]

8:5 The letter *he* preceding the word "council" has been erased in 1QS.[13]

---

[8] Cf. Qimron, HDSS, 25–26.

[9] So already Puech, "Review of *Textual Development*," 449. For the same argument on syntactical grounds and the disruption of the biblical dictum, see Alexander and Vermes, DJD 26:143.

[10] See García Martínez and Tigchelaar, DSSSE, 88.

[11] Puech, "Écriture de 1QS VII–VIII," 40 and Qimron, DSSHW 1:224.

[12] See also 1QS 9:5 and 9:19 below as well as 1.5.1.3 above.

[13] Cf. García Martínez and Tigchelaar, DSSSE, 88 and Qimron, DSSHW 1:224.

8:5 4Q259 2:14 reads "eternal [judg]ment" where 1QS has "eternal plant." Alexander and Vermes draw attention to the superlinear correction of the same word in 1QS 8:5 and suggest the possibility of a misreading caused by an attempt to copy an imperfect manuscript.[14]

8:6 Remains of three letters are added above the line ostensibly to complete "Aaron" in 4Q259 2:14. Based on the recent image B-295972 by Shai Halevi published by the LLDSSDL the superlinear remains appear to be of a damaged or partly erased *resh* followed by *resh* and *yod*.[15] There is no sign of final *nun* whereas superlinear *resh*(s) repeat the original *resh* in the line below. Overall this looks like a poorly executed effort on the part of the scribe responsible for the original text and the addition.[16]

8:6 The reading "the chosen of" (בחירי) is the result of a scribal correction, perhaps from "those who choose" (בוחרי), in 1QS with an intial second letter *yod* or attempt at *vav* erased and transposed superlinearly to follow after *khet*. The erased letter is read by Qimron as *yod*.[17] It is noteworthy that an oscillation between the active and passive participle of the same root is attested in 1QS 9:17 "Those who have chosen the way" (בוחרי) where 4Q258 8:2 and 4Q259 3:16 read "the chosen of the way" (בחירי).[18] The participle is reconstructed in the comparable though not identical wording of 4Q265 (Miscellaneous Rules) 7:8.[19]

8:8 There is a larger than expected space after the second *mem* in "from their place" (ממקומם) in 1QS. The first medial *mem* is presented in final form.[20] In addition to the broader disruptions that seem to have affected the inscription of this column and this line in 1QS, the particular hesitation here might also be due to an aborted haplography given the two opening and closing letters currently appear identical.

8:8 The variant reading "dwelling" (מעון) in 1QS over against 4Q259's "refuge" (מעוז) can again be attributed to a visual error.[21] It is possible that 1QS and 4Q258, which shares 1QS's reading, both misread a *Vorlage* like 4Q259 or that 1QS drew on 4Q258 here. While a visual error is likely at some stage in the textual history of this passage Alexander and Vermes rightly stress that both readings make sense in the present context.[22]

---

[14] Alexander and Vermes, DJD 26:143 and 8.4.2 below.

[15] Cf. Qimron, DSSHW 1:225.

[16] See also Alexander and Vermes, DJD 26:139, 141 and Puech, "Review of *Textual Development*," 449 who read *vav nun* above the line. García Martínez and Tigchelaar, DSSSE, 530 read *resh, vav, nun* superlinearly and propose an erased *tav* underlying the correction.

[17] Qimron, DSSHW 1:224; see also Wernberg-Møller, "Reflections," 64 n. 1 and García Martínez and Tigchelaar, DSSSE, 88.

[18] See Puech, "Écriture de 1QS VII–VIII," 39.

[19] See Baumgarten, DJD 35:70. See also 1QSa 1:16 and Reymond, *Qumran Hebrew*, 25–26.

[20] Cf. Martin, *Scribal Character of the Dead Sea Scrolls*, 2:463.

[21] See 1.5.6.2 and Table 3 above.

[22] Alexander and Vermes, DJD 26:144.

8:9 García Martínez and Tigchelaar propose emending "all of their (כולם) knowledge" to "eternal (עולם) knowledge."[23]

8:9 On the elision of *he* in the infinitive *hiphil* לקריב in 1QS see *ad* 1QS 5:10 above.

8:9 "Odour" (ריח) is added above the line in 1QS.[24]

8:9 The final *tav* of the final word "house of" in 4Q259 2:17 is generously drawn in order to end the line flush with the line above, something Malachi Martin labelled "marginal fitting."[25]

8:10 A short paragraphos in 1QS is positioned, unusually, at the same height as the inscription of this line rather than just below the line. This marginal paragraphos coincides with a line where 1QS attests a superlinear plus over against 4Q259 2 as well as a transition between two sub-sections.[26]

8:10 Puech attributes the substantial superlinear addition in 1QS to the second hand, Scribe B.[27]

8:10 A superlinear addition above the first word of this line has been erased in 1QS. Initial *bet* and remains of a subsequent *lamed* can be identified.

8:10 The spelling of "to establish" is fuller in 4Q258 6:3 (להקים) than in 1QS (להקם).

8:10 "The statutes of" (חו{ת}קות) is corrected in 1QS with an erasure of *tav* and the letters *qoph* and *vav* have been added above the line.

8: 10 The uninscribed space clearly preserved both at the beginning and end of 4Q259 2:19 supports the suggestion of Alexander and Vermes that this line was left blank.[28] In addition, I identify a *vacat* at the end of 4Q259 2:18.

8:10: The superlinear text in 1QS includes the remains of a second erasure of the phrase "with perfect conduct" (בתמים דרך). All of the superlinear addition is lacking in 4Q259 2:18 as clearly indicated by the preservation of the final *mem* of "eternal" (עולם) in "eternal statutes" which is followed immediately by the words "When these are established" (בהכין אלה) in 4Q259.[29] 4Q258 6:4–5, while fragmentary, does seem to attest sufficient space for the superlinear addition in 1QS 8:10 as part of its main text.[30]

---

[23] García Martínez and Tigchelaar, DSSSE, 88. See already Wernberg-Møller, *Manual of Discipline*, 33 and 127.

[24] See Qimron, DSSHW 1:224 and Puech, "Écriture de 1QS VII–VIII," 41. For the suggestion that 4Q259 2:17 also attests the remains of superlinear text see PTSDSSP 1:86 and Puech, "Review of *Textual Development*," 450. Alexander and Vermes ascribe the apparent position of the remains to the effects of "distortion and shrinkage of the skin at the torn edge," see Alexander and Vermes, DJD 26:141.

[25] Martin, *Scribal Character of the Dead Sea Scrolls*, 1:109.

[26] See also 1QS 5:13; 5:25; 8:13 as well as 1.5.1.3 above.

[27] Puech, "Écriture de 1QS VII–VIII," 42.

[28] Alexander and Vermes, DJD 26:142.

[29] See Alexander and Vermes, DJD 26:106 in the context of a discussion of 4Q258 6:4 and Pl. 15 and Puech, "Écriture de 1QS VII–VIII," 41.

[30] Cf. Alexander and Vermes, DJD 26:105–106.

8:10 1QS and 4Q258 share the plus "and without injustice" (ואין עולה) over against 4Q259. In 1QS these words are added above the line. This is a further instance where 1QS and 4Q258 agree over against a shorter text in 4Q259. However, it is important to acknowledge that prior to the superlinear supplementation 1QS corresponded to 4Q259.

8:10–11 The digital images reveal a further erasure partly overwritten by "with perfect conduct" (בתמים דרך) at the end of 1QS 8:10. After intitial *bet* the remaining letters are written just below the regular line. Qimron has identified the erasure now overwritten as "they shall be set apart" (יבדלו), a reading which is now added superlinearly at the beginning of 1QS 8:11 with damage to the top stroke of *lamed*.[31]

8:11 The article *he* has been added superlinearly to "that has been hidden" (הנסתר) in 1QS.

8:12 As discussed briefly in 1.5.6.1 above, Milik first deciphered the reading "*in Israel* " in cryptic letters in 4Q259 3, a reading scrutinised in detail and confirmed by Puech.[32] According to Puech the cryptic word goes back to a second hand correcting an earlier unencrypted reading "in the yahad."

The last two cryptic letters (*aleph* and *lamed*) of "*in Israel*" are written above the line.[33] Stegemann has drawn attention to a number of cases in 1QSa where the theophoric element of "Israel" is written in "some kind of reverential writing of the name ישראל."[34] It looks as though the theophoric element in Israel in 1QS has been written at an angle. The way the divine name element appears in 1QS is, however, more likely due to the text of its *Vorlage*. As we saw above, 4Q259 3:3 – which may have been consulted by the scribe of 1QS – attests the theophoric element of Israel written above the line in cryptic script which may have caused the scribe of 1QS to pause before adding the divine name element. Whether the scribe of 4Q259 was operating out of reverence or simply for pragmatic reasons is hard to know. Pragmatic reasons such as having to make the cryptic phrase fit into a space left by a scribe copying the Hebrew are compelling.[35]

---

[31] Qimron, DSSHW 1: 224; see also Qimron, PTSDSSP 1:34 n. 242; García Martínez and Tigchelaar, DSSSE, 88 and Puech, "Écriture de 1QS VII–VIII," 41.

[32] Milik, "Le travail d'édition."

[33] Puech, "L'alphabet cryptique A." Further, Uwe Glessmer, "The Otot-Texts (4Q319) and the Problem of Intercalations in the Context of the 364-Day Calendar," in *Qumranstudien: Vorträge und Beiträge der Teilnehmer des Qumranseminars auf dem internationalen Treffen der Society of Biblical Literature, Münster, 25–26. Juli 1993*. Edited by Heinz-Josef Fabry, Armin Lange and Hermann Lichtenberger. Schriften des Institutum Judaicum Delitzschianum 4 (Göttingen: Vandenhoeck & Ruprecht, 1996), 125–164, 133–134.

[34] Stegemann, "Some Remarks," 485–486 as well as 1QSa 1:1, 6, 20; 2:2, 14, 20.

[35] See Puech, "L'alphabet cryptique A."

It is noteworthy that both the words "in Israel" and the encrypted phrase "people of [injustice] in 4Q259 3:4 (see the note on **8:13** below) occur in regular square Hebrew script elsewhere in 4Q259.[36]

8:12–13 Two superlinear additions attested in 1QS are lacking from 4Q258 6:6 and 4Q259 3:3 and are attributed by Puech to a second hand B.[37]

8:13 The letters in "from the midst of" (מתוך) show signs of reshaping in 1QS.

8:13 As Puech has shown, 4Q259 preserves further letters in the Cryptic A script at the start of 4Q259 3:4 for the designation "*people of [injustice]*."[38] Alexander and Vermes express their reservations about the identification of the script as cryptic.[39] Recent multi-spectral images by Shai Halevi and published by the LLDSSDL as B-295966 and B-314657 support the readings of Milik and Puech.

8:13 The phrase "the people of" (הנשי) is spelled with initial *he* rather than *aleph* in 1QS. While there are philological explanations that may account for this,[40] I suggested above that it is also possible that the scribe at work in 1QS misread the transition from cryptic *aleph* to *nun* in the *Vorlage* 4Q259 as *he*.[41]

8:14 4Q258 lacks the explicit quotation of Isa 40:3 here. The citation and the same introductory formula are, however, attested in 4Q259 3:4–5 with the significant variant reading to prepare "the way of truth."

8:14 The divine name is represented by four dots in 1QS. This practice is also attested in 4Q175 (4QTestimonia) and 4Q53 (4QSam^c), two manuscripts copied by the same scribe as 1QS.[42] In 4Q258 8:9 and 9:8 the divine name *el* is written in paleo-Hebrew script.

8:16 In the opening word of this line in 1QS the preposition *kaph* appears to have been reshaped.

8.4 Commentary

8.4.1 Expectations for the Emerging Community (1QS 8·1–4b // 4Q259 2:9b–13a)

What is said about the council of the community here leaves little doubt that the language is highly theological. The group comprises twelve members of the laity and three priests. This combination of a lay element alongside members who

---

[36] For further discussion see Glessmer, "The Otot-Texts," 141; Hempel, "Profile and Character" and 1.5.6.1 above.

[37] Puech "Écriture de 1QS VII–VIII," 40 and 8.4 below.

[38] Puech, "L'alphabet cryptique A;" also Metso, *Textual Development*, 53–54 and Qimron, DSSHW 1:225.

[39] Alexander and Vermes, DJD 26:145–146.

[40] See, e. g., Kutscher, *Language*, 509.

[41] See 1.5.6 above. Cf. also 4Q259 4:6 and the Textual Note on 1QS 9:24 in 14.3 below.

[42] Cf. Tigchelaar, "Scribe" and 1.5.1.2 above.

represent the priesthood is very familiar from Chapters 5, 6 and 7 above. The number twelve symbolically represents the twelve tribes, and the three priestly representatives stand for the three clans of Levi referred to in Num 3:17 which reads "The following were the sons of Levi by their names: Gershon, Kohath and Merari." Knibb has encapsulated the picture painted here as describing "an Israel in miniature."[43] The numerical make-up of the council is referred to by the sum total of fifteen members in 4Q265 (Miscellaneous Rules) 7:7. Having introduced a theologically charged account of an emerging community our passage develops a strong claim to this group's commitment to uphold everything revealed from the law before developing the case for their exemplary conduct by means of a pastiche of biblical references esp. Micah 6:8 and Ps 51:19 (English verse 17). Significantly, each of these passages reveals ethical behaviour that is presented as on a par with sacrifices. The core values expressed here closely mirror the values associated with the community according to 5.2.5.

8:3 The expression "broken spirit" is taken from Ps 51:19 (English 51:17). As was the case in Micah 6:8, Ps 51:19 is very critical of the standards of current cultic practice. The phrase "make up for trespasses" (רצה עון) draws on Lev 26:41, 43 and can mean "to atone."[44]

8:3 The plus "with humility" in 4Q259 is likely secondary.[45]

8:4b The references to "their conduct with all" and "the rule of time" display terminological overlap with the introductory words of the statutes for the Maskil in 1QS 9:12 // 4Q259 3:6–7.[46]

8.4.2 The Emerging Community is Likened to a Temple in a Context of Looming Judgment (1QS 8:4c–7a// 4Q258: 6:1 // 4Q259 2:13b–16a)

The emerging community is here described by means of a rich and overlaid cluster of figurative and aspirational concepts beginning with an emphasis on the establishment of the new community in truth against the background of an anticipated eternal judgment.[47] The reference to eternal judgment has been misread by the scribe of 1QS 8:5 as "an eternal plant."[48] The identification of the

---

[43] Knibb, *Qumran Community*, 130.

[44] For a discussion of Lev 26 and the present passage see Robert Kugler, "A Note on Lev 26:41, 43; 4Q434 1 ii 3 and 4Q504 1–2 Recto 5–6 and 1QS 8:3 (Par. 4Q259 2:12): On Human Agency in the Divine Economy at Qumran," in *Prayer and Poetry in the Dead Sea Scrolls and Related Literature: Essays in Honor of Eileen Schuller on the Occasion of her 65th Birthday.* Edited by Jeremy Penner, Ken M. Penner and Cecilia Wassén. STDJ 98 (Leiden: Brill, 2011), 245–250.

[45] See further 8.3 above.

[46] Cf. Chapter 14 below.

[47] On the importance of judgment in 1QS 8 and 9 see already Milik, *Ten Years of Discovery*, 116.

[48] See also 8.3 above.

community with an eternal plant[49] is a common theme in the Scrolls and other early Jewish literature.[50] The terminology also occurs in an account of God's granting communion with the angels to the chosen ones in 1QS 11:8.[51] The reference to eternal judgment in 4Q259 is, however, entirely intelligible and better integrated into the role that is ascribed to the emerging community in God's judgment across both manuscripts at this point. Given the visual similarity between the words "plant" and "judgment" coupled with the scribal correction in 1Q, I suggest the scribe of the latter manuscript was working with a damaged *Vorlage* and resorted to the familiar phrase "eternal plant."[52] The context of judgment explains a second reference to the new community as witnesses to truth. A second cluster of ideas describes the new community in cultic terms as holy and a means to atone for the land.[53] A recurring feature of the narrative is the description of the priestly and lay elements of the new community in terms of Aaron and Israel.[54]

8.4.3 The Emerging Community is Likened to a Fortified City (1QS 8:7b–8a // 4Q258: 6:2b // 4Q259 2:16b)

The image of the community representing the cultic benefits of the Temple gives way to a description of the emerging community as a fortified city based on Isa 28:16.[55] This subtle development of metaphors was noted by Klinzing in a perceptitve early analysis of this material.[56] The sense that the imagery developed here constitutes an interlude in the middle of two passages that describe the community in cultic terms is mirrored materially in 1QS where two sizeable *vacats* set this statement apart from the surrounding text.

The nominal form of זוע which occurs in Isa 28:19 with referenece to terror is reminiscent of the language of a wavering or shaking (זוע) spirit in the penal code in 1QS 7:18b. In our comments on the latter passage I argued that the verb likely refers to an offender's physical symptoms which would have enabled detection

---

[49] Cf. Isa. 60:21; 61:3.

[50] See especially CD 1:7 and 1 Enoch 93:9–10 as well as Patrick A. Tiller, "The 'Eternal Planting' in the Dead Sea Scrolls," *DSD* 4 (1997): 312–335.

[51] Further, 15.2.8.

[52] In a perceptive footnote Tiller acknowledges the scribal correction in 1QS and considers its reading a secondary development of what we find in 4Q259, see "'Eternal Planting,'" 326 n. 38. For the suggestion that 4Q259 may haves served as one of the *Vorlagen* for 1QS see 1.5.6.2 above.

[53] Cf. also 8.4.4 and Chapter 11 below.

[54] See 8.1 above.

[55] See Brownlee, *The Dead Sea Manual*, 33 and Tzoref, "Use of Scripture." Isa 28:16 can thus be added to Isa 2:22 and Isa 40:3 as another part of Isaiah read by the scribes behind the Community Rules as profoundly reflecting the place of the movement in God's plan, see Brooke, "Isaiah in Some of the Non-Scriptural Dead Sea Scrolls," 251–254.

[56] Klinzing, *Umdeutung des Kultus*.

and punishment.[57] Whereas in Isa 28 it is the Temple that offers safety and stability in the face of the power of a recurring scourge, the Community Rules represented in 8.2.3 portray the emerging community in comparable terms as a safe have. Consequently, anyone who departs or lacks commitment is exposing themselves to danger.[58]

8.4.4 The Emerging Community is Likened to a Temple as Part of a Covenantal Relationship (1QS 8:8b–10a // 4Q258: 6:2c–4a // 4Q259 2:16c–18a)

After the sizeable *vacat* that frames the material discussed in 8.4.3 in 1QS we return here to the topic of the community's likeness to a Temple. Both in terms of content and structure this material appears to repeat and expand on what is said in 8.4.2.[59] Both passages begin by stressing the holiness of the Temple and end with a reference to the judgment of the wicked. A new emphasis here on the covenant is reminiscent of the plus in 1QS 5:5–6.[60] As I argued in 8.4.3 above, the material evidence supports the literary analysis of cumulative growth here since these particular lines attest to the highest level of secondary supplementation within 1QS. Moreover, 4Q259 offers evidence of a shorter account that lacks the texts added above the line in 1QS 8:10 which Puech attributes to a second hand B.[61]

A number of scholars have rightly stressed the need to take the metaphorical context of the account of the emerging community more seriously.[62] The slippage towards a literal reading of the cultic elements in this account has been particularly pronounced. Recent research has rightly challenged the suggestion that the movement behind the Scrolls turned its back on the Jerusalem Temple.[63]

---

[57] See 1.2.1 and 7.2.6.3 above.

[58] A comparable portrayal of the solid foundation of the assembly has been identified by Asaf Gayer in the Final Hymn, see Gayer, "The Centrality of Prayer and the Stability of Trust: An Analysis of the Hymn of the Maskil; in 1QS IX,25b–XI,15a," in *Ancient Jewish Prayers and Emotions: Emotions Associated with Jewish Prayer In and Around the Second Temple Period.* Edited by Stefan Reif and Renate Egger-Wenzel (Berlin: De Gruyter, 2015), 317–334.

[59] See also Collins, "Construction of Israel," 32–33 and Klinzing, *Umdeutung des Kultus,* 61.

[60] For a discussion of overlapping terminology and concerns between this passage and the account of community emergence in 1QS 5 as well as 4Q265 (Miscellaneous Rules) 7 see Hempel, *Qumran Rule Texts in Context,* 79–96. On the plusses in 1QS 5 see 1.5.1.4.2 above.

[61] See Puech, "Écriture de 1QS VII–VIII," 42 and 1.5.1.2 and 8.3 above.

[62] See, e. g., Newsom, *Self and Symbolic Space* and Cecilia Wassén, "Do You Have to Be Pure in a Metaphorical Temple? Sanctuary Metaphors and Construction of Sacred Space in the Dead Sea Scrolls and Paul's Letters," in *Purity, Holiness, and Identity in Judaism and Christianity: Essays in Memory of Susan Haber.* Edited by Carl S. Ehrlich, Anders Runesson and Eileen Schuller. WUNT 305 (Tübingen: Mohr Siebeck, 2013), 55–86.

[63] See also 11.4 below

8.4.5 A Sub-Group is Set Apart as Holy and to be Granted Access to the Findings of the Scholar (1QS 8:10b–12a // 4Q258 6:4b–6a // 4Q259 2:18b–3:3a)

This passage describes the emergence of a sub-group within the council of the community after a period of two years. The length of this period of "probation" for the wider community mirrors the two probationary years that are expected of aspiring members keen to join the many according to 6.5.2.3. As was the case in 5.2.3, the early history of the community is characterised by internal tensions. The newly emerging group is portrayed as keen to share the findings of the scholar who is able to access legal interpreations hidden from Israel. The texts reflect a sense of anxiety on the part of the off-shoot group of being excluded from such insights on the grounds of the dangers posed by a renegade spirit. While a concern with the correct interpretation of the law and its observance runs across the diverse sections of this chapter, this is the only example where a group who claim an elevated status within the original community are portrayed as in need of guidance that may be withheld from them out of a concern about betrayal. The scholar (איש הדורש) appears to be a student of the law who does not belong to the sub-group whose emergence is described here or, if he does, operates without transparency.[64]

Whereas the opening lines of column 8 spoke of a group of the future that emerged from within Israel, this statement presupposes an elite sub-group within the council of the community. 1QS 8:10 leaves no doubt that some time, two years at a minimum, had elapsed from the earliest days. It seems likely that the present passage goes back to a later time than the surrounding material.

8.4.6 The Emerging Council is to Keep Apart from the People of Injustice and Devote Themselves to the Study of the Law (1QS 8:12b–16a // 4Q258 6:6a–8a // 4Q259 3:3b–6a)

This passage is closely related to the admonitions to keep separate from the people of injustice in Chapters 5 and 6.1 above.[65] Both there and in the present passage the separation from the people of injustice is intimately connected with

---

[64] For further discussion of the material on the interpretation of scripture in the Community Rules see Steven D. Fraade, "Interpretive Authority in the Studying Community at Qumran," *JJS* 44 (1993): 46–69 and Hempel, "Interpretative Authority" and further bibliography there. On the role of controlling knowledge in the ancient knowledge economy reflected in the Dead Sea Scrolls see Hempel, "Bildung und Wissenswirtschaft."

[65] See also George J. Brooke, "Isa 40:3 and the Wilderness Community," in *New Qumran Texts and Studies: Proceedings of the First Meeting of the International Organization for Qumran Studies, Paris 1992.* Edited by George J. Brooke and Florentino García Martínez. STDJ 15 (Leiden: Brill, 1994), 117–132.

an account of communal origins that suggests a schismatic context. I was able to show, on the basis of the kinds of interactions that are forbidden with the people of injustice, that the members of this group were considered by some as authoritative and as part of an in-group with whom one may consider sharing property and food. 1QS offers a longer text that includes more explicit references to scripture over against 4Q258 in the present passage and in Chapters 5 and 6.1. Moreover, both passages share the same introductory formula, "as it is written."[66] Finally, the context in both passages is the challenging separation from the people of injustice at a crucial point in the movement's formation. Whereas the issue of this separation is shared across all three preserved manuscripts, the reference to Isa 40:3 occurs only in 1QS and 4Q259. The use of the cryptic script in 4Q259 in this context intimates the need for protecting insights from this group.[67]

Against the background of the assumed appeal of the people of injustice as sources of authority in matters of law[68] the insertion of an explicit citation in 1QS and 4Q259 is meant to bolster the expertise of the author's group and challenge the claims to authority of the people of injustice in those matters. It is significant that obedience to the law of Moses, which characterises good leadership according to the account of community formation and separation from the people of injustice in 6.1, also implies a wilderness discourse in relation to the revelation of the law at Sinai.[69] Moreover, emphasis on legal interpretation emerges as a contentious area even *within* the movement associated with the Scrolls from Qumran as recent research on 4QMMT and other legal texts has suggested.[70] As I will argue below on 1QS 8:13 in particular, the reading "the way of truth" in 4Q259 is intrinsically connected to the rejection of injustice.

The reference to preparing the way of the Lord in the wilderness draws on Isa 40:3 and has for a long time been associated with the withdrawal of the movement behind the Community Rules to Qumran.[71] We find a second reference to Isa 40:3 in the Statutes for the Maskil.[72] It is noteworthy that

---

[66] Cf. Metso, "Biblical Quotations," 84–86.

[67] For further discussion see Hempel, "Profile and Character" and 8.3 above.

[68] See 6.1 above.

[69] For an analysis of the Sinai event for the portrayal of the community in the Community Rules see James C. VanderKam, "Sinai Revisited," in *Biblical Interpretation at Qumran.* Edited by Matthias Henze. Studies in the Dead Sea Scrolls and Related Literature (Grand Rapids, MI: Eerdmans, 2005), 44–60; see also Kampen, "Torah."

[70] Cf. Steven Fraade, "To Whom It May Concern: *4QMMT* and Its Addressee(s)," *RevQ* 19 (2000): 507–526; Maxine Grossman, "Reading *4QMMT*: Genre and History," *RevQ* 20 (2001): 3–21 and Charlotte Hempel, " 4QMMT in the Context of the Dead Sea Scrolls and Beyond," in *Qumran 4QMMT: Some Precepts of the Law.* Edited by Reinhard G. Kratz et al. Sapere (Tübingen: Mohr Siebeck, forthcoming).

[71] For recent discussion and further literature see Schofield, *From Qumran to the Yaḥad,* 159–162.

[72] Cf. 1QS 9:19–20 // 4Q256 18:3 // 4Q258 8:4 // 4Q259 3:19 and Chapter 14 below.

the gap between our passage and the second reference to Isa 40:3 in the Statutes for the Maskil is dramatically shorter in 4Q259 where the Statutes follow immediately after the current passage.[73] However, recent research has rightly highlighted the metaphorical context of the reference to the wilderness in this passage. As Dimant has shown, the interpretation of Isa 40:3 formally resembles the Qumran commentary form known as *pesher* by employing a pronoun (היא) "this is" to introduce the interpretation of the biblical lemma. As Dimant rightly emphasizes, the key import of this reference to Isa 40:3 is the interpretation of the preparation of the way in the wilderness as "this is the study of the law."[74] Moreover, Hindy Najman has demonstrated the conceptualisation of the wilderness as a place of revelation in ancient Judaism more broadly.[75] Finally, both Brooke and Schofield have fruitfully drawn on critical spatiality studies to demonstrate the multivalent use of the desert in this passage.[76] Beyond the pronounced exegetical framework drawn out by Dimant, such exegetical reflections would have been read afresh by those members of the movement associated with the Community Rules who at some point settled in the vicinity of Qumran. As Schofield eloquently put it, "The wilderness became [...] where [...] imagined utopian space met lived space."[77]

8:13 The divine name has been replaced with a third person personal pronoun in 1QS 8:13 whereas four dots are used in the following line.[78] As observed by Metso this pronoun is syntactically unusual.[79] It is commonly supposed, moreover, that 4Q259's reading to prepare "the way of truth" (אמת) also represents an effort to avoid the divine name.[80] It is more likely, however, that the reference to truth is part of a polemical statement that sets the community's own foundation in contrast to the charge of injustice that is levelled against a group called

---

[73] See Metso, "Biblical Quotations," 85.

[74] Dimant, "Not Exile in the Desert but Exile in Spirit: The Pesher of Isa 40:3 in the *Rule of the Community* and the History of the Scrolls Community," in *History, Ideology and Bible Interpretation at Qumran*, 455–464 and fulsome further bibliography there. See also the chapter entitled "4Q159 Fragment 5 and the 'Desert Theology' of the Qumran Sect," in Moshe Bernstein, *Reading and Re-Reading Scripture at Qumran: Law, Pesher and the History of Interpretation.* STDJ 107/2 (Leiden: Brill, 2013), 2:540–553.

[75] Hindy Najman, "Towards a Study of the Uses of the Concept of Wilderness in Ancient Judaism," *DSD* 13 (2006): 99–113 and further literature cited there.

[76] See George J. Brooke, "Room for Interpretation: An Analysis of Spatial Imagery in the Qumran Pesharim," in *The Dead Sea Scrolls: Texts and Context.* Edited by Charlotte Hempel. STDJ 90 (Leiden: Brill, 2010), 309–324 and Alison Schofield, "Re-Placing Priestly Space: The Wilderness as Heterotopia in the Dead Sea Scrolls," in *A Teacher for All Generations: Essays in Honor of James C. VanderKam.* Edited by Eric Mason et al. JSJSup 153/1 (Leiden, Brill, 2012) 1: 469–490.

[77] Schofield, "Wilderness as Heterotopia," 90.

[78] Cf. Stegemann, "Gottesbezeichnungen in den Qumrantexten;" Tov, *Scribal Practices*, 218–221 and 7.4.2.3 above.

[79] Metso, *Textual Development*, 71.

[80] See, e. g., Alexander and Vermes, DJD 26:146 and Maier, *Qumran-Essener*, 1:188.

the people of injustice in several foundation accounts in the Community Rules, including the present passage. Since it is rather odd that 1QS should be using alternative ways of avoiding the tetragrammaton in such quick succession, I raised the possibility that the scribe of 1QS misread a reference to "the truth" in 4Q259 as part of a larger picture of comparable reading lapses between the two manuscripts.[81] Finally, "truth" is a key notion in the Community Rules beginning with its first mention in 1QS 1:5 where it supplements the series of virtues endorsed in Micah 6:8.

8:15: Immediately after the reference to and interpretation of Isa 40:3 that ends in 1QS 8:15b // 4Q258 6:7 the heading introducing the Statutes for the Maskil follows in 4Q259 3:6a. This offers clear evidence that the latter manuscript lacked the material found in 1QS 8:15b–9:11 and parallels which extends to almost an entire column in 1QS.[82]

In sum, the evidence of the different witnesses to this passage in the Community Rules preserves a form of the account that lacked the explicit citation of Isa 40:3 and is represented by 4Q258. We then have the distinctive admonition in advance of the citation of Isa 40:3 in 4Q259 that refers to preparing the way of "truth." I argued that in its immediate context of an admonition to keep apart from "the people of injustice," this use of the antonym "the way of truth" is highly significant. Readings that privilege the text of 1QS and perceive a desire to avoid the divine name in 4Q259[83] have overlooked the compelling rhetorical thrust of this passage in 4Q259.

---

[81] Cf. 1.5.6.2 above.

[82] For details see 1.5.6 above.

[83] See, e. g., Metso, "Biblical Quotations," 85.

9. Deliberate Failure to Obey a Commandment (1QS 8:16b–19 // 4Q258 6:8b–11a // Lacking in 4Q259)

9.1 Introduction

The material in this chapter and the one that follows picks up highly developed procedures and concerns that characterise the meetings and judicial concerns of the many in 6.5. This impression is confirmed by a reference to the many which associates this short passage with a rabbim cluster I identified above.[1]

This short piece of disciplinary law deals with a deliberate breach of the commandments which is punished with exclusion from the purity of the people of holiness. The concern for the observance of the torah, the preservation of the exclusive purity of the people of holiness, denying access to deliberation and a distancing from injustice all share a great deal with Chapter 10 below as well as the account of admission into the community by oath in 6.1 above. Moreover, a number of scholars have identified CD 20:1b–8a as a closely related passage to the material in Chapters 9 and 10 here.[2]

1QS 8:18b–19a introduces the many and the council as designations for the community that are distinct from the language in the opening lines where we have "the people of the community, the covenant of the community" in 1QS, "the people of the covenant of [the community]" in 4Q258 and "the people of holiness." The terminology found in 1QS 8:18b–19a resembles the penal code and looks like an interpolation here. In terms of violations this passage is concerned with the torah and its commandments rather than infringements against the values and principles of the community as was the case in the penal code.[3] Moreover, the penal code is concerned with the purity of the many and does not attest the designation "the people of holiness." The final clause in 1QS 8:19b // 4Q258 6:10 picks up the designation "community" (יחד) with which the passage began and suggests the section as a whole combines the themes of admission into the community alongside disciplinary matters. In terms of structure this short

---

[1] Cf. 5.4.4; 6.2 and 6.5 above.

[2] For a close analysis of that relationship and further bibliography see Hempel, *Qumran Rule Texts in Context*, 123–136.

[3] See Chapter 7 above.

passage resembles the sequence of disciplinary issues followed by the topic of admission attested also in 4Q265 (Miscellaneous Rules) 4 i–ii.

9.2 Translation

1QS 8	4Q258 6
[16b]No person from among *the people of the community, the covenant of* [17]*the community,*	[8b][No per]son from among *the people of the covenant of the [community*

1QS 8
who fails to observe any of the commandments deliberately shall touch the purity of the people of holiness, [18]nor shall he have knowledge of any of their deliberation until his actions *vacat* have been cleansed from any injustice and he conducts himself perfectly. Then they shall allow him to approach [19]the council on the authority of the many and afterwards he shall be enrol{.}[ed] according to his rank.

1QS 8	4Q258 6
This law shall apply to everyone who joins the community.	[10][This law shall apply to everyone [11]who joins] the community.

9.3 Textual Notes

8:19 The final *bet* of "he shall be enrolled" (יכת{.}ב) has been written above the line after the erasure of an orginal letter. Wernberg-Møller suggests the orginal reading was יכתיו whereas Puech reads the uncorrected text as יכתה.[4]

9.4 Commentary

This short passage displays both thematic and terminological unevenness. The bulk of the passage in 1QS 8:16b–19a // 4Q258 6:8b is concerned with community members who are temporarily excluded after infringement of the law. Once reformed such candidates may be re-admitted and re-ranked. The closing statement adds that this process applies to new members also. Newsom suggests that this sections deals with probationers.[5] This interpretations accounts well

---

[4] See Wernberg-Møller, *Manual of Discipline*, 42 and Puech, "Écriture de 1QS VII–VIII," 42.
[5] Cf. Newsom, *Self as Symbolic Space*, 163–164.

for the final statement on joining the community but sits more awkwardly with the opening statement which refers to a person from amongst the people of the community.

8:17 The concern about touching the purity is not accompanied by a reference to pure liquids as is the case in 6.5.2.3. In this respect the present passage is closer to 6.1.2.1, especially the prohibition for the people of injustice – on our reading temporarily or permanently excluded former members – of touching the purity of the people of holiness.[6]

8:18 The reference to "injustice" (עול) reinforces the thematic connection established with regard to the people of injustice in 6.1.2.1.[7]

8:19a The re-enrolment process that concludes this disciplinary process is described in the same terms as the conclusion to Chapter 10 below.

---

[6] Cf. 1QS 5:13 // 4Q256 9:8–9 // 4Q258 1:7–8.
[7] See also 8.2.6 and 8.4.6 above.

10. Rules of Conduct and Discipline for the People of Perfect Holiness (1QS 8:20–9:2 // 4Q258 6:12; 7:1–3 // Lacking in 4Q259)

10.1 Introduction

The framing of this chapter describes the community in elevated terms such as "the people of perfect holiness," "the people of holiness" and "the council of holiness" whose conduct is "perfect." However, once we look beyond this powerful rhetorical framework we find a set of regulations that deal with serious shortcomings which are dealt with along the lines of the penal code in Chapter 7 above. The core of this passage employs language that reverts to administrative bodies we are familiar with from 6.5 such as "the council of the community" and "the many." However, with reference to community members who are instructed to ostracise those excluded, the elevated designation "council of holiness" is retained.

However, the idealised picture is raptured with the very first case that is introduced. The passage begins with the case of a member of the council of holiness whose conduct is perfect with respect to God's commandments who, rather paradoxically, has either deliberately or inadvertently infringed the law. On the perfection rhetoric that opens this scenario such a situation – especially if the infringement was deliberate – is an oxymoron. We then learn of the punitive consequences of such behaviour which are developed at some length and include a number of apparent contradictions. Initially, a categorical exclusion from the council of the community is proposed in 1QS 8:22b–24a for both offences despite the significant difference of intent. This is followed by instructions to ostracise those excluded in respect of their property and counsel. Given that members' property only features in those sections of the Community Rules that envisage shared use, we are left wondering how property that had been handed over to the community upon joining can be shared by those who are left behind? It is clear that there are nuances presupposed in the regulations on the pooling of property that are hard to unravel on the basis of the evidence we have. Such nuances might apply to the property of excluded and ostracised members in particular with little clarity on whether their property was "ostracised" within the pooled property or handed back in so far as this was possible.

10.2 Translation

1QS 8

[20]*Vacat*. These are the regulations according to which the people of perfect holiness shall conduct themselves each one with his neighbour.

1QS 8	4258 6
[21]Every member of the	[12]Everyone me [mber of] the

1QS 8

council of holiness whose conduct is perfect according to that which He has commanded – each one from among them – [22]who has deliberately or inadvertently transgressed any part of the law of Moses they shall send him away from the council of the community [23]never to return again. And no person from among the people of holiness shall share his property or his counsel regarding any [24]matter. And if he has acted inadvertently

1QS 8–9	4Q258 7
he shall be excluded	[1]*they shall exclude him*
from the purity and from (exchanging) counsel,	from the purity, from (exchanging) counsel,
and they shall resort to the rule[25]*which (states): He shall not judge or be consulted concerning any counsel*	*and from judgment*
for two years.	for tw[o year]s.
(This applies) on condition that his conduct is perfect [26]*in meetings,*	*And he shall return*
study and in counsel	to study and (exchanging) counsel
[accor]ding to the many,	
if he does not commit a further inadvertent sin until he has completed the two	if he does not commit a further [2]inadvertent sin until he has completed the two
[27]years *Vacat* – 9[1]for it is on account of	years – for it is on account of one inad-
{.} one inadvertent sin that he shall be	vertent sin that he shall be punished for
punished for two (years).	two years.
But the one who has acted deliberately	*But in the case of deliberate sin*
shall never return again.	he shall never return again.
Only the one who has sinned inadvertently	*Nevertheless* [3]*he*
[2]shall be tested for two years with regard	shall be tested for two [y]ears with regard
to the perfection of his conduct and his	to the perfection of his conduct and his
counsel according to the many	counsel according to the many
and afterwards	*and*
he shall be enrolled according to his rank	he shall be enrolled according to his rank
in the community of holiness.	in the community of holiness. *Vacat.*

10.3 Textual Notes

8:23 The first *vav* in "with his property" (בהונו) has been added above the line in 1QS.

8:26 Whereas 1QS refers to refraining from repeated inadvertent transgressions with the clause (אם לוא שגג עוד), 4Q258 7:1–2 employs a slighter longer phrase (אם לוא הלך עוד בשגגה).

8:26 The infinitive construct *qal* of "to fill" is spelled differently in 1QS (מולאת) from 4Q258 7:2 (מלאות) with the former attesting the phenomenon of proto-Semitic short *u* represented by *vav* rather than *shewa*.[1]

8:27 Here 1QS attests a longer text (ימים)[2] followed by the rest of this line left blank, even though the sentence continues into 1QS 9:1.

9:1 The first two words are written contiuously in 1QS. Immediately afterwards there is a smudge suggesting a *shin* was erased when the ink was still wet. It would appear the scribe originally left insufficient space before inscribing the following word and started again.

9:2 In 1QS the re-enrolment of candidates is couched in a third person singular imperfect *qal* ("he shall write") or, conceivably, a *niphal* imperfect with plene spelling and introduced with "and afterwards." The shorter text in 4Q258 7:3 begins more concisely with the conjunction which appears to have been damaged by a crack in the leather.

10.4 Commentary

As mentioned in our analysis of the material in Chapter 9 as well as in 6.1 above, all three passages share a number of themes such as the designation of the in-group as the people of holiness, a concern with disciplining members and strong boundaries around the in-group's purity and deliberations to which property is added here.[3] In addition, a comparable sequence is shared by Chapters 9 and 10 by beginning with disciplinary matters followed by regulations on (re)admission into the community.[4] The sequence differs in 6.1 which begins with admission by oath before describing what amounts to a reversed admission process for a group called "the people of injustice." Such a reversal is, in practice, a disciplinary matter. Whereas Chapter 9 and 6:1 endorse keeping away from "any injustice" (1QS 8:18) and "the people of injustice" (1QS 5:10 // 4Q256 9:8 // 4Q258 1:7)

---

[1] Cf. Alexander and Vermes, DJD 26:112 and Qimron, HDSS, 35–36.

[2] See Qimron, DSSHW 1:224.

[3] On the connection of this section with the Penal Code dealt with in Chapter 7 above see Metso, *Textual Development*, 124–128 and Shemesh, "Scriptural Background of the Penal Code," 193–194.

[4] See Chapter 9 above as well as 4Q265 (Miscellaneous Rules) 4 i–ii.

respectively, the present passage is concerned with infringements within the community between "each one and his neighbour" (1QS 8:20). Restrictions on sharing property feature both here and in 6.1. Importantly, disobedience to the law of Moses – rather than communal rules – is at issue across all three passages.[5] The more serious intentional disobedience to the law ("with a high hand") occurs in a plus in 1QS 5:12, in 1QS 8:17 and at 1QS 8:22 here. This more serious infringement does not occur in the shorter text of 4Q256 9 and 4Q258 1 dealt with in 6.1 above.

While the present passage deals explicitly with disobedient members of the in-group, our analysis of 6.1 above has demonstrated that the much-maligned people of injustice are also former members. Moreover, as is clear particularly from the longer text in 1QS 5:11–12, they are being ostracised based on legal disagreements. I concluded, moreover, that in order for the issue of potential access to property and deliberation to arise, the people of injustice must be envisaged as living or meeting in proximity to the people of holiness.[6] In light of the significant overlap between this passage and 6.1 it is clear that the people of injustice in 6.1 are, in fact, ostracised members of the in-group who have been temporarily or permanently excluded on the basis of disobedience to the law. The emphasis on the correct application of hidden and revealed law in 1QS 5:11–12 demonstrates that the infringements relate to differences in the interpretation of the law rather than blatant disregard for a generally agreed upon commandment.

8:24–25 As Alexander and Vermes observe, the plus in 1QS cites what appears to be a ruling of the movement.[7] As is the case with scriptural quotations at other times 4Q258 lacks the direct quotation.

8:25–26 While there is a plus in 1QS that refers to the authority of the many, the preservation of a reference to the many across both manuscripts in 1QS 9:2 // 4Q258 7:3 also needs to be acknowledged. Finally, the longer account of 1QS 8:25–26 seems convoluted compared to the streamlined text of 4Q258.[8]

---

[5] Compare 1QS 8:22 with 1QS 5:8 // 4Q256 1:6–7 // 4Q258 9:7; 1QS 5:11–12 in 6.1 and 1QS 8:17 in Chapter 9.

[6] See 1QS 5:13 // 4Q256 9:8–9 // 4Q258 1:7–8.

[7] Alexander and Vermes, DJD 26:112.

[8] On the assessment of Alexander and Vermes the shorter text preserved in 4Q258 is "compressed […] though occasionally its individual readings are superior," DJD 26:112.

11. The Community and the Cultic Realm
(1QS 9:3–6 // 4Q258 7:4–7a // Lacking in 4Q259)

11.1 Introduction

This passage has for some time been read as a clear indication that the movement portrayed in the Community Rules had turned its back on the Jerusalem Temple in favour of prayer.[1] A close reading of the text suggests that such a reading is unfounded. In particular, I translate the preposition *min* in a key phrase on securing atonement in 1QS 9:4 with "by means of the flesh of burnt offerings and by means of the fat of sacrifices"[2] rather than "without the flesh of burnt offerings and without the fat of sacrifices."[3] Our translation results in an emphasis in this passage on prayer alongside sacrifices on which more will be said in the Commentary below.[4]

In the Community Rules that include the Final Hymn, as is the case for both manuscripts represented here, the significance of prayer can hardly be over-estimated. What we have here is a fulsome advocation of prayer alongside sacrifice – and the language used of the sacrificial cult expresses the community's aspiration towards restoring the cultic efficacy of sacrificial worship. The elevation of praise as an efficient means to achieve salvation alongside acceptable sacrifice offers an effective build-up to the grand finale represented in a number Community Rules in the form of the Final Hymn.

This passage revisits themes explored in Chapter 8. It is not attested in 4Q259 which may be the result of a secondary elaboration of 4Q259's shorter text in both 1QS and 4Q258.[5] Moreover the material presented here has been recognized as a re-presentation of ideas introduced earlier.[6]

---

[1] Cf., e. g., Joseph M. Baumgarten, "Sacrifice and Worship among the Jewish Sectarians of the Dead Sea (Qumrân) Scrolls," *HTR* 46 (1953): 141–159; Brownlee, *Dead Sea Manual*, 34 and Wernberg-Møller, *Manual of Discipline*, 133.

[2] See also Wise, DSSANT, 139.

[3] So, e. g., García Martínez and Tigchelaar, DSSSE, 91.

[4] Cf. also Penner, *Patterns of Daily Prayer*, 122–124.

[5] See Metso, "Primary Results" and Metso, *Textual Development*, 71–73.

[6] Cf. John J. Collins, "The Yaḥad and 'The Qumran Community,'" in *Biblical Traditions in Transmission*. Edited by Hempel and Lieu, 81–96, 89 and Hempel, *Qumran Rule Texts in Context*, 85–92.

11.2 Translation

1QS 9	4Q258 7
[3]*Vacat.* When these exist in Israel	[4][When] these [exis]t in Israel *as a community*
according to all these rules as a foundation of the spirit of holiness and eternal [4]truth in order to atone for the guilt of wrongdoing and the betrayal of sin so that the land may be accepted by means of the flesh of burnt offerings and *by means of the fat* of sacrifices. *And a holy offering* of [5]the lips fittingly (offered) is like a soothing (odour) of righteousness and [perfect]	*according to* these rules as a [foun]dation of the spirit of holiness and eternal truth in order to atone for the guilt of wrongdoing [5][and the betray]al of [si]n so that the lan[d] may be accepted [by means of the flesh of] burnt offerings and *the fat* of sacrifices. *And holy offerings and freewill-offerings* of the lips fit[tingly] (offered) are like a soothing (odour) [6][of righteousness and perfect] conduct is like a [pl]easing free[will-offering].
conduct is like a pleasing freewill offering. At that time *the people of the community shall be* [6]*set apart as a holy house for Aaron,* so that they may come together in utmost holiness and as a house of community for Israel whose conduct is perfect.	*Vacat.* At that time *they shall set themselves apart as a house of Aaron to be holy for all* […] [7]and those whose conduct is perfe[ct and together for Is]rael.

11.3 Textual Notes

9:3 A *vacat* opens this line in 1QS. A new beginning is also marked by a composite marginal sign comprised of a paragraphos with paleo-Hebrew *zayin* and *samek*.[7] The beginning of the line is not preserved in 4Q258 7:4 but the preceding line ended with a *vacat*.

9:4 4Q258 7:5 lacks the second occurrence of *mem* "without" and attests a plural over against 1QS's singular for "sacrifices." Given the singular is likely a collective there is little difference in meaning.

9:4 The last two words in this line are written without a space between them in 1QS despite the fact that the second word "A holy offering" (תרומה) marks the beginning of new sentence or sub-clause. There is no evidence of any damage to the surface of the leather in 1QS, nor would the line length including an inter-word space be unusual in this column. Regular word spaces are preserved in 4Q259 7:5 where we also find the plural "holy offerings" followed by the plus "and free will offerings" (ונדבת).

---

[7] See Tov, *Scribal Practices*, 207 and 1.5.1.3.2.

9:5 4Q258 7:6 attests a clear *vacat* before the phrase "At this time" whereas 1QS runs on. 4Q258 attests another *vacat* before the almost identical phrase (בעת [הזאת]) at 4Q258 8:4 that is again lacking in 1QS 9:20. This is also one of three instances in 1QS where a marginal paragraphos appears to mark a passage that refers to a particularly potent moment in time.[8]

9:5 The second *he* in the phrase "at that time" (בעת ההיאה) appears to have been corrected in 1QS. The same letter is damaged in 4Q258 7:6 by a deep crease in the parchment.

9:5 1QS reads the *hiphil* of the verb בדל over against the *niphal* in 4Q258.[9] Brownlee considers the possibility of a *niphal* with *yod* representing *tsere* in 1QS, an option favoured by both Wernberg-Møller and Qimron.[10] The *niphal* is clear in 4Q258 7:6.

9:6 With Qimron I read "to come together" (להיחד) in 1QS.[11]

9:6 Alexander and Vermes presuppose a somewhat shorter text for the lacuna in 4Q258.[12]

11.4 Commentary

As indicated above this passage was initially read as the clearest expression of the community's understanding of itself as a replacement of the Temple and its cult.[13] Current research has offered some compelling arguments against such a reading. Martin Goodman pointed to the strong anti-cultic polemic attested in a number of prophetic passages from the Hebrew Bible and stressed the likelihood that such disagreements belong to multi-faceted inner-Jewish debates on halakhic matters pertaining to the cult.[14] Moreover, Falk has demonstrated that the offering of the lips offers points of connection with the Temple liturgy rather than representing a "replacement" of it.[15] Our translation in 1QS 9:4 above with "by means of flesh" rather than "without flesh" is of a piece with that view.

9:3: This is the third and final occurrence of a heading which includes the phrase "When these exist in Israel" in 1QS. Significantly 4Q258 7:4 attests a longer text than 1QS by including the words "as a community."

---

[8] See also 1QS 9:11 and 9:19 below as well as 1.5.1.3 above.

[9] Cf. HAWTTM 1:231–233 and Alexander and Vermes, DJD 26:113.

[10] Cf. Brownlee, *Dead Sea Manual*, 35 n. 9; Wernberg-Møller, *Manual of Discipline*, 133 and Qimron, HDSS, 19. In HDSS the reference is erroneously given as 1QS 9:6.

[11] Qimron, DSSHW 1:226.

[12] Alexander and Vermes, DJD 26:113–114.

[13] See, e. g., Wernberg-Møller, *Manual of Discipline*, 133.

[14] Goodman, "The Qumran Sectarians and the Temple in Jerusalem," in *The Dead Sea Scrolls: Texts and Context*. Edited by Charlotte Hempel. STDJ 90 (Leiden: Brill, 2010), 277–87.

[15] Falk, *Daily, Sabbath and Festival Prayers*, 218.

9:5 For a discussion of the verb נדב to refer to a fervent commitment see 5.4 above.

9:6 The translation "holy of holies" for קודש קודשים, for which we would expect a definite article, has been convincingy challenged by Markus Bockmuehl.[16] In light Bockmuehl's discussion I translate the phrase with "utmost holiness." The claim to a degree of holiness for the community that is customarily the preserve of the Temple suggests these are the elevated claims of a priestly group. Though the rhetoric points to inner-Jewish and probably inter-priestly disputes, these are compatible with a plea for cultic reform without implying a rejection of the Temple.

9:6 The prominence of the language of perfection in 1QS 8–9 has been explored in detail by Anja Klein who rightly notes the cultic background of the terminology which is particularly to the fore in 9:6.[17]

---

[16] Bockmuehl, "Redaction and Ideology in the Rule of the Community (1QS/4QS)," *RevQ* 18 (1998): 541–560, 555.

[17] See Klein, "Right Spirit," 186 and 5.4.2 above.

12. The Authority of the Sons of Aaron
(1QS 9:7 // 4Q258 7:7b // Lacking in 4Q259)

12.1 Introduction

This passage stands out from much of the Community Rules by emphatically appointing the sons of Aaron alone as the authority figures in matters of judgment and property.

12.2 Translation

1QS 9	4Q258 7
[7]Only the sons of Aaron shall rule with regard to judgment and property *and on their authority decisions shall be taken concerning any rule of the people of the community.*	[7b][Only the sons of Aa]ron [shall ru]l[e with regard to] judgment and property. *Vacat*

12.3 Textual Notes

9:7b The shorter text preserved in 4Q258 results in a smooth catchword link to the beginning of the material in Chapter 13 on the shared topic of "property." This catchword link is less clear in 1QS after its text was secondarily expanded.

12.4 Commentary

The unequivocal authority of the sons of Aaron over matters of judgment and property advocated here contrasts markedly with other parts of the Community Rules. Thus, in 1QS 5 it is the sons of Zadok (1QS) and the many (4QS) respectively who deal with such matters.[1] According to Chapter 10 "the many" are

---

[1] See especially Chapter 5 above.

expected to rule in matters of property in relation to the people of holiness. It seems likely that this short statement was placed here on the basis of a catchword link with Aaron in the previous line.[2] Finally, the emphatic use of "only" suggests that whoever composed or included this regulation was aware of alternative views or practices on this matter. The sons of Aaron are allocated a pre-eminent position also in 4Q279 (4QFour Lots; *olim* 4QTohorot D) 4Q279 5:4.[3]

---

[2] Cf. Chaper 11 above.
[3] For details see Alexander and Vermes, DJD 26:217–223.

13. The Conduct of the People of Holiness and the People of Deceit (1QS 9:8–11 // 4Q258 7:7c–9 // Lacking in 4Q259)

13.1 Introduction

This passage returns to the theme of laying down rules on the conduct of the people of holiness that was also the subject of Chapter 10 above. As in the former chapter, the in-group is described in elevated terms as the people of holiness whose conduct is perfect. As was the case in Chapter 10, a close look at what is said about the people of holiness, and especially their relationship to the children of deceit, reveals a more chequered picture.[1] A first sub-section advocates firm boundaries between the property of the people of holiness and the people of deceit which is followed by an indirect warning aimed at the people of deceit.

13.2 Translation

13.2.1 The Property of the People of Holiness (1QS 9:7–9a // 4Q258 7:7c–8)

1QS 9	4Q258 7
[8]And the property of the people of holiness whose conduct is perfect shall not be mixed with the property of the people of deceit who [9a]have not cleansed their conduct to keep away from injustice and to conduct themselves perfectly.	[7c]And the property of [the people of holiness [8]whose condu]ct is perfect shall not be mi[xed with] the property of [the people of de]cei[t] who have not cleans[ed their conduct […] [9a][…] and to conduct themselves [perfectly.

---

[1] See also 1.4 above.

13.2.2 A Warning to the People of Deceit (1QS 9:9b–11a // 4Q258 7:9b)

1QS 9	4Q258 7
[9b]They shall not deviate from any counsel of the law	[9b]They shall not deviate from any counsel of the law
so as to walk [10]*in all the hardness of their heart,*	SHORTER TEXT
but they shall be judged by the first rules	but they shall be judged by the [first] ru[les]

1QS
according to which the people of the community began to be disciplined [11]until the coming of the p[ro]phet and the messiahs of Aaron and Israel. *Vacat.*

13.3 Textual Notes

9:9b–10a 4Q258 offers a shorter and likely more original text than 1QS. Moreover, the language of the plus in 1QS is consistent with comparable plusses in that manuscript.[2]

9:11a The *bet* in "prophet" has been added above the line in 1QS.

13.4 Commentary

13.4.1 The Property of the People of Holiness (1QS 9:7–9a // 4Q258 7:7c–8)

While the boundaries between the people of holiness and the people of deceit appear at first sight sharply drawn, it is important to note that holding property in common is a practice only to be considered with members of the same movement. In fact, the root ערב "to mix," which is used here, occurs several times in community-internal contexts.[3] In particular, 1QS 7:22–25 // 4Q259 2:5b–9a deals with the punishment for a long-standing member who has betrayed the community.[4] The punishment for such an offence in the penal code focuses, as here, on purity and property. This suggests that what is described here are boundaries between two groups that are, or were, very close. The issues are likely continued economic interactions with members who have turned their backs on the community. Such a scenario is comparable to what we learn about

---

[2] See also 1.5.1.4 above.
[3] See 6.5 above.
[4] See further 7.4.6.4.

the people of injustice in Chapter 5 as well as section 6.1 where boundaries are again described in terms of preserving purity and property. The terminological overlap is particularly close with 1QS 5:13–14 // 4Q256 9:8–9 // 4Q258 1:7–8 and the reference to ritual immersion which I identified in 4Q256 9:10–11 // 4Q258 1:9–10. In both passages it is the purity and the property of a group called "the people of holiness" that is at stake. While distinctive designations are used to refer to internal opponents in both passages, a subtle terminological connection is also discernible. While the people of injustice are described as operating "deliberately" (ביד רמה), the present passage refers to "the people of deceit" (אנשי הרמיה). The use of biliteral roots that resemble each other may be significant. Support for this comes from the use of such roots for exegetical purposes both in the Hebrew Bible (e. g. Jer 8:13 and Zeph 1:2) as well as by the translators of the Septuagint as suggested by Emanuel Tov.[5] I suggest that such an exegetical allusion is at work here also. A comparable group is referred to as the people of destruction in the Statutes for the Maskil.[6]

9:8: The catchword property (הון) offers a link between this section and Chapter 12. This connection is much more proximate in the shorter text of 4Q258 which ends on the term property in 4Q258 7:7b.[7] In 1QS the terminology shifts back to the people of holiness after the previous line ended with the designation the people of the community.[8] Moreover, the topic moves on to deal with boundaries rather than authority in both 1QS and 4Q258. In terms of terminology this material also echoes Chapter 10 and may reflect a comparable stage in the development of the community and the literature.

13.4.2 A Warning to the People of Deceit (1QS 9:9b–11a // 4Q258 7:9b)

I take this second warning as addressing infringements on the part of the people of deceit who are admonished not to deviate from the counsel of the law. The issue of legal interpretation identified here as placing a wedge between the authors of this passage and the people of deceit offers yet another connection to the acrimonious account of relations with the people of injustice in Chapter 5 and 6.1 above. The antecedent of the third person masculine plural verb in the opening statement of this sub-section is, however, somewhat ambiguous. In any

---

[5] See Emanuel Tov, "Biliteral Exegesis of Hebrew Roots in the Septuagint?" in *Reflection and Refraction: Studies in Biblical Historiography in Honour of A. Graeme Auld*. Edited by Robert Rezetko, Timothy H. Lim and W. Brian Aucker. VTSup 113 (Leiden: Brill, 2006) 459–82. I am grateful to Noam Mizrahi for the bibliographical reference.

[6] Further, 14.2.2 and 14.4.2 below.

[7] See Chapter 12 above and Philip R. Davies, *Sects and Scrolls: Essays on Qumran and Related Topics*. South Florida Studies in the History of Judaism 134 (Atlanta, GA: Scholars Press, 1996), 139–150, 144.

[8] Cf. 12.2 above.

case, this group is to be judged by the community's first rules in the interim until the final judgment which is expected to be inaugurated by the arrival of an eschatological prophet and the messiahs of Aaron and Israel. Whereas comparable messianic references occur more frequently in the Damascus Document, this is the only such instance in the Community Rules. Moreover, the passage as a whole – including the reference to messianic expectations – is lacking from 4Q259.[9]

9:10: A second point of contact with the Damascus Document is the notion of earlier and later rules. This line clearly indicates an awareness that a considerable amount of time has elapsed since the founding of the community and the formulation of its first rules. Moreover, the designation for the community has shifted again to the people of the community. It is difficult to be sure what body of earlier laws is meant here but it seems conceivable that the legislation preserved in the rules of the related movement described in the Damascus Document are in view here based on the close connections to the Damascus Document (CD 20:31–32) that have been identified in this relatively short sub-section of the Community Rules. The relationship between 1QS 9:9–10 and CD 20:31 has been aptly described by Philip Davies as

... the most explicit connection between 1QS and CD that is to be found, and the strongest piece of evidence in 1QS and CD that the communitites reflected in each text shared (to whatever extent and however briefly) a common set of regulations or laws.[10]

In addition to Davies's remarks I have drawn attention to the significance of the shared context of indiscipline on the part of lax members or former members in both passages where the first rules are mentioned.[11] This again suggests a moment of schism over the interpretation of the law as emerged from accounts of key moments of community formation in Chapters 5 and 8.2.5 above. The paragraphos just after 1QS 9:11 comes at a cesura reflecting the literary growth in the manuscripts. It marks the point just before the shorter text of 4Q259 converges with four other manuscripts. It is possible that this paragraphos also draws attention to the potent period of time that is indicated by the reference to the prophet and the messiahs of Aaron and Israel. I identified paragraphoi accompanying points where diverging manuscripts converge as well as instances where paragraphoi highlight a passage describing a significant moment in time.[12]

---

[9] See 1.5 above.

[10] Davies, *Sects and Scrolls,* 141.

[11] Cf. Hempel, *Qumran Rule Texts in Context,* 123–136.

[12] For a summary see 1.5.1.3 and Table 1 above.

14. The Statutes for the Maskil (1QS 9:12–25 // 4Q256 18:1–7 // 4Q258 7:15–8:9 // 4Q259 3:6b–4:8 // 4Q260 1:1–2)

14.1 Introduction

Whereas the Maskil is referred to at a number of crucial junctures in the Community Rules manuscripts and the Dead Sea Scrolls more widely, it is the material introduced here that tells us more about this figure than any other text from Jewish antiquity. The Maskil emerges as a multi-tasker par excellence with expertise and a remit in matters liturgical and calendrical,[1] apotropaic,[2] spiritual,[3] cryptic[4] as well as halakhic concerns with human conduct.[5] It is noteworthy that the Maskil's halakhic dimension which emerged from our discussion of the heading "Midrash for the Maskil over the people of law" in 4Q258 1:1[6] is also evident in the opening words of the current section. The new topic is introduced here with the heading "These are the statutes (חוקים) for the Maskil to walk (התהלך) in them (in his dealings) with all the living" in 1QS 9:12 // 4Q259 3:6. The multi-faceted responsibilities of the Maskil are of a piece with an understanding of humanity vis-à-vis God and his creation as an organic whole. Thus, the heavenly bodies are in tune with times for prayer and festivals[7] as well as events of the distant past[8] and recent history.[9] Such an inter-connectedness also characterises an anthropology where an individual's spiritual make-up and their

---

[1] Cf. Chapter 15 below.

[2] See 4Q510–4Q511 Songs of the Maskil and 1.2.1 above.

[3] Further, 14.2.2 below, Chapter 4 above and Hempel, *Qumran Rules Texts in Context*, 303–337. I conclude an analysis of several striking features of the material to come out of Cave 4 by stressing the learned and eclectic nature of the contents of this cave which in turn mirrors the polymathic remit of the Maskil.

[4] Cf. 4Q298 (Words of the Maskil to the Sons of Dawn) and 1.5.6 above.

[5] Compare 5.4 above as well as Anderson, "The Use of *Ruah*," 296–297.

[6] See 5.4 above.

[7] Cf. 15.1.1 below.

[8] Note, for instance, the calendrical alignment of the flood in 4Q252 (Commentary on Genesis A).

[9] The references to Hasmonean rulers Salome Alexandra and Hyrcanus II in 4Q332 (Historical Text D) are a good example.

actions are of a piece[10] and accounts for the universalism ("all the living") that might otherwise surprise in a text largely concerned with particular groups.[11]

The beginning of the new section is clearly marked in 1QS 9:12. The remainder of the previous inscribed line 1QS 9:11 is left empty followed by a full empty and unnumbered line and a *vacat* at the beginning of 1QS 9:12 alongside a paragraphos hook in the right margin. In fact, this is the most emphatic indication of a new beginning in 1QS. The large interlinear gap in the Penal Code (1QS 7:7–8) is not related to a new beginning and thus represents a different phenomenon.[12] The combination of an open section followed by an empty line as we find in 1QS 9:11 is described by Tov as "the greatest section division."[13] The sense that this juncture marks a meeting point of tectonic plates in the Community Rules is reinforced further by the witness of 4Q259 which sets in here after a significant minus corresponding to 1QS 8:15b–9:11 // 4Q258 6:7–7:9.[14] Finally, the same heading occurs verbatim, though without any stipulations following it, in the Laws of the Damascus Document.[15] Martin proposes this was one of the sources used by the scribe of 1QS which was added secondarily.[16] This convergence with the Damascus Document indicates that a form of this material circulated independently of its incorporation into the Community Rules. Whereas the notion of successive revelation is common in the Dead Sea Scrolls, it is particularly prominent in these opening lines.[17] The section as a whole can be divided into fours parts, each with a distinctive flavour as indicated in 14.2 and 14.4 below.

---

[10] See 1QS 9:14–15 // 4Q259 3:10–12.

[11] Consider also the penchant for vocabulary that indicates an overriding comprehensiveness such as "all, every" (כול איש; איש ואיש). See also Newsom, *Self and Symbolic Space*, 81 who draws out the significance of such language in the Teaching on the Two Spirits.

[12] For details see Chapter 7 above.

[13] Tov, *Scribal Practices*, 147.

[14] See further 1.1 and 1.5.6 above.

[15] Cf. CD 12:20–21 // 4Q266 (4QDᵃ) 9 ii 7–8 and Hempel, *Laws of the Damascus Document*, 105–106, 114–121, 189.

[16] Martin, *Scribal Character of the Dead Sea Scrolls*, 55.

[17] See also Devorah Dimant, "Time, Torah and Prophecy at Qumran," in *History, Ideology and Bible Interpretation at Qumran*, 301–314 and Glessmer, "The Otot-Texts," 134–141.

14.2 Translation[18]

14.2.1 The Maskil's Role among Humanity Supported by Successive Revelations (1QS 9:12–14a // 4Q259 3:6b–10a)

1QS 9	4Q259 3
EMPTY LINE	

1QS 9	4Q259 3
[12]*Vacat.* These are the statutes for the Maskil to walk in them (in his dealings) with all the living according to the rule for each time and according to the weight of each person. [13]He shall execute the will of God according to everything that has been revealed from time to time. He shall acquire every insight which has been found *according to the times* and [14a]the statute of time.	[6b]These are the sta[tutes] [7]for the Mas[kil to walk in] them (in his dealings) with all the living according to the rule for each [time] [8]and according to the wei[ght of each person. He shall exe]cute the will of God according to everything that has been revealed [from time to time]. [9]H[e shall acquire every insight] which has been found *in previous times* and the [statute] [10a]of time.

14.2.2 Establishing Boundaries (1QS 9:14b–18a // 4Q256 18 1a // 4Q258 7:15–8:3a // 4Q259 3:10b–16a)

1QS 9	4Q259 3
[14b]He shall separate and weigh *the sons of the Zadok vacat* according to their spirit. He shall sustain the chosen ones of the time according to [15]His will according to that which He has commanded. He shall execute judgment on each person according to his spirit.	[10b][He shall separate and] weigh *the children of righteousness* according to their sp[i]rit. [11][He shall sustain the chosen ones of the time] according to His will according to that which He has commanded. [He shall execute [12]judgment on] each person [according to his spirit.]

1QS 9	4Q258 7–8	4Q259 3
He shall bring near each person according to the cleanness of his hands [16]*and* according to his insight allow him to approach.	7[15][He shall bring near each person] according to the cleanness of [his] ha[nds] 8[1]*and* according to his insight allow him to approach.	He shall bring near each person according to the cleanness of his hands, acc[ording to [13]his insight allow him to approach.]

---

[18] On the principles behind the "Transparent Composite Text" for the translation of 4Q256 and 4Q258 from this point see 1.7 above. In short, text preserved <u>in 4Q256 only</u> is <u>single underlined</u> and text preserved <u>in 4Q258 only</u> is <u>double underlined</u>. In addition, the line numbers of each manuscript are identified in the body of the translation by indicating the distinctive column numbers in 4Q256 and 4Q258 alongside line numbers. Note, in addition, the Textual Note on 1QS 9:22 // 4QS in 14.3 below.

1QS 9	4Q258 7–8	4Q259 3
And equally his love and his hatred. *Vacat.* He shall not rebuke or get into an argument with the people of destruction [17]but conceal *the counsel of the law* in the midst of the people of injustice. He shall discipline with true knowledge and righteous judgment *those who have chosen* [18]*the way,* each according to his spirit, according to	And equally his love and his hatred. *Vacat.* He shall not rebuke or get into an argument with the people of destruction [2]but conceal *his/His counsel* in the midst of the people of injustice. He shall discipline with true knowledge and righteous judgment *the chosen of the way* each according to his spirit and according to	[And equally] his [lo]ve and his hatred. He shall not [rebuke] [14]or [get into an argument with the peo]ple of destruction but conceal *the coun[sel of]* [15]*the law* [in the midst of the people of injustice. He shall] discipline with true knowledge and righteous [16]judgment *the cho[sen of the way,* each] according to his spirit and according to

1QS 9	4Q256 18 and 4Q258 8	4Q259 3
the *rule* of time.	18[1]the *rule* of 8[3]time.	the *rules* of time.

14.2.3 The Maskil in the Midst of the Yahad (1QS 9:18b–21a // 4Q256 18:1b–4a // 4Q258 8:3b–5a // 4Q259 3:16b–4:2a)

1QS 9	4Q256 18 and 4Q258 8	4Q259 3–4
He shall guide them with knowledge and thus instruct them *in the wonderful and true mysteries in the midst of* [19]*the people of the community* so that they may conduct themselves perfectly each with *his neighbour* according to all that has been revealed to them. This is the time to prepare the way [20]*to* the wilderness. *He shall instruct them (with)* all that has been found to do	He shall guide them with knowledge and thus instruct them 18[2]*in the wonderful and true mysteries in the midst of the people of the community* so that they may conduct themselves perfectly each with 8[4]*his neighbour* according to all 18[3][that has] been revealed to them. This is the time to prepare the way *in* the wilderness. *He shall instruct them in* all that has been continue double underline below *in* found to do. *Vacat*	He shall guide them [17]with knowledge [and thus instruct them in] *the wonderful mysteries.* *And if the way of the alliance of the community* [18]*reaches perfection,* they shall con[duct themselves perfectly each] with *his neighbours* according to all that has been revealed to them. [19]This is [the time to prepare the way] *in* the wilderness. *He shall facilitate their mastery over* all 4[1][that has been found to do]

1QS 9	4Q256 18 and 4Q258 8	4Q259 3–4
at this time, and they shall keep away from everyone who has not averted his path [21]from all injustice. *Vacat.*	18[4]*At [this]* 8[5]*time* [they shall keep away] from everyone who has not averted his path(s) from all injustice. *Vacat*	*at th[is] time* [and] they shall keep [away from everyone who has not averted his path(s) [2a]from all injustice. *Vacat.*]

14.2.4 The Rules of Conduct for the Maskil (1QS 9:21b–25 // 4Q256 18:4b–7 // 4Q258 8:5b–9 // 4Q259 4:2b–6 // 4Q260 1:1–2)

1QS 9	4Q256 18 and 4Q258 8	4Q259 4
These are the rules of conduct for the Maskil during these times with regard to his love and his hatred. (He shall direct) eternal hatred [22]towards the people of destruction with a spirit of secretiveness. He shall leave to them property and wages like a servant to his master (displaying) humility before [23]his ruler.	These are 18[5]the rules of conduct for the Maskil during [these] 8[6]tim[es with regard to his love and] his hatred. (He shall direct) eternal hatred towards 18[6]the people of destruction with a spirit of secretiveness. He shall leave to them property, gain 8[7][and wages like a servant to] his [m]aster (displaying) humility before 18[7]his ruler.	[2b]These are the rules of [condu]ct for the Maskil [during these times with regard to his love] [3]and [his] hatred. [(He shall direct) eter]nal [hatred] to[wards the people of destruction] with a sp[i]rit of secretiveness. He shall lea[ve] [4]to them property [and wages like a servant to his master (displaying) humility] before his ruler.

1QS 9	4Q258 8	4Q259 4
He shall be a person who is dedicated to the statute	He shall be a person who is dedicated to the statute	He shall [be] [5]a person who is dedi[cated to the statute]

1QS 9	4Q258 8	4Q259 4	4Q260 1
and ready for a day of vengeance. He shall perform the will (of God) in everything he does [24]and in everything that is under his control (he) shall comply with that which He has commanded.	and ready for a day of [vengeance.] He shall [perform [8]the will (of God) in everything he does and in] everything that is under his control (he) shall comply with that whi[ch He has commanded.	[and rea]dy for a day of [vengeance. He shall perform the will (of God) in every]thing he do[es] [6]and in [ev-ery]thing [that is under his control (he shall comply with)] that which [He has comman-ded.	[1][and ready for a day of vengeance. He shall perform the will (of God) in everythi]ng he [2]do[es and in every-thing that is under his control (he shall comply with) that which He has com-manded.]

1QS 9	4Q258 8	4Q260 1
Everything he encounters	Every]thing he encounters	Everything he encounters

1QS 9	4Q258 8
shall readily delight him and he shall derive no pleasure except from the will of God. [25][A] ll His words shall delight him, and he shall not desire anything that He has not comman[ded]. He shall continually look out for God's judgment.	shall readily delight him and [he shall derive no pleasure] [9]except from the will of [God. All His words shall delight him, and he shall not desire anything th]at [He] has not [commanded. He shall] con[tinually] look out [for] God's [judgme]nt.

14.3 Textual Notes

9:13 In 4Q259 3:8 the horizontal bottom stroke of initial *kaph* opening the phrase "according to all that has been revealed" runs into the second *kaph*. Moreover, the thickness of strokes in this manuscript varies a good deal with the initial *kaph* appearing noticeably thicker than the remaining letters.

9:13 "From time to time" has been written continuously in 1QS.

9:13 4Q259 3:9 reads "in previous times (לפני העתים)" where 1QS attests "according to the times" (לפי העתים).[19] Despite the fact that 4Q259 is damaged at a place where two now separate parts of a composite of smaller fragments meet, the top of *nun* is clear.[20]

9:14 1QS reads "the sons of the Zadok" (sic) which seems rather out of place here. Nor would we expect the definite article with a proper noun. Curiously, the scribe of 1QS left a larger space both before and especially after the words "the sons of Zadok." This was motivated either by visible damage to the surface of the parchment or a deliberate lacuna provoked perhaps by a deficient exemplar manuscript.[21] Gaster's early suggestion to emend to "the sons of righteousness" has now found material support in 4Q259 3:10 where we also find a nota accusativi that is absent in 1QS. While the reading in 4Q259 is clear, both *he* and *tsade* are damaged alongside other letters in this fragment. What looks initially like a possible deletion dot above "the Zadok" (sic) in 1QS emerges from the digital image at magnification as a small hole in the leather.

---

[19] Cf. Alexander and Vermes, DJD 26:146. Metso and Qimron miss the remains of *nun* and read לפי in 4Q259 also, see Metso, *Textual Development*, 53 and Qimron, PTSDSSP 1:88. Note, however, that in his more recent edition Qimron includes the *nun* in לפני, see DSSHW 1:226.

[20] See especially PAM 43.263 as digitised on LLDSSEL B-284709. For our interpretation of this significant reading in 4Q259 as it stands see 14.4.1 below as well as 1.5.6 and Table 3 above.

[21] Cf. Martin, Scribal Practices, 2:466. Gaster's view on this material is noted in Brownlee, *Dead Sea Manual*, 37.

9:14 The possessive suffix in "their spirit" is spelled רוחם in 1QS and ר[ו]חמה in 4Q259 3:10.[22]

9:16: There is a clear *vacat* in the middle of this line in 1QS and, slightly less pronounced, also in 4Q258 8:1 whereas the text runs on in 4Q259 3:13.

9:16 "Destruction" (השחת) is corrected twice in 4Q258 8:1 by adding *shin* above the line and marking a penultimate *ayin* for deletion with a correction dot above. Alexander and Vermes also identify a correction of original *dalet* to *khet* and identify an original reading of "the knowledge" (הדעת).[23]

9:18 I take 4Q259 3:16 to read a construct plural "the rules of time" where 1QS, 4Q256 and 4Q258 have a singular. Alexander and Vermes read final *vav* in 4Q259 (תכונו) and propose the possibility of a scribal lapse.[24] Given the crude script of 4Q259[25] the reading of final *yod* seems possible.[26]

9:18: The *tav* of להנחותם "he shall guide them" was corrected in 1QS with traces of correction dots visible above and below the preceding *vav* even if somewhat effaced. The remains of a horizontal stroke at the bottom of the letter suggest a correction from final *mem* to *tav*.

9:18–19 There is a syntactical divergence in 4Q259 3:17–18 which reads "and if the alliance of the community reaches perfection" which Wise incorporates into the translation of 1QS.[27]

9:19–20 A paragraphos appears to mark this reference to the time at which the community is to prepare the way of the Lord (Isa 40:3).[28] Moreover, as noted in the Textual Note on 1QS 9:5 above, 4Q258 8:4 attests a clear *vacat* before the reference to "at that time" both here and at 4Q258 7:6 // 1QS 9:5.

9:20 Whereas 1QS reads "to the wilderness," the remains of the preposition preserved in 4Q258 8:4 and 4Q259 3:19 are more consistent with initial *bet* than *lamed*. In 4Q258 we would expect to see parts of the top of *lamed*, and the clear trace of ink near the bottom right corner of initial *mem* in 4Q259 is hard to reconcile with a *lamed*, see LLDSSDL 295980 (Shai Halevi).

9:20 4Q259 3:19 reads the *hiphil* of משל "he shall facilitate their mastery over." The *hiphil* of משל occurs repeatedly in 4QInstruction.[29]

9:20 4Q256 and 4Q259 read בכול and בכל respectively where 1QS attests כול.

9:20 Both 1QS and 4Q256 read the singular possessive suffix "his path" whereas 4Q258 attests the plural suffix "his paths." It is also possible that both 1QS and 4Q256 attest a plural suffix with contraction of *āw>ō*, see Reymond, *Qumran Hebrew*, 144–145.

---

[22] See further Qimron, DSSHW 1:226.

[23] Alexander and Vermes, DJD 26:115.

[24] Cf. Alexander and Vermes, DJD 26:144–149.

[25] See further 1.5.6.1 above.

[26] See also Qimron, DSSHW 1:226 who allows for *vav* or *yod* in 4Q259.

[27] Wise, DSSANT, 140

[28] See further 1.5.1.3 above as well as 1QS 9:5 and 1QS 9:11.

[29] See Murphy, *Wealth in the Dead Sea Scrolls*, 199–200 and n. 153 as well as Alexander and Vermes, DJD 26:149.

9:21 Both 1QS and 4Q258 attest a *vacat* before the new sub-heading "These are the rules of conduct for the Maskil during these times with regard to his love and his hatred."[30] There is enough space for the *vacat* to be mirrored in 4Q256 and 4Q259 also.[31] Despite being followed by a new sub-heading across the manuscripts the *vacat* is less pronounced in 1QS 9:21 than in 1QS 9:16 above. Parts of the sub-heading appear, moreover, rather squeezed in 1QS 9:21, especially when we come to the term Maskil. It is possible that the scribal correction of *yod* in Maskil may have led to more constrained spacing.[32] The *vacat* in 4Q258 8: 5 is generous by comparison. Confusion may have arisen for the scribe of 1QS because the words "his love and his hatred" occur just before the *vacat* in 1QS 9:16 and then again in 1QS 9:21 as part of a new sub-heading.

9:22 The term "gain" is a plus in 4Q258 8:7 over against 1QS. This passage is a rare case where 4Q256 and 4Q258 appear to diverge since there is insufficient space to include 4Q258's further item "wages" in the reconstruction 4Q256 18:6.[33]

9:23 1QS is commonly read as referring to "the statute and its time" (עתו) which is reminiscent of the language in 1QS 9:14 // 4Q259 3:10 above.[34] However, given the difficulty of distinguishing *vav* and *yod* in this and other manuscripts from Qumran, the neat hand of 4Q258 8:7 now offers the superior reading עתי "ready for" in 1QS, 4Q259 and a credible restoration for 4Q260. Qimron is certain that 4Q259 also reads *yod*.[35] I, therefore, read and translate the admonition for the Maskil across all three preserved manuscripts with "dedicated for the statute and ready for a day of vengeance."

9:24 The relative pronoun is spelled with initial *he* in 4Q259 4:6, a likely consequence of the common weakening of the gutturals.[36]

9:24 The words "everything he encounters" are written in smaller script in 4Q260 1:2 as is clearly visible in LLDSSDL B-361659.[37]

9:25 "God" (אל) is written in paleo-Hebrew letters in 4Q258 8:9 and in 4Q258 9:8 below.

---

[30] Cf. Tov, *Scribal Practices*, 151.

[31] See Alexander and Vermes, DJD 26:57–58 and 150–151.

[32] Cf. Qimron, DSSHW1:226.

[33] See Alexander and Vermes, DJD 26:58 and 1QS 5:20 and parallels above.

[34] Cf., e. g., Burrows, *Dead Sea Scrolls*, n. p.; Habermann, *Three Scrolls*, 82; García Martínez and Tigchelaar, DSSSE, 92 and Maier, *Qumran-Essener*, 1:193.

[35] Qimron, DSSHW 1:226–227, see also Alexander and Vermes, DJD 26:115, 119, 150–151.

[36] See the fragment 4d on the left of the group of smaller fragments at the bottom right of the image LLDSSDL B-281230. Cf. also the Textual Note on 1QS 8:13 in 8.3 above.

[37] See also DJD 26:159.

14.4 Commentary

14.4.1 The Maskil's Role among Humanity Supported by Successive Revelation (1QS 9:12–14a // 4Q259 3:6b–10a)

We are immediately struck by a strong universal perspective as the references to the Maskil's dealing "with all the living" and "the weight of each person" indicate. In this first part of the Statutes for the Maskil universalism is unfettered, and these lines lack any reference to a particular community by designations found across the Community Rules including in association with the Maskil in 1QS 3:13 ("the children of light") and 4Q256 9:1 // 4Q258 1:1 ("the people of the law"). This universalistic strand is one of several shared emphases of this part of the Community Rules with portions of the Teaching on the Two Spiritis.[38]

In addition to these distinctive features the theme of predetermined time-liness for potent events, such as revelations introduced here, runs right across this section as a whole.[39]

9:12 I have commented on the figure of the Maskil in 4.4.1, 5.4.1 and 14.1 above.[40]

9:12 The phrase "all the living" occurs in the Teaching on the Two Spirits (1QS 4:26), here and in the Final Hymn (1QS 10:16 and 1QS 10:18 and parallels).[41] The phrase is is entirely absent from 1QS 5–8 and paralles.

9:12 It is difficult to be sure what is meant by the instruction for the Maskil to adjust his dealings with others on the basis of "the weight of each person" though some kind of diagnostic process may be presupposed.[42]

9:13 1QS reads "He shall acquire every insight which has been found *according to* the times (לפי העתים)" where 4Q259 3:9 refers to "every insight which has been found *in previous* times (לפני העתים)."[43] While 4Q259 employs almost

---

[38] Cf. 4.1.4 above.

[39] See Heinz-Josef Fabry, "עֵת *'et*," ThWQ 3:243–253 and Gerhard von Rad, "The Divine Determination of Times (Excursus)," in *Wisdom in Israel* (London: SCM, 1975), 263–283. On the broader sense of the term תכון including in relation to divinely ordained times see Bakker "תָּכֵן *tākan*" and Kister, "Physical and Metaphorical Measurements," 167–169. On the sapiential flavour of this section, and the Community Rules more widely, see Tanzer, "Sages," 176.

[40] Wernberg-Møller suggests that the term refers to "a member of the pious community" especially in the current passage, see *Manual of Discipline*, 66.

[41] For an overview over the occurrences of the phrase in the Dead Sea Scrolls and the Bible see Tigchelaar, *Increase Learning*, 97–98. On the related Maskil heading in the Damascus Document and the material features marking a new beginning at 1QS 9:12 see 14.1 above.

[42] For some proposals see Alexander, "Physiognomy, Initiation, and Rank" and Jonathan Ben-Dov, "Ideals of Science: The Infrastructure of Scientific Activity in Apocalyptic Literature and in the Yahad," in *Ancient Jewish Sciences and the History of Knowledge*. Edited by Jonathan Ben-Dov and Seth Sanders (New York, NY: New York University Press, 2014), 109–152 who explores astrology and physiognomy as possible scenarios.

[43] Wise translates both prepositions with "of earlier times," see Wise, DSSANT, 139.

identical language its reading makes a subtle but important point that deserves to be taken seriously. Given the reference to successive "revelations from time to time (הנגלה לעת בעת)" in the previous line, 4Q259's concern with insights found at earlier times reflects the expectation that the Maskil must be au fait not only with current revelations but also with a repertoire of significant insights gained from previous disclosures. On our reading it is just as likely that the scribe of 1QS missed a subtlety – either aurally or literarily – and was perhaps influenced by the phrase "according to their spirit" in the following line. Discrepancies, including the presence or lack of *vacat*s, are part of a pattern of variation alongside some continuity across the manuscripts on the topic of עת "time."[44]

14.4.2 Establishing Boundaries (1QS 9:14b–18a // 4Q256 18 1a // 4Q258 7:15–8:3a // 4Q259 3:10b–16a)

The instruction to separate and weigh a group referred to as "the sons of the Zadok" in 1QS 9:14 and "the sons of righteousness" in 4Q259 3:10 indicates we have left the universalistic framework of the introductory lines behind. In whatever way we read the two variant manuscripts, we have a clear reference to a particular group that is soon followed by a second socially-selected entity referred to as "the chosen ones of the time." However, if our reading and inter-pretation of 4Q255 A:4 is correct, then 4Q255 preserves a version of the in-struction to weigh the spirits of humankind that reflects a universalistic frame-work.[45]

9:14 An instruction to separate, though frequent in the Community Rules, sets a more particularist tone than the opening lines of this section.

9:14: The concern here is with an assessment of individuals' spiritual make-up. The notion of weighing is applied to a particular group rather than humanity more broadly.[46]

9:14 The phrase the sons of Zadok occurs with reference to a priestly group in 1QS 5:2, 9.[47] In both instances 4Q256 and 4Q258 lack the reference to the sons of Zadok and refer instead to "the many" in the first and to "the council of the people of the community" in the second instance. This has led Robert Kugler to argue that the same hand that was at work in 1QS 5 is also responsible for a

---

Alexander and Vermes suppose a slip of the pen on the part of the scribe of 4Q259, see DJD 26:146, 148.

[44] See the Textual Notes and Commentary on 1QS 9:18, 20, 23 above.

[45] Cf. 1.5.2.3 above.

[46] Compare the Commentary on 1QS 9:12 // 4Q259 3:8 above.

[47] See Chapter 5 and 6.1 above and Hempel, *Qumran Rule Texts in Context*, 210–227 for more discussion and further bibliography. On the readings "the sons of the Zadok" (1QS) and "the sons of righteousness" in 4Q259 3:10 see 14.3 above.

Zadokite revision here in 1QS 9:14.[48] Others have taken 1QS's ungrammatical reading ("the sons of the Zadok") as a typographical error.[49] The superior reading of 4Q259 has received much less attention. In context, the leadership figure here is the Maskil and the territory we are in is one of election and spiritual qualities rather than the interpretation of the torah which is associated with the sons of Zadok in 1QS 5. In my view 4Q259's reading is to be preferred. The designation "sons of righteousness" describes a group that is chosen of the time with an anticipated judgment in view. While the reading in 1QS 9:14 is suggestive in light of what we find 1QS 5, I suggest it is the result of the scribe of 1QS struggling with a *Vorlage* that contained a text like 4Q259. Since the scribe of 1QS was familiar with 1QS 5 he associated the remains in front of him with a familar phrase. We argued above that 4Q259 was one of the *Vorlagen* used by the scribe of 1QS.[50]

9:14 "The chosen ones of the time" in 1QS must be taken alongside "the chosen ones of the way" referred to in 4Q258 8:2 and 4Q259 3:16 where 1QS 9:17–18 reads "those who have chosen the way" below.

9:15: On "cleanness of his hands" see 1QH[a] 8:28 and 30 which reads, "cleansing me by your spirit of holiness and bringing me near according to your will."[51]

9:16b–17a Both rebuke and exchanging counsel are activities that characterise the movement's internal processes. The fact that they are activities that must not extend to the people of destruction is intended to manage the influence of former members, a group elsewhere referred to as "the people of injustice."[52] In addition, I identified the same group behind the designation "the people of deceit" in Chapter 13 above.

14.4.3 The Maskil in the Midst of the Yahad (1QS 9:18b–21a // 4Q256 18:1b–4a // 4Q258 8:3b–5a // 4Q259 3:16b–4:2a)

This is the only instance where walking in perfection is put into an inter-personal frame of reference by admonishing community members to conduct themselves perfectly with one another. In all other cases where we come across the notion of perfectly in the Community Rules it refers to an absolute virtue to be attained by an individual or characteristic of a collective.[53]

---

[48] Cf. Kugler, "A Note on 1QS 9:14."

[49] So Qimron and Charlesworth, PTSDSSP 1:40; Knibb, *Qumran Community*, 141–142; Lohse, *Texte aus Qumran*, 34–35; Abegg's edition reads "Zadok" but tags "righteousness," see "Qumran Non-Biblical Manuscripts."

[50] See 1.5.6 and 8.4.2 above.

[51] See also 1QS 4:21 and 4.2.6 above.

[52] Cf. further Hempel, "The Community and Its Rivals" and Chapters 5 and 6.1 above.

[53] See 1.4.1 above.

9:18–19: The phrase "in the midst of the people of the community" in 1QS and 4Q258 is unusual in the context of this section. It does, however, provide a connection with other parts of S which suggests this is probably a secondary addition here. 4Q259 3:17 has a different syntax in several parts of this portion of the Statutes of the Maskil and also reads "the alliance (סוד) of the community."[54] García Martínez and Tigchelaar take סוד with "path" and translate "secret path."[55]

9:19–21 The Maskil is here transposed to the period of preparing the way to the wilderness (cf. Isa 40:3).[56]

14.4.4 The Rules of Conduct for the Maskil (1QS 9:21b–25 // 4Q256 18:4b–7 // 4Q258 8:5b–9 // 4Q259 4:2b–6 // 4Q260 1:1–2)

A new sub-heading ("These are the rules of conduct for the Maskil during these times with regard to his love and his hatred.") and a *vacat* mark the beginning of this section.[57] The *vacat* is clearly preserved in 1QS and 4Q258. Curiously a paragraphos in the margin precedes this new heading by two lines and seems to highlight the recourse to an earlier citation of Isa 40:3 in 1QS 9:19–20 // 4Q256 18:3 // 4Q258 8:4 // 4Q259 3:19. The theme of the Maskil's love and hatred also picks up an earlier theme.[58] As has been shown by Ari Mermelstein, love and hate are not individual emotive responses but socially constructed.[59] The argument suggests that members of the movement's love and hate are rooted in a theological disposition.[60] Note also the instruction to love the children of light and hate the children of darkness in 1QS 1:9–10.

The scribe of 1QS, and perhaps a *Vorlage*, made an effort to present this sub-section as a new beginning. However, both the heading and a great deal of the material that follows recapitulate familiar content that deals again with the Maskil's conduct, remit and firm boundaries with outsiders such as the people of destruction.[61]

---

[54] Cf. 1QS 6:19 and 1.5.6.2 above. On the syntactical divergence of 4Q259 from the remaining witnesses see 14.3 above. As suggested by Alison Schofield, the text of 4Q259 introduces a conditional element, see *From Qumran to the Yaḥad*, 161.

[55] See García Martínez and Tigchelaar, DSSSE, 531. The translation by Wise appears to draw on the text of 4Q259 in translating 1QS by incorporating a conditional element, see "if then the secret Way is perfected," DSSANT, 140. On knowledge control in the Dead Sea Scrolls see also Hempel, "Bildung und Wissenswirtschaft" and Stone, *Secret Groups*.

[56] Cf. Brooke, "Isa 40:3 and the Wilderness Community," 125.

[57] Compare 1QS 9:21b // [4Q256 18:4] // 4Q258 8:5 // [4Q259 4:2] and see Alexander and Vermes, DJD 26:58 and 151.

[58] See 14.4.2 above.

[59] Mermelstein, "Love and Hate at Qumran: The Social Construction of Sectarian Emotion," *DSD* 20 (2013): 237–263.

[60] Cf. 1QS 1:3–4 // 4Q255 1:4–5 and CD 2:15 // 4Q266 2 ii 14–15.

[61] See 14.2.1 and 14.2.2 above.

As indicated in 14.3 above 4Q258 8:7 attests a longer text than 1QS 9:22 and 4Q256 18:6. If Alexander and Vermes are correct that 4Q258 refers to "property, gain, [and wages]" over against 1QS's "property and wages" and 4Q256's "property and gain" we would have a case where 4Q258 departs from both 1QS and 4Q256.[62] Moreover, the context is compatible with the more extensive plus in 4Q258 1:12–13 since the concern here is for the Maskil to distance himself from the property and economic remit of the people of the pit. The reservations about economic engagement and sharing of property with this group is reminiscent of the material on the people of injustice who are described as endowed with potentially desirable goods according to Chapter 6 above.[63] While the people of the pit emerge as a problematic entity, it is striking how the text then adopts a softer and rather subservient tone by encouraging the Maskil to leave to them their property as a servant or slave might.

The idea of judgment is introduced sharply across all four manuscripts as part of the Maskil's remit in 1QS 9:23 and parallels which introduce – on the superior reading across the manuscripts[64] – the need for the Maskil to be ready for a day of vengeance. Finally, the climactic concluding statement in the Statutes is an admonition for the Maskil to continually look out for God's judgment in 1QS 9:25 // 4Q258 8:9. This transition forms a potent reminder of the consequences of divine wrath. It also offers a powerful transition to the partially preserved rubric introducing the Hymn and its blessings and acknowledgements of God's greatness. The latter liturgical elements were considered as a potent means of protection from malevolent forces.[65]

---

[62] Alexander and Vermes, DJD 26:58; see also 1QS 5:20 and Chapter 6 above.

[63] See, especially, 6.1.2.1; 6.1.3 and 6.1.4.1. We can draw further support from 1QS 10:19–20 // 4Q260 4:7–9, see 15.2.4 below.

[64] See also 14.3 above.

[65] Further, 1.2.1; 3.1; 3.4.2; 5.4.2 and 14.1 above as well as 15.1.2 below.

15. Hymn (1QS 9:26–11:22 // 4Q256 19:1–6; 20:2–7; 23:1–3 // 4Q258 8:10–10:8a; 12:4; 13:1–3 // 4Q260 2:1–5; 3:1–3; 4:1–5:7 // 4Q264 1:1–10)

15.1 Introduction

The Final Hymn is most fully preserved in 1QS. 4Q260 and 4Q264 both constitute small-scale and perhaps portable scrolls that preserve remains of the Final Hymn.[1] The single fragment that survives of 4Q264 may belong to a liturgical anthology.[2] The precise beginning of the Hymn is unclear because the bottom of column 9 and its parallel in 4Q258 are damaged, see 1QS 9:26 // 4Q258 8:10. It is clear, however, that the material in 1QS 9:26–10:1a // 4Q258 8:10–11a forms a transition between the Statutes for the Maskil and the Hymn. I take this transition as an introductory rubric to the Hymn. Asaf Gayer identifies the beginning of the Hymn in 1QS 9:25b based on the prominence of the theme of judgment in the framework of the Hymn.[3] As I have shown, the theme of judgment also plays a crucial role in the Statutes for the Maskil which would make the topic pertinent in either of these two inter-related parts of some Community Rules.[4] The admonition to "bless his maker" that opens the preserved remains of the rubric makes it clear that the following material is presented as associated with the figure of the Maskil.[5] Elsewhere Goedhart refers to the Hymn's "warm personal tone" ("warme persoonlijke toon").[6] Such an interpretation suggests a rather romanticised reading of the Hymn as providing access to the innermost feelings of the Maskil, analogously with the approach to the so-called Teacher Hymns in the Hodayot.[7] Moreover, the approach recently championed by Jaqueline Vayntrub to think of speeches in the Hebrew Bible in literary terms as

---

[1] Cf. Alexander and Vermes, DJD 26:154.

[2] See Alexander and Vermes, DJD 26:201.

[3] Gayer, "Centrality of Prayer and the Stability of Trust," 319.

[4] Cf. 14.2.2 and 14.4.2 above. See also 8.2.3 and 8.4.3.

[5] See already Goedhart, *Slothymne*, 333–338.

[6] Goedhart *Slothymne*, 9.

[7] For a critique of the latter see Angela K. Harkins, "Who is the Teacher of the Teacher Hymns? Re-Examining the Teacher Hymns Hypothesis Fifty Years Later," in *A Teacher for All Generations: Essays in Honor of James C. VanderKam*. Edited by Eric Mason et al. JSJSup 153 (Leiden: Brill, 2012), 449–467.

"character speeches" offers a more nuanced lense also here.[8] The Maskil figure thus functions as an exemplaric model of liturgical piety.[9]

While we are retaining the customary designation "the Hymn," what we have is more accurately described as an anthology of disparate material.[10] In particular, the first section that follows the introductory rubric has been taken by a number of experts as containing a liturgical calendar[11] On our reading this calendric material is now well integrated into the dominant framework of blessing and praise and forms part of what Noam Mizrahi has called the "literary liturgy" in various forms of the Community Rules.[12]

15.1.1 The Final Hymn and the Calendrical Anthology 4Q259 4–7 (4Otot [4Q319])

One manuscript of the Community Rules (4Q259) continues after the equivalent of 1QS 9:25 with the calendrical anthology 4QOtot (4Q319).[13] Strictly speaking the transition from the end of the Statutes for the Maskil and 4Q259 4:9 (4Q319) is not preserved in 4Q259 4.[14] 4QOtot comprises a collection of calendrical material.[15] Its contents present the longest and most complex calendrical cycle among all the calender texts from Qumran by combining the six-year cycle of priestly courses with a cycle of sabbatical years and jubilee years (seven cycles of seven years=49 years) making up a total of 294 years (49x6).[16]

4QOtot was published separately from the Community Rules in DJD 21, a volume devoted to Calendrical Texts. In his most recent edition of the Com-

---

[8] Vayntrub, *Beyond Orality: Biblical Poetry on its Own Terms* (London: Routledge, 2019).

[9] See also Eva Mroczek, "The Hegemony of the Biblical in the Study of Second Temple Literature," *JAJ* 6 (2015): 1–35, 6 on David's "exemplary liturgical and calendrical legacy" and Hindy Najman, *Seconding Sinai: The Development of Mosaic Discourse in Second Temple Judaism*. JSJSup 77 (Leiden: Brill 2003) on the exemplarity of Moses. On the figure of the Maskil see further Charlotte Hempel, "Biblical Views: Where are the Scribes in the Dead Sea Scrolls?," *BAR* July/August (2018): 52, 68 and especially also Newsom, *Self as Symbolic Space*.

[10] See Leaney, *Rule of Qumran*, 115 and Falk, *Daily, Sabbath and Festival Prayers*, 101. Arjen Bakker refers to "a series of hymns" see "The Figure of the Sage," 98.

[11] Compare already Milik, *Ten Years of Discovery*, 107–118 and Leaney, *Rule of Qumran*, 17–26 and 80–107 as well as 15.4.2 below.

[12] Noam Mizrahi, "Liturgy, Hebrew of the Dead Sea Scrolls," in *Encyclopedia of Hebrew Language and Linguistics*. Edited by Geoffrey Khan (Leiden: Brill, 2013), 2:558–561, 558.

[13] See Alexander and Vermes, DJD 26:129–152; Talmon, Ben-Dov and Glessmer, DJD 21:196–201; Glessmer, "The Otot-Texts;" Metso, *Textual Development*, 48–54; Milik, *Books of Enoch*, 62–64; James C. VanderKam, *Calendars in the Dead Sea Scrolls: Measuring Time* (London: Routledge, 1998), 80–84 and 1.5.6 above.

[14] Cf. Alexander and Vermes, DJD 26:150–151.

[15] See Talmon, Ben-Dov and Glessmer, DJD 21:201 and Ben-Dov, *Head of All Years: Astronomy and Calendars at Qumran in Their Ancient Context*. STDJ 78 (Leiden: Brill, 2008), 147.

[16] See Talmon, Ben-Dov and Glessmer, DJD 21:201 and Ben-Dov, *Head of All Years*, 17–18.

munity Rules Qimron appends 4QOtot (4Q319).[17] The initial decision to publish this part of 4Q259 separately from the remainder of the Community Rules was no doubt influenced by the initial impression that calendrical material is only loosely part of compositions of different genres. The example of 4Q394 (4QMMTª) is another case in point where calendrical material is prefaced to halakhic exposition.[18] It also allowed experts on calendric matters to tackle this part of the Community Rules. Commendable exceptions are the *Dead Sea Scrolls Study Edition* where 4Q319 (Otot) is presented as part of 4Q259 as well as the translation by Maier who presents the calendrical material entirely as part of 4Q259 starting somewhat later with 4Q259 5.[19]

The term '*otot* (signs) goes back to the account of the creation of the luminaries on the fourth day (Gen 1:14–19), a passage which establishes a nexus between the heavenly lights and calendrical matters such as seasons, days and years.[20] In fact, Gen 1:14–19 is an important point of reference both for 4Q319 and the Calendar of Praise that introduces the Hymn. A creation context is introduced, furthermore, immediately in the opening rubric of the Hymn where the Maskil is instructed to bless God the creator ("he shall bless his maker"). Moreover, both 4Q319 and the opening lines of the Hymn are concerned with the heavenly luminaries.[21] In 4Q259 4:9–11 (Otot) we find an introduction to the calendrical rosters proper in the form of a reference to the creation of light on the fourth day which, according to both 4Q259/4Q319 and 4Q320 (Calendrical Document / Mishmarot A), set a calendrical mega-cycle in motion.[22]

A number of scholars, including Uwe Glessmer, have acknowledged a calendrical connection between Otot and the Hymn.[23] Thus, Stern notes on the Maskil's Hymn in relation to Otot that it includes "calendrical material, at least with a cursory reference to the times of the day, new moons, festivals and four days of remembrance when various prayers are to be recited [...] and thus occupies a similar function."[24] However, as I have shown, the connections between the Final Hymn and the contents of 4Q259–4Q319 (Otot) range more widely. In short, both the Hymn and 4Q259–4Q319 (Otot) share an emphasis on

---

[17] See Qimron, DSSHW 1:231–234; also Martone, *Regola*, 54–80.

[18] See 4Q394 3–7 i and Qimron and Strugnell, DJD 10:7–13. For a concise recent overview cf. Helen Jacobus, "Calendars," in CDSS, 435–448.

[19] See García Martínez and Tigchelaar, DSSSE, 532–533 and Maier, *Qumran-Essener*, 2:210–213, 277.

[20] Cf. VanderKam, *Calendars*, 3–4.

[21] See the references to "the rule of light," "the watches of darkness," "the heavenly lights," and "the new moon" in 1QS 10:1b–4a // 4Q256 19:1–2a // 4Q258 8:11b–13 // 4Q260 2:1–3. For more details refer to 15.2.1 and 15.2.2.

[22] See Talmon, Ben-Dov and Glessmer, DJD 21:201.

[23] Cf. Glessmer, "The Otot-Texts," 129–132.

[24] Sacha Stern, *Calendars in Antiquity: Empires, States, and Societies* (Oxford: Oxford University Press, 2012), 68, see also Talmon, Ben-Dov and Glessmer, DJD 21:214–215 and Alexander and Vermes, DJD 26:20–24.

the heavenly lights in conjunction with divinely ordained times as well as instructions to utter blessings.[25] In addition, the crucial term *'ot* ("sign") which is found in Gen 1:14 and frequently in 4Q319 also occurs in the Hymn in the context of a section on praise at appointed times and festivals.[26] A connection between hymns of blessing, calendrical observance, the creation of the luminaries and the term *'ot* is also attested in 4Q408 3+3a Apocryphon of Moses[c]?[27] and 1QH[a] 20:7–12, a hymn associated with the Maskil (cf. 4Q427 [H[a]] 20:[4], 11).[28] Finally, the prose composition David's Compositions that forms part of the Qumran Psalms Scroll (11Q5 27:2–11) also establishes a connection between the 364-day year and prayer. In short, Gen 1:14, a broader creation context, timeliness and calendrical concerns go to the heart of 4Q259 4–7 (4QOtot) and the opening rubric and first section of the Final Hymn.[29] The fact that scholars have studied the Community Rules and Otot in isolation has obscured a number of these intriguing connections. Beyond the Final Hymn defining moments in time such the emergence of the movement, divine revelations and, ultimately, the final judgment and the eschaton indicate that prayer, liturgical time and the calendar are closely intertwined in the theology and world view of the movement behind the Community Rules.[30]

It would be wrong, on the other hand, not to acknowledge some distinctiveness between 4Q259 4–7 (4Otot [4Q319]) and the Final Hymn such as the interest in priestly courses in 4Q319. In fact, the combination of calendrical rosters with other significant events such as priestly courses, festivals or historical events is attested more commonly at Qumran and has led to fluctuating designations for calendrical material.[31] In sum, the judgment by the editor of 4QOtot that "the variance of subject-matter between the organizational-legal material of Serekh ha-Yaḥad and the technical *otot* schedule, seems conclusive"[32] needs to be chastened since it fails to take into account the palpable shared interests in the calendar, the heavenly luminaries, as well as creation in disparate parts of the Final Hymn.

---

[25] See 1QS 9:26; 4Q259 (4Q319) 4:9 and Talmon, Ben-Dov and Glessmer, DJD 21:214–215.

[26] See 1QS 10:4 // 4Q256 19:2 // 4Q258 9:1.

[27] Steudel, DJD 36:304–308. See also Liora Goldman, "4Q408 Prayers," in Ariel Feldman and Liora Goldman, *Scripture and Interpretation: Qumran Texts that Rework the Bible*. Edited and Introduced by Devorah Dimant. BZNW 449 (Berlin: De Gruyter, 2014), 323–350.

[28] The reference to the Maskil in 1QH 20:7 is poorly preserved but the reconstruction is supported by 4Q427 8 ii 10 and 4Q428 [H[b]] 12 ii; see Newsom, Stegemann and Schuller, DJD 40:250–260, esp. 255.

[29] See also Penner, *Patterns of Daily Prayer*.

[30] Cf., e. g., Chapters 8, 11; and 13 as well as 14.2.3 and 15.1.3. See further Brooke, "Aspects of the Theological Significance of Prayer" and Carol Newsom's description of "the construction of time" as part of "the configured world of the *Serek ha-Yahad*," *Self as Symbolic Space*," 174.

[31] See Hempel, *Qumran Rule Texts in Context*, 319–329 and 4.4.1 above.

[32] Cf. Ben-Dov, DJD 21:196 and compare 5.4.1 above.

15.1.2 The Apotropaic Function of Praise

Given the centrality of praise as a means of terrifying malevolent spirits in the apotropaic Songs of the Maskil (4Q510–511)[33] there are good reasons to consider the significance of ending several manuscripts of the Community Rules with the Final Hymn of the Maskil in this light.[34] Moreover, counterbalanced with the Covenant Ceremony as well as the Teaching on the Two Spirits in the opening columns, the Hymn creates a framework in what I have called "the long text of S" that addresses a struggle with the forces of evil.[35] The same is true on a larger scale of the Scroll of 1QS-1QSa-1QSb which also ends with blessings, though a fuller treatment of that Scroll is beyond the scope of this Commentary.

As I argued in 1.2.1 above, an apotropaic framework is established already by the emphasis on keeping away from all evil in the programmatic opening lines of 1QS 1 (1QS 1:4 // [4Q255 1:5–6]). Strikingly the demand for a fervent commitment "to turn back from all evil" – while shared by 1QS 5:1 and 4Q256 9:1 – constitutes the opening requirement in 4Q258 1:1 at the beginning of this manuscript.[36] The evidence of 4Q258 makes it clear that even prior to the supplementation of the Covenant Ceremony and the Teaching on the Two Spirits the shorter text of the Communite Rule represented by 4Q258 already attests a framework that opens with a prominent reference to turning away from all evil and ends with blessing and the Final Hymn. Thus, the dangers emanating from malevolent powers shape otherwise distinctive witnesses of the complex Rule tradition. In addition, several shared elements illustrate a common cultural context behind the Hymn and apotropaic texts from Qumran including the reference to the lyre (1QS 10:9 and 4Q511 10:8); an emphasis on the speaker's lowly humanity (1QS 11:9–10.21–22 and 4Q511 28–29); a stress on divinely sourced knowledge (1QS 11:15–16 and 4Q511 28–29 3) and references to a cycle of liturgical time (1QS 10:1–8 // parallels and 4Q511 2 i 9). In sum, in our estimation the liturgical collection that makes up the Final Hymn in several manuscripts of the Community Rules ought to be recognized as a further exemplar of apotropaic hymns. Daniel Falk's assessment of this category of hymn as

---

[33] Cf. Nitzan, *Qumran Prayer and Religious Poetry*, 227–272.

[34] See Charlotte Hempel, "The Apotropaic Function of the Final Hymn in the Community Rule," in *Petitioners, Penitents, and Poets: On Prayer and Praying in Second Temple Judaism.* Edited by Ariel Feldman and Timothy Sandoval. BZAW (Berlin: De Gruyter, forthcoming). On the increased role of praise in Second Temple Jewish liturgy see Mika Pajunen, "The Praise of God and His Name as the Core of the Second Temple Liturgy," *ZAW* 127 (2015): 475–488, 484–487.

[35] Cf. 1.2.1 above.

[36] See Chapter 5 above.

intended for "regulized use for general protection of the community from evil"
is particularly apposite for our reading of the function of the Hymn.[37]

15.1.3 The Hymn and the Covenant Ceremony

A number of scholars have drawn attention to a series of shared concerns
and terminological correspondences between the Hymn and the material on
the Admission into and Reaffirmation of the Covenant.[38] The most comprehensive treatment by Weise concludes that the Hymn would have featured in the
initiation ceremony that took place during the Covenant Ceremony described
in 1QS 1:18b–2:18 and parallels.[39] The following terminological and thematic
connections, several of which I identify as secondary expansions in 1QS, are
noteworthy.

a. Statutes / Commandments

Hymn

> 1QS 10:1
>   Divinely decreed times (opening rubric)
> 10:5
>   Statutes engraved forever
> 10:6c–7a
>   Established statute
> 10:8b
>   Engraved statute with reference to praise
> 10:10
>   I shall recount His statutes.
> 10:11 // [4Q258 9:11–12]
>   My wrongdoing shall be engraved like a statute before my eyes.
> 10:25–26 // No parallels
>   I will prescribe a statute according to the measuring line of the times.

Covenant Ceremony

> 1QS 1:17 // 4Q256 2:1–2
>   All that He has commanded

---

[37] Falk, "Material Aspects of Prayer Manuscripts," 71. See also Daniel K. Falk, "The Contribution of the Qumran Scrolls to the Study of Ancient Jewish Liturgy," in *The Oxford Handbook of the Dead Sea Scrolls*. Edited by Timothy H. Lim and John J. Collins (Oxford: OUP,
2010), 617–651, 635.

[38] See 3.2.2 and 3.4.2 above.

[39] Cf., e. g., Weise *Kultzeiten*, 61–112; further Falk, *Daily, Sabbath and Festival Prayers*,
110–111, 237–238 who draws particular attention to the close relationsip between 1QS 10:9–
11:22 and 1QS 1:18–2:18; Murphy, *Wealth in the Dead Sea Scrolls*, 128 and Puech, *La croyance Esséniens*, 2:422 who assigns both the Teaching and the Hymn to the third and final stage
in the growth of 1QS.

1QS 3:8–9 // 4Q255 2:2–3 // 4Q257 3:11–12
  Profound humility towards all the divine statutes
1QS 3:9–10 // 4Q255 2:5–6 // 4Q257 313–14
  Walking perfectly in all God's ways, as He has commanded
1QS 3:10–11 // 4Q255 2:7
  Admonition to adhere to all of God's commandments

b. Blessings

Hymn

  10:13 // 4Q258 10:2
    I will bless His name
  10:14 // 4Q256 20:2 // 4Q258 10:2
    I shall bless Him
  10:16 // [4Q256 20:4] // [4Q258 10:4] // [4Q260 4:1]
    […] bless (at onset of fear etc.)
  11:15 // 4Q264 3
    Blessed are You, my God

Covenant Ceremony

  1:18–19 // 4Q256 2:3–4
    The priests and the levites shall bless the God of salvation and all His true works.
  2:1–2 // No parallels
    The priests shall bless all the people of the lot of God.

c. God's Righteous and Powerful Acts

Hymn

  1QS 10:11–12 // 4Q258 9:12–13
    The speaker proclaims God's knowledge, strength and glory.
  1QS 10:16 // 4Q256 20:4–5 // [4Q258 10:4–5] // 4Q260 4:2–3[40]
    God's marvellous acts, might and loving acts
  10:23 // 4Q260 5:5–6
    The speaker's tongue is to recount God's righteous deeds continually alongside
    the treachery of humanity until the end of their wrongdoing.
  11:3 // No parallel
    God's wonders and righteous acts
  11:5 // No parallel
    God's marvellous mysteries
  11:12–15 // 4Q258 13:1–3 // 4Q264 1–3
    God's loving acts, righteousness, goodness and glory are juxtaposed to the
    speaker's fleshly sinfulness.
  11:18–20 // 4Q264 6–8
    God's wonders along with the His strength, glory and wonderful works are de-
    scribed followed by a final account of human lowliness.

---

[40] See the Textual Note on 1QS 10:16 below.

Covenant Ceremony

> 1QS 1:21–22 // 4Q256 2:5–6
> The priests enumerate God's righteous deeds, loving acts and kindness juxtaposed
> with Israel's shortcomings recited by levites – not unlike a collective abasement.
> 1QS 2:1 // No parallels
> God's kind love from eternity to eternity

d. Fear and Terror Followed by Blessing and Account of God's Marvellous Acts

Hymn

> 1QS 10:15–16 // [4Q256 20:4] // [4Q258 10:3–4] // 4Q260 4:1
> God is blessed at the onset of fear and terror.

Covenant Ceremony

> 1QS 1:17–18 // 4Q256 2:2–3
> Admonition not to turn one's back on God because of all the dread, terror and
> testing that characterize the rule of Belial[41]
> 1QS 2:5–6 // [4Q256 2:13–3:1] // 4Q257 2:2–3
> The levites' curse includes the entreaty that God hand over those addressed (to)
> terror at the hand of all those who wreak vengeance.

e. Belial/Worthlessness

Hymn

> 10:21 // 4Q260 5:2
> The speaker commits not to keep Belial/worthlessness in their heart.

Covenant Ceremony

> 1QS 1:18 // [4Q256 2:3]
> The rule of Belial
> 1QS 1:23–24 // No parallels
> The rule of Belial
> 1QS 2:4 // [4Q256 2:12–13] // 4Q257 2:1
> The levites shall curse all the people of the lot of Belial.
> 1QS 2:19 // No parallels
> A reference to "all the days of the rule of Belial"

f. Judgment / Salvation and the Liminal Space in Betweeen[42]

Hymn

> 10:11 // [4Q258 9:11]
> The speaker will pronounce His judgment.

---

[41] Cf. Isa 24:17; Prov 3:24–25 and 4Q525 (Beatitudes) 2–3 ii 4–6.

[42] On the prominence of judgment in the Final Hymn see also Gayer, "Centrality of Prayer
and Stability of Trust."

10:16–17 // 4Q256 20:5–6 // [4Q258 10:5] // 4Q260 4:3
  The judgment of all the living is in God's hand.
10:18 // 4Q256 20:7 // [4Q258 10:7] // 4Q260 4:5–6
  With God lies the judgment of all the living.
10:20 // 4Q260 4:9
  Reference to a time when God has dispensed judgment
10:25 // No parallels
  The speaker pledges to preserve faithfulness and strong judgment for God's
  righteousness.
11:2 // No parallels
  The speaker acknowledges that his justice lies with God.
11:10 // No parallels
  Judgment belongs to God.

Covenant Ceremony

  1QS 1:26 // No parallels
    God's judgment
  1QS 2:6–8 // 4Q256 2:13–3:2 // 4Q257 2:2–5
    The levites' curse refers to divine punishment with destruction at the hand of all
    those who requite retribution as well as eternal damnation.
  1QS 2:15 // No parallels
    God's anger and the wrath of His judgments shall flare up against the insincere
    convert for eternal destruction.
  1QS 3:5–6 // 4Q257 3:7–8 // 4Q262 1:3–4
    Consequences of the denial of God's judgment on the part of the one refusing to
    enter the covenant

g. Apostates

Hymn

  10:21 // 4Q260 5:1
    Those who rebel against the way
  11:1 // No par.
    Among other terms "those whose spirits go astray"

Covenant Ceremony

  1QS 2:12 // No parallels
    The one entering this covenant (who) places the stumbling block of his sinfulness
    before him so that he backslides.
  1QS 2:25–26 // No parallels
    Anyone who refuses to enter [the covenant of Go]d in order to walk with a
    hardened heart

h. Perfection

Hymn

> 11:2 // No parallels
> The speaker's perfection is in God's hand.
> 11:17 // 4Q264 4–5
> Without God no conduct is perfect.

Covenant Ceremony

> 1QS 2:1–2 // No parallels
> The priests shall bless all the people of the lot of God who walk perfectly in all
> His ways.
> 1QS 3:9–10 // 4Q255 2:5–6 // 4Q257 3:13–14
> The reformed renegade shall direct his steps to walk perfectly in all God's ways.

In sum, distinctive features attested in the Covenant Ceremony are the explicit reference to the rule of Belial and the anchoring in Israel's history in the shape of the reference to "our fathers" which are both lacking from the Hymn. Overall, the number of correspondences are striking.

15.1.4 The Hymn and the Statutes for the Maskil

A significant number of connections have been identified between the emphases and concerns expressed in the Final Hymn and parts of the Community Rules that describe the Maskil's sphere of influence.[43] The following terminological and thematic links are noteworthy: the root *ḥqq* and the notion of engraving;[44] a shared emphasis on time and timeliness;[45] a universalistic frame of reference;[46] and, finally, the connection between instructional and liturgical realms associated with the figure of the Maskil noted by Carol Newsom.[47]

---

[43] So already Weise, *Kultzeiten*, 3. Some consider the Hymn as forming part of the Statutes for the Maskil, see, e. g., VanderKam, *Calendars*, 46.

[44] See, e. g., 1QS 9:23 // 4Q258 8:7 // [4Q259 4:5] and 1QS 10:10 // [4Q258 9:10] // [4Q260 3:3]; 1QS 10:26 and Newman, *Before the Bible*, 114–115.

[45] Cf. Jacob Licht, "Time and Eschatology in Apocalyptic Literature and at Qumran," *JJS* 16 (1965): 177–182.

[46] See Daniel Falk, "Religious Life at Qumran," in *Celebrating the Dead Sea Scrolls: A Canadian Collection.* Edited by Peter W. Flint, Jean Duhaime and Kyung S. Baek. EJL 30 (Atlanta, GA: SBL, 2011), 253–286 and 4.4.1 above.

[47] Newsom, "The Sage in the Literature of Qumran: The Functions of the Maskil," in *The Sage in Israel and the Ancient Near East.* Edited by James G. Gammie and Leo G. Perdue (Winona Lake, IN: Eisenbrauns, 1990), 373–382.

15.1.5 The Hymn and the Hodayot

The close relationship of the Final Hymn to the Hodayot has long been recognized by scholars, and Eileen Schuller has referred to the Final Hymn in the Community Rules as "a very '*Hodayot*-like' psalm."[48] Over the course of the scholarly investigation of the Hodayot it has become clear that the manuscripts attest clusters of hymns. While there is disagreement on the details, most scholars concur that the Final Hymn is most closely reminiscent of the hymns customarily but rather loosely labelled Hymns of the Community.[49] The close relationship between the Final Hymn and the Hodayot is particularly manifest when the Hymn is compared to 1QH[a] 20:7–22:34.[50]

15.2 Translation

15.2.1 Introductory Rubric (1QS 9:26–10:1a // 4Q258 8:10–11a)

1QS 9–10	4Q258 8
[26][ ] *qh* he shall bless his maker and re[count] everything that comes to pass [... with an offering of the] lips he shall bless Him [10a]at *vacat* the times which God has decreed.	[10][he shall bless his maker and re]count [everything that comes to pass ... with an offering of the lips he shall] bless Him at [the times] [11a][which God has decreed.]

15.2.2 A Calendar for Praise (1QS 10:1b–8 // 4Q256 19:1–6 // 4Q258 8:11b–9:7a // 4Q260 2:1–5)

1QS 10	4Q258 8
[1b]At the beginning of the rule of light at its turning point and when it is gathered to its assigned place.	[11b][At the beginning of the rule of light a]t [its] turning [point and when] it is gathered to [its] assigned place.

---

[48] Schuller, "Recent Scholarship on the Hodayot 1993–2010," *CurrBR* 10 (2011): 119–162, 143; see also Goedhart, *Slothymne*, 344–348.

[49] See Schuller, "Recent Research," 142.

[50] Here I am following the delineation proposed by Émile Puech, "Quelques aspects de la restauration," 52–53; see also Puech, "Hodayot," in EDSS 1.366–67, 52–53; see now the convenient edition by Eileen Schuller and Carol Newsom, *The Hodayot (Thanksgiving Psalms): A Study Edition of 1QH[a]*. EJL 36 (Atlanta, GA: SBL, 2012), 62–65. Further, Penner, *Patterns of Daily Prayer*, 137–164.

1QS 10	4Q258 8	4Q260 2
[1c]At the beginning of [2]the watches of darkness when He opens its storehouse and spreads it out over <the world> and at its turning point when it is gathered before the light when	[11c]At the beginning of [the watches of [12]darkness when He opens its storehouse and spreads it out over <the world> and at] its [turning point when it is gathered be]fore the light when	[1]At the beginning of the w[at]ches of [darkness when He opens its storehouse and spreads it out over <the world> and together with] its turning point [2]when it is gathered be[fore the light when]

1QS 10	4Q256 19	4Q258 8	4Q260 2
[2]the heavenly lights [3]shine forth from *the* holy height and are gathered at the place of glory.	[1]the heavenly lights [shine forth] from *His* holy height and are gathered at the place of glory.	[12][the heavenly lights] shine forth [from the holy [13]h]eight [and are gathered at the place of glory.	[2] [the heavenly lights shine forth from the holy height and] are [gather]ed at the place of [3]glory.
At the onset of the appointed times on the days of the new moon at their turning point when [4]one succeeds the other. The time of their renewal is a great day for the holy of holies and a sign *n vacat* for the outpouring of *His* eternal love at the beginning of [5]the appointed times at all periods to come.	*At the onset of* the appointed times ^on ^the ^days ^of the new moon at [2]their turning point when one succeed[d]s the other. The time of their renewal is a great day for the holy of holies and a sign [3]for the outpouring of eter[na]l lo[ve at the be]ginning of the appointed times at all periods to come.	At the onset of the appointed times on the days of the new moon at their turning point when one succeeds the other.] [9][1]The time of their renewal is a great day for the holy of holies and a sign for the outpouring of eternal love [2]at the beginning of the appointed times at all periods to come.	*When the* [ap-pointed times] *arrive* [on the days of the new moon together at their turning point when o]ne [succeeds] the other. [4]The time of [their] renew[al is a great day for the holy of holies and a sign *vacat (?)* for the outpouring of] eternal [love] [5]at the begin[in]g [of the appointed times at all periods to come.
At the beginning of months according to their appointed times and their established holy days	At the beg^inning of months according to their appointed times[4] and [their established holy] days	At the beginning of months accord-ing to their appointed times and their established holy [3]days	At the beginning of months according to their appointed times and their established hol]y [days]

1QS 10	4Q256 19	4Q258 9
[5]for remembrance, at their appointed times [6](with) an offering of the lips I will bless Him according to the statute engraved forever. At the beginning of {.} years and at the turning point of their appointed times when their established statute [7]is fulfilled on each day according to its law one after the other. At harvest time until summer, *vacat* at sowing time *until* the time of growth, at the appointed times of years until their year weeks,	[4][for re]membrance, at their appointed times (with) an offering of the lips I will bless Him according to the sta[tute] engraved forever. [5][At the beginning of years and at the turning] point of appointed times when their established statute is fulfilled on each day according to [its] l[aw one after the other. [6]At harvest time until summer, at sowing time *and*] the ti[m]e of growth, at the appointed times of ye[ars until their year weeks]	[1]for remembrance, at [their] appointed times (with) an [offering of] the lip[s] I will bless Him according to the statute [4][en]graved forever. At the beginning of years and at the turning p[oint of their appointed times when their established statute [is ful]filed on each day according to its law one after the other. At [harvest] tim[e until summer, at so]wing [time] *and* the time of [6]growth, at the appointed times of ye[ar]s until [their] year weeks,

1QS 10	4Q258 9
[8]at the beginning of their year weeks until the time of release. For as long as I live a statute is engraved on my tongue regarding the fruit of praise and the portion of my lips. {…}	[6][at the beginning of] their [ye]ar weeks until the appointed time of release. [7a]For as long as I live a statute is [en]graved on [my tongue regarding the fruit of] praise and the por[tion of] my lips.

15.2.3 Timely Music and Praise of God (1QS 10:9–16a // 4Q256 20:2–5a[51] // 4Q258 9:7b–10:5a // 4Q260 3:1–3; 4:1–3a)

1QS 10	4Q258 9
[9]{.} Let me perform music with accomplishment, and all my music shall be for the glory of God.	[7b]Let me perform music [8]with accomplishment, and all my music shall be for the glory of 𝕲𝖔𝖉.

1QS 10	4Q258 9	4Q260 3
My *lyre and* harp (shall play) for His holy scheme, and I will raise up the flute of my lips in accordance	*Let me play* [my] harp [for his holy] scheme, [and the flute of [9]my lips I will] raise up in accordance with	[1]*Let me play* [my] harp for [his holy scheme, and the flute of my lips I will] raise up in accordance with the

---

[51] On the considered exclusion of 4Q256 fragment 7b which covers 4Q256 20:1 in this translation see the Textual Note on 1QS 10:13 in 15.3 below.

1QS 10	4Q258 9	4Q260 3
with the measuring line of His fitting pattern. [10]With the arrival of day and night I shall (re)enter the covenant of God and with the departure of evening and morning I shall recount His statutes. And on the basis of them *I shall set up* [11]my boundaries so that there is no (scope for) turning back.	the measuring [line of] His [fitting pa]ttern. Wi[th the arrival of] day [and] ni[gh]t I shall (re)enter the covenant of [10][God and with the departure of evening and morning I shall recount His statutes.] And on the basis of them *I will re-establish* [11][my boundaries so that there is no (scope for) turning back.]	measuring line of His fitting pattern. [2]With [the arrival of day and night I shall (re)enter the covenant of God and wi]th the departure of evening [3]and morning I shall re[count His statutes. And on the basis of them I will re-establish (?) my boundaries s]o that there is no (scope for) turning back.

1QS 10	4Q258 9–10
[11]I will pronounce His judgment according to my corruption, and my wrongdoing shall be engraved like a statute before my eyes. To God I will call out "my righteousness" [12]and to the Most High "architect of my wellbeing, fountain of knowledge, spring of holiness, pinnacle of glory, almighty strength with eternal splendour." I will choose that which [13]He teaches me and I will take delight in the way He disciplines me. Be{.}fore I stir my hands and feet I will bless His name,	[11][I will pronounce His judgment according to my corruption, and] my [wrong]doing [shall be engraved like a statute] [12]before my eyes. [To God I will call out "my righteousness" and to the Most High "arch]itect of my wellbeing, foun[tain of [13]knowledge, spring of holiness, pinnacle of glory, almighty strength with eternal splendour." I will choose] 10[1] that which He teaches [me and I will take delight in the way He disciplines me. Before I stir my hands] [2]and feet I will bless [His name]

1QS 10	4Q256 20[52]	4Q258 10
[13]before going out and coming in, [14]settling or rising and while I lie on my bed I shall rejoice for Him. I shall bless Him with the holy offering emanating from my lips from among the lines of people [15a]before I raise my hand to taste the delights of the fruits of the earth.	[2][before going out and coming in, settling or rising and while I lie on my bed] I shall rejoice for Him. I shall [bless Him [3]with the holy offering emanating from my lips from among the lines of people before I raise my hand] to taste the delights of the fruits of [4][the earth.]	SHORTER TEXT [2][before I raise my hand to taste] [3]the delights of the fru[its of the earth]

---

[52] On 4Q256 20:1 see the comments on 1QS 10:13 in 15:3 below.

1QS 10	4Q256 20	4Q258 10	4Q260 4
[15b]At the onset of fear and terror and in the place of distress (filled) with desolation [16]I shall bless Him *on account of performing* exceedingly marvellous acts, I will ponder *His might* and lean on His loving acts all day long.	[4][At the onset of fear and terror and in the place of distress (filled) with desolation I shall bless] Him *on account of performing* exceedingly marvellous acts, [I will ponder] [5a]*His might* [and lean on His loving acts all day long.	[3][At the onset of fear and terror and in the place of distress] [4](filled) wi[th desolation I shall bless Him on account of performing exceedingly marvellous acts, I will ponder His might and] lea[n on [5]His loving acts all day long.]	[1][At the on]set of fear and terror [and in the place of] distress (filled) with desolation [I shall bless Him] [2]*and (His)* exceedingly marvellous acts, [I will] ponder [His] *mighty deeds* and [lean on His] loving acts, [3]all day long.

15.2.4 God's Judgment and the Psalmist's Anger (1QS 10:16b–24b // 4Q256 20:5b–7 // 4Q258 10:5b–8a // 4Q260 4:3b–5:7)

1QS 10	4Q256 20	4Q258 10	4Q260 4
[16b]*I know that* the judgment of all the living [17]and the truth of *all* His actions lie in His hand.	[5b]*I] know th[at]* the judgment of all the living and the tru[th of *all*] [6][His actions lie in] His [ha]nd.	[5b][I know that the judgment of all the living and the truth of *all* His actions lie in His hand.]	SHORTER TEXT [3b]The judgment of all the living [and the truth of His ac]tions [lie in His hand].
When distress is set free I shall praise Him and on account of His salvation I shall exalt Him also. I shall not repay a person[18] with evil, but I shall pursue the individual with kindness. For with God lies the judgment of all the living and it is He who will render a person his reward.	[When distress is set free I shall praise Him and on account of] His [salvat]ion I shall [exalt Him also. I shall] no[t repay a person [7]with evil, but I shall pursue the individual with kindness. For with God lies the ju]dgment of all the living and it is He [who will render a person his reward.]	[6]When [distress] is set [free I shall praise Him and on account of His salvation I shall exalt Him also. I shall not re]pay [7][a person with evil, but I shall pursue the individual with kindness. For with God lies the judgment of all the living and it is He] [8]who will render [a person his reward.]	When distress [4]is s[et free] I shall praise Him and on account of [His] salvation [I shall exalt Him al]so. I shall not re [pay] [5]a person with evil, [but I shall pursue] the individual with kindness. F[or] with God [lies the judgment of] [6]all the living and it is He who will render a per[son] his [rewa]rd.

1QS 10	4Q260 4–5
[18c]I shall not display jealousy in a spirit of [19]wickedness, and my soul shall not desire property acquired through violence. I shall not {…} seize (opportunities to) quarrel with a person (intent on) [de]struction until the day of vengeance. I shall not deflect [20]my anger from the people of injustice, and I will not be satisfied until He has dispensed judgment. I will not bear a *raging* grudge against those who turn away from wrongdoing, but I will have no compassion [21]with all those who rebel against the way, nor will I comfort the stricken until their conduct is perfect. I will not keep Belial/worthlessness in my heart. Frivolousness and sinful deception [22]shall not be heard in my mouth, treachery and lies shall not be found on my lips. Fruits of holiness shall be on my tongue, but abhorrent (words) [23]shall not be found on it. With praise I shall open my mouth, and my tongue shall recount God's righteous deeds continually alongside the treachery of humanity until the end of [24]their wrongdoing. I will banish emptiness from my lips, impurities and distortions from the knowledge of my heart.	[6]I shall not display jealou[sy] in [a spirit of] [7]wickedness, and my soul [shall not desire] property acquired through violen[ce]. I shall n[o]t seize (opportunities to) qua[rrel with a person (intent on)] destruction un[til the day of venge]ance. I shall no[t deflect] my anger [9]from the people of injustice, and I will n[o]t [be satisfied until He has disp]ensed judgment. [I will not] [10]bear a grudge against those who tu[rn] away from wrongdoing […] *people of* [and I will have no] 5[1][com]passion with all those who rebel against the way, nor will I comfort the stricken until their con[duct] [2]is perfect. I will not keep Belial/worthlessness in my heart. Frivolousness and sinful deception [3]shall not be heard in my mouth, [trea]chery and lies shall not be found on my lips. [4]Fruits of holiness shall be on my tongue *vacat* but abhorrent (words) shall not be found [5]on it. With prai[se I shall o]p[en] *vacat* my mouth, [and] my tongue shall re[count] God's righteous [6]deeds continu[ally alongside the treachery of] humanity un[til the e]nd of their wrongdoing. [I will banish [7]emptiness from my lips, impurities and distortions] from [the knowledge of my heart.]

15.2.5 Secrecy (1QS 10:24c–11:2a)

1QS 10–11

10[24c] With sound counsel I will {conceal} re[co]unt knowledge, [25]with prudent knowledge I will fence […] *h* with a firm boundary in order to preserve faithfulness and strong judgment for God's righteousness. I will prescribe [26]a statute according to the measuring line of the times. [   ] righteousness and devoted love towards the humble, but a firm hand against those who hast[en to make known] 11[1] insights to those whose spirits go astray and to teach those who grumble, to answer humbly in front of the haughty and with a broken spirit to the people of [2a]perversion who point (their) finger and spread wicked talk *vacat* and acquire property.

15.2.6 The Psalmist's Relationship to God (1QS 11:2b–5b)

[2b]As for me, my justice lies with God, in His hand (He holds) the perfection of my conduct as well as the uprightness of my heart. [3]Through His righteous acts he blots out my wrongdoing, for He set free His light from the source of His knowledge, and my eyes have seen His wonders, the light of my heart the mystery of [4]being and happenings of eternity. My right hand is supported, and the path of my steps is on sound rock which will not tremble under any circumstances. For God's truth is [5]the rock of my steps, and His strength is the support of my right hand. From the source of His righteousness emanates my justice, a light shines in my heart because of His marvellous mysteries.

15.2.7 The Psalmist's Privileged Access to Revelation (1QS 11:5c–7a)

My eyes have seen [6]happenings of eternity, wisdom which is hidden from humanity, knowledge and prudent thoughts (concealed) from human[ki]nd, a source of righteousness and a reservoir of [7]strength as well as a spring of glory (undisclosed to) the assembly of flesh.

15.2.8 An Elevated Community in Communion with the Heavenly Realm (1QS 11:7b–9a // 4Q258 12:4)

Those who{ . }[m] God has chosen He has established as an eternal possession

1QS 11	4Q258 12
and He bestowed upon them as an inheritan{ . }[c]e a share in the lot of [8]the holy ones.	[4] [and he bestowed upon] them [as an inheri]tance a share in the lo[t of the holy ones.]

1QS 11
[8]And he united their assembly with the children of heaven to (form) a joint council, the foundation of a holy structure and an eternal planting for all [9]time to come.

15.2.9 The Speaker's Lowly Humanity and Shortcomings Contrasted with Divine Providence and Righteousness (1QS 11:9b–15b // 4Q258 13:1–3 // 4Q264 1–3a)

But I belong to wicked humanity and to the assembly of unjust flesh. My trespasses, my wrongdoings, my sins { . . .} as well as my perverted heart [10]belong to an assembly of worms and those who walk in darkness. For a human being does not determine its path, nor humankind its steps, but judgment belongs to God and from His hand [11]perfect conduct (is granted), on account of His knowledge everything has come into being. He arranges every event according to His plan and without Him nothing is achieved. As for me, when [12]I stagger God's loving acts are my salvation for ever, and if I stumble because of fleshly sinfulness my justice stands in perpetuity on account of God's righteousness. [13]And though He sets free my distress He will deliver me from destruction and guide my steps onto the path.

1QS 11	4Q264
[13]With His kind acts He drew me close and through His loving acts my justice [14]will emerge. With His true righteousness He has judged me and with His abundant goodness	[1][With His kind acts He drew me close and through His loving acts my justice will emerge. With] His true [righteousness] He has judged me and with [His] abundant good[ness]

1QS 11	4Q258 13	4Q264
[14]He will atone for all my trespasses. With His righteousness He will cleanse me from human [15]uncleanness and (from) the sin of human beings so that I may praise God for His righteousness	[1][He will a]tone [2][for all] my [trespass]es. [With His righteousness He will cleanse me from human uncleanness and (from) the sin of hu]man be[ings] [3][so that I may praise God for] His [ri]ghteousness	[2][He will atone for all my trespasses. With His righteousness He will cleanse me from] hu[man uncleanness] and (from) the sin of human beings so that I may praise [God [3]for His righteousness

1QS 11	4Q264
and the Most High for His glory.	and the Most High for His glory.]

15.2.10 A Final Blessing and Restatement of Creaturely Frailty (1QS 11:15c–22 // 4Q256 23:1–3 // 4Q264 3b–10)

1QS 11	4Q264
[15c]Blessed are You, my God, who opens the heart [16]of Your servant to knowledge. Prepare with righteousness all his deeds and raise up the child of Your handmaid according to Your satisfaction with the elect of humanity so that they may take their stand [17]before You forever. For without You no conduct is perfect and without Your approval nothing is accomplished. You have taught [18]all knowledge and every event has occurred with Your approval. There is no other apart from You	[3b][Blessed are You, my God, who opens] the heart of Your servant [to knowledge]. Prepare with [righteous]ness all [his] deed[s [4]and raise up the child of Your handmaid according to Your satisfaction with the elect of humanity so that they may take] their stand before You forever. For without You [5][no conduct is perfect and without Your approval nothing is accomplished. You have] taught all knowledge and every event [6][has occurred with Your approval. There is no other apart from

1QS 11	4Q264
to reply to Your counsel, to comprehend [19]all of Your holy plan, to look upon the depth of Your mysteries and to understand all Your wonders along with the might of [20]Your strength. Who is able to grasp Your glory and what, indeed, is the human being amongst Your wonderful works? [21] What is one born of a woman to reply before You? One fashioned from dust, whose home is food for worms, one created from a piece of [22]nipped off clay	You to reply to] Your [couns]el, to comprehend all of [Your holy] [7]plan, [to look upon the depth of Your mysteries and to understand] all Your wonders along with the might of Your strength. [8][Who is able to grasp Your glory and what, indeed, is the human] being amongst Your wonderful works? [What is] [9]one born of a woman [to reply before You? One fashioned from dust,] whose home is [food for wor]ms, one created from a piece of [9][nipped off] [10]clay

1QS 11	4Q256 23	4Q264
whose predilection is for the dust? What can clay reply and what counsel can one formed by hand convey? *Vacat*	[1][whose predilection is for the dust? What can clay reply? And] what [counsel can one formed by hand] convey? *Vacat* [2][ ]*according to everything* wh[ich] [3][ ] *l* [ ]	[whose predilection is for the dust? What can clay reply?] And what counsel can [one formed by ha]nd convey? *Vacat*

15.3 Textual Notes

9:26 The beginning of this line is damaged until the remains of *qoph* and *he* precede more substantially preserved text. The downstroke of *qoph* was lost after the top layer of parchment peeled away.[53] 4Q258 8:10 does not preserve the missing beginning of 1QS 9:26. The proposed restoration of part of the lacuna in the middle of the line draws on 1QS 10:6 // 4Q256 19:4.

9:26 The form עושיו, literally "his makers," is odd in 1QS. Alexander and Vermes suggest a phonetic spelling for עושהו "his maker."[54] In Ps 149:2 the same spelling occurs[55] in a comparable liturgical context of praise which suggests a shared linguistic environment.

10:1 The scribe left extra space between the first and second word in 1QS (עם קצים) "at the times," perhaps to avoid a damaged part of parchment.[56] A com-

---

[53] For a discussion of various conjectural restorations see Weise, *Kultzeiten*, 6 n. 4.
[54] Alexander and Vermes, DJD 26:116. See also Licht, *Rule Scroll*, 199.
[55] Cf. Wernberg-Møller, *Manual of Discipline*, 139 n. 60.
[56] Cf. Qimron, DSSHW 1:228.

parison of the 1948 photograph by Trever with the recent digital images made available by the Shrine of the Book shows the extent to which the damage after this word has progressed.[57] It is also conceivable that the scribe marked the start of a new column before stepping away and interrupting his labour temporarily.[58]

10:1 The final letter *resh* of the relative pronoun is the result of a scribal correction from *he* in 1QS.[59]

10:1 The form חקקא "He has decreed" attested in 1QS is difficult, and the translation above follows the view that the final *aleph* stands for God (*elohim or el*).[60] The crucial words have not survived in 4Q258 8:11, but the sense is clear.

10:1 The two Hebrew words על מעון "to its place" are written continuously in 1QS. 4Q258 8:11 reads the preposition אל .

10:1 and 5 In 1QS 10:1 and 5 ברשית is spelled without *aleph* in contrast to 4Q258 and 4Q260 which preserve the fuller orthography. In 4Q256 19:3 *aleph* is added above the line.[61]

10:1 The translation and meaning of תקופה in 1QS and 4Q258 8:11 and frequently in the remainder of the Hymn as "turning point" refers to the sun's course in the context of the arrival of daylight and darkness.[62]

10:2 The first word in 1QS, אשמורי "watches of," is an unusual masculine plural construct of a word otherwise attested in the feminine as in 4Q260 2:1.[63]

10:2 With many scholars I supplement the additional space left after the letters עלת in 1QS to read על תבל "over <the world>." Philip Alexander suggests this was caused by a poorly executed draft master text. He raises the possibility that the master copy was the crudely written papyrus manuscript 4Q255.[64] In our view there is stronger cumulative evidence that 1QS copied from a manuscript that resembled 4Q259. It is unfortunate that neither 4Q258 nor 4Q260 preserve this crucial passage. Maier, referring to 2 Sam 22:12 and Ps 3:7, translates וישתהו עלת "sie zu einer Hülle macht" ("makes it into a covering").[65]

10:2 4Q260 2:1 lacks the inseparable preposition and conjunction "and at its turning point" in ובתקופתו, though the lost text immediately preceding in 4Q260 may have attested a preposition as suggested tentatively by Alexander and Vermes.[66] The editors also note the odd space left between *vav* and *pe* in the

---

[57] See Trever, *Scrolls from Qumrân Cave 1*, 144–145.

[58] See 5.1.2 above.

[59] Cf. García Martínez and Tigchelaar, DSSSE, 94.

[60] See, e. g., Brownlee, *Dead Sea Manual*, 38; also Wernberg-Møller, *Manual of Discipline*, 140; Weise, *Kultzeiten*, 8–9 and Maier, *Qumran-Essener* 1, 193 n. 542.

[61] See also 4Q256 20:1 and an 1QS 10:13 below.

[62] Cf. Weise, *Kultzeiten*, 20–22.

[63] Cf. Alexander and Vermes, DJD 26:161 and Qimron, DSSHW 1:228.

[64] Alexander, "Literacy among Jews," 18.

[65] Maier, *Qumran-Essener* 1:194 n. 546; see further Wernberg-Møller, *Manual of Discipline*, 141 n. 7.

[66] Alexander and Vermes, DJD 26:161.

middle of the word.[67] The resulting neat alignment with the vertical ruling may have been a factor for this meticulous scribe.

10:2 The spelling of the infinitive *hiphil* construct באופיע "when (the heavenly lights) shine forth" with *aleph* in 1QS is a further instance of weakened gutturals.[68] The spelling in 4Q258 8:12 with *he* and without *yod* illustrates that not all S manuscripts conform to the full orthography of 1QS.

10:3 4Q256 19:1 reads "His holy height" over against 1QS's "holy height."

10:3 1QS 10:3 and 4Q256 19:1 attest the noun במבוא over against 4Q260 2:3 which reads the infinitive בבוא.

10:3 "On the days of" (לימי) is added above the line in 4Q256 19:1.

10:3–4 On the syntax compare Ps 49:3, 11.[69]

10:4 The *vav* in מסרותם "they succeed" is damaged by a vertical crease in 1QS.

10:4 Burrows and Habermann read הם גדול in 1QS.[70] The reading יום גדול is now confirmed by all three manuscripts from Cave 4 and is followed by recent editions.[71]

10:4 The *gimel* in גדול "great" in 4Q256 19:2 is damaged by a scratch on the surface of the parchment.

10:4 1QS attests a mysterious letter *nun* followed by a *vacat* after the term "sign." Neither the *vacat* nor the *nun* are found in 4Q256 19:2–3 or 4Q258 9:1. This passage is not preserved in 4Q260 but the manuscript has enough space for the *vacat* and/or *nun*. Based on considerations of space Alexander and Vermes tentatively propose restoring נאמנה in 4Q260 2:4,[72] but it is just as possible that 4Q260 included a *vacat* and the ominous *nun* attested in 1QS 10:4. Philip Alexander suggests that the scribe of 1QS copied a poorly legible exemplar that attested an original נאמן "assured."[73]

10:4 The pronominal suffix "His (eternal) love" חסדיו in 1QS is lacking in 4Q258 9:1.

10:5 On the superlinear correction in 4Q256 19:3 see the note on 1QS 10:1 and 5 above.

10:5 Only tiny traces of the tops of the letters of וימי "days" survive at the beginning of 4Q256 19:4.

10:6 At the beginning of this line I identify the remains of an erased composite marginal sign in 1QS that includes a paragraphos at the top. In terms of size the

---

[67] Alexander and Vermes, DJD 26:157, 159.

[68] Cf. Qimron, HDSS, 25.

[69] See Weise, *Kultzeiten*, 33–34 and Wernberg-Møller, *Manual of Discipline*, 141–142.

[70] Cf. also Weise, *Kultordung*, 40–42 for fulsome discussion.

[71] See Qimron, PTSDSSP 1:42; Qimron, DSSHW 1:228 and Alexander and Vermes, DJD 26:123.

[72] Alexander and Vermes, DJD 26:160.

[73] Alexander, "Literacy among Jews," 18 and see on 10:2 above; also Alexander and Vermes, DJD 26:123; Leaney, *Rule of Qumran*, 238; Tov, *Scribal Practices*, 28 and Weise, *Kultzeiten*, 44–45.

erasure is comparable to the marginal sign at 1QS 9:3 This erased sign would have indicated the beginning of the prayer in the first person. Tigchelaar suggests a faintly preserved paragraphos is what we may call collateral damage which occurred when the scribe erased letters at the beginning of this line.[74] However, the area covered by the erasure is compatible with a large marginal sign since it goes beyond the beginning of 1QS 10:6 by protruding into the margin and all the way down to the line below.[75]

10:6 The *he* pefix in "I will bless Him" הברכנו in 1QS is best seen as a consequence of the weakening of the gutturals attested in the DSS.[76] 4Q256 19:4 and 4Q258 9:3 both read אברכנו.[77]

10:6 1QS preserves evidence of an erasure of what looks like wet ink before "years."

10:7 Both here and in 1QS 10:4 "one after the other" is written as one word in contrast to 4Q256 19:2 and 4Q258 9:5.

10:7 *Zayin* in "sowing" is obscured in 1QS as a result of a crack in the parchment. 4Q256 19:6 likely reads the conjunction after "sowing." There are no remains of the top of *lamed*, cf. DJD 26:60–61

10:8 "Fruit of praise" is again written as one word in 1QS.

10:8–9 Several letters are erased at the end of line 8 and the beginning of line 9 in 1QS. Qimron deciphers אשא at the end of line 8 but does not offer a reading for the erasure in line 9. García Martínez and Tigchelaar propose to read an erased *sin* at the start of 1QS 9.[78] It is possible that the scribe started the next word "Let me perform music," now in line 9, with *sin* rather than *zayin* at the end of line 8.[79]

10:9 "God" is written in paleo-Hebrew script in 4Q258 9:8 as was the case in 4Q258 8:9.

10:9 1QS literally reads "the lyre of my harp." 4Q258 9:8 reads a first person impf. *hiphil* of נכה (אכה) "to play an instrument" with initial *aleph* damaged.[80] The poorly preserved first word of 4Q260 3:1 may agree with 4Q258 9:8.[81]

---

[74] Tigchelaar, "Scribe," 442 and Falk, "In the Margins," 23–24.

[75] Cf. also 1.5.1 above and 15.4.2 below.

[76] Cf. Qimron, HDSS, 24–25.

[77] See Alexander and Vermes, DJD 26:123. Reymond offers a number of examples of a confusion between *aleph* and *he* already in the MT, see *Qumran Hebrew*, 104–105; 1QS 8:13 above and 1QS 10:12 below.

[78] García Martínez and Tigchelaar, DSSSE, 94.

[79] See Charlesworth, PTSDSSP 1:45 n. 261.

[80] So already Józef T. Milik, "Texte des variantes des dix manuscrits de la Règle de la Communauté trouvés dans la Grotte 4: Recension de P. Wernberg-Møller, The Manual of Discipline," *RB* 67 (1960): 410–416, 415; also Alexander and Vermes, DJD 26:124.

[81] See Alexander and Vermes, DJD 26:162 and Qimron, DSSHW 1:228.

10:10 The translation of the infinitive of "to be" with preposition *bet* with "on the basis of them" (i. e. the statutes) draws on the context.[82]

10:10 The penultimate letter of אבואה "I shall (re)enter" has been corrected from *he* to *aleph* in 1QS.[83]

10:10 1QS has a different verb, אשים "I shall set up," from 4Q258 9:10 which reads אשיב "I shall re-establish." One can easily imagine a copyist error when copying the final letter.

10:12 There is no need to emend the *he* prefix in הבחרה "I will choose," as this can be regarded as the same phenomenon discussed for הברכנו in 1QS 10:6 above.

10:13 4Q256 7a preserves a generous top margin and the remains of ברייש]ית "before; at the beginning." Neither Qimron nor Martone include fragment 7a in their presentation of 4Q256.[84] Metso identifies the remains of fragment 7a (numbered fragment 9) as paralleling 1QS 7:7 ברוש]ו ("in full").[85] García Martínez and Tigchelaar identify the remains of 4Q256 7a with the occurrence of ברישית in 4Q256 20:1.[86] No reservations are expressed by Alexander and Vermes about the identification of fragment 7a[87] in contrast to their position on fragment 8.[88] While it is possible that fragment 7a is part of 4Q256 its precise identification remains uncertain. The radically different physical appearance of fragment 7a from the top right of fragment 7b, where both Alexander and Vermes and García Martínez and Tigchelaar would place it – is particularly discernible on the LLDSSDL's multi-spectral colour image B-366904 (4Q256 7a) compared to B-366902 (4Q256 7b). The new images make an identification in parallel with 1QS 10:13 unlikely. On the basis of the uncertainty of its identification 4Q256 7a has not been included in the translation of 4Q256 above.

10:13 In the first of the two occurrences of בראשית "before" in 1QS *aleph* is the result of a scribal correction, perhaps from *shin*.[89] As a result the spacing is unusual within this word.

10:13–14 The preserved remains of 4Q258 10:2–3 which consist of the beginning of the lines suggest a text that is shorter than 1QS. There is enough space, however, in 4Q256 20 to accommodate the text of 1QS resulting in a rare divergence between 4Q256 and 4Q258.[90]

---

[82] Cf. Wernberg-Møller, *Manual of Discipline*, 145 and Lohse, *Texte aus Qumran*, 37 who translates "durch ihr Dasein."

[83] See Qimron, DSSHW 1:228 and García Martínez and Tigchelaar, DSSSE 1:94.

[84] See Qimron, PTSDSSP 1:66; Qimron, DSSHW 1:230 and Martone, *Regola*, 50, 52.

[85] Metso, *Textual Development*, 23, 29.

[86] García Martínez and Tigchelaar, DSSSE 1:516.

[87] Alexander and Vermes, DJD 26:40, 61–63; similarly Abegg, "Qumran Non-Biblical Manuscripts."

[88] Alexander and Vermes, DJD 26:40, 63–64 and see the note on 1QS 11:22 below.

[89] Cf. Wernberg-Møller, *Manual of Discipline*, 43 and the note on 1QS 10:1 and 5 above.

[90] See DJD 26:125–126.

10:15 Brownlee, following a suggestion by W. F. Albright, reads ברשות "in the realm of."[91]

10:16 Qimron's reading והפלא in 4Q260 4:2 is to be preferred to בהפלא read by Alexander and Vermes.[92] 4Q260 4:2 attests a plural noun with suffix ובגבורות]יו.[93]

10:16 *Aleph* has elided in מודה "very."[94]

10:16 The phrase ואדעה כי "I know that" attested in 1QS and 4Q256 is lacking from 4Q260.

10:19 With Wernberg-Møller I read *ryb* "quarrel."[95]

10:19 The expected final *yod* in the construct plural "people of destruction" is lacking in 1QS which reads "a person (intent on) destruction."[96]In addition, initial *shin* of "destruction" was omitted due to haplography and subsequently added superlinearly.[97] The crucial word "a person" is not preserved in 4Q260 4:7. Nor is there sufficient space in 4Q260 for the article in "destruction." The term "humanity" (אנוש) occurs in the Hymn in 1QS 11:6, 10; 1QS 11:15 // 4Q264 2.

10:19 The words "seize (opportunities to)" and "until the day of" are added above the line in 1QS after an erasure of several words. García Martínez and Tigchelaar decipher the remains of the erasure as "I shall not {bear a grudge against those who return/repent.}"[98]

10:20 1QS includes a reference to באף "raging" that is lacking from 4Q260.

10:20 4Q260 4:10 attests a longer text than 1QS, though it is not possible to offer any reconstruction with confidence based on the only remaining word "the people of."[99]

10:21 4Q260 5:1 reads "I will have no compassion on the straightforward ones" בנכוחים where 1QS has בנכאים "the stricken" with *aleph* rather than *khet*. Alexander and Vermes acknowledge a likely corruption in 4Q260.[100] Our translation presupposes emending to בנכוהים "the stricken" also in 4Q260. The cause of the corruption might have been homoioteleuton with the ending of the preceding verb (נחם).

10:21 Several letters (*vav, yod* and *ayin*) in "and Belial/worthlessness" have been crudely corrected in 1QS.[101] The noun Belial seems to be the reference here

---

[91] Brownlee, *Dead Sea Manual*, 40–41; also Levy, *Wörterbuch* 4:472.

[92] Alexander and Vermes, DJD 26:162–163.

[93] Cf. Qimron, DSSHW 1:228. A plural with a contracted third masc. plural suffix in 1QS and 4Q256 is also possible, cf. on 1QS 11:3 below and DJD 26:164.

[94] See Qimron, HDSS, 25 and 1QS 4:1 above.

[95] Wernberg-Møller, "Reflections," 49.

[96] See "אנוש I" in HAWTTM 1:148–150, 150.

[97] Cf. Alexander and Vermes, DJD 26:163 and Reymond, *Qumran Hebrew*, 24.

[98] García Martínez and Tigchelaar, DSSSE, 96–97.

[99] Alexander and Vermes, DJD 26:165.

[100] Alexander and Vermes, DJD 26:166–167.

[101] Cf. Qimron, DSSHW 1:228.

rather than the proper name. Brownlee has drawn attention to Deut 15:9 for a similar usage.[102]

10:22 Several letters (second *vav* and *nun*) in עוון "sin" have again been corrected in 1QS.[103] Inspecting the digital images at high magnification reveals that the parchment is worn out and the skin looks flawed at this point. The same is true above and below the previous word כחש "deception."

10:22–23 Both *vacat*s in 4Q260 5:4–5 are caused by a flaw in the leather.[104]

10:24 The only surviving trace preserved of 4Q260 5:7 are the remains of the letter *mem*.[105]

10:24 The penultimate word in this line has been corrected in 1QS. The *tav* of an original אסתר "I shall conceal" has been marked for deletion and replaced above the line with *pe* yielding the antonym אספר "I shall recount." Both readings yield good sense, though the corrected text destroys the parallelism with the phrase that follows and contradicts the message of the section.[106]

10:25 Our reading "I will prescribe" for the last word of this line follows Qimron.[107]

10:26 Our reading and reconstruction of the last two words again follow Qimron.[108]

11:1–2 The codicological features of 1QS 11 are exceptional.[109]

11:1: *Kaph* is substituted for *gimel* in "grumbling."[110]

11:1–2 On the designation "people of perversion" see Ezek 9:9.[111]

11:2 The empty space in 1QS does not make sense from a content point of view. There is no visible damage to the surface of the skin though the first two letters of the following phrase, "acquiring wealth," appear to be written with a freshly dipped pen, see also the word immediately above in 11:1.

11:3 The plural suffix in "His righteous acts" has contracted.[112]

11:4 The translation "they will not tremble" follows an emendation to יזדעזע proposed by Brownlee who credits comments by H. L. Ginsberg.[113]

11:6 *Vav* has been added above the line in "humankind" (אנוש) in 1QS, cf. 1QS 10:19.

---

[102] See Wernberg-Møller, *Manual of Discipline*, 148 n. 68.

[103] Cf. Qimron, DSSHW 1:228.

[104] See Alexander and Vermes, DJD 26:166 and Plate 17. On 1QS 10:23 see further Wernberg-Møller, "Reflections," 45.

[105] Cf. Alexander and Vermes DJD 26:166.

[106] For discussion and further literature see Wernberg-Møller, *Manual of Discipline*, 149.

[107] Qimron, PTSDSSP 1:46.

[108] Qimron, DSSHW 1:228.

[109] See 1.5 above.

[110] Cf. Qimron, HDSS, 27.

[111] See also Wernberg-Møller, *Manual of Discipline*, 150 n. 4.

[112] Further, Reymond, *Qumran Hebrew*, 144–145.

[113] See Brownlee, *Dead Sea Manual*, 43 as well as 1QS 8:7–8 and parallels in Chapter 8 above.

11:7 Final *resh* in the relative pronoun has been added above the line in 1QS after an erasure.

11:7 *Lamed* has been added above the line after an erasure in 1QS in "He bestowed upon them as an inheritance a share" (ינחילם). The space available for the correction is overgenerous which suggests hesitation on the part of the scribe as he was copying this word, perhaps because he was struggling with a damaged *Vorlage*.

11:9 There is evidence of three erased letters after "my sins" in 1QS.

11:15 The preposition *lamed* in לאל is partially effaced in 1QS in what looks like smudged ink that reaches to the line immediately above.

11:15 The transition to the Final Blessing is marked by a paragraphos in 1QS as well as an in-text dicolon.[114]

11:16 The translation "child of Your truth" favoured by Lohse destroys the parallelism between עבד "servant" and אמת "maidservant."[115]

11:20 The phrase "what indeed is the human being" resembles 1QH[a] 18:5 where אף הואה is written as one word (אפהו).[116] The article in "the human being" has been added above the line in 1QS. In 1QH[a] 18:5 the term human being (*adam*) is not determined.

11:21 Note the two cancellation dots in "what is one born of a woman to reply" which are positioned to indicate or clarify the separation of the two words.[117]

11:21 The form "he was fashioned" מגבלו is not attested in Biblical Hebrew. However, Wernberg-Møller draws attention to the Peshitta's rendering of Gen 2:7 with the root *gbl*.[118]

11:21 The phrase "His home is food for worms" is best understood figuratively as a reference to the human body.

11:21 The last word in this line in 1QS has given rise to a series of readings. Alexander and Vermes read מצוורדק and translate "formed from semen," taking רוק "spit" as a euphemism.[119] Wernberg-Møller reads מצי רוק and translates "he who is saliva which has been emitted."[120] On this reading the construct is written continuously. The letters which Wernberg-Møller and others take to be a second

---

[114] Cf. Tov, *Scribal Practices*, 211.

[115] Lohse, *Texte aus Qumran*, 43.

[116] See Kutscher, *Language*, 440.

[117] So already Milik as quoted Wernberg-Møller, *Manual of Discipline*, 154 who reads "what can he who is born of a woman be reckoned," drawing on Isa 29:16 and based on the suggestion that an intial root letter *khet* dropped out as a consequence of a weakening of the gutturals. The same verb recurs in 1QS 11:22 where Wernberg-Møller translates similarly. Alexander and Vermes restore 4Q264 and translate line 9 (1QS 11:21) along the same lines as Wernberg-Møller, but then restore and translate the analogous phrase in line 10 (1QS 11:22) as I do, see DJD 26:203–206. Leaney also translates each occurrence distinctly "how shall he that is born of woman dwell" (1QS 11:21) and "what answer shall clay give" (1QS 11:22), *Rule of Qumran*, 236.

[118] Wernberg-Møller, *Manual of Discipline*, 154.

[119] Alexander and Vermes, DJD 26:203–206.

[120] Wernberg-Møller, *Manual of Discipline*, 39, 43.

noun "saliva" (רוק) are written at a downwards tilting angle in 1QS, perhaps in an effort to fit the word in at the end of the line. The reading is confirmed by 4Q264 9 as well as 4Q511 (Songs of the Maskil) 28–29 3–4 and 1QH[a] (Hodayot) 20:35–36.[121] Curiously, all three witnesses present the construct also written continuously. Crucially, the infra-red image of 4Q264 by Shai Halevi LLDSSDL B-360432 suggests that the final words of 4Q264 9 are written without any inter-word space (מצי/ורוקחמר). The material evidence of both 1QS 11:21 and 4Q264 line 9 can be accommodated by reading מצורוק with Émile Puech.[122] Puech takes the form not as a construct but as a noun of the root צרק prefaced by the pre-position "from." His reading results in a construct with "clay" that can be trans-lated "one created from a piece of clay." Puech notes the semantic connection between the roots צרק "a small piece of dough or clay" and the inverted con-sonants in the root קרץ "to mould, pinch." The entire construct phrase is written continuously in 4Q264. The imagery, both here and in the subsequent line, draws on the work of the potter.[123]

11:22 The translation "whose predilection is for the dust" for ולעפר תשוקתו is based on the results of the detailed philological analysis of תשוקה in the Hebrew Bible, the ancient Versions and the Dead Sea Scrolls by Andrew Macintosh.[124]

11:22 Alexander and Vermes raise serious doubts about the identification of 4Q256 fragment 8 which they present as parallel to 11:22.[125] The presence of remains of additional text in 4Q256 8:2–3 that is not attested in any other S manuscript, following what is clearly the end of 1QS, is significant. Alexander and Vermes argue that the presence of "additional text" is a key consideration in raising doubts about the identification of 4Q256 8.[126] A number of scholars do not include this fragment in their editions.[127] However, any reservations about the identification of this fragment ought to be based on material consid-erations rather than the inclusion here of text not found in other S manuscripts which privileges some witnesses over others. Alexander and Vermes comment on the shape of *lamed* in 4Q256 8:2 and also suspect a "decapitation" of the letter.[128] Our examination of the most recent multi-spectral digital images and the original fragment confirm a sizeable hole where the top of the *lamed* would

---

[121] See also 1QH[a] 23:28, 36 and Schuller and Newsom, *Hodayot*, 64–65, 70–71.

[122] Puech, "Note de lexicographie de hébraïque qumrânienne (*m-ṣw/yrwq, mḥšbym, śwṭ*)," in *Solving Riddles and Untying Knots: Biblical, Epigraphic, and Semitic Studies in Honor of Jonas C. Greenfield*. Edited by Ziony Zevit, Seymour Gitin and Michael Sokoloff (Winona Lake, IN: Eisenbrauns, 2005), 181–189, here 181–184. Puech notes the semantic connection between the root צרק and the inverted consonants in the root קרץ.

[123] I am grateful to Noam Mizrahi for a private conversation on this passage.

[124] Andrew Macintosh, "The Meaning of Hebrew תשוקה," *JSS* 61 (2016): 365–387.

[125] Alexander and Vermes, DJD 26:46, 63–64.

[126] Alexander and Vermes, DJD 26:63.

[127] See, e. g., Qimron, PTSDSSP 1:66; Qimron, DSSHW 1:230; García Martínez and Tigchelaar, DSSSE 1:516 and Martone, *Regola* 50, 52, 115.

[128] Alexander and Vermes, DJD 26:63–64.

have been.[129] Metso's suggestion that the additional words are the remains of a closing statement is appealing though impossible to verify.[130]

The only other manuscript to preserve the end of the Final Hymn is 4Q264 which also attests the remains of stitching that indicates the presence of a further sheet.[131]

15.4 Commentary

Different themes characterize this Hymn which is more accurately described as a liturgical anthology. As a result the material below is divided into a number of sub-sections. This presentation does not preclude considerable thematic connections between the sub-sections. The textual picture is, on the whole, stable and supported by five manuscripts. The most substantial point of textual divergence occurs in 1QS 10:13–15 // 4Q256 20:1–3 // 4Q258 10:2–4 where 4Q256 and 4Q258 cover the same ground but appear to diverge. This is noteworthy given the substantial proximity of these two manuscripts where they cover the same material, see 15.3 and 1.5 above. Taking into account that this divergence occurs in a liturgical context such variation between two manuscripts that are otherwise closely affiliated may tell us more about their liturgical source material that the author-compilers drew upon. Another possibility is that shared source material was either shortened in 4Q258 or expanded in 4Q256.

15.4.1 Introductory Rubric (1QS 9:26b–10:1a // 4Q258 8:10–11a)

It is difficult to establish the beginning of this new section with certainty because of the fragmentary nature of 1QS 9:26 // 4Q258 8:10–11a. However, it seems clear that what is preserved of 1QS 9:26b–10:1a // 4Q258 8:10–11a introduces the topic of prayer and may therefore be taken as an introduction to the Hymn that follows. The person instructed to praise in the third person and the first person voice we hear in the Hymn is the Maskil in the three witnesses that attest references to this figure (1QS, 4Q 256 and 4Q 258). It seems likely that the hymnic material originated independently, at least in part, and became secondarily associated with the Maskil and incorporated into some manuscripts of the Rule. This figure is the antecedent of the third person singular admonition to praise in 1QS 9:26. The Hymn is, therefore, also referred to as the Maskil's Hymn.[132]

---

[129] The relatively distinctive wording מה יבין followed by a sizeable *vacat* supports the tentative identification upheld in DJD 26 and Abegg, "Qumran Non-Biblical Manuscripts."

[130] Metso, *Textual Development*, 23 where the fragment is numbered 12.

[131] See 1.5.11 above.

[132] For a discussion of significant connections and concerns expressed in the Final Hymn and parts of the Community Rules that describe the Maskil's sphere of influence see 15.1.4 above.

9:26 The reference to God as "his maker" in a call to praise and rejoicing is reminiscent of Ps 149:2.[133] Similar language is also used in the blessing that forms part of the expulsion ceremony at the end of the Damascus Document in 4Q266 11:9.[134]

10:1a It is noteworthy that the root "to engrave" (חקק), which often refers to the halakhic sphere, is here associated with blessing rather than statutes. It is clear that the boundaries between these two channels of relating to the divine will are not absolute and certainly both fall within the remit of the Maskil.[135]

15.4.2 Calendar for Praise (1QS 10:1b–8 // 4Q256 19:1–6 // 4Q258 8:11b–9:7a // 4Q260 2:1–5)

Commentators are divided on whether or not 1QS 9:26b–10:8 // 4QS is part of the Final Hymn. Thus, Weise treats 1QS 9:26b–10:8 as a an originally independent unit (a "Kultordnung") which was incorporated here by the author of 1QS to precede the Final Hymn.[136] Similarly Knibb identifies 1QS 10:1b–8a as "a liturgical calendar" which he considers as a separate section.[137] While the calendar of praise is distinctive, it is clear that the Hymn is composite and draws on several sub-sections that have been blended together by a redactor.

A number of passages (1QS 10:4b–5a; 6a; 6c–7a and 8b) stand apart from the calendar proper and offer expansions that disrupt the pattern of listing daily and seasonal times. Thus, Weise recognized early on that the liturgical calendar ("die eigentliche Kultordnung") has been supplemented at the point of its integration in the Community Rules.[138] The formulaic language of the calendar suggests the integration of a pre-existing liturgical source.[139] A comparable liturgical calendar is found in 1QHᵃ 20:7–12 // 4Q427 8 ii // 4Q428 12 ii.[140] The latter calendar is similarly associated with the Maskil as clearly preserved in 4Q427 8 ii 10 and 4Q428 12 ii 3. The expansions mentioned above broaden the calendric interest of the scheme to include a future and eternal perspective and repeatedly refer to the speaker as bound by statutes engraved forever. The formally distinct nature

---

[133] See further Ps 95:6, Job 35:10 and 15.3 above.

[134] Cf. 3.1 above and on the increased emphasis on creation in liturgical texts from the Second Temple period see Pajunen, "Praise of God."

[135] See 5.4 above.

[136] Weise, *Kultzeiten*, 8–9, 57.

[137] Knibb, *Qumran Community*, 144; see further Gayer, "Centrality of Prayer and Stability of Trust," 320–321; Goedhart, *Slothymne*, 8–9; Penner, *Patterns of Daily Prayer*, 137–140; Talmon, *Qumran from Within*, 212–224 and Tanzer, "Sages," 164.

[138] Weise, *Kultzeiten*, 56–57 where he identifies additions in 1QS 10:6a, 8b that are related to the introductory rubric, see 15.4.1 above and Falk, *Daily, Sabbath and Festival Prayers*, 104.

[139] So Weise, *Kultzeiten*, 47.

[140] See 15.1.5 above; Schuller and Newsom, *Hodayot*, 62–65; Falk, *Daily, Sabbath and Festival Prayers*, 100–103 and Weise, *Kultzeiten*, 12–20.

of 1QS 10:4 is recognised by Alexander and Vermes who describe it as "a parenthesis within the list of times of prayer."[141]

As Falk has argued, the admonition to offer blessings at dawn and dusk suggests that prayer was more likely a part of the Temple liturgy than a substitute.[142] Given the insights we have gained about an acute awareness of exposure to malevolent forces at liminal times such as when day gives way to night and vice versa it is likely that both sacrifices and prayers at such times would have offered a sense of security.[143]

Prayer is also associated with the annual seasons, as well as months and sabbaths, both in the Final Hymn and in the prayer corpus that has survived from Qumran including Daily Prayers (4Q503), the Words of the Luminaries (4Q504; 4Q506) which refer to prayers for the days of the week including the sabbath, as well as Festival Prayers (1Q34+34bis, 4Q507, 4Q508 and 4Q509+505). The non-Masoretic prose text David's Compositions that forms part of the Qumran Psalms Scroll refers to prayers for every day of the year (365).[144] A sabbath liturgy is presupposed in the Songs of the Sabbath Sacrifice and again in David's Composition which refers to 52 songs associated with the Sabbath (11QPsalms^a [11Q5] 27:7). The calendar for praise includes the beginnings of the year (1QS 10:6b // 4QS), year weeks (seven-year periods) that culminate in the year of release or sabbatical year (1QS 10:7c–8a // 4QS). This calendrical scheme is interspersed with a reference to the major points in the agricultural year such as sowing, growth and harvest (1QS 10:7b // 4QS on which compare 4Q509 3:6; 8:4 // 4Q508 22+23:3 [Festival Prayers]). Similar references to daily praise alongside a more longitudinal framework feature also in the War Scroll (1QM 14:13–14).

Overall, the emphasis is on a well-ordered temporal axis where the cosmos, the heavens, time and prayer all form a comforting and orderly whole. Moreover, I argued in 5.4.1 above that obedience to the law is likewise organically connected to such a scheme and the figure of the Maskil in 4Q256 9:1 // 4Q258 1:1. Bilhah Nitzan has drawn attention to "cosmological hymns that create an experience of harmony with the entire universe through the performance of God's law at the appointed times."[145] A view that promotes the idea of a well-ordered cosmos intrinsically connected to liturgical and legal practices tapped into a fundamental desire for exerting control over an unpredictable world. The same sentiment is expressed in 1QH^a 9:18–19, 26.

10:1b–3a The psalmist is instructed to pray at dawn and dusk – or conveivably pledges to do so based on the switch from a third person singular framework

---

[141] Alexander and Vermes, DJD 26:123.

[142] Falk, *Daily, Sabbath and Festival Prayers*, 218 and Chapter 11 above.

[143] Cf. 1.2.1 and 15.1.2 above.

[144] See 11QPsalms^a (11Q5) 27:2–11 and Falk, *Daily, Sabbath and Festival Prayers*, 95–96.

[145] Bilhah Nitzan, "Harmonic and Mystical Characteristics in Poetic and Liturgical Writings from Qumran," *JQR* 85 (1994): 163–183, esp. 183.

established in 9:26–10:1a to the first person in 1QS 10:8 // 4Q258 9:7. Such a practice is advocated in a number of sources including 4Q503 (Daily Prayers) and 4Q504; 4Q506 (Words of the Luminaries).[146] As Bilhah Nitzan has observed these times line up with the cycle of morning and evening sacrifice.[147] Such liminal times when darkness gives way to light and vice versa would have exposed the psalmist and his fellow Jews to the fear of an attack from demonic forces. Thus, Penner has observed that 1QM 18:5 locates the prayer at the climax of the eschatological battle at sunset and stresses the importance of prayer in the War Scroll as the climactic final confrontation with the forces of evil comes into view.[148]

10:3b–4a The significant celestial turning points of months ("new moons") are now in focus. Some have suggested that these lines refer to the seasons.[149] It is preferable, however, to take the references to "the days of the new moon" (ימי חודש) at face value.

10:5–6 The reference to "the beginning of the months" (ברשית ירחים) refers to solar months in distinction from new moons. The appointed times and holy days for rememberance have been interpreted in various ways including as festivals which are associated more widely with remembrance in Num 10:10.[150]

10:6 In the context of the annual cycle "the turning point of their appointed times" is best taken to refer to the solstices and equinoxes.

10:6 The opening words of this line display close verbal correspondences with the opening rubric introducing the Hymn which strengthens the case for regarding statements such as these that interrupt the liturgical calendar proper as secondary expansions.[151] In the Textual Notes above I identify the presence of an erased composite scribal sign that marks the point at which the voice of the psalmist is first heard.[152] Given the potent position of the uncorrected marginal sign at the point where the speaker is first given a voice in the Hymn, it is likely that the original sign was purposefully positioned here. It may be compared to the two erased paragraphoi in the Covenant Ceremony that mark the point at which priests and levites begin to speak after a double amen.[153]

---

[146] See Esther Chazon, "4QDibHam: Liturgy or Literature?" *RevQ* 15 (1992): 447–455; Falk, *Daily, Sabbath, and Festival Prayers*, 59–124 and Weise, *Kultzeiten*, 25–27.

[147] Bilhah Nitzan, "The Dead Sea Scrolls and the Jewish Liturgy," in *The Dead Sea Scrolls as Background to Postbiblical Judaism and Early Christianity: Papers from an International Conference in St Andrews in 2001*. Edited by James Davila. STDJ 46 (Leiden: Brill, 2003), 195–219, 207.

[148] Penner, *Patterns of Daily Prayer*, 161–162 and n. 53.

[149] Weise, *Kultzeiten*, 32–46 and Holm-Nielsen, *Hodayot*, 203 note 30.

[150] See Falk, *Daily, Sabbath and Festival Prayers*, 189–190 and Nitzan, *Qumran Prayer*, 89–109.

[151] See also 1QS 10:8.

[152] Cf. 1.5.1.3 and 15.3 above.

[153] Cf. our discussion of 1QS 1:20 and 1QS 2:10 in 1.5.1.3 and Chapter 3 above. See further Falk, "In the Margins," 24.

10:7 The seasonality of the year features unambiguously here where we have references to sowing, growth and harvest.

10:4 As the Hymn proceeds, the term אות "sign" is used with reference to the creation of evening, morning and blessing, a combination that also occurs in 4Q408 (Apocryphon of Moses^c). The precise meaning of the term *'ot* – so crucial in 4Q319 as discussed in 15.1.1 above – has been disputed over centuries in scholarship. It occurs in Jer 10:2 where Jeremiah is warning against the learning of the nations who are disturbed by the signs of the heavens. Ben-Dov speaks of an "entire school of cosmological thought in Second Temple Judaism" that goes against prophetic reservations expressed in Jeremiah.[154]

10:6a A good case has been made suggesting that the tone of the words "(with) an offering of the lips I will bless Him according to the statute engraved forever" stands apart from the enumeration of cultic times in the surrounding material. Weise assigns this passage to the author of 1QS ("der Verfasser von 1QS").[155]

10:6–7 Noteworthy here are references to "statute" (חוק) and "judgment" (משפט) in the context of 1QS 10:6–7 // 4Q256 19:5 // 4Q258 9:3–5.[156]

10:8 1QS and 4Q258 9:7 read "portion of my lips" (מנחת שפתי) here rather than "offering of the lips" (תרומת שפתים) which we find in 1QS 10:6 // 4Q256 19:4 above. Also noteworthy is the preceding reference to "the fruit of praise" (פרי תהילה) which establishes a connection to the firstfruits (cf. Deut 26:2) or especially the fourth year produce which is described as a praise offering (הלולים) in Lev 19:24.[157]

10:8 Many commentators advocate a caesura after 10:8.[158] Based on their assessment of the calendarical material as a separate composition and not part of the Final Hymn Weise and Knibb take 1QS 10:8b // 4Q258 9:7a as the transition between the liturgical calendar and the Hymn proper.[159]

15.4.3 Timely Music and Praise of God (1QS 10:9–16a // 4Q256 20:2–5a // 4Q258 9:7b–10:5a // 4Q260 3:1–3; 4:1–3a)

This section of the Hymn still deals with timely praise of God but focuses on particular liturgical actions and their motivations. The section begins in 1QS 10:9 // 4Q258 9:7b with the psalmist's commitment to musical offerings in

---

[154] See Ben-Dov, DJD 21:209.

[155] Weise, *Kultzeiten*, 56–57. On the idea of an engraved statute which here refers to the cosmic order see Weise, *Kultzeiten*, 29–30, 49–51.

[156] On the study of the law at a time of trials see 4Q525 (Beatitudes) 2–3 ii 6; also and 1.2.1 as well as 6.4.4.3 above.

[157] On the significance of the language of an "engraved statute" on the lips of the Maskil see Newman, *Before the Bible*, 114–115.

[158] Cf. 15.4.2 above.

[159] Weise, *Kultzeiten*, 9–10, 57 and Knibb, *Qumran Community*, 144.

praise of God's glory and in accordance with God's judgment. 1QS 10:10–12b // 4Q258 9:9b–13a // 4Q260 3:2–3 juxtaposes the speaker's sense of covenantal obligations and inadequacies with God's splendour as a source of his wellbeing. 1QS 10:12c–16a outlines times for praise as well reflections on the reassurance of God's mighty deeds when coming and going, sleeping and waking, enjoying food and times of distress. A number of these occasions are liminal times when securing divine protection was deemed particularly necessary and beneficial.[160]

10:9 For Goedhart this marks the beginning of the Final Hymn which can be divided into four psalms. The first psalm runs from 1QS 10:9–17 and is classified as dealing with Praise.[161]

10:9 The references to lyre and harp suggest instrumental music was part of liturgical practice envisaged here. The lyre also occurs in the apotropaic Songs of the Maskil in 4Q511 10:7–8.[162]

10:9 Our translation of משפטו "His fitting pattern" here follows Kister.[163]

10:10 The Maskil commits to a daily (re)entry into the covenant in the morning alongside a recitation of the commandments in the evening.

10:11 The reference to divine judgment initiates a theme that is developed further elsewhere in the Hymn.[164]

10:12 The divine epithet "Most High" occurs also in 1QS 4:22; 10:12; 11:15 and parallels.

10:13b–14a These lines allude to Deut 6:7.[165] Shemaryahu Talmon has argued that the psalmist's words represent the view that the day began at sunrise rather than sunset as presupposed in Deut 6:7.[166] Weise concludes that the Hymn reflects times for the recital of the Shema here.[167]

10:13–14 The shorter text attested by 4Q258 is likely more original than 1QS and 4Q256.

---

[160] Cf. Esther G. Chazon, "'The Road Not Taken:' Prayer in Rabbinic and Nonrabbinic Sources," in *The Faces of Torah: Studies in the Texts and Contexts of Ancient Judaism in Honor of Steven Fraade.* Edited by Michal Bar-Asher Siegal, Tzvi Novick and Christine Hayes. JAJSup 22 (Göttingen: Vandenhoeck & Ruprecht, 2017), 603–618. On the role of prayer and praise in keeping malevolent forces at bay see also 15.1.2 above.

[161] Goedhart, *Slothymne*, 8–10, 18–67; see also Tanzer, "Sages," 164.

[162] See 1 Sam 16 and Guerra, "Encountering Evil," 187–189. See also Eva Mroczek, "Hegemony of the Biblical," 6 on David's "exemplary liturgical and calendrical legacy;" Mrozcek, "Hymns" in *The Dictionary of the Bible and Ancient Media.* Edited by Tom Thatcher et al. (London: Bloomsbury, 2017), 180–183, 181 and Najman, *Past Renewals*, 189–204 on exemplarity. On the figure of the Maskil see further Hempel, "Biblical Views."

[163] Kister, "Physical and Metaphorical Measurements," 155

[164] Cf. "the judgment of all the living" in 1QS 10:16–17 // 4Q256 20:5 // [4Q258 10:5] // 4Q260 4:3; "[the judgment of] all the living" in 1QS 10:18 // 4Q256 20:7 // [4Q258 10:7] // [4Q260 4:5–6]) and "the judgment of the people of injustice" in 1QS 10:20 // 4Q260 4:9.

[165] See Falk, "Qumran Prayer Texts and the Temple," 116.

[166] Shemaryahu Talmon, *The World of Qumran from Within: Collected Studies* (Jerusalem: Magnes; Leiden: Brill, 1989), 175–178.

[167] Weise, *Kultzeiten*, 30–32.

10:13–14 For the idea of praying upon waking see Sir. 39:5.

10:14 The description of the psalmist's prayer emanating as an offering of the lips "from among the lines of people" refers to neatly arranged lines and suggests a collective liturgical event. The term "arrangement, battle line" (מערכה) is found frequently in the War Scroll with reference to battle formations. It is suggestive to imagine an allusion to the carefully stratified communal hierarchy in prayer. Given 4Q258's shorter text at this point the reference to this collective act of worship appears to be lacking in that manuscript.

10:15a Rather than the characteristic term בראשית "before" this line reads בטרם, otherwise attested only one more time at 1QS 6:5 // [4Q258 2:9] also in a liturgical context. Moreover, all three manuscripts (1QS; 4Q256; 4Q258) attest the only occurrence of עדן "delight" here in the Community Rules. Taken together the vocabulary employed here is somewhat distinctive.

10:15 It is striking how "the onset of fear and terror" (ברשית פחד ואימה) is presented as a routinely experienced, regular state of unrest to be neutralised with a disarming liturgical response of praise.[168]

15.4.4 God's Judgment and the Psalmist's Anger (1QS 10:16b–24b // 4Q256 20:5b–7 // 4Q258 10:5b–8a // 4Q260 4:3b–5:7)

This material deals with God's judgment. Others have proposed a different delimitation (1QS 10:17b–11:2a).[169]

15.4.5 Secrecy (1QS 10:24c–11:2a)

This sub-section is made up of a polemical account dealing with secrecy, betrayal and property.[170] On discretion as a quality expected of the Maskil see 1QS 9:21–22 // 4Q258 8:6–7 // 4Q259 4:3–4 above and 15.4.7 below.

15.4.6 The Psalmist's Relationship to God (1QS 11:2b–5b)

The speaker describes his position as elevated both in terms of his conduct and access to refined knowledge and mysteries in the form of a first person account.

---

[168] See 15.1.2; cf. also 1QS 1:17 // 4Q256 2:2 (see 3.4.1 above) and 1QS 3:14 (see 4.4.1 above).

[169] Goedhart, *Slothymne*, 8–10, 68–125 and Tanzer, "Sages," 164. Tanzer describes the context as dealing with "the role of the righteous man in God's scheme of judgment." See also Gayer, "Centrality of Prayer and the Stability of Trust" as well as 5.4.6 and 8.4.2 above.

[170] On the emphasis on secrecy in the context of ancient prayer traditions see Matthias Klinghardt, "Prayer Formularies for Public Recitation: Their Use and Function in Ancient Religion," *Numen* 46 (1999): 1–52, 41–45.

15.4.7 The Psalmist's Elevated Access to Revelation (1QS 11:5c–7a)

The theme of the psalmist's privileged access to revelation is developed further with a more focused emphasis on his ability to access esoteric knowledge. The language here has been aptly described by Joseph Angel as a "discourse of knowledge" associated with the Maskil both here and in 4Q511 (Songs of the Sage) 28–29 3.[171]

15.4.8 An Elevated Community in Communion with the Heavenly Realm (1QS 11:7b–9a // 4Q258 12:4)

This textual unit no longer employs universal language but picks up themes from the central columns of the Community Rules such as "council of a community," the idea of the community as signifying a holy structure and the figure of the eternal planting.[172] This passage interrupts the first person account and is likely an interpolation.

The idea of a liturgical union found here is attested in a number of texts from Qumran including the Songs of the Sabbath Sacrifice (e. g. 4Q400 2:1, 6), the Hodayot (e. g. 1QHᵃ 11:21–23) and the Rule of Blessings (1QSb 4.24–26).[173]

15.4.9 The Speaker's Lowly Humanity and Shortcomings Contrasted with Divine Providence and Righteousness (1QS 11:9b–15b // 4Q258 13:1–3 // 4Q264 1–3a)

This account of the speaker's lowly state is again framed in universal human terms. The speaker locates his low estate as part an assembly of unjust flesh. Scholars have long drawn attention to the self-deprecating statements that are attested in the Final Hymn, the Songs of the Maskil (4Q511)[174] as well as the Hodayot.[175] By contrast, the psalmist's claim to privileged revelation in

---

[171] Angel, "Maskil, Community, and Religious Experience," 6.

[172] Cf. 8.2.2 and 8.4.2 above.

[173] See Gideon Bohak, "Mystical Texts, Magic, and Divination," in CDSS, 457–466, 458–462; Falk, *Daily, Sabbath and Festival Prayers*, 126–149; Michael R. Jost, "Yaḥad, Maśkil, Priests and Angels: Their Relation in the Community Rule (1QS)," in *Law, Literature, and Society in Legal Texts from Qumran.* Edited by Jutta Jokiranta and Molly Zahn. STDJ 128 (Leiden: Brill, 2019), 207–229 and Pajunen, "Praise of God," 484–487.

[174] See, e. g., 4Q511 28–29 3–4.

[175] See already Heinz-Wolfgang Kuhn, *Enderwartung und gegenwärtiges Heil: Untersuchungen zu den Gemeindeliedern von Qumran.* SUNT 4 (Göttingen: Vandenhoeck & Ruprecht, 1966), 27–29. More recently cf. Carol Newsom, "Deriving Negative Anthropology Through Exegetical Activity: The Hodayot as Case Study," in *Is There a Text in this Cave? Studies in the Textuality of the Dead Sea Scrolls in Honour of George J. Brooke.* Edited by Ariel Feldman, Maria Cioată and Charlotte Hempel. STDJ 119 (Leiden: Brill, 2017), 258–274.

15.4.7 above located the rest of humanity emphatically outside of this privileged domain. Such inconsistencies further support the view that the Hymn is a composite anthology that includes a range of material and lacks a sense of conceptual consistency.

11:9–12 These lines have been considered as particulary illuminating for the Palestinian Jewish background to Paul's writing on grace.[176]

15.4.10 A Final Blessing and Restatement of Creaturely Frailty (1QS 11:15c–22 // 4Q256 23:1–3 // 4Q264 3b–10)

This blessing forms a climactic moment in the Final Hymn. Despite the ubiquitous emphasis on the timeliness and content of blessing and praise, this is the first direct address to God.[177] The final blessing acknowledges the elevation of the psalmist to a group referred to as "the elect of humanity." This extra-ordinary phrase combines both the universal language that characterises much of the Hymn with the idea of a select sub-group. The speaker makes an appeal for divinely facilitated knowledge and righteous behaviour. He also looks forward to a time when the elect of humanity will stand before God in perpetuity. This climactic moment is followed by a final juxtaposition of God's mysterious plans, wondrous deeds and unfathomable glory with the lowly place of humanity.[178]

This blessing, which constitutes the end of the Hymn in two of the three pre-served manuscripts, forms a fitting conclusion to the Community Rules in those manuscripts. The prospect of permanent security as one of a select group be-fore God signals the possibility of closure regarding the precarious liminality that characterises the community and individual members in much of the Rules, see 1.2.1 and 1.4 above. The language used to refer to this chosen group as "the elect of humanity" – while distinctive within the Rules – builds on the idea of the fundamental remoteness of the human condition from the glorious divine realm. That the moment of the speaker's elevation should be described in terms that acknowledge his shared humanity dramatically bridges the prevelant an-thropological-theological divide that underlies much of the Hymn. A return, in closing, to affirm humanity's creaturely frailty now reads as if the psalmist felt he over-reached himself but also reinforces the sense that the elevation that is hoped for has not yet been achieved.

---

[176] See Joseph Fitzmyer S. J., *The Dead Sea Scrolls and Christian Origins* (Grand Rapids, MI: Eerdmans, 2000), 28–29.

[177] Cf. also Newsom, *Self and Symbolic Space*, 173.

[178] For an analysis of the language "one born of a woman" attested in 1QS 11:21 and the book of Job see Newsom, "Deriving Negative Anthropology," 268.

Bibliography*

Abegg, Martin G. Jr., *The Dead Sea Scrolls Concordance. Volume One: The Non–Biblical Texts from Qumran [Parts 1–2]* (Leiden: Brill, 2003).

–, "Qumran Non-Biblical Manuscripts (QUMRAN)," Accordance module, Version 4.5 (Altamonte Springs, FL: OakTree Software, 1999–2018).

Adler, Yonatan, "Second Temple Period Ritual Baths Adjacent to Agricultural Installations: The Archaeological Evidence in Light of Halakhic Sources," *JJS* 59 (2008): 62–72.

–, "The Hellenistic Origins of Jewish Ritual Immersion," *JJS* 69 (2018): 1–21.

Aitken, James K., *The Semantics of Blessing and Cursing in Ancient Hebrew* (Leuven: Peeters, 2007).

Aksu, Ayhan, "A Palaeographical and Codicological (Re)assessment of the Opisthograph 4Q433a/4Q255," *DSD* 26 (2019): 170–188.

Alexander, Philip, S., "Literacy among Jews in the Second Temple Period: Reflections on the Evidence from Qumran," in *Hamlet on a Hill: Semitic and Greek Studies Presented to Professor T. Muraoka on the Occasion of his Sixty-Fifth Birthday.* Edited by Martin F. J. Baasten and Wido Th. van Peursen. Orientalia Lovaniensia Analecta 118 (Leuven: Peeters, 2003), 3–25.

–, "Physiognomy, Initiation, and Rank in the Qumran Community," in *Geschichte – Tradition – Reflexion. Festschrift Martin Hengel. Volume 1: Judentum.* Edited by Hubert Cancik, Hermann Lichtenberger and Peter Schäfer (Tübingen: Mohr Siebeck, 1996), 1:385–394.

–, "The Redaction-History of *Serekh ha-Yahad*: A Proposal," *RevQ* 17 (1996): 437–453.

–, "The Demonology of the Dead Sea Scrolls," in *The Dead Sea Scrolls After Fifty Years. Volume II: A Comprehensive Assessment.* Edited by Peter W. Flint and James C. VanderKam (Leiden: Brill, 1999), 331–353.

–, "'Wrestling against Wickedness in High Places:' Magic in the Worldview of the Qumran Community," in *The Scrolls and the Scriptures: Qumran Fifty Years After.* Edited by Stanley E. Porter and Craig A. Evans. JSP Supplements 26 (Sheffield: Sheffield Academic Press, 1997), 318–337.

Anderson, Arnold A., "The Use of *Ruah* in 1QS, 1QH, and 1QM," *JSS* 7 (1962): 293–303.

Angel, Joseph L., "Maskil, Community, and Religious Experience in the Songs of the Sage (4Q510–511)," *DSD* 19 (2011): 1–27.

Arnold, Russell C. D., *The Social Role of Liturgy in the Religion of the Qumran Community.* STDJ 60 (Leiden: Brill, 2006).

Avermarie, Friedrich, "'Tohorat Ha-Rabbim' and 'Mashqeh Ha-Rabbim:' Jacob Licht Reconsidered," in *Legal Texts and Legal Issues: Proceedings of the Second Meeting of*

---

* For frequently cited works see Abbreviations Including Frequently Cited Sources above, XXI–XXII.

the IOQS in Honor of Joseph M. Baumgarten. Edited by Moshe Bernstein, Florentino García Martínez and John Kampen. STDJ 23 (Leiden: Brill, 1997), 215–229.

Baker, Cynthia, "When Jews were Women," *History of Religions* 45 (2005): 114–134.

Bakker, Arjen, "תָּכַן *tākan*," ThWQ 3:1123–1128.

–, "The Figure of the Sage in *Musar le-Mevin* and *Serek ha-Yahad*" (PhD diss., Katholieke Universiteit Leuven, 2015).

Barkay, Gabriel et al., "The Amulets from Ketef Hinnom: A New Edition and Evaluation," *BASOR* 334 (2004): 41–71.

Barthélemy, Dominique O. P., "Notes en marge de publications récentes sur les manuscrits de Qumran," *RB* 59 (1952): 187–218.

Baumgärtel, Friedrich, "Zur Liturgie der 'Sektenrolle' vom Toten Meer," *ZAW* 65 (1953): 263–265.

Baumgarten, Albert I., "Graeco-Roman Voluntary Organizations and Ancient Jewish Sects," in *Jews in a Graeco-Roman World*. Edited by Martin Goodman (Oxford: Oxford University Press, 1999), 93–111.

–, "Information Processing in Ancient Jewish Groups," in *Sectarianism in Early Judaism: Sociological Advances*. Edited by David Chalcraft (Cambridge: Cambridge University Press, 2014), 246–255.

–, *The Flourishing of Jewish Sects in the Maccabean Era: An Interpretation*. JSJSup 55 (Leiden: Brill, 1997).

Baumgarten, Joseph M., "Sacrifice and Worship among the Jewish Sectarians of the Dead Sea (Qumrân) Scrolls," *HTR* 46 (1953): 141–159.

–, "Scripture and Law in 4Q265," in *Biblical Perspectives: Early Use and Interpretation of the Bible in Light of the Dead Sea Scrolls*. Edited by Michael E. Stone and Esther G. Chazon. STDJ 28 (Leiden: Brill, 1998), 25–33.

–, "The Cave 4 Versions of the Qumran Penal Code," *JJS* 43 (1992): 268–276.

–, "The Duodecimal Courts of Qumran, Revelation, and the Sanhedrin," *JBL* 95 (1976): 59–78.

Beall, Todd S., *Josephus' Description of the Essenes Illustrated by the Dead Sea Scrolls*. SNTSMS 58 (Cambridge: Cambridge University Press, 1988).

Becker, Michael, "תִּירוֹשׁ *tîrôš*," ThWQ 3:1118–1120.

Ben-Dov, Jonathan, *Head of All Years: Astronomy and Calendars at Qumran in Their Ancient Context*. STDJ 78 (Leiden: Brill, 2008).

–, "Ideals of Science: The Infrastructure of Scientific Activity in Apocalyptic Literature and in the Yahad," in *Ancient Jewish Sciences and the History of Knowledge*. Edited by Jonathan Ben-Dov and Seth Sanders (New York, NY: New York University Press, 2014), 109–152.

Ben-Dov, Jonathan and Daniel Stökl Ben Ezra, "4Q249 Midrash Moshe: A New Reading and Some Implications," *DSD* 21 (2014): 131–149.

Bergmeier, Roland, *Die Essenerberichte des Flavius Josephus: Quellenstudien zu den Essenertexten im Werk des jüdischen Historiographen* (Kampen: Kok Pharos, 1993).

Berner, Christoph, "'Mind the Step' (Exod. 20:26), or, even better: 'Wear Breeches!' (Exod. 28:42–43): The Issue of (Un)Covering One's 'Shame' in Cultic Legislation," in *Clothing and Nudity in the Hebrew Bible*. Edited by Christoph Berner et al. (London: Bloomsbury, 2019), 417–434.

Bernstein, Moshe, *Reading and Re-Reading Scripture at Qumran: Law, Pesher and the History of Interpretation*. STDJ 107/2 (Leiden: Brill, 2013).

Betz, Otto, *Offenbarung und Schriftforschung in der Qumransekte*. WUNT 6 (Tübingen: Mohr Siebeck, 1960).

Beyerle, Stefan and Andreas Ruwe, "A Comparison of the 'Penal Code' in the Damascus Document and in the Serekh ha-Yaḥad from a Literary Perspective," *DSD* 25 (2018): 359–384.

Blenkinsopp, Joseph, "Interpretation and the Tendency to Sectarianism: An Aspect of Second Temple History," in *Jewish and Christian Self-Definition*. Edited by Ed P. Sanders (Philadelphia, PA: Fortress, 1981), 2:1–26.

Bockmuehl, Markus, "Redaction and Ideology in the Rule of the Community (1QS/4QS)," *RevQ* 18 (1998): 541–560.

Bohak, Gideon, *Ancient Jewish Magic: A History* (Cambridge: Cambridge University Press, 2008).

–, "Mystical Texts, Magic, and Divination," in CDSS, 457–465.

Brand, Miryam, *Evil Within and Without: The Source of Sin as Portrayed Within Second Temple Literature*. JAJSup 9 (Berlin: De Gruyter, 2013).

Brooke, George J., "4Q341: An Exercise for Spelling and for Spells?" in *Writing and Ancient Near Eastern Society: Papers in Honour of Alan R. Millard*. Edited by Piotr Bienkowski, Christopher Mee and Elizabeth Slater (London: T&T Clark, 2005), 271–282.

–, "Aspects of the Theological Significance of Prayer and Worship in the Qumran Scrolls," in *Prayer and Poetry in the Dead Sea Scrolls and Related Literature: Essays in Honor of Eileen Schuller on the Occasion of Her 65th Birthday*. Edited by Jeremy Penner, Ken M. Penner and Cecilia Wassén. STDJ 98 (Leiden: Brill, 2012), 35–54.

–, "Between Scroll and Codex? Reconsidering the Qumran Opisthographs," in *On Stone and Scroll: Essays in Honour of Graham Ivor Davies*. Edited by James K. Aitken, Katharine J. Dell and Brian A. Mastin. BZAW 420 (Berlin: De Gruyter, 2011), 123–138.

–, "Choosing Between Papyrus and Skin: Cultural Complexity and Multiple Identities in the Qumran Library," in *Jewish Cultural Encounters in the Ancient Mediterranean and Near Eastern World*. Edited by Mladen Popović, Myles Schoonover and Marijn Vandenberghe. JSJSup 178 (Leiden: Brill, 2017), 119–135.

–, *Exegesis at Qumran: 4QFlorilegium in Its Jewish Context*. JSOTSup 29 (Sheffield: JSOT, 1985).

–, "Isa 40:3 and the Wilderness Community," in *New Qumran Texts and Studies: Proceedings of the First Meeting of the International Organization for Qumran Studies, Paris 1992*. Edited by George J. Brooke and Florentino García Martínez. STDJ 15 (Leiden: Brill, 1994), 117–132.

–, "Isaiah in Some of the Non-Scriptural Dead Sea Scrolls," in *Transmission and Interpretation of the Book of Isaiah in the Context of Intra- and Interreligious Debates*. Edited by Florian Wilk and Peter Gemeinhardt. BETL 280 (Leuven: Peeters, 2016), 243–260.

–, "Reading, Searching and Blessing: A Functional Approach to Scriptural Interpretation in the יחד," in *The Temple in Text and Tradition: A Festschrift in Honour of Robert Hayward*. Edited by George J. Brooke and Timothy McLay. LSTS 83 (London: Continuum, 2015), 140–156.

–, *Reading the Dead Sea Scrolls: Essays in Method*. EJL 39 (Atlanta, GA: SBL, 2013).

–, "Room for Interpretation: An Analysis of Spatial Imagery in the Qumran Pesharim," in *The Dead Sea Scrolls: Texts and Context*. Edited by Charlotte Hempel. STDJ 90 (Leiden: Brill, 2010), 309–324.

–, *The Dead Sea Scrolls and the New Testament* (Minneapolis, MN: Fortress, 2005).

Brownlee, William H., *The Dead Sea Manual of Discipline: Translation and Notes*. BASOR Supplementary Studies 10–12 (New Haven, CT: ASOR, 1951).

Burrows Millar with the assistance of John C. Trever and William H. Brownlee, *The Dead Sea Scrolls of St. Mark's Monastery. Volume II, Fascicle 2: Plates and Transcription of the Manual of Discipline* (New Haven, CT: ASOR, 1951).

Callegher, Bruno, "The Coins of Khirbet Qumran from the Digs of Roland de Vaux: Returning to Henri Seyrig and Augustus Spijkermann," in *The Caves of Qumran: Proceedings of the International Conference, Lugano 2014*. Edited by Marcello Fidanzio. STDJ 118 (Leiden: Brill, 2017), 221–235.

Carmignac, Jean, "Conjecture sur la première ligne de la Règle de la Communauté," *RevQ* 2 (1959): 85–87.

Chan, Michael J., "יָשַׁב jāšab," ThWQ 2:302–309.

Charlesworth, James H., ed., *The Dead Sea Scrolls: Hebrew, Aramaic, and Greek Texts with English Translations. Rule of the Community and Related Documents* (PTSDSSP 1), Tübingen/Louisville, KY: Mohr Siebeck/Westminster John Knox, 1994.

Chazon, Esther G., "'The Road Not Taken:' Prayer in Rabbinic and Nonrabbinic Sources," in *The Faces of Torah: Studies in the Texts and Contexts of Ancient Judaism in Honor of Steven Fraade*. Edited by Michal Bar-Asher Siegal, Tzvi Novick and Christine Hayes. JAJSup 22 (Göttingen: Vandenhoeck & Ruprecht, 2017), 603–618.

–, "4QDibHam: Liturgy or Literature?," *RevQ* 15 (1992): 447–455.

Christian, Meike, "The Literary Development of the 'Treatise of the Two Spirits' as Dependent on Instruction and the Hodayot," in *Law, Literature and Society in Legal Texts from Qumran*. Edited by Jutta Jokiranta and Molly Zahn. STDJ 128 (Leiden: Brill, 2019), 153–184.

Cohen, Yehudah, *Tangled Up in Text: Tefillin and the Ancient World*. BJS 351 (Providence RI: Brown University, 2008).

Collins, John J., *Beyond the Qumran Community: The Sectarian Movement of the Dead Sea Scrolls* (Grand Rapids, MI: Eerdmans, 2010).

–, "Cosmos and Salvation: Jewish Wisdom and Apocalyptic in the Hellenistic Age," *HR* 17 (1977): 121–142.

–, "Prayer and the Meaning of Ritual in the Dead Sea Scrolls," in *Prayer and Poetry in the Dead Sea Scrolls and Related Literature: Essays in Honor of Eileen Schuller on the Occasion of Her 65th Birthday*. Edited by Jeremy Penner, Ken M. Penner and Cecilia Wassén. STDJ 98 (Leiden: Brill, 2012), 69–85.

–, "Proverbial Wisdom and the Yahwist Vision," in *Gnomic Wisdom*. Edited by John D. Crossan. Semeia 17 (Chico, CA: Scholars Press, 1980), 1–17.

–, "The Construction of Israel in the Sectarian Rule Books,' in *Judaism in Late Antiquity Part 5: The Judaism of Qumran. A Systemic Reading of the Dead Sea Scrolls*. Edited by Alan J. Avery-Peck, Jacob Neusner and Bruce D. Chilton. HdO 57 (Leiden: Brill, 2001) 1:25–42.

–, "The Nature and Aims of the Sect Known from the Dead Sea Scrolls," in *Flores Florentino: Dead Sea Scrolls and Other Early Jewish Studies in Honour of Florentino García Martínez*. Edited by Anthony Hilhorst, Émile Puech and Eibert Tigchelaar. JSJSup 122 (Leiden: Brill, 2007), 31–52.

–, "The Yaḥad and 'The Qumran Community,'" in *Biblical Traditions in Transmission: Essays in Honour of Michael A. Knibb*. Edited by Charlotte Hempel and Judith Lieu. JSJSup 111 (Leiden: Brill, 2006), 81–96.

–, "Wisdom Reconsidered, in Light of the Scrolls," *DSD* 4 (1997): 265–281.

Conklin, Blane W., "Alleged Derivation of the Dead Sea Scroll Term *Serek*," *JSS* 52 (2007): 45–57.

Coser, Lewis A., *Greedy Institutions: Patterns of Undivided Commitment* (New York, NY: The Free Press, 1974).

Cothenet, Édouard, "Le Document de Damas," in *Les Textes de Qumrân*. Edited by Jean Carmignac, Édouard Cothenet and Hubert Lignée (Paris: Letouzey et Ané, 1963), 2:129–204.

Crawford, Sidnie White, *Scribes and Scrolls at Qumran* (Grand Rapids, MI: Eerdmans, 2019).

–, *The Temple Scroll and Related Texts*. CQS 2 (Sheffield: Sheffield University Press, 2000).

Cross, Frank M., "Introduction," in John C. Trever, *Scrolls from Qumrân Cave I: The Great Isaiah Scroll-The Order of the Community-The Pesher to Habakkuk*. Edited by Frank Moore Cross, David Noel Freedman and James A. Sanders (Jerusalem: The Albright Institute of Archaeological Research and the Shrine of the Book, 1972), 1–5.

–, "The Development of the Jewish Scripts," in *The Bible and the Ancient Near East: Essays in Honor of William Foxwell Albright*. Edited by G. Ernest Wright; London: Routledge and Kegan Paul, 1961), 133–202.

–, "The Paleographical Dates of the Manuscripts," PTSDSSP1: 57.

Cross, Frank M. and Esther Eshel, "Ostraca from Khirbet Qumrân," *IEJ* 47 (1997): 17–28.

Dahmen, Ulrich, "צָדוֹק *ṣādôq*," ThWQ 3:379–383.

David-Barrett, Tammas and Robin I. Dunbar, "Fertility, Kinship and the Evolution of Mass Ideologies," *Journal of Theoretical Biology* 427 (2017): 20–27.

Davies, Philip R., *Sects and Scrolls: Essays on Qumran and Related Topics*. South Florida Studies in the History of Judaism 134 (Atlanta, GA: Scholars Press, 1996).

Davila, James R., *Liturgical Works*. Eerdmans Commentaries on the Dead Sea Scrolls (Grand Rapids, MI: Eerdmans, 2000).

Delcor, Mathias, "V. Doctrines des Esséniens I. L'Instruction des Dieux Esprits," *DBSup* 9:960–970.

Dimant, Devorah, "נָדַב *nādab*," ThWQ 2:879–883.

–, "The Composite Character of the Qumran Sectarian Literature as an Indication of Its Date and Provenance," *RevQ* 88 (2006): 615–30.

–, *History, Ideology and Bible Interpretation at Qumran: Collected Studies*. FAT 90 (Tübingen: Mohr Siebeck, 2014).

–, "Time, Torah and Prophecy at Qumran," in *History, Ideology and Bible Interpretation at Qumran: Collected Studies*. FAT 90 (Tübingen: Mohr Siebeck, 2014), 301–314

–, "The Volunteers in the Rule of the Community – A Biblical Notion in Sectarian Garb," *RevQ* 23 (2007): 233–245.

Dombrowski, Bruno W. W., *Wider die Hellenisierung jüdischer Religion: Die Qumran-Assoziation nach dem 'Manual of Discipline' (QS)*. Qumranica Mogilanensia (Krakow: Enigma, 1998).

Drawnel, Henryk, "Qumran and the Ancient Near East," in CDSS, 109–118.

Duhaime, Jean, "Les voies des deux esprits (1QS iv 2–14): Une analyse structurelle," *RevQ* 75 (2000): 349–67.

–, "L'instruction sur les deux esprits et les interpolations dualistes a Qumrân," *RB* 84 (1977): 566–94.

Dupont-Sommer, André, "L'instruction sur les deux Esprits dans le 'Manuel de Discipline,'" *RHR* 142 (1952): 5–35.

–, *The Dead Sea Scrolls: A Preliminary Survey*. Trans. Margaret Rowley (Oxford: Blackwell, 1952).

Eckhardt, Benedikt, "Meals and Politics in the *Yaḥad*: A Reconsideration," *DSD* 17 (2010): 180–209.

–, "The Yahad in the Context of Hellenistic Group Formation," in CDSS, 86–96.

Elgvin, Torleif, "מַשְׂכִּיל," ThWQ 2:802–806.

–, "The Yahad is More than Qumran," in *Enoch and Qumran Origins: New Light on a Forgotten Connection*. Edited by Gabriele Boccaccini (Grand Rapids, MI: Eerdmans, 2005), 273–279.

Eshel, Esther, "Apotropaic Prayers in the Second Temple Period," in *Liturgical Perspectives: Prayer and Poetry in Light of the Dead Sea Scrolls*. Edited by Esther Chazon with Ruth Clements and Avital Pinnick. STDJ 48 (Leiden: Brill, 2003), 69–88.

–, "4Q477: The Rebukes by the Overseer," *JJS* 45 (1994): 111–122.

Evans, Paul S., "Creating a New 'Great Divide:' The Exoticization of Ancient Culture in Some Recent Applications of Orality Studies to the Bible," *JBL* 136 (2017): 749–764.

Fabry, Heinz-Josef, "אָסַף 'āsap," ThWQ 1:251–255.

–, "עֵת 'et," ThWQ 3:243–253.

–, "קוּם qûm," ThWQ 3:509–516.

Falk, Daniel K., "Berakhot," in CDSS, 289–301.

–, *Daily, Sabbath and Festival Prayers in the Dead Sea Scrolls*. STDJ 27 (Leiden: Brill, 1998).

–, "In the Margins of the Dead Sea Scrolls," in *Bible as Notepad: Tracing Annotations and Annotation Practices in Late Antique and Medieval Biblical Manuscripts*. Edited by Liv I. Lied and Marilena Maniaci. Manuscripta Biblica 3 (Berlin: De Gruyter, 2018), 10–38.

–, "Liturgical Texts," in CDSS, 422–434.

–, "Material Aspects of Prayer Manuscripts at Qumran," in *Literature or Liturgy? Early Christian Hymns and Prayers in the Literary and Liturgical Context in Antiquity*. Edited by Clemens Leonhard and Helmut Löhr (Tübingen: Mohr Siebeck, 2014), 33–87.

–, "Religious Life at Qumran," in *Celebrating the Dead Sea Scrolls: A Canadian Collection*. Edited by Peter W. Flint, Jean Duhaime and Kyung S. Baek. EJL 30 (Atlanta, GA: SBL, 2011), 253–286.

–, "The Contribution of the Qumran Scrolls to the Study of Ancient Jewish Liturgy," in *The Oxford Handbook of the Dead Sea Scrolls*. Edited by Timothy H. Lim and John J. Collins (Oxford: OUP, 2010), 617–651.

Fatkin, Danielle Steele, "Invention of a Bathing Tradition in Hasmonean Palestine," *JSJ* 50 (2019): 155–177.

Feldman, Ariel, "On Amulets, Apotropaic Prayers, and Phylacteries: The Contribution of Three New Texts from the Judean Desert," in *Petitioners, Penitents, and Poets: On Prayer and Praying in Second Temple Judaism*. Edited by Ariel Feldman and Timothy Sandoval. BZAW (Berlin: De Gruyter, forthcoming).

Feldman, Ariel and Faina, "4Q147: An Amulet?" *DSD* 26 (2019): 1–29.

–, "4Q148 (4QPhylactère U): Another Amulet from Qumran?," *JSJ* 50 (2019): 197–222.

Feldman, Ariel, Maria Cioată and Charlotte Hempel (eds), *Is There a Text in this Cave? Studies in the Textuality of the Dead Sea Scrolls in Honour of George J. Brooke*. STDJ 119 (Brill, Leiden, 2017).

Fitzgerald, Aloysius F. S. C., "MTNDBYM in 1QS," *CBQ* 36 (1974): 495–502.

Fitzmyer, Joseph A. S. J., *The Dead Sea Scrolls and Christian Origins* (Grand Rapids, MI: Eerdmans, 2000).

Flusser, David, *Judaism of the Second Temple Period: Volume 1. Qumran and Apocalypticism*. Trans. Azzan Yadin (Grand Rapids, MI: Eerdmans; Jerusalem: Magnes, 2007).

–, "Qumrân and Jewish 'Apotropaic' Prayers," *IEJ* 16 (1966): 194–205.

Fox, Michael V., *Proverbs 1–9*. AB 18 (New Haven, CT: Yale University Press, 2000).

Fraade, Steven D., *Legal Fictions: Studies of Law and Narrative in the Discursive Worlds of Ancient Jewish Sectarians and Sages*. JSJSup 147 (Leiden: Brill, 2011).

–, "Interpretive Authority in the Studying Community at Qumran," *JJS* 44 (1993) 46–69.

–, "Midrashim," in EDSS 1:548–552.

–, "Rhetoric and Hermeneutics in Miqṣat Maʿaśeh ha-Torah (4QMMT): The Case of the Blessings and Curses," *DSD* 10 (2003): 150–161.

–, "To Whom It May Concern: 4QMMT and Its Addressee(s)," *RevQ* 19 (2000): 507–526.

Fredriksen, Paula, "Did Jesus Oppose the Purity Laws," *Bible Review* 11 (1995): 18–25.

Freedman, David N. and Kenneth A. Mathews, *The Paleo-Hebrew Leviticus Scroll (11QPaleoLev)* (Winona Lake, IN: Eisenbrauns for ASOR, 1985).

Freidenreich, David M., "Food and Table Fellowship," in *The Jewish Annotated New Testament*. Edited by Amy-Jill Levine and Marc Zvi Brettler (New York, NY: Oxford University Press, 2011), 521–24.

Frey, Jörg, "Different Patterns of Dualistic Thought in the Qumran Library," in *Legal Texts and Legal Issues: Proceedings of the Second Meeting of the International Organization for Qumran Studies Published in Honour of Joseph M. Baumgarten*. Edited by Moshe Bernstein, Florentino García Martínez and John Kampen. STDJ 23 (Leiden: Brill, 1997), 275–335.

Furstenberg, Yair, "Controlling Impurity: The Natures of Impurity in Second Temple Debates," *Dine Israel* 30 (2015): 163–196.

García Martínez, Florentino, "¿Sectario, no-sectario, o qué? Problemas de una taxonomía correcta de los textos qumránicos," *RevQ* 23 (2008): 383–394.

Gaster, Theodor, *The Scriptures of the Dead Sea Sect in English Translation* (London: Secker & Warburg, 1957).

Gayer, Asaf, "The Centrality of Prayer and the Stability of Trust: An Analysis of the Hymn of the Maskil in 1QS IX,25b–XI,15a," in *Ancient Jewish Prayers and Emotions: Emotions Associated with Jewish Prayer In and Around the Second Temple Period*. Edited by Stefan Reif and Renate Egger-Wenzel (Berlin: De Gruyter, 2015), 317–334.

Gillihan, Yonder Moynihan, *Civic Ideology, Organization, and Law in the Rule Scrolls: A Comparative Study of the Covenanters' Sect and Contemporary Voluntary Associations in Political Context*. STDJ 97 (Leiden: Brill, 2011).

–, "Posture or Gesture? A Note on לשח/לשוח in the Qumran Penal Codes," *RevQ* 24 (2009): 291–296.

Glessmer, Uwe, "The Otot-Texts (4Q319) and the Problem of Intercalations in the Context of the 364-Day Calendar," in *Qumranstudien: Vorträge und Beiträge der Teilnehmer des Qumranseminars auf dem internationalen Treffen der Society of Biblical Literature, Münster, 25–26. Juli 1993*. Edited by Heinz-Josef Fabry, Armin Lange and Hermann Lichtenberger. Schriften des Institutum Judaicum Delitzschianum 4 (Göttingen: Vandenhoeck & Ruprecht, 1996), 125–164.

Goedhart, Hendrik, *De Slothymne van het Manual of Discipline: A Theological-Exegetical Study of 1QS X,9–XI,22* (Rotterdam: Bronder Offset, 1965).

Golden, Mark, "Did the Ancients Care When Their Children Died?," *Greece and Rome* 35 (1988): 152–163.

Goldman, Liora, "4Q408 Prayers," in Ariel Feldman and Liora Goldman, *Scripture and Interpretation: Qumran Texts that Rework the Bible*. Edited and Introduced by Devorah Dimant. BZNW 449 (Berlin: De Gruyter, 2014), 323–350.

Goodman, Martin, "The Qumran Sectarians and the Temple in Jerusalem," in *The Dead Sea Scrolls: Texts and Context*. Edited by Charlotte Hempel STDJ 90 (Leiden: Brill, 2010), 277–87.

Greenfield, Jonas, Michael E. Stone and Esther Eshel, *The Aramaic Levi Document: Edition, Translation, Commentary*. SVTP 19 (Leiden: Brill, 2004).

Grossman, Maxine L., "Inferring Holy Perfection in a Wholly Imperfect World: Cognitive Approaches to Perfection Structures in the Dead Sea Scrolls," Paper Presented at the Annual Meeting of the SBL. San Antonio, TX. 20 November 2016.

–, *Embodying Perfection: Sex, Gender, and the Social World of the Qumran Rule Scrolls*, forthcoming.

–, "Postmodern Questions and Sexuality Studies," in CDSS, 246–256.

–, "Reading 4QMMT: Genre and History," *RevQ* 20 (2001): 3–21.

Guerra, Tupá, "Encountering Evil: Apotropaic Magic: in the Dead Sea Scrolls," (PhD diss., University of Birmingham, 2017).

Guilbert, Pierre, "La Règle de la Communauté," in Jean Carmignac and Pierre Guilbert, *Les Textes de Qumran: Traduit et Annotés* (Paris: Letouzey et Ané, 1961), 11–80.

Gzella, Holger, "פלג *plg*," ThWQ 3:287–292.

Habermann, Abraham Meir, ʿ*Edah We-ʿEduth: Three Scrolls from the Judaean Desert. The Legacy of a Community* (Jerusalem: Maḥbaroth Le-Sifruth, 1952).

Hachlili, Rachel, "Communal Meals at Qumran Revisited," *RevQ* 28 (2016): 215–256.

Harding, Gerald Lankester, "Introductory," DJD 1:3–7.

Harkins, Angela K., "Who is the Teacher of the Teacher Hymns? Re-Examining the Teacher Hymns Hypothesis Fifty Years Later," in *A Teacher for All Generations: Essays in Honor of James C. VanderKam*. Edited by Eric Mason et al. JSJSup 153 (Leiden: Brill, 2012), 449–467.

Harrington, Hannah, "Purity," EDSS 2:724–728.

–, *The Purity Texts*. CQS 5 (London: T & T Clark, 2004).

Hartog, Pieter B., *Pesher and Hypomnema: A Comparison of Two Commentary Traditions from the Hellenistic Roman Period*. STDJ 121 (Leiden: Brill, 2017).

Hawley, Robert, "On Maśkil in the Judean Desert," *Henoch* 28 (2006): 43–77.

Hempel, Charlotte, "4QMMT in the Context of the Dead Sea Scrolls and Beyond," in *Qumran 4QMMT: Some Precepts of the Law*. Edited by Reinhard G. Kratz et al. Sapere (Tübingen: Mohr Siebeck, forthcoming).

–, "סֶרֶךְ *særæk*," ThWQ 2:1111–1117.

–, "Biblical Views: Where are the Scribes in the Dead Sea Scrolls?," *BAR* July/August (2018): 52, 68.

–, "Bildung und Wissenswirtschaft im Judentum zur Zeit des Zweiten Tempels," in *Was ist Bildung in der Vormoderne?* Edited by Peter Gemeinhardt (Tübingen: Mohr Siebeck, 2019), 229–244.

–, "Curated Communities: Refracted Realities on Social Media and at Qumran," in *The Dead Sea Scrolls and Ancient Media Culture*. Edited by Travis Williams, Chris Keith and Loren Stuckenbruck. STDJ (Leiden: Brill, forthcoming).

–, "Cutting the Cord with the Familiar: What Makes 4Q265 Miscellaneous Rules Tick?" in *Sibyls, Scriptures, and Scrolls: John Collins at Seventy.* Edited by Joel Baden, Hindy Najman and Eibert Tigchelaar. JSJSup 175 (Brill, Leiden, 2016), 534–541.

–, "Interpretative Authority in the Community Rule Traditions," *DSD* 10 (2003): 59–80.

–, *Qumran Rule Texts in Context: Collected Studies.* TSAJ 154 (Tübingen: Mohr Siebeck, 2013).

–, "Reflections on Literacy, Textuality, and Community in the Qumran Dead Sea Scrolls," in *There a Text in this Cave?* Edited by Feldman, Cioată and Hempel, 69–82.

–, "Rules," in CDSS, 405–412.

–, "Self-Fashioning in the Dead Sea Scrolls: Thickening the Description of What Rule Texts Do," in *Social History of the Jews within the Ancient World.* Edited by Jonathan Ben-Dov and Michal Bar-Asher Siegal. TSAJ (Tübingen: Mohr Siebeck, forthcoming).

–, "Shared Traditions: Points of Contact Between S and D." in *The Dead Sea Scrolls: Transmission of Traditions.* Edited by Metso, Najman and Schuller, 115–131.

–, "The Apotropaic Function of the Final Hymn in the Community Rule," in *Petitioners, Penitents, and Poets: On Prayer and Praying in Second Temple Judaism.* Edited by Ariel Feldman and Timothy Sandoval. BZAW (Berlin: De Gruyter, forthcoming).

–, "The Community and Its Rivals According to the Community Rule from Caves 1 and 4," *RevQ* 21 (2003): 47–81.

–, *The Damascus Texts.* CQS 1 (Sheffield: Sheffield Academic Press, 2000).

–, "The Dead Sea Scrolls: Challenging the Particularist Paradigm," in *Torah, Temple, Land: Ancient Judaism(s) in Context.* Edited by Bernd Schröter. TSAJ (Tübingen: Mohr Siebeck, forthcoming).

–, "The Earthly Essene Nucleus of 1QSa," *DSD* 3 (1996): 253–269 [reprinted as Chapter 3 in Hempel, *Qumran Rule Texts in Context*].

–, "The Essenes," in *Religious Diversity in the Graeco-Roman World.* Edited by Dan Cohn-Sherbok and John M. Court (Sheffield: Sheffield Academic Press, 2001), 65–80.

–, "The Gems of DJD 36: Reflections on Some Recently Published Texts," *JJS* 54 (2003): 146–152.

–, *The Laws of the Damascus Document: Sources, Tradition and Redaction.* STDJ 29 (Leiden: Brill, 1998).

–, "The Literary Development of the S-Tradition: A New Paradigm," *RevQ* 22 (2006): 389–401 [reprinted as Chapter 7 in Hempel, *Qumran Rule Texts in Context*].

–, "The Long Text of the *Serekh* as Crisis Literature," *RevQ* 27 (2015): 3–24.

–, "The Penal Code Reconsidered," in *Legal Texts and Legal Issues: Proceedings of the Second Meeting of the International Organization for Qumran Studies, Published in Honour of Joseph M. Baumgarten.* Edited by Moshe Bernstein, Florentino García Martínez and John Kampen. STDJ 23 (Leiden: Brill, 1997), 337–348.

–, "The Profile and Character of Qumran Cave 4Q: The Community Rule Manuscripts as a Test Case," in *The Caves of Qumran: Proceedings of the International Conference, Lugano 2014.* Edited by Marcello Fidanzio. STDJ 118 (Leiden: Brill, 2017), 74–80.

–, "The Treatise on the Two Spirits and the Literary Development of the Rule of the Community,' in *Dualism in Qumran.* Edited by Géza G. Xeravits. LSTS 76 (London: T&T Clark, 2010), 102–120.

–, "Who is Making Dinner at Qumran?" *JTS* 63 (2012): 49–65.

–, "Wisdom and Law in the Hebrew Bible and at Qumran," *JSJ* 48 (2017): 1–27.

Hengel, Martin, "Qumran und der Hellenismus," in *Qumrân: Sa piété, sa théologie et son milieu*. Edited by Mathias Delcor. BETL 46 (Paris-Gembloux: Duculot; Leuven: University Press, 1978), 333–372.

Henten, Jan Willem van and Luuk Huitink, "Josephus," in *Characterization in Ancient Greek Literature: Studies in Ancient Greek Narrative 4*. Edited by Koen De Temmerman and Evert van Emde Boas. Mnemosyne Supplements 411 (Leiden: Brill, 2018), 251–270.

Himmelfarb, Martha, "Impurity and Sin in 4QD, 1QS, and 4Q512," *DSD* 8 (2001): 9–37.

–, *A Kingdom of Priests: Ancestry and Merit in Ancient Judaism* (Philadelphia, PA: University of Pennsylvania Press, 2006).

Hinojosa, Kamilla Skarström, "A Synchronic Approach to the Serek ha-Yahad (1QS): From Text to Social and Cultural Context" (PhD diss., Umeå University, Sweden, 2016).

Holm-Nielsen, Svend, *Hodayot: Psalms from Qumran* (Aarhus: Universitetsforlaget, 1960).

Horbury, William, "Jews and Christians on the Bible: Demarcation and Convergence" in *Christliche Exegese zwischen Nicaea und Chalkedon*. Edited by Johannes van Oort and Ulrich Wickert (Leuven: Peeters, 1998), 72–103.

Hultgren, Stephen, *From the Damascus Document to the Covenant of the Community: Literary, Historical, and Theological Studies in the Dead Sea Scrolls*. STDJ 66 (Leiden: Brill, 2007).

Jacobs, Jarod, "עָמַד *ʿāmad*," ThWQ 3:146–150.

Jacobus, Helen R., "4Q318: A Jewish Zodiac Calendar at Qumran," in *The Dead Sea Scrolls in Context*. Edited by Charlotte Hempel. STDJ 90 (Leiden: Brill, 2010), 365–395.

–, "Calendars," in CDSS, 435–448.

Japhet, Sara, *I & II Chronicles: A Commentary*. OTL (Louisville, KY: Westminster/John Know Press, 1993).

Jassen, Alex, "The Presentation of the Ancient Prophets as Lawgivers at Qumran," *JBL* 127 (2008): 307–337.

Johnson, Michael, "One Work or Three? A Proposal for Reading 1QS-1QSa-1QSb as a Single Composite Work," *DSD* 25 (2018): 141–177.

Johnson, William A., *Readers and Reading Culture in the High Roman Empire: A Study of Elite Communities* (New York: Oxford University Press, 2010).

Jokiranta, Jutta, "בֶּן *ben*," ThWQ 1:462–473.

–, "Black Sheep, Outsiders, and the Qumran Movement: Social-Psychological Perspectives on Norm-Deviant Behaviour," in *Social Memory and Social Identity in the Study of Early Judaism and Early Christianity*. Edited by Samuel Byrskog, Raimo Hakola and Jutta Jokiranta. NTOA/WUNT 116 (Göttingen: Vandenhoeck & Ruprecht, 2016), 151–174.

–, "Ritualization and the Power of Listing in 4QBerakhot³ (4Q286), in *Is There a Text in this Cave?* Edited by Feldman, Cioată and Hempel, 438–458.

–, "Thinking about Ancient Manuscripts as Information Processing," in *Sibyls, Scriptures, and Scrolls: John Collins at Seventy*. Edited by Joel Baden, Hindy Najman and Eibert Tigchelaar. JSJSup 175 (Leiden: Brill, 2017), 1: 611–635.

–, "Towards a Cognitive Theory of Blessing: Dead Sea Scrolls as Test Case," in *Functions of Psalms and Prayers in the Late Second Temple Period*. Edited by Mika S. Pajunen and Jeremy Penner. BZAW 486 (Berlin: De Gruyter, 2017), 25–47.

Jokiranta, Jutta and Hanna Vanonen, "Multiple Copies of Rule Texts or Multiple Rule Texts? Boundaries of the S and M Documents," in *Crossing Imaginary Boundaries: The*

Dead Sea Scrolls in the Context of Second Temple Judaism. Edited by Mika S. Pajunen and Hanna Tervanotko. PFES 108 (Helsinki: Finnish Exegetical Society, 2015), 11–60.

Jokiranta, Jutta and Cecilia Wassén, "A Brotherhood at Qumran? Metaphorical, Familial Language in the Dead Sea Scrolls," in *Northern Lights on the Dead Sea Scrolls: Proceedings of the Nordic Qumran Network 2003–2006*. Edited by Anders Klostergaard Petersen et al. STDJ 80 (Leiden: Brill, 2009), 173–203.

Jokiranta, Jutta and Molly Zahn, eds., *Law, Literature and Society in Legal Texts from Qumran*. STDJ 128 (Leiden: Brill, 2019).

Jonge, Marinus de, "The *Testaments of the Twelve Patriarchs* and the "Two Ways," in *Biblical Traditions in Transmission: Essays in Honour of Michael A. Knibb*. Edited by Charlotte Hempel and Judith Lieu. JSJSup 111 (Leiden: Brill, 2006), 179–194.

Jost, Michael R., "Yaḥad, Maśkil, Priests and Angels: Their Relation in the Community Rule (1QS)," in *Law, Literature, and Society in Legal Texts from Qumran*. Edited by Jutta Jokiranta and Molly Zahn. STDJ 128 (Leiden: Brill, 2019), 207–229.

Kampen, John "'Torah' and Authority in the Major Sectarian Rules Texts from Qumran," in *The Scrolls and Biblical Traditions: Proceedings of the Seventh Meeting of the IOQS in Helsinki*. Edited by George J. Brooke et al. STDJ 103 (Leiden: Brill, 2012), 231–254.

Keady, Jessica M., *Vulnerability and Valour: A Gendered Analysis of Everyday Life in the Dead Sea Scrolls Communities*. LSTS 91 (London: Bloomsbury T&T Clark, 2017).

Keith, Chris, *Jesus's Literacy: Scribal Culture and the Teacher from Galilee*. LNTS (London: T&T Clark, 2011).

Kister, Menahem, "Commentary to 4Q298," *JQR* 85 (1994): 237–249.

–, "Divorce, Reproof, and Other Sayings in the Synoptic Gospels: Jesus Traditions in the Context of 'Qumranic' and Other Texts," in *Text, Thought and Practice in Qumran and Early Christianity*. Edited by Ruth A. Clements and Daniel R. Schwartz. STDJ 84 (Leiden: Brill, 2009, 195–209.

–, "Physical and Metaphysical Measurements Ordained by God in the Literature of the Second Temple Period," in *Reworking the Bible: Apocryphal and Related Texts at Qumran*. Edited by Esther Chazon, Ruth Clements and Devorah Dimant. STDJ 58 (Leiden: Brill, 2005), 153–176.

–, "The Root NDB in the Scrolls and the Growth of Qumran Texts: Lexicography and Theology," *Meghillot* 11–12 (2015): 111–130 [Hebrew].

Klawans, Jonathan, *Impurity and Sin in Ancient Judaism* (New York, NY: Oxford University Press, 2000).

Klein, Anja, "From the 'Right Spirit' to the 'Spirit of Truth:' Observations on Ps 51 and the Community Rule," in *The Dynamics of Language and Exegesis at Qumran*. Edited by Devorah Dimant and Reinhard G. Kratz. FAT 35 (Tübingen: Mohr Siebeck, 2009), 171–191.

Klinghardt, Matthias, *Gemeinschaftsmahl und Mahlgemeinschaft: Soziologie und Liturgie frühchristlicher Mahlfeiern*. TANZ 13 (Tübingen: Francke, 1996).

–, "Prayer Formularies for Public Recitation: Their Use and Function in Ancient Religion," *Numen* 46 (1999): 1–52.

Klinzing, Georg, *Die Umdeutung des Kultus in der Qumrangemeinde und im Neuen Testament*. SUNT 7 (Göttingen: Vandenhoeck & Ruprecht, 1971).

Knibb, Michael A., "Interpreter of the Law," EDSS 1:383–384.

–, *The Qumran Community*. Cambridge Commentaries on Writings of the Jewish and Christian World 200 BC to AD 200 (Cambridge: Oxford University Press, 1987).

Kooij, Arie van der, "The *Yahad* – What is in a Name?" *DSD* 18 (2011): 109–128.

Kraemer, David, *Jewish Eating and Identity Through the Ages* (New York, NY: Routledge, 2007).

Kraft, Robert A., "Setting the Stage and Framing Some Central Questions," *JSJ* 32 (2001): 371–395.

Kratz, Reinhard G., "Der *Penal Code* und das Verhältnis von *Serekh ha-Yachad* (S) und *Damaskusschrift* (D)," *RevQ* 25 (2011): 199–227.

–, "Laws of Wisdom: Sapiential Traits in the Rule of the Community (1QS 5–7)," in *Hebrew in the Second Temple Period: The Hebrew of the Dead Sea Scrolls and of Other Contemporary Sources*. Edited by Steven E. Fassberg, Moshe Bar-Asher and Ruth A. Clements. STDJ 108 (Leiden: Brill, 2013), 133–145.

–, "The Teacher of Righteousness and His Enemies," in *Is There a Text in this Cave?* Edited by Feldman, Cioată and Hempel, 515–532.

Kratz, Reinhard G., ed., *Qumran 4QMMT: Some Precepts of the Law*. Sapere (Tübingen: Mohr Siebeck, forthcoming).

Kugel, James, "On Hidden Hatred and Open Reproach: Early Exegesis of Leviticus 19:17," *HTR* 80 (1987):43–61.

Kugler, Robert A., "A Note on 1QS 9:14: The Sons of Righteousness or the Sons of Zadok," *DSD* 3 (1996): 315–320.

–, "A Note on Lev 26:41, 43; 4Q434 1 ii 3 and 4Q504 1–2 Recto 5–6 and 1QS 8:3 (Par. 4Q259 2:12): On Human Agency in the Divine Economy at Qumran," in *Prayer and Poetry in the Dead Sea Scrolls and Related Literature: Essays in Honor of Eileen Schuller on the Occasion of her 65th Birthday*. Edited by Jeremy Penner, Ken M. Penner and Cecilia Wassén. STDJ 98 (Leiden: Brill, 2011), 245–250.

–, "Ethnicity: A Fresh Religious Context for the Scrolls," in CDSS, 77–85.

–, "Making All Experience Religious: The Hegemony of Ritual at Qumran," *JSJ* 33 (2002): 131–152.

–, "Priests," in EDSS 2:688–293.

Kuhn, Heinz-Wolfgang, *Enderwartung und gegenwärtiges Heil: Untersuchungen zu den Gemeindeliedern von Qumran*. SUNT 4 (Göttingen: Vandenhoeck & Ruprecht, 1966).

–, "Zum 2. Korintherbrief: Drei wichtige Parallelen zur Qumrangemeinde (Gemeinde Gottes, neuer Bund und Neuschöpfung)," *ZNW* 110 (2019): 42–83.

Kutscher, Edward Y., *The Language and Linguisitc Background of the Isaiah Scroll (1QIsaᵃ)*. STDJ 6 (Leiden: Brill, 1974).

Lange, Armin, "גּוֹרָל *gôrāl*," ThWQ 1:593–600.

–, *Handbuch der Textfunde vom Toten Meer* (Tübingen: Mohr Siebeck, 2009).

–, *Weisheit und Prädestination: Weisheitliche Urordnung und Prädestination in den Textfunden von Qumran*. STDJ 18 (Leiden: Brill, 1995).

Lange, Armin, Hermann Lichtenberger and K. F. Diethard Römheld, eds., *The Demonology of Israelite-Jewish and Early Christian Literature in Context of Their Environment* (Tübingen: Mohr Siebeck, 2003).

Laperrousaz, Ernest-Marie, "Le cadre chronologique de l'existence à Qoumrân de la communauté Essénienne du maître de justice," in *Qoumrân et les manuscrits de la Mer Morte: Un Cinquantenaire* (Paris: Cerf, 1997), 71–97.

Lapin, Hayim, "The Law of Moses and the Jews: Rabbis, Ethnic Marking, and Romanization," in *Jews, Christians, and the Roman Empire: The Poetics of Power in Late Antiquity*. Edited by Annette Yoshiko Reed and Natalie B. Dohrmann. Jewish Culture and Contexts (Philadelphia: University of Pennsylvania Press, 2013), 79–92.

Leaney, Alfred R. C., *The Rule of Qumran and Its Meaning*. NTL (London: SCM, 1966).

Leonhardt-Balzer, Jutta, "Evil at Qumran," in *Evil in Second Temple Judaism and Early Christianity*. Edited by Chris Keith and Loren T. Stuckenbruck. WUNT 2.317 (Tübingen: Mohr Siebeck, 2016), 17–33.

–, "Scrolls and Non-Jewish Hellenistic Literature," in CDSS, 156–163.

Levinson, Bernard M., *"The Right Chorale:" Studies in Biblical Law and Interpretation*. FAT 54 (Tübingen: Mohr Siebeck, 2008).

Levy, Jacob, *Wörterbuch über die Talmudim und Midraschim*. 4 Volumes (Berlin: Benjamin Harz, 1924).

Licht, Jacob, "An Analysis of the Treatise on the Two Spirits in DSD," *Scripta Hierosolymitana* 4 (1958): 88–100.

–, "Some Terms and Concepts of Ritual Purity in the Qumran Writings," in *Studies in the Bible Presented to Professor M. H. Segal*. Edited by J. M Grintz and Jacob Liver (Jerusalem: Kiryat Sefer, 1964), 300–309 [Hebrew].

–, *The Rule Scroll* (Jerusalem: Bialik, 1965) [Hebrew].

–, "Time and Eschatology in Apocalyptic Literature and at Qumran," *JJS* 16 (1965): 177–182.

Lieberman, Saul, *Hellenism in Jewish Palestine: Studies in the Literary Transmission, Beliefs and Manners of Palestine in the I Century B. C. E.–IV Century C. E.* (New York: Jewish Theological Seminary of America, 1962).

–, "The Discipline of the So-Called Dead Sea Manual of Discipline," *JBL* 71 (1952): 199–206.

Lied, Liv, "Text-Work-Manuscript: What is an 'Old Testament Pseudepigraphon'?" *JSP* 25 (2015): 150–165,

Lieu, Judith M., *Christian Identity in the Jewish and Graeco-Roman World* (Oxford: Oxford University Press, 2004).

Lim, Timothy H., *Pesharim*. CQS 3 (Sheffield: Sheffield Academic Press, 2002).

Loader, James A., "The Model of the Priestly Blessing in 1QS," *JSJ* 14 (1983): 11–17.

Luther, Rebekka and Idan Dershowitz, "Four Identified Fragments from 4QJob^a (4Q99)," *RevQ* forthcoming.

Lohse, Eduard, *Die Texte aus Qumran: Hebräisch und Deutsch* (Darmstadt: Wissenschaftliche Buchgesellschaft, 1971).

MacDonald, Nathan, *Priestly Rule: Polemic and Biblical Interpretation in Ezekiel 44*. BZAW 476 (Berlin: De Gruyter, 2015).

Macintosh, Andrew A., "The Meaning of Hebrew תשוקה," *JSS* 61 (2016): 365–387.

Magness, Jodi, *Stone and Dung, Oil and Spit: Jewish Daily Life in the Time of Jesus* (Grand Rapids, MI: Eerdmans, 2011).

–, *The Archaeology of Qumran and the Dead Sea Scrolls* (Grand Rapids, MI: Eerdmans, 2002).

–, "Were Sacrifices Offered at Qumran?" *JAJ* 7 (2016): 5–34.

Maier, Johann, "דָּרַשׁ dāraš; מִדְרָשׁ midrāš," ThWQ 1:726–738.

–, *Die Qumran-Essener: Die Texte vom Toten Meer*. 2 Volumes. UTB (München: Reinhardt, 1995).

–, "Early Jewish Biblical Interpretation in the Qumran Literature," in *Hebrew Bible/Old Testament: The History of Its Interpretation. Volume 1: From the Beginnings to the Middle Ages (Until 1300)*. Edited by Magne Sæbø (Göttingen: Vandenhoeck & Ruprecht, 1996) 108–129.

Martin, Malachi, *The Scribal Character of the Dead Sea Scrolls*. Two Volumes (Louvain: Publications Universitaires, 1958).

Martone, Corrado, *La "Regola della Comunità:" Edizione critica* (Turin: Silvio Zamorani, 1995).

Mason, Steve, "Essenes and Lurking Spartans in Josephus' *Judean War*: From Story to History," in *Making History: Josephus and Historical Method*. Edited by Zuleika Rogers (Leiden: Brill, 2007), 219–261.

Mébarki, Farah and Émile Puech, *Les manuscrits de la mer Morte* (Arles: Éditions du Rouergue, 2002).

Mendels, Doron, "Hellenistic Utopia and the Essens," *HTR* 72 (1979): 207–222.

Mermelstein, Ari, "Love and Hate at Qumran: The Social Construction of Sectarian Emotion," *DSD* 20 (2013): 237–263.

Metso, Sarianna, "Biblical Quotations in the Community Rule," in *The Bible as Book: The Hebrew Bible and the Judaean Desert Discoveries*. Edited by Edward D. Herbert and Emanuel Tov (London: The British Library, 2002), 81–92.

–, "The Primary Results of the Reconstruction of 4QS^e," *JJS* 44 (1993): 303–308.

–, *The Serekh Texts*. CQS 9 (London: T&T Clark, 2007).

–, *The Textual Development of the Qumran Community Rule*. STDJ 21 (Leiden: Brill, 1997).

–, "Whom Does the Term Yaḥad Identify?" in *Biblical Traditions in Transmission: Essays in Honour of Michael A. Knibb*. Edited by Charlotte Hempel and Judith Lieu. JSJSup 111 (Leiden: Brill, 2006), 213–235.

Metso, Sarianna, Hindy Najman and Eileen Schuller, eds., *The Dead Sea Scrolls: Transmission of Traditions and Production of Texts*. STDJ 92 (Leiden: Brill, 2010).

Meyer, Nicholas A., "תבמים *tkmjm*," ThWQ 3:1121–1123.

Milik, Józef T., "Manuale Disciplinae," *Verbum Domini* 29 (Rome: Pontificium Institutum Biblicum, 1951), 129–158.

–, "Milkî-ṣedeq et Milkî-rešaʿ dans les anciens écrits juifs et chrétiens," *JJS* 23 (1972): 95–144.

–, "Numération des feuilles des roulaux dans le scriptorium de Qumrân," *Semitica* 27 (1977): 75–81.

–, "Le travail d'édition des fragments manuscrits de Qumrân," *RB* 63 (1956): 49–67.

–, *Ten Years of Discovery in the Wilderness of Judaea* (London: SCM, 1959).

–, "Texte des variantes des dix manuscrits de la Règle de la Communauté trouvés dans la Grotte 4: Recension de P. Wernberg-Moeller, The Manual of Discipline," *RB* 67 (1960): 410–416.

–, *The Books of Enoch: Aramaic Fragments of Qumrân Cave 4* (Oxford: Oxford University Press, 1974).

Mizrahi, Noam, "תבמי בשר 'Body Parts:' The Semantic History of a Qumran Hebrew Lexeme," in *The Reconfiguration of Hebrew in the Hellenistic Period: Proceedings of the Seventh International Symposium on the Hebrew of the Dead Sea Scrolls and Ben Sira at Strasbourg University, June 2014*. Edited by Jan Joosten, Daniel Machiela and Jean-Sébastien Rey. STDJ 124 (Leiden: Brill, 2018), 123–157.

–, "Liturgy, Hebrew of the Dead Sea Scrolls," in *Encyclopedia of Hebrew Language and Linguistics*. Edited by Geoffrey Khan (Leiden: Brill, 2013), 2:558–561.

–, "Priests of *Qoreb*: Linguistic Enigma and Social Code in the *Songs of the Sabbath Sacrifice*," in *Hebrew of the Late Second Temple Period: Proceedings of a Sixth International Symposium on the Hebrew of the Dead Sea Scrolls and Ben Sira*. Edited by Eibert Tigchelaar and Pierre van Hecke. STDJ 114 (Leiden: Brill, 2015), 37–64.

–, "Saturation, that is, Drunkenness: The Interpretation of 1QpHab 11:8–16 and Its Linguistic Background," *Meghillot* 14 (2019): 105–117 [Hebrew].

Mizzi, Dennis, "Qumran Period I Reconsidered: An Evaluation of Several Competing Theories," *DSD* 22 (2015): 1–42.

Morgenstern, Matthew, "A New Clue to the Original Length of the Genesis Apocryphon," *JJS* 47 (1996): 345–347.

–, "A 'Reconstructionist' Approach to the Dead Sea Scrolls: E. Puech's Edition of Discoveries in the Judean Desert XXV," *JJS* 55 (2004): 347–353.

Mroczek, Eva, "Hymns" in *The Dictionary of the Bible and Ancient Media*. Edited by Tom Thatcher et al. (London: Bloomsbury, 2017), 180–183.

–, "The Hegemony of the Biblical in the Study of Second Temple Literature," *JAJ* 6 (2015): 1–35.

Muraoka, Takamitsu, "Community Rule (1QS)," *in Encyclopedia of Hebrew Language and Linguistics*. Edited by Geoffrey Khan (Leiden: Brill, 2013), 1:493–495.

–, "Sirach 51:13–30: An Erotic Hymn to Wisdom," *JSJ* 10 (1979): 166–178.

Murphy, Catherine M., *Wealth in the Dead Sea Scrolls and in the Qumran Community*. STDJ 40 (Leiden: Brill, 2002).

Murphy-O'Connor, Jerome, "La genèse littéraire de la Règle de la Communauté," *RB* 76 (1969): 528–549.

Najman, Hindy, *Past Renewals: Interpretative Authority. Renewed Revelation and the Quest for Perfection in Jewish Antiquity*. JSJSup 53 (Leiden: Brill, 2010).

–, *Seconding Sinai: The Development of Mosaic Discourse in Second Temple Judaism*. JSJSup 77 (Leiden: Brill 2003).

–, "The Vitality of Scripture Within and Beyond the 'Canon,'" *JSJ* 43 (2012): 497–518.

–, "Towards a Study of the Uses of the Concept of Wilderness in Ancient Judaism," *DSD* 13 (2006): 99–113.

Najman, Hindy and Eibert Tigchelaar, "A Preparatory Study of Nomenclature and Text Designation in the Dead Sea Scrolls," *RevQ* 26 (2014): 305–325.

Nati, James, "The *Community Rule* or *Rules* for the Community," in *Sibyls, Scriptures, and Scrolls: John Collins at Seventy*. Edited by Joel Baden, Hindy Najman and Eibert Tigchelaar. JSJSup 175 (Leiden: Brill, 2017), 2: 916–939.

Newman, Judith H., *Before the Bible: The Liturgical Body and the Formation of Scriptures in Early Judaism* (New York, NY: Oxford University Press, 2018).

–, "Speech and Spirit: Paul and the Maskil as Inspired Interpreters of Scripture," in *The Holy Spirit, Inspiration, and the Cultures of Antiquity: Multidisciplinary Perspectives*. Edited by Jörg Frey and John R. Levison. Ekstasis 5 (Berlin: De Gruyter, 2014), 243–66.

Newsom, Carol, "Apocalyptic and the Discourse of the Qumran Community," *JNES* 49 (1990): 135–144.

–, "Deriving Negative Anthropology Through Exegetical Activity: The Hodayot as Case Study," in *Is There a Text in this Cave?* Edited by Feldman, Cioată and Hempel, 258–274.

–, "The Sage in the Literature of Qumran: The Functions of the Maskil," in *The Sage in Israel and the Ancient Near East*. Edited by James G. Gammie and Leo G. Perdue (Winona Lake, IN: Eisenbrauns, 1990), 373–382.

–, *The Self as Symbolic Space: Constructing Identity and Community at Qumran*. STDJ 52 (Leiden: Brill, 2004).

Nitzan, Bilhah, "4Q280. 4QCurses," in DJD 29:1–8.

–, "4Q286–290. Berakhot[a-e]," in DJD 11:1–74.

–, "Blessings and Curses," in EDSS 1:95–100.

–, "Education and Wisdom in the Dead Sea Scrolls in Light of their Background in Antiquity," in *New Perspectives on Old Texts: Proceedings of the Tenth International Symposium of the Orion Center for the Study of the Dead Sea Scrolls and Associated Literature, 9–11 January 2005*. Edited by Esther G. Chazon, Betsy Halpern-Amaru and Ruth A. Clements. STDJ 88 (Leiden: Brill, 2010), 97–116.

–, "Harmonic and Mystical Characteristics in Poetic and Liturgical Writings from Qumran," *JQR* 85 (1994): 163–183.

–, *Qumran Prayer and Religious Poetry*. Trans. Jonathan Chipman. STDJ 12 (Leiden: Brill, 1994).

–, "The Dead Sea Scrolls and the Jewish Liturgy," in *The Dead Sea Scrolls as Background to Postbiblical Judaism and Early Christianity: Papers from an International Conference in St Andrews in 2001*. STDJ 46 (Leiden: Brill, 2003), 195–219.

Noam, Vered, "4QMMT and Rabbinic Halakhah," in *Qumran 4QMMT: Some Precepts of the Law*. Edited by Reinhard G. Kratz (Tübingen: Mohr Siebeck, forthcoming).

Novick, Tzvi, "Overt Acknowledgement of Practical Considerations in Legal Texts from Qumran," *DSD* 21 (2014): 64–81.

Osten-Sacken, P. von der, *Gott und Belial: Traditionsgeschichtliche Untersuchungen zum Dualismus in den Texten aus Qumran* (Göttingen: Vandenhoeck & Ruprecht, 1969).

Pajunen, Mika S., "The Praise of God and His Name as the Core of the Second Temple Liturgy," *ZAW* 127 (2015): 475–488.

Palmer, Carmen, *Converts in the Dead Sea Scrolls: The Gēr and Mutable Ethnicity*. STDJ 126 (Leiden: Brill, 2018).

Penner, Jeremy, *Patterns of Daily Prayer in Second Temple Judaism*. STDJ 104 (Leiden: Brill, 2012).

Pfann, Stephen, "4Q249 Midrash Sefer Moshe," in *Legal Texts and Legal Issues: Proceedings of the International Organization for Qumran Studies Published in Honour of Joseph M. Baumgarten*. Edited by Moshe Bernstein, Florentino García Martínez and John Kampen. STDJ 23 (Leiden: Brill, 199), 11–18.

Ploeg, Johannes van der, "Le 'Manuel de Discipline' des Roulaux de la Mer Morte," *BO* 8 (1951): 113–126.

Popović, Mladen, "Networks of Scholars: The Transmission of Astronomical and Astrological Learning Between Babylonians, Greeks and Jews," in *Ancient Jewish Sciences and the History of Knowledge*. Edited by Jonathan Ben-Dov and Seth Sanders (New York, NY: New York University Press, 2014), 153–195.

–, *Reading the Human Body: Physiognomics and Astrology in the Dead Sea Scrolls*. STDJ 67 (Leiden: Brill, 2007).

Porzig, Peter, "The Place of the 'Treatise of the Two Spirits' (1QS 3:13–4:26) within the Literary Development of the Community Rule," in *Law, Literature and Society*. Edited by Jokiranta and Zahn, 127–151.

Pouilly, Jean, *La Règle de la Communauté de Qumrân: Son évolution littéraire*. Cahiers de la Revue Biblique 17 (Paris: Gabalda, 1976).

Puech, Émile, "Hodayot," in EDSS 1:366–367.

–, "L'alphabet cryptique A en *4QSᵉ (4Q259)*," *RevQ* 18 (1998): 429–35.

–, *La croyance des Esséniens en la vie future: Immortalité, resurrection, et vie éternelle*. 2 vols (Paris: Gabalda, 1993).

–, "Note de lexicographie de hébraïque qumrânienne (*m-ṣw/yrwq, mḥšbym, śwṭ*)," in *Solving Riddles and Untying Knots: Biblical, Epigraphic, and Semitic Studies in Honor of Jonas C. Greenfield*. Edited by Ziony Zevit, Seymour Gitin and Michael Sokoloff (Winona Lake, IN: Eisenbrauns, 2005), 181–189.

–, "Quelques aspects de la restauration du rouleau des hymnes (1QH)," *JJS* 39 (1988): 38–55.

–, "Remarques sur l'écriture de 1QS VII–VIII," *RevQ* 10 (1979): 35–43.

–, "Review of *The Textual Development of the Qumran Community Rule* by Sarianna Metso," *RevQ* 18 (1998): 448–453.

Qimron, Elisha, "Notes on the 4Q Zadokite Fragments on Skin Disease," *JJS* 42 (1991): 256–259.

–, *The Hebrew of the Dead Sea Scrolls* (Atlanta, GA: Scholars Press, 1986).

Rabin, Chaim, *The Zadokite Documents: I. The Admonition II. The Laws* (Oxford: Oxford University Press, 1954).

Rad, Gerhard von, *Wisdom in Israel* (London: SCM, 1975).

Reed, Annette Yoshiko and Natalie B. Dohrmann, "Rethinking Romanness, Provincialising Christendom," in *Jews, Christians, and the Roman Empire: The Poetics of Power in Late Antiquity*. Edited by Annette Yoshiko Reed and Natalie B. Dohrmann. Jewish Culture and Contexts (Philadelphia: University of Pennsylvania Press, 2013), 1–22.

Reed, Annette and Adam Becker, eds., *The Ways that Never Parted: Jews and Christians in Late Antiquity and the Early Middle Ages* (Minneapolis, MN: Fortress, 2007).

Regev, Eyal, "יַחַד *jaḥad*," ThWQ 2:121–130.

Rendsburg, Gary, "Qumran Hebrew (with a Trial Cut [1QS])," in *The Dead Sea Scrolls at 60: Scholarly Contributions of New York University Faculty and Alumni*. Edited by Lawrence H. Schiffman and Shani Tzoref. STDJ 89 (Leiden: Brill, 2010), 217–246.

Reymond, Eric D., *Qumran Hebrew: An Overview of Orthography, Phonology, and Morphology*. RBS 76 (Atlanta, GA: SBL, 2014).

–, "The Scribe of 1QS, 1QSa, 1QSb, 4Q53 (4QSam^c), 4Q175 and Three Features of Orthography and Phonology," *DSD* 25 (2018): 238–254.

Rofé, Alexander, "A Neglected Meaning of the Verb כול and the Text of 1QS vi:11–13," in *"Shaʿarei Talmon:" Studies in the Bible, Qumran, and the Ancient Near East Presented to Shemaryahu Talmon*. Edited by Michael A. Fishbane and Emanuel Tov (Winona Lake, IN: Eisenbrauns, 1992), 315–321.

–, "The Piety of the Torah-Disciples at the Winding-Up of the Hebrew Bible: Josh. 1:8; Ps 1:2; Isa. 59:21," in *Bibel in jüdischer und christlicher Tradition: Festschrift für Johann Maier zum 60. Geburtstag*. Edited by Helmut Merklein, Karlheinz Müller and Günter Stemberger (Frankfurt a. M.: Hain, 1993), 75–85.

Sacchi, Paolo, *Regola della Comunitá: Introduzione, traduzione e comment a cura di*. Studi Biblici 150 (Brescia: Paideia, 2006).

Sanders, Ed P., "The Dead Sea Sect and Other Jews," in *The Dead Sea Scrolls in Their Historical Context*. Edited by Timothy H. Lim et al. (Edinburgh: T&T Clark, 2000), 7–43.

Scheepstra, S. E., "True and Righteous are all the Works of God: A Proposal for the Reconstruction of 1QS I, 26," *RevQ* 16 (1995): 641–646.

Schiffman, Lawrence H., "Communal Meals at Qumran," *RevQ* 10 (1979): 45–56.

–, "Legislation Concerning Relations with Non-Jews in the *Zadokite Fragments* and in Tannaitic Literature," *RevQ* 11 (1983): 379–389.

–, *Reclaiming the Dead Sea Scrolls: The History of Judaism, the Background to Christianity, the Lost Library of Qumran* (Philadelphia, PA: Jewish Publication Society, 1994).

–, *Sectarian Law in the Dead Sea Scrolls: Courts, Testimony and the Penal Code.* BJS 33 (Chico, CA: Scholars Press, 1983).

–, "Sectarian Rule (5Q13)," in PTSDSSP 1:132–143.

–, *The Eschatological Community of the Dead Sea Scrolls.* SBLMS 38 (Atlanta, GA: Scholars Press, 1989).

–, *The Halakhah at Qumran.* SJLA 16 (Leiden: Brill, 1975).

Schlenke, Barbara, "משל II," ThWQ 2:819–826.

Schofield, Alison, *From Qumran to the Yaḥad: A New Paradigm of Textual Development for the Community Rule.* STDJ 77 (Leiden: Brill, 2009).

–, "Re-Placing Priestly Space: The Wilderness as Heterotopia in the Dead Sea Scrolls," in *A Teacher for All Generations: Essays in Honor of James C. VanderKam.* Edited by Eric Mason et al. JSJSup 153/1 (Leiden, Brill, 2012) 1: 469–490.

–, "Wilderness," in EDEJ, 1337–1338.

Schuller, Eileen, "Recent Scholarship on the Hodayot 1993–2010," *CurrBR* 10 (2011): 119–162.

–, "Some Observations on Blessings of God in Texts from Qumran," in *Of Scribes and Scrolls: Studies on the Hebrew Bible, Intertestamental Judaism, and Christian Origins.* Edited by Harold H. Attridge, John J. Collins and Thomas H. Tobin (Lanham, MD: University of America, 1990), 133–43.

Schuller, Eileen and Carol Newsom, *The Hodayot (Thanksgiving Psalms): A Study Edition of 1QH^a.* EJL 36 (Atlanta, GA: SBL, 2012).

Scott, Ian W., "Sectarian Truth: The Meaning of אמת in the *Community Rule*," in *Celebrating the Dead Sea Scrolls: A Canadian Collection.* Edited by Peter W. Flint, Jean Duhaime and Kyung S. Baek. EJL 30 (Atlanta, GA: SBL, 2011), 303–343.

Scott, James M., "Covenant," in EDEJ, 491–494.

Shemesh, Aharon, "Expulsion and Exclusion in the Community Rule and the Damascus Document," *DSD* 9 (2002): 44–74.

–, "The Scriptural Background of the Penal Code in the *Rule of the Community* and *Damascus* Document," *DSD* 15 (2008): 191–224.

Skjærvø, Prods Oktor, "Zoroastrian Dualism," in *Light Against Darkness: Dualism in Ancient Mediterranean Religion and the Contemporary World.* Edited by Armin Lange et al. JAJSup 2 (Göttingen: Vandenhoeck & Ruprecht, 2011), 55–91.

Smelik, Willem F., "The Use of הזכיר בשם in Classical Hebrew: Josh 23:7; Isa 48:1; Amos 6:10; Ps 20:8; 4Q504 III 4; 1QS 6:27," *JBL* 118 (1999): 321–332.

Smith, Morton, "The Common Theology of the Ancient Near East," *JBL* 71 (1952): 135–147.

Snyder, H. Gregory, *Teachers and Texts in the Ancient World: Philosophers, Jews and Christians* (London: Routledge, 2000).

Sonne, Isaiah, "Remarks on 'Manual of Discipline' Col. VI,6–7," *VT* 7 (1957): 405–408.

Stegemann, Hartmut, *Die Essener, Qumran, Johannes der Täufer und Jesus* (Freiburg im Breisgau: Herder, 1993).

–, "Religionsgeschichtliche Erwägungen zu den Gottesbezeichnungen in den Qumrantexten," in *Qumrân: Sa piété, sa théologie et son milieu.* Edited by Mathias Delcor et al. (Paris: Gembloux; Leuven: Leuven University Press, 1978), 195–217.

–, "Some Remarks to *1QSa*, to *1QSb*, and to Qumran Messianism," *RevQ* 17 (1996): 479–505.

–, *The Library of Qumran: On the Essenes, Qumran, John the Baptist, and Jesus* (Grand Rapids, MI: Eerdmans, 1998).

–, "Zu Textbestand und Grundgedanken von 1QS III, 13–IV. 26," *RevQ* 13 (1988): 95–131.

Stern, Sacha, *Calendars in Antiquity: Empires, States, and Societies* (Oxford: Oxford University Press, 2012).

–, "Qumran Calendars and Sectarianism," in OHDSS, 232–253.

Steudel, Annette, "Reading and Reconstructing Manuscripts," in CDSS, 186–191.

–, "The Damascus Document (D) as a Rewriting of the Community Rule (S)," *RevQ* 25 (2012): 605–620.

Stone, Michael E., "Amram," in EDSS 1:23–24.

–, *Ancient Judaism: New Visions and Views* (Grand Rapids, MI: Eerdmans, 2011).

–, *Secret Groups in Ancient Judaism* (Oxford: Oxford University Press, 2018).

Strine, Casey, "The Study of Involuntary Migration as a Hermeneutical Guide for Reading the Jacob Narrative," *Biblical Interpretation* 26 (2018): 485–498.

Strugnell, John, "Notes on 1QS 1, 17–18; 8, 3–4 and 1QM 17, 8–9," *CBQ* 29 (1967): 580–582.

Stuckenbruck, Loren T., "The Demonic World of the Dead Sea Scrolls," in *Evil an the Devil*. Edited by Ida Fröhlich and Erkki Koskenniemi (London Bloomsbury, 2013), 51–70.

–, "The 'Heart' in the Dead Sea Scrolls: Negotiating Between the Problem of Hypocrisy and Conflict within the Human Being," in *The Dead Sea Scrolls in Context: Integrating the Dead Sea Scrolls in the Study of Ancient Texts, Languages, and Cultures*. Edited by Armin Lange, Emanuel Tov and Matthias Weigold (Leiden: Brill, 2011), 437–453.

–, "The Interiorization of Dualism Within the Human Being in Second Temple Judaism: The Treatise of the Two Spirits in its Tradition-Historical Context," in *Light Against Darkness: Dualism in Ancient Mediterranean Religion and the Contemporary World*. Edited by Armin Lange et al. JAJSup 2 (Göttingen: Vandenhoeck & Ruprecht, 2011), 145–168.

Sutcliffe, Edmund F., "The General Council of the Qumran Community," *Biblica* 40 (1959): 971–983.

Talmon, Shemaryahu, *The World of Qumran from Within: Collected Studies* (Jerusalem; Leiuden: Magnes; Brill, 1989).

Tanzer, Sarah, "The Sages at Qumran: Wisdom in the 'Hodayot'" (PhD diss., Harvard, 1986).

Taylor, Joan E., *The Essenes, the Scrolls and the Dead Sea* (Oxford: Oxford University Press, 2012).

–, "Women, Children, and Celibate Men in the Serekh Texts," *HTR* 104 (2011): 171–190.

Taylor, Joan E., Dennis Mizzi and Marcello Fidanzio, "Revisiting Qumran Cave 1Q and Its Archaeological Assemblage," *PEQ* 149 (2017): 295–325.

Thomas, Samuel, "בְּלִיַּעַל *beлijjaʿal*," ThWQ 1:452–458.

Tigchelaar, Eibert J. C., "A Newly Identified 11QSerekh ha-Yaḥad Fragment (11Q29)?," in *The Dead Sea Scrolls Fifty Years After Their Discovery 1947–1997*. Edited by Lawrence H. Schiffman, Emanuel Tov and James C. VanderKam (Jerusalem: IES, 2000), 285–292.

–, "Changing Truths: אֱמֶת and קֹשֶׁט as Core Concepts in the Second Temple Period," in *Congress Volume Stellenbosch 2016*. Edited by Louis C. Jonker, Gideon R. Kotzé and Christl M. Maier. VTSup 177 (Leiden: Brill, 2017), 395–415.

–, "Dittography and Copying Lines in the Dead Sea Scrolls: Considering George Brooke's Proposal about 1QpHab 7:1–2," in *Is There a Text in this Cave?* Edited by Feldman, Cioată and Hempel, 293–302.

–, *To Increase Learning for the Understanding Ones: Reading and Reconstructing the Fragmentary Early Jewish Sapiential Text 4QInstruction.* STDJ 44 (Leiden: Brill, 2001).

–, "The Scribe of 1QS," in *Emanuel: Studies in Hebrew Bible, Septuagint, and the Dead Sea Scrolls in Honor of Emanuel Tov.* Edited by Shalom Paul et al. VTSup 94 (Leiden: Brill, 2003), 439–452.

–, "The Scribes of the Scrolls," in CDSS, 524–532.

–, "'These are the Names of the Spirits of …': A Preliminary Edition of *4QCatalogue of Spirits* (4Q230) and New Manuscript Evidence for the *Two Spirits Treatise* (4Q257 and 1Q29a)," *RevQ* 21 (2004): 529–548.

Tiller, Patrick A., "The 'Eternal Planting' in the Dead Sea Scrolls," *DSD* 4 (1997): 312–335.

Tov, Emanuel, "Biliteral Exegesis of Hebrew Roots in the Septuagint?" in *Reflection and Refraction: Studies in Biblical Historiography in Honour of A. Graeme Auld.* Edited by Robert Rezetko, Timothy H. Lim and W. Brian Aucker. VTSup 113 (Leiden: Brill, 2006) 459–82.

–, *Scribal Practices and Approaches Reflected in Texts Found in the Judean Desert.* STDJ 54 (Leiden: Brill, 2004).

–, *Textual Criticism of the Hebrew Bible* (2nd ed. Minneapolis, MN: Fortress; Assen: van Gorcum, 2001).

Trever, John C., *Scrolls from Qumrân Cave I: The Great Isaiah Scroll-The Order of the Community-The Pesher to Habakkuk.* Edited by Frank Moore Cross, David Noel Freedman and James A. Sanders (Jerusalem: The Albright Institute of Archaeological Research and the Shrine of the Book, 1972).

–, *The Untold Story of Qumran* (London: Pickering and Inglis, 1965).

Tucker, James M., "From Ink Traces to Ideology: A Reassessment of 4Q256 (4QSerekh ha-Yahad[b]) Frags. 5 a–b and 1QS 6:16–17," in *Law, Literature and Society in Legal Texts from Qumran.* Edited by Jutta Jokiranta and Molly Zahn. STDJ 128 (Leiden: Brill, 2019), 185–206.

Tzoref, Shani, "The Use of Scripture in the Community Rule," in *A Companion to Biblical Interpretation in Early Judaism.* Edited by M. Henze (Grand Rapids, MI: Eerdmans, 2012), 203–234.

Ulrich, Eugene, "4QSam[c]: A Fragmentary Manuscript of 2 Samuel 14–15 from the Scribe of the Serek hay-yahad (1QS)," *BASOR* 235 (1979):1–25.

Uusimäki, Elisa, *Turning Proverbs Towards Torah: An Analysis of 4Q525.* STDJ 117 (Leiden: Brill, 2016).

VanderKam, James C., *Calendars in the Dead Sea Scrolls: Measuring Time* (London: Routledge, 1998).

–, "Messianism in the Scrolls," in *The Community of the Renewed Covenant.* Edited by Eugene Ulrich and James C. VanderKam, Christianity and Judaism in Antiquity 10 (Notre Dame, IN: University of Notre Dame Press, 1994), 211–234.

–, "Sinai Revisited," in *Biblical Interpretation at Qumran.* Edited by Matthias Henze. Studies in the Dead Sea Scrolls and Related Literature (Grand Rapids, MI: Eerdmans, 2005), 44–60.

–, *The Dead Sea Scrolls and the Bible* (Grand Rapids, MI: Eerdmans, 2012).

–, "The Oath and the Community," *DSD* 16 (2009): 416–432.

Vaux, Roland de, *Archaeology and the Dead Sea Scrolls: The Schweich Lectures 1959* (Oxford: Oxford University Press; The British Academy, 1973).

Vayntrub, Jaqueline, *Beyond Orality: Biblical Poetry on its Own Terms* (London: Routledge, 2019).

Vermes, Geza, "Preliminary Remarks on Unpublished Fragments of the Community Rule from Qumran Cave 4," *JJS* 42 (1991): 250–255.

–, "The Leadership of the Qumran Community: Sons of Zadok-Priests-Congregation," in *Geschichte – Tradition – Reflexion: Festschrift für Martin Hengel zum 70. Geburtstag.* Edited by Hubert Cancik, Hermann Lichtenberger and Peter Schäfer (Tübingen: Mohr Siebeck, 1996), 1: 375–384.

Vermes, Geza and Martin D. Goodman, *The Essenes According to the Classical Sources.* Oxford Centre Textbooks 1 (Sheffield: JSOT Press, 1989).

Wassén, Cecilia, "זָקֵן zāqen," ThWQ 1:865–869.

–, "Daily Life," in CDSS, 547–558.

–, "Do You Have to Be Pure in a Metaphorical Temple? Sanctuary Metaphors and Construction of Sacred Space in the Dead Sea Scrolls and Paul's Letters," in *Purity, Holiness, and Identity in Judaism and Christianity: Essays in Memory of Susan Haber.* Edited by Carl S. Ehrlich, Anders Runesson and Eileen Schuller. WUNT 305 (Tübingen: Mohr Siebeck, 2013), 55–86.

–, "Purity and Holiness," in CDSS, 513–523.

–, "Purity Laws for Men and Women in the Dead Sea Scrolls: A Comparison of Ideals and Praxis," in *Frauen im antiken Judentum und frühen Christentum.* Edited by Jörg Frey and Nicole Rupschus. WUNT 2.489 (Tübingen: Mohr Siebeck, 2019), 57–84.

–, "The (Im)purity Levels of Communal Meals within the Qumran Movement," *JAJ* 7 (2016): 102–122.

Weinfeld, Moshe, *The Organizational Pattern and the Penal Code of the Qumran Sect: A Comparison with Guilds and Religious Associations of the Hellenistic Roman Period.* NTOA 2 (Göttingen: Vandenhoeck & Ruprecht; Fribourg: Éditions Universitaires, 1986).

Weise, Manfred, *Kultzeiten und kultischer Bundesschluss in der "Ordensregel" vom Toten Meer.* SPB 3 (Leiden: Brill, 1961).

Weissenberg, Hanne von, "God(s), Angels and Demons," in CDSS, 490–495.

–, "Miqṣat Maʿaśeh ha-Torah," in CDSS, 325–328.

Wernberg-Møller, Preben, "Observations on the Interchange of *Ayin* and *Ḥet* in the Manual of Discipline," *VT* 3 (1953) 104–107.

–, "A Reconsideration of the Two Spirits in the Rule of the Community," *RevQ* 3 (1961): 413–441.

–, "Some Reflections on the Biblical Material in the Manual of Discipline," *ST* 9 (1955): 40–66.

–, *The Manual of Discipline.* STDJ 1 (Leiden: Brill, 1957).

Williamson, Hugh, *1 and 2 Chronicles.* NCBC (Grand Rapids, MI: Eerdmans; London: Marshall, Morgan & Scott, 1982).

–, *Ezra, Nehemiah.* Word Biblical Commentary 16 (Waco, TX: Word Books, 1985).

Wilson, Andrew and Lawrence Wills, "Literary Sources of the Temple Scroll," *HTR* 75 (1982): 275–288.

Wise, Michael O., *A Critical Study of the Temple Scroll from Qumran Cave 11* (Chicago, IL: Oriental Institute of the University of Chicago, 1990).

–, "Review of Michael A. Knibb, The Qumran Community," *JNES* 49 (1990): 200–202.

Wright, Benjamin G. III, "The Dead Sea Scrolls and the Study of the Ancient World," in CDSS, 216–227, 220–221.

Yadin, Yigael. *The Temple Scroll: Volume Two Text and Commentary* (Jerusalem: IES, 1983).

Yalon, Hanoch, *The Dead Sea Scrolls: Linguistic Studies* (Jerusalem: Shrine of the Book, 1967) [Hebrew].

Yardeni, Ada, "A Draft of a Deed on an Ostracon from Khirbet Qumrân," *IEJ* 47 (1997): 233–237.

Index of Ancient Sources

Prepared by Michael DeVries

References to the Community Rules manuscripts are given only where the passage in question is not part of the primary text treated in the relevant chapter of the Commentary.

Hebrew Bible

Genesis
1:14	113, 268
1:14–19	33, 267
2:7	290
7:5	81

Exodus
18:21	89
18:25	89
19:1	67
19:7	180
20:26	213
22	81
28:42–43	213
32–34	133
35	133
35:21	132
35:29	132

Leviticus
5:21 [6:2]	201
12:18	210
14	129
15:8	212
15:16	14
18:27	203
19	214
19:17	155, 210
19:24	296
20:23–24	203
22:16	157
25:22	79
26	82, 90, 91, 226
26:15	91
26:15–43	90
26:16	77
26:43	78, 91
26:44–45	90, 93

Numbers
3:17	226
6:24–26	7, 83
10:10	295
14:43	81
16	135
16–17	214
16:20–21	135
19	94
25:13	95
35	133, 138
35:21	133
35:29	133

Deuteronomy 87
6:7	297
6:17–18	62
6:18	60, 63
15:9	289
17:6	157
19:15	157

Apocrypha and Septuagint

Pseudepigrapha

New Testament

Dead Sea Scrolls

   Index of Ancient Sources

PAM Images

LLDSSLD Images

Miscellaneous Photographs

Josephus and Philo

Philo   Athos ms. *e*   59

Good Person
84   12
85–88   12

Rabbinic Literature

m. Bikkurim   *t. Demai*
3:2   168   2:2–3:10   181

m. Demai
2:2–3   12, 181

Index of Modern Authors

Prepared by Michael DeVries